CLYMER®

HONDA

XR400R • 1996-2000

The world's finest publisher of mechanical how-to manuals

INTERTEC PUBLISHING

P.O. Box 12901, Overland Park, Kansas 66282-2901

Copyright ©2001 Intertec Publishing

FIRST EDITION
First Printing March, 2001

Printed in U.S.A.

CLYMER and colophon are registered trademarks of Intertec Publishing.

ISBN: 0-89287-776-6

Library of Congress: 20011086729

Technical photography by Ron Wright.

Technical illustrations by Stephen Amos and Robert Caldwell.

Special thanks to Clawson Motorsports, Fresno, California, for their assistance with this book.

COVER: Photographed by Mark Clifford, Mark Clifford Photography, Los Angeles, California. Honda XR400R courtesy of Rice Motorsports, La Puente, California.

PRODUCTION: Holly Messinger.

CLYMER PUBLICATIONS
Intertec Directory & Book Division
Chief Executive Officer Timothy M. Andrews
President Ron Wall
Vice President, Directory & Book Division Rich Hathaway

EDITORIAL

Editorial Director
Mark Jacobs

Editor
Mike Hall

Associate Editor
James Grooms

Technical Writers
Ron Wright
Ed Scott
George Parise
Mark Rolling
Michael Morlan
Jay Bogart
Ronney Broach

Production Manager
Shirley Renicker

Editorial Production Supervisor
Dylan Goodwin

Editorial Production Coordinators
Greg Araujo
Dennis Conrow
Shara Pierceall-Meyer

Editorial Production Assistants
Susan Hartington
Holly Messinger
Darin Watson

Technical Illustrators
Steve Amos
Robert Caldwell
Mitzi McCarthy
Bob Meyer
Michael St. Clair
Mike Rose

MARKETING/SALES AND ADMINISTRATION

Group Publisher
Randy Stephens

Advertising & Promotions Manager
Elda Starke

Advertising & Promotions Coordinator
Melissa Abbott

Associate Art Directors
Chris Paxton
Tony Barmann

Sales Manager/Marine
Dutch Sadler

Sales Manager/Motorcycles
Matt Tusken

Sales Coordinator
Paul Cormaci

Customer Service Manager
Terri Cannon

Fulfillment Coordinator
Susan Kohlmeyer

Customer Service Representatives
Ardelia Chapman
Donna Schemmel
Kim Jones
April LeBlond

Warehouse & Inventory Manager
Leah Hicks

The following books and guides are published by Intertec Publishing.

CLYMER SHOP MANUALS
Boat Motors and Drives
Motorcycles and ATVs
Snowmobiles
Personal Watercraft

ABOS/INTERTEC/CLYMER BLUE BOOKS AND TRADE-IN GUIDES
Recreational Vehicles
Outdoor Power Equipment
Agricultural Tractors
Lawn and Garden Tractors
Motorcycles and ATVs
Snowmobiles and Personal Watercraft
Boats and Motors

AIRCRAFT BLUEBOOK-PRICE DIGEST
Airplanes
Helicopters

AC-U-KWIK DIRECTORIES
The Corporate Pilot's Airport/FBO Directory
International Manager's Edition
Jet Book

I&T SHOP SERVICE MANUALS
Tractors

INTERTEC SERVICE MANUALS
Snowmobiles
Outdoor Power Equipment
Personal Watercraft
Gasoline and Diesel Engines
Recreational Vehicles
Boat Motors and Drives
Motorcycles
Lawn and Garden Tractors

CONTENTS

QUICK REFERENCE DATA

VEHICLE HISTORY DATA

MODEL:_____ YEAR:_____

VIN NUMBER:_____

ENGINE SERIAL NUMBER:_____

CARBURETOR SERIAL NUMBER OR I.D. MARK:_____

Record the numbers here for your reference.

MAINTENANCE TORQUE SPECIFICATIONS

	N•m	in.-lb.	ft.-lb.
Banjo bolt at oil strainer	37	–	27
Brake lever adjuster locknut	6	53	–
Crankcase oil drain bolt	25	–	18
Crankshaft hole cap	7	62	–
Down tube oil drain bolt	39	–	29
Driven sprocket	32	–	24
Fuel valve mounting bolt	9	80	–
Oil strainer screen	54	–	40
Rear axle nut	88	–	65
Rim lock	13	115	–
Spark plug	18	–	13
Timing mark hole cap	10	88	7
Valve adjusting locknut	24	–	18
Valve covers	15	–	11

RECOMMENDED LUBRICANTS AND FUEL

Engine oil	Honda GN4 or HP4 10W-40 or 20W-50 API SF or SG
Air filter	Foam air filter oil
Drive chain[1]	Pro Honda Chain Lube or other non-tacky O-ring chain lubricant
Brake fluid	DOT 4
Steering and suspension lubricant	Multipurpose grease
Fuel	Pump gasoline with Octane rating of 92 or higher
Control cables[2]	Cable lube

1. Use kerosene to clean O-ring drive chain.
2. Do not use chain lube to clean and lubricate control cables.

ENGINE OIL CAPACITY

	Liters	U.S. qt.	Imp. qt.
Oil change only	1.7	1.8	1.5
Oil and filter change	1.8	1.9	1.6
After engine disassembly	2.2	2.3	1.9

SPARK PLUG TYPE AND GAP

Spark plug type	
Standard	NGK DPR8Z
	Denso X24GPR-U
Colder plug for high speed riding	NGK DPR9Z
	Denso X27GPR-U
Spark plug gap	0.6-0.7 mm (0.023-0.028 in.)

ENGINE COMPRESSION

Engine compression	686-980 kPa (100-142 psi) @ 450 rpm

VALVE CLEARANCE

Intake valve	0.081-0.121 mm (0.0032-0.0048 in.)
Exhaust valve	0.106-0.147 mm (0.0042-0.0058 in.)

ENGINE IDLE SPEED

Engine idle speed	1200-1400 rpm

DRIVE CHAIN SLIDER SPECIFICATIONS

Drive chain slack	35-45 mm (1 1/3-1 3/4 in.)
Stock drive chain size/link	DID 520V8/108
	RK 520MOZ6/108
Drive chain length at 41 pins/40 links service limit	638 mm (25.1 in.)

TIRE INFLATION PRESSURE

	psi (kPa)
Front and rear tire	15 (100)

CLYMER®

HONDA

XR400R • 1996-2000

CHAPTER ONE

GENERAL INFORMATION

This detailed and comprehensive manual covers the Honda XR400R model from 1996-2000.

The text provides complete information on maintenance, tune-up, repair and overhaul. Hundreds of photos and drawings guide the reader through every job.

A shop manual is a reference tool and as in all Clymer manuals, the chapters are thumb tabbed for easy reference. Important items are indexed at the end of the book. All procedures, tables and figures are designed for the reader who may be working on the Honda for the first time. Frequently used specifications and capacities from individual chapters are summarized in the *Quick Reference Data* at the front of the book.

Tables 1-8 are at the end of this chapter.

Table 1 lists models and serial numbers.

Table 2 lists vehicle dimensions.

Table 3 lists vehicle weight.

Table 4 lists decimal and metric equivalents.

Table 5 lists conversion tables.

Table 6 lists general torque specifications.

Table 7 lists technical abbreviations.

Table 8 lists metric tap and drill sizes.

MANUAL ORGANIZATION

All dimensions and capacities are expressed in metric and U.S. standard units of measurement.

This chapter provides general information on shop safety, tool use, service fundamentals and shop supplies. The tables at the end of the chapter include general vehicle information.

Chapter Two provides methods for quick and accurate diagnosis of problems. Troubleshooting procedures present typical symptoms and logical methods to pinpoint and repair the problem.

Chapter Three explains all routine maintenance necessary to keep the vehicle running well. Chapter Three also includes recommended tune-up procedures, eliminating the need to constantly consult the chapters on the various assemblies.

Subsequent chapters describe specific systems such as engine, transmission, clutch, drive system, fuel and exhaust systems, suspension and brakes. Each disassembly, repair and assembly procedure is discussed in step-by-step form.

Some of the procedures in this manual specify special tools. In most cases, the tool is illustrated in use. Well-equipped mechanics may be able to substitute similar tools or fabricate a suitable replacement. However, in some cases, the specialized equipment or expertise may make it impractical for the home mechanic to attempt the procedure. When necessary, such operations are identified in the text with the recommendation to have a dealership or specialist perform the task. It may be less expensive to have a professional perform these jobs, especially when considering the cost of the equipment.

WARNINGS, CAUTIONS AND NOTES

The terms, WARNING, CAUTION and NOTE have specific meanings in this manual.

A WARNING emphasizes areas where injury or even death could result from negligence. Mechanical damage may also occur. WARNINGS *are to be taken seriously.*

A CAUTION emphasizes areas where equipment damage could result. Disregarding a CAUTION could cause permanent mechanical damage, though injury is unlikely.

A NOTE provides additional information to make a step or procedure easier or clearer. Disregarding a NOTE could cause inconvenience, but would not cause equipment damage or personal injury.

SAFETY

Professional mechanics can work for years and never sustain a serious injury or mishap. Follow these guidelines and practice common sense to safely service the vehicle.

1. Do not operate the vehicle in an enclosed area. The exhaust gasses contain carbon monoxide, an odorless, colorless, and tasteless poisonous gas. Carbon monoxide levels build quickly in small enclosed areas and can cause unconsciousness and death in a short time. Make sure the work area is properly ventilated or operate the vehicle outside.

2. *Never* use gasoline or any extremely flammable liquid to clean parts. Refer to *Cleaning Parts* and *Handling Gasoline Safely* in this chapter.

3. *Never* smoke or use a torch in the vicinity of flammable liquids, such as gasoline or cleaning solvent.

4. If welding or brazing on the vehicle, remove the fuel tank, carburetor and shock to a safe distance at least 50 ft. (15 m) away.

5. Use the correct type and size of tools to avoid damaging fasteners.

6. Keep tools clean and in good condition. Replace or repair worn or damaged equipment.

7. When loosening a tight fastener, be guided by what would happen if the tool slips.

8. When replacing fasteners, make sure the new fasteners are of the same size and strength as the original ones.

9. Keep the work area clean and organized.

10. Wear eye protection *anytime* the safety of your eyes is in question. This includes procedures involving drilling, grinding, hammering, compressed air and chemicals.

11. Wear the correct clothing for the job. Tie up or cover long hair so it can not get caught in moving equipment.

12. Do not carry sharp tools in clothing pockets.

13. Always have an approved fire extinguisher available. Make sure it is rated for gasoline (Class B) and electrical (Class C) fires.

14. Do not use compressed air to clean clothes, the vehicle or the work area. Debris may be blown into your eyes or skin. *Never* direct compressed air at yourself or someone else. Do not allow children to use or play with any compressed air equipment.

15. When using compressed air to dry rotating parts, hold the part so it can not rotate. Do not allow the force of the air to spin the part. The air jet is capable of rotating parts at extreme speed. The part may be damaged or disintegrate, causing serious injury.

16. Do not inhale the dust created by brake pad and clutch wear. These particles may contain asbestos. In addition, some types of insulating materials and gaskets may contain asbestos. Inhaling asbestos particles is hazardous to health.

17. Never work on the vehicle while someone is working under it.

18. When placing the vehicle on a stand, make sure it is secure before walking away.

Handling Gasoline Safely

Gasoline is a volatile flammable liquid and is one of the most dangerous items in the shop.

Because gasoline is used so often, many people forget that it is hazardous. Only use gasoline as fuel for gasoline internal combustion engines. Keep in mind, when working on a vehicle, gasoline is always present in the fuel tank, fuel line and carburetor. To avoid a disastrous accident when working around the fuel system, carefully observe the following precautions:

1. *Never* use gasoline to clean parts. See *Cleaning Parts* in this chapter.

2. When working on the fuel system, work outside or in a well-ventilated area.

3. Do not add fuel to the fuel tank or service the fuel system while the vehicle is near open flames, sparks or where someone is smoking. Gasoline vapor is heavier than air. It collects in low areas and is more easily ignited than liquid gasoline.

4. Allow the engine to cool completely before working on any fuel system component.

5. When draining the carburetor, catch the fuel in a plastic container and then pour it into an approved gasoline storage devise.

6. Do not store gasoline in glass containers. If the glass breaks, a serious explosion or fire may occur.

7. Immediately wipe up spilled gasoline with rags. Store the rags in a metal container with a lid until they can be properly disposed of, or place them outside in a safe place for the fuel to evaporate.

8. Do not pour water onto a gasoline fire. Water spreads the fire and makes it more difficult to put out. Use a class B, BC or ABC fire extinguisher to extinguish the fire.

9. Always turn off the engine before refueling. Do not spill fuel onto the engine or exhaust system. Do not overfill the fuel tank. Leave an air space at the top of the tank to allow room for the fuel to expand due to temperature fluctuations.

Cleaning Parts

Cleaning parts is one of the more tedious and difficult service jobs performed in the home garage. There are many types of chemical cleaners and solvents available for shop use. Most are poisonous and extremely flammable. To prevent chemical exposure, vapor buildup, fire and serious injury, observe each product warning label and note the following:

1. Read and observe the entire product label before using any chemical. Always know what type of chemical is being used and whether it is poisonous and/or flammable.

2. Do not use more than one type of cleaning solvent at a time. If mixing chemicals is called for, measure the proper amounts according to the manufacturer.

3. Work in a well-ventilated area.

4. Wear chemical-resistant gloves.

5. Wear safety glasses.

6. Wear a vapor respirator if the instructions call for it.

7. Wash hands and arms thoroughly after cleaning parts.

8. Keep chemical products away from children and pets.

9. Thoroughly clean all oil, grease and cleaner residue from any part that must be heated.

10. Use a nylon brush when cleaning parts. Metal brushes may cause a spark.

11. When using a parts washer, only use the solvent recommended by the manufacturer. Make sure the parts washer is equipped with a metal lid that will lower in case of fire.

Warning Labels

Most manufacturers attach information and warning labels to the vehicle. These labels contain instructions that are important to personal safety when operating, servicing, transporting and storing the vehicle. Refer to the owner's manual for the description and location of labels. Order replacement labels from the manufacturer if they are missing or damaged.

SERIAL NUMBERS

Serial numbers are stamped onto the frame and engine. Record these numbers in the *Quick Reference Data* section at the front of the book. Have these numbers available when ordering parts.

The frame number (**Figure 1**) or vehicle identification number (VIN) is stamped on the steering tube.

The engine number (**Figure 2**) is stamped on a pad on the lower side of the left crankcase.

Table 1 lists model years and numbers.

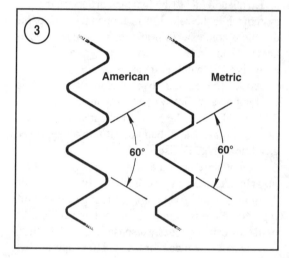

FASTENERS

Proper fastener selection and installation is important to ensure that the vehicle operates as designed, and can be serviced efficiently. The choice of original equipment fasteners is not arrived at by chance. Make sure that replacement fasteners meet all the same requirements as the originals.

Threaded Fasteners

Threaded fasteners secure most of the components on the vehicle. Most are tightened by turning them clockwise (right-hand threads). If the normal rotation of the component being tightened would loosen the fastener, it may have left-hand threads. If a left-hand threaded fastener is used, it is noted in the text.

Two dimensions are required to match the size of the fastener: the number of threads in a given distance and the outside diameter of the threads.

Two systems are currently used to specify threaded fastener dimensions: the U.S. Standard system and the metric system (**Figure 3**). Pay particular attention when working with unidentified fasteners; mismatching thread types can damage threads.

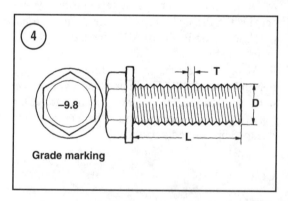

Grade marking

NOTE
To ensure that the fastener threads are not mismatched or cross-threaded, start all fasteners by hand. If a fastener is hard to start or turn, determine the cause before tightening with a wrench.

The length (L, **Figure 4**), diameter (D) and distance between thread crests (pitch) (T) classify met-

ric screws and bolts. A typical bolt may be identified by the numbers, 8—1.25 × 130. This indicates the bolt has diameter of 8 mm, the distance between thread crests is 1.25 mm and the length is 130 mm. Always measure bolt length as shown in **Figure 4** to avoid purchasing replacements of the wrong length.

The numbers located on the top of the fastener (**Figure 4**) indicate the strength of metric screws

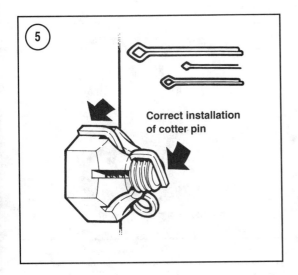

Correct installation of cotter pin

and bolts. The higher the number, the stronger the fastener is. Unnumbered fasteners are the weakest.

Many screws, bolts and studs are combined with nuts to secure particular components. To indicate the size of a nut, manufacturers specify the internal diameter and the thread pitch.

The measurement across two flats on a nut or bolt indicates the wrench size.

> *WARNING*
> *Do not install fasteners with a strength classification lower than what was originally installed by the manufacturer. Doing so may cause equipment failure and/or damage.*

Torque Specifications

The materials used in the manufacture of the vehicle may be subjected to uneven stresses if the fasteners of the various subassemblies are not installed and tightened correctly. Fasteners that are improperly installed or work loose can cause extensive damage. It is essential to use an accurate torque wrench, described in this chapter, with the torque specifications in this manual.

Specifications for torque are provided in Newton-meters (N•m), foot-pounds (ft.-lb.) and inch-pounds (in.-lb.). Refer to **Table 5** for torque conversions and **Table 6** for general torque specifications. To use **Table 6**, first determine the size of the fastener as described in *Fasteners* in this chapter. Torque specifications for specific components

are at the end of the appropriate chapters. Torque wrenches are covered in the *Basic Tools* section.

Self-Locking Fasteners

Several types of bolts, screws and nuts incorporate a system that creates interference between the two fasteners. Interference is achieved in various ways. The most common type is the nylon insert nut and a dry adhesive coating on the threads of a bolt.

Self-locking fasteners offer greater holding strength than standard fasteners, which improves their resistance to vibration. Most self-locking fasteners cannot be reused. The materials used to form the lock become distorted after the initial installation and removal. It is a good practice to discard and replace self-locking fasteners after their removal. Do not replace self-locking fasteners with standard fasteners.

Washers

There are two basic types of washers: flat washers and lockwashers. Flat washers are simple discs with a hole to fit a screw or bolt. Lockwashers are used to prevent a fastener from working loose. Washers can be used as spacers and seals, or to help distribute fastener load and to prevent the fastener from damaging the component.

As with fasteners, when replacing washers make sure the replacement washers are of the same design and quality.

Cotter Pins

A cotter pin is a split metal pin inserted into a hole or slot to prevent a fastener from loosening. In certain applications, such as the rear axle on an ATV or motorcycle, the fastener must be secured in this way. For these applications, a cotter pin and castellated (slotted) nut are used.

To use a cotter pin, first make sure the diameter is correct for the hole in the fastener. After correctly tightening the fastener and aligning the holes, insert the cotter pin through the hole and bend the ends over the fastener (**Figure 5**). Unless instructed to do so, never loosen a torqued fastener to align the holes. If the holes do not align, tighten the fastener just enough to achieve alignment.

Cotter pins are available in various diameters and lengths. Measure length from the bottom of the head to the tip of the shortest pin.

Circlips and E-clips

Circlips (**Figure 6**) are circular-shaped metal retaining clips. They are required to secure parts and gears in place on parts such as shafts, pins or rods. External type circlips are used to retain items on shafts. Internal type circlips secure parts within housing bores. In some applications, in addition to securing the component(s), circlips of varying thickness also determine endplay. These are usually called selective circlips.

Two basic types of circlips are used: machined and stamped circlips. Machined circlips (**Figure 7**) can be installed in either direction, since both faces have sharp edges. Stamped circlips (**Figure 8**) are manufactured with a sharp edge and a round edge. When installing a stamped circlip in a thrust application, install the sharp edge facing away from the part producing the thrust.

E-clips are used when it is not practical to use a circlip. Remove E-clips with a flat blade screwdriver by prying between the shaft and E-clip. To install an E-clip, center it over the shaft groove and push or tap it into place.

Observe the following when installing circlips:
1. Remove and install circlips with circlip pliers. See *Circlip Pliers* in this chapter.
2. In some applications, it may be necessary to replace circlips after removing them.
3. Compress or expand circlips only enough to install them. If overly expanded, they lose their retaining ability.
4. After installing a circlip, make sure it seats completely.
5. Wear eye protection when removing and installing circlips.

SHOP SUPPLIES

Lubricants and Fluids

Periodic lubrication helps ensure a long service life for any type of equipment. Using the correct type of lubricant is as important as performing the lubrication service, although in an emergency the wrong type is better than none. The following sec-

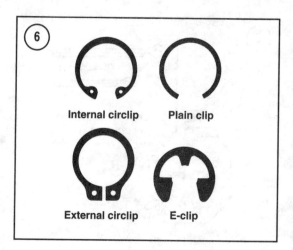

Internal circlip   Plain clip

External circlip   E-clip

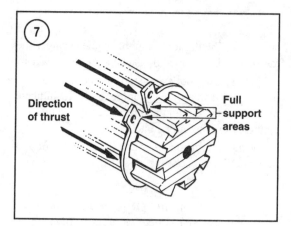

Direction of thrust

Full support areas

tion describes the types of lubricants most often required. Make sure to follow the manufacturer's recommendations for lubricant types.

Engine oils

Engine oil is classified by two standards: the American Petroleum Institute (API) service classification and the Society of Automotive Engineers (SAE) viscosity rating. This information is on the oil container label. Two letters indicate the API service classification. The number or sequence of numbers and letter (10W-40 for example) is the oil's viscosity rating. The API service classification and the SAE viscosity index are not indications of oil quality.

The service classification indicates that the oil meets specific lubrication standards. The first letter in the classification (*S*) indicates that the oil is for gasoline engines. The second letter indicates the

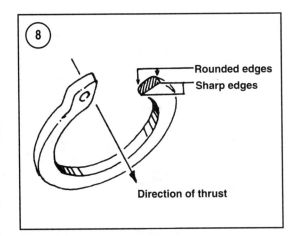

Rounded edges
Sharp edges
Direction of thrust

standard the oil satisfies. The classification started with the letter (*A*) and is currently at the letter (*J*).

Always use an oil with a classification recommended by the manufacturer. Using an oil with a classification different than that recommended can cause engine damage.

Viscosity is an indication of the oil's thickness. Thin oils have a lower number while thick oils have a higher number. Engine oils fall into the 5- to 50-weight range for single-grade oils.

Most manufacturers recommend multigrade oil. These oils perform efficiently across a wide range of operating conditions. Multigrade oils are identified by a (*W*) after the first number, which indicates the low-temperature viscosity.

Engine oils are most commonly mineral (petroleum) based; however synthetic and semi-synthetic types are used more frequently. When selecting engine oil, follow the manufacturer's recommendation for type, classification and viscosity.

Greases

Grease is lubricating oil with thickening agents added to it. The National Lubricating Grease Institute (NLGI) grades grease. Grades range from No. 000 to No. 6, with No. 6 being the thickest. Typical multipurpose grease is NLGI No. 2. For specific applications, manufacturers may recommend water-resistant type grease or one with an additive such as molybdenum disulfide (MoS_2).

Brake fluid

Brake fluid is the hydraulic fluid used to transmit hydraulic pressure (force) to the wheel brakes. Brake fluid is classified by the Department of Transportation (DOT). Current designations for brake fluid are DOT 3, DOT 4 and DOT 5. This classification appears on the fluid container.

Each type of brake fluid has its own definite characteristics. Do not intermix different types of brake fluid. DOT 5 fluid is silicone-based. DOT 5 is not compatible with other fluids or in systems for which it was not designed. Mixing DOT 5 fluid with other fluids may cause brake system failure. When adding brake fluid, *only* use the fluid recommended by the manufacturer.

Brake fluid will damage any plastic, painted or plated surface it contacts. Use extreme care when working with brake fluid and remove any spills immediately with soap and water.

Hydraulic brake systems require clean and moisture free brake fluid. Never reuse brake fluid. Keep containers and reservoirs properly sealed.

> *WARNING*
> *Never put a mineral-based (petroleum) oil into the brake system. Mineral oil will cause rubber parts in the system to swell and break apart, resulting in complete brake failure.*

Chain lubricant

There are many types of chain lubricants available. Which type of chain lubricant to use depends on the type of chain.

On O-ring (sealed) chains, the lubricant keeps the O-rings pliable and prevents corrosion. The actual chain lubricant is enclosed in the chain by the O-rings. Recommended types include aerosol sprays specifically designed for O-ring chains, and conventional engine or gear oils. When using a spray lubricant, make sure it is suitable for O-ring chains.

Do not use a high-pressure washer, solvents or gasoline to clean an O-ring chain; clean only with kerosene.

Foam air filter oil

Filter oil is specifically designed for use in foam air filters. The oil is blended with additives making it easy to pour and apply evenly to the filter. These additives evaporate quickly, making the filter oil very tacky. This allows the oil to remain suspended within the foam pores, trapping dirt and preventing it from being drawn into the engine.

Do not use engine oil as a substitute for foam filter oil. Engine oils will not remain in the filter. Instead, they will be drawn into the engine, leaving the filter ineffective.

Cleaners, Degreasers and Solvents

Many chemicals are available to remove oil, grease and other residue from the vehicle.

Before using cleaning solvents, consider how they will be used and disposed of, particularly if they are not water-soluble. Local ordinances may require special procedures for the disposal of many types of cleaning chemicals. Refer to *Safety and Cleaning Parts* in this chapter for more information on their use.

Use brake parts cleaner to clean brake system components when contact with petroleum-based products will damage seals. Brake parts cleaner leaves no residue. Use electrical contact cleaner to clean electrical connections and components without leaving any residue. Carburetor cleaner is a powerful solvent used to remove fuel deposits and varnish from fuel system components. Use this cleaner carefully, as it may damage finishes.

Generally, degreasers are strong cleaners used to remove heavy accumulations of grease from engine and frame components.

Most solvents are designed to be used in a parts washing cabinet for individual component cleaning. For safety, use only nonflammable or high flash point solvents.

Gasket Sealant

Sealants are used in combination with a gasket or seal and are occasionally used alone. Follow the manufacturer's recommendation when using sealants. Use extreme care when choosing a sealant different from the type originally recommended. Choose sealants based on their resistance to heat, various fluids and their sealing capabilities.

One of the most common sealants is RTV, or room temperature vulcanizing sealant. This sealant cures at room temperature over a specific time pe-

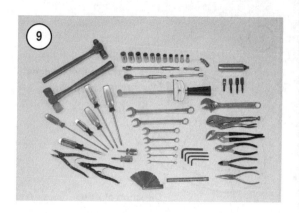

riod. This allows the repositioning of components without damaging gaskets.

Moisture in the air causes the RTV sealant to cure. Always install the tube cap as soon as possible after applying RTV sealant. RTV sealant has a limited shelf life and will not cure properly if the shelf life has expired. Keep partial tubes sealed and discard them if they have surpassed the expiration date.

Applying RTV sealant

Clean all old gasket residue from the mating surfaces. Remove all gasket material from blind threaded holes; it can cause inaccurate bolt torque. Spray the mating surfaces with aerosol parts cleaner and then wipe with a lint-free cloth. The area must be clean for the sealant to adhere.

Apply RTV sealant in a continuous bead 2-3 mm (0.08-0.12 in.) thick. Circle all the fastener holes unless otherwise specified. Do not allow any sealant to enter these holes. Assemble and tighten the fasteners to the specified torque within the time frame recommended by the RTV sealant manufacturer.

Gasket Remover

Aerosol gasket remover can help remove stubborn gaskets. This product can speed up the removal process and prevent damage to the mating surface that may be caused by using a scraping tool. Most of these types of products are very caustic. Follow the gasket remover manufacturer's instructions for use.

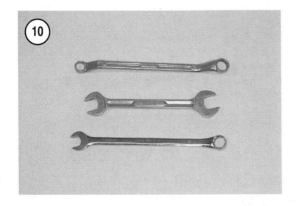

Threadlocking Compound

A threadlocking compound is a fluid applied to the threads of fasteners. After tightening the fastener, the fluid dries and becomes a solid filler between the threads. This makes it difficult for the fastener to work loose from vibration, or heat expansion and contraction. Some threadlocking compounds also provide a seal against fluid leakage.

Before applying threadlocking compound remove any old compound from both thread areas and clean them with aerosol parts cleaner. Use the compound sparingly. Excess fluid can run into adjoining parts.

Threadlocking compounds are available in different strengths. Follow the particular manufacturer's recommendations regarding compound selection. Two manufacturers of threadlocking compound are ThreeBond and Loctite. They both offer a wide range of compounds for various strength, temperature and repair applications.

BASIC TOOLS

Most of the procedures in this manual can be carried out with simple hand tools and test equipment familiar to the home mechanic. Always use the correct tools for the job at hand. Keep tools organized and clean. Store them in a tool chest with related tools organized together.

Quality tools are essential. The best are constructed of high-strength alloy steel. These tools are light, easy to use and resistant to wear. Their working surface is devoid of sharp edges and the tool is carefully polished. They have an easy-to-clean finish and are comfortable to use. Quality tools are a good investment.

When purchasing tools to perform the procedures covered in this manual, consider the tools potential frequency of use. If a tool kit is just now being started, consider purchasing a basic tool set (**Figure 9**) from a large tool supplier. These sets are available in many tool combinations and offer substantial savings when compared to individually purchased tools. As work experience grows and tasks become more complicated, specialized tools can be added.

Screwdrivers

Screwdrivers of various lengths and types are mandatory for the simplest tool kit. The two basic types are the slotted tip (flat blade) and the Phillips tip. These are available in sets that often include an assortment of tip sizes and shaft lengths.

As with all tools, use a screwdriver designed for the job. Make sure the size of the tip conforms to the size and shape of the fastener. Use them only for driving screws. Never use a screwdriver for prying or chiseling metal. Repair or replace worn or damaged screwdrivers. A worn tip may damage the fastener, making it difficult to remove.

Wrenches

Open-end, box-end and combination wrenches (**Figure 10**) are available in a variety of types and sizes.

The number stamped on the wrench refers to the distance between the work areas. This size must match the size of the fastener head.

The box-end wrench is an excellent tool because it grips the fastener on all sides. This reduces the chance of the tool slipping. The box-end wrench is designed with either a 6 or 12-point opening. For stubborn or damaged fasteners, the 6-point provides superior holding ability by contacting the fastener across a wider area at all six edges. For general use, the 12-point works well. It allows the wrench to be removed and reinstalled without moving the handle over such a wide arc.

An open-end wrench is fast and works best in areas with limited overhead access. It contacts the fastener at only two points, and is subject to slipping under heavy force, or if the tool or fastener is worn.

A box-end wrench is preferred in most instances, especially when breaking loose and applying the final tightness to a fastener.

The combination wrench has a box-end on one end, and an open-end on the other. This combination makes it a very convenient tool.

Adjustable Wrenches

An adjustable wrench or Crescent wrench (**Figure 11**) can fit nearly any nut or bolt head that has clear access around its entire perimeter. Adjustable wrenches are best used as a backup wrench to keep a large nut or bolt from turning while the other end is being loosened or tightened with a box-end or socket wrench.

Adjustable wrenches contact the fastener at only two points, which makes them more subject to slipping off the fastener. The fact that one jaw is adjustable and may loosen only aggravates this shortcoming. Make certain the solid jaw is the one transmitting the force.

Socket Wrenches, Ratchets and Handles

Sockets that attach to a ratchet handle (**Figure 12**) are available with 6-point (A, **Figure 13**) or 12-point (B) openings and different drive sizes. The drive size indicates the size of the square hole that accepts the ratchet handle. The number stamped on the socket is the size of the work area and must match the fastener head.

As with wrenches, a 6-point socket provides superior-holding ability, while a 12-point socket needs to be moved only half as far to reposition it on the fastener.

Sockets are designated for either hand or impact use. Impact sockets are made of thicker material for more durability. Compare the size and wall thickness of a 19-mm hand socket (A, **Figure 14**) and the 19-mm impact socket (B). Use impact sockets when using an impact driver or air tools. Use hand sockets with hand-driven attachments.

> *WARNING*
> *Do not use hand sockets with air or impact tools, as they may shatter and cause injury. Always wear eye protection when using impact or air tools.*

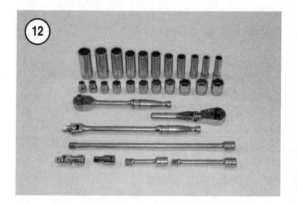

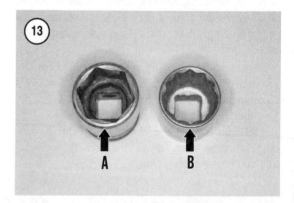

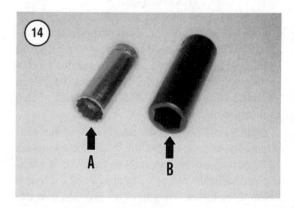

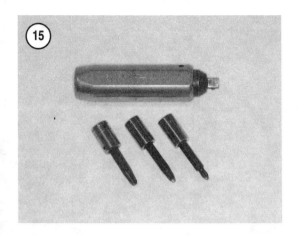

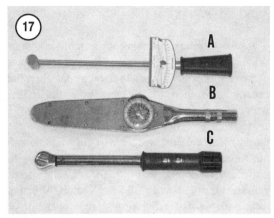

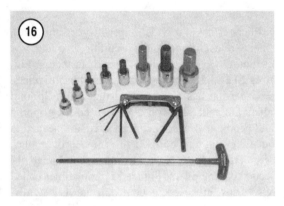

Various handles are available for sockets. The speed handle is used for fast operation. Flexible ratchet heads in varying lengths allow the socket to be turned with varying force, and at odd angles. Extension bars allow the socket setup to reach difficult areas. The ratchet is the most versatile. It allows the user to install or remove the nut without removing the socket.

Sockets combined with any number of drivers make them undoubtedly the fastest, safest and most convenient tool for fastener removal and installation.

Impact Driver

An impact driver provides extra force for removing fasteners, by converting the impact of a hammer into a turning motion. This makes it possible to remove stubborn fasteners without damaging them. Impact drivers and interchangeable bits (**Figure 15**) are available from most tool suppliers. When using a socket with an impact driver make sure the socket is designed for impact use. Refer to *Socket Wrenches, Ratchets and Handles* in this section.

> *WARNING*
> *Do not use hand sockets with air or impact tools as they may shatter and cause injury. Always wear eye protection when using impact or air tools.*

Allen Wrenches

Allen or setscrew wrenches (**Figure 16**) are used on fasteners with hexagonal recesses in the fastener head. These wrenches are available in L-shaped bar, socket and T-handle types. A metric set is required when working on most vehicles. Allen bolts are sometimes called socket bolts.

Torque Wrenches

A torque wrench is used with a socket, torque adapter or similar extension to tighten a fastener to a measured torque. Torque wrenches come in several drive sizes (1/4, 3/8, 1/2 and 3/4) and and have various methods of reading the torque value. The drive size indicates the size of the square drive that accepts the socket, adapter or extension. Common methods of reading the torque value are the deflecting beam (A, **Figure 17**), the dial indicator (B) and the audible click (C).

When choosing a torque wrench, consider the torque range, drive size and accuracy. The torque specifications in this manual provide an indication of the range required.

A torque wrench is a precision tool that must be properly cared for to remain accurate. Store torque wrenches in cases or separate padded drawers within a toolbox. Follow the manufacturer's instructions for their care and calibration.

Torque Adapters

Torque adapters or extensions extend or reduce the reach of a torque wrench. The torque adapter shown in **Figure 18** is used to tighten a fastener that cannot be reached due to the size of the torque wrench head, drive, and socket. If a torque adapter changes the effective lever length (**Figure 19**), the torque reading on the wrench will not equal the actual torque applied to the fastener. It is necessary to recalibrate the torque setting on the wrench to compensate for the change of lever length. When a torque adapter is used at a right angle to the drive head, calibration is not required, since the effective length has not changed.

To recalculate a torque reading when using a torque adapter, use the following formula, and refer to **Figure 19**.

$$TW = \frac{TA \times L}{L + A}$$

TW is the torque setting or dial reading on the wrench. TA is the torque specification and the actual amount of torque that will be applied to the fastener. A is the amount that the adapter increases (or in some cases reduces) the lever length as measured along the centerline of the torque wrench (**Figure 19**). L is the lever length of the wrench as measured from the center of the drive to the center of the grip. The effective length of the torque wrench is the sum of L and A.

Example:

TA = 20 ft.-lb.
A = 3 in.
L = 14 in.

$$TW = \frac{20 \times 14}{14 + 3} = \frac{280}{17} = 16.5 \text{ ft. lb.}$$

In this example, the torque wrench would be set to the recalculated torque value (TW = 16.5 ft.-lb.). When using a beam-type wrench, tighten the fastener until the pointer aligns with 16.5 ft.-lb. In this example, although the torque wrench is preset to 16.5 ft.-lb., the actual torque is 20 ft.-lb.

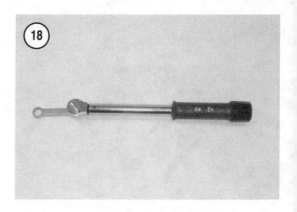

Pliers

Pliers come in a wide range of types and sizes. Pliers are useful for holding, cutting, bending, and crimping. Do not use them to turn fasteners. **Figures 20 and 21** show several types of useful pliers. Each design has a specialized function. Slip-joint pliers are general-purpose pliers used for gripping and bending. Diagonal cutting pliers are needed to cut wire and can be used to remove cotter pins. Needlenose pliers are used to hold or bend small objects. Locking pliers (**Figure 21**), sometimes called Vise-grips, are used to hold objects very tightly. They have many uses ranging from holding two parts together, to gripping the end of a broken stud. Use caution when using locking pliers, as the sharp jaws will damage the objects they hold.

Circlip Pliers

Circlip or snap ring pliers (**Figure 22**) are specialized pliers with tips that fit into the ends of circlips to remove and install them.

Circlip pliers are available with a fixed action (either internal or external) or convertible (one tool works on both internal and external circlips). They may have fixed tips or interchangeable ones of various sizes and angles. For general use, select a convertible type plier with interchangeable tips.

WARNING
Circlips can slip and fly off when removing and installing them. Also, the circlip plier tips may break. Always wear eye protection when using circlip pliers.

⑲ **HOW TO MEASURE TORQUE WRENCH EFFECTIVE LENGTH**

L   A

L   A

L + A = Effective length

L

L = Effective length

L

No calculation needed

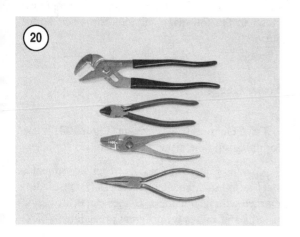

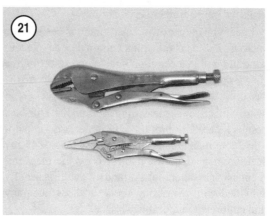

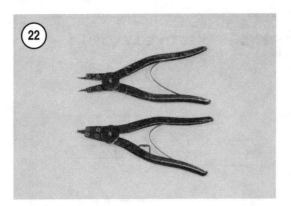

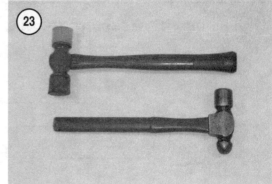

Hammers

Various types of hammers (**Figure 23**) are available to fit a number of applications. A ball-peen hammer is used to strike another tool, such as a punch or chisel. Soft-faced hammers are required when a metal object must be struck without damaging it. *Never* use a metal-faced hammer on engine and suspension components, as damage will occur in most cases.

Always wear eye protection when using hammers. Make sure the hammer face is in good condition and the handle is not cracked. Select the correct hammer for the job and make sure to strike the object squarely. Do not use the handle or the side of the hammer to strike an object.

PRECISION MEASURING TOOLS

The ability to accurately measure components is essential to successfully rebuild an engine. Equipment is manufactured to close tolerances, and obtaining consistently accurate measurements is essential to determining which components require replacement or further service.

Each type of measuring instrument is designed to measure a dimension with a certain degree of accuracy and within a certain range. When selecting the measuring tool, make sure it is applicable to the task.

As with all tools, measuring tools provide the best results if cared for properly. Improper use can damage the tool and result in inaccurate results. If any measurement is questionable, verify the measurement using another tool. A standard gauge is usually provided with measuring tools to check accuracy and calibrate the tool if necessary.

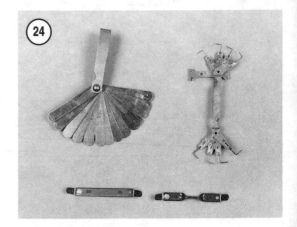

Precision measurements can vary according to the experience of the person performing the procedure. Accurate results are only possible if the mechanic possesses a feel for using the tool. Heavy-handed use of measuring tools may produce inaccurate results. Hold the tool gently by the fingertips so the point at which the tool contacts the object is easily felt. This feel for the equipment will produce more accurate measurements and reduce the risk of damaging the tool or component. Refer to the following sections for specific measuring tools.

Feeler Gauge

The feeler or thickness gauge (**Figure 24**) is used for measuring the distance between two surfaces.

A feeler gauge set consists of an assortment of steel strips of graduated thickness. Each blade is marked with its thickness. Blades can be of various lengths and angles for different procedures.

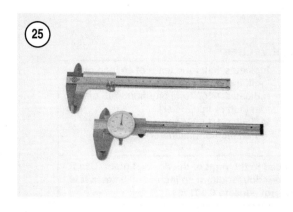

(25)

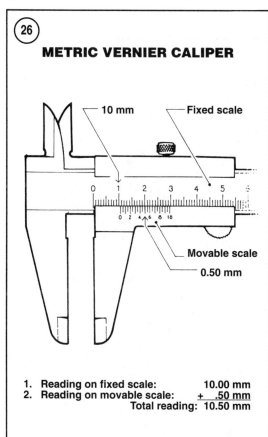

(26)

METRIC VERNIER CALIPER

10 mm

Fixed scale

0   1   2   3   4   5

0 2 4 6 8 10

Movable scale

0.50 mm

1. Reading on fixed scale: 10.00 mm
2. Reading on movable scale: +   .50 mm
                     Total reading: 10.50 mm

A common use for a feeler gauge is to measure valve clearance. Wire (round) type gauges are used to measure spark plug gap.

Calipers

Calipers (**Figure 25**) are excellent tools for obtaining inside, outside and depth measurements. Although not as precise as a micrometer, they allow reasonable precision, typically to within 0.05 mm (0.001 in.). Most calipers have a range up to 150 mm (6 in.).

Calipers are available in dial, vernier or digital versions. Dial calipers have a dial readout that provides convenient reading. Vernier calipers have marked scales that must be compared to determine the measurement. The digital caliper uses an LCD to show the measurement.

Properly maintain the measuring surfaces of the caliper. There must not be any dirt or burrs between the tool and the object being measured. Never force the caliper closed around an object; close the caliper around the highest point so it can be removed with a slight drag. Some calipers require calibration. Always refer to the manufacturer's instructions when using a new or unfamiliar caliper.

To read a vernier caliper refer to **Figure 26**. The fixed scale is marked in 1 mm increments. Ten individual lines on the fixed scale equal 1 cm. The moveable scale is marked in 0.05 mm (hundredth) increments. To obtain a reading, establish the first number by the location of the 0 line on the movable scale in relation to the first line to the left on the fixed scale. In this example, the number is 10 mm. To determine the next number, note which of the lines on the movable scale align with a mark on the fixed scale. A number of lines will seem close, but only one will align exactly. In this case, 0.50 mm is the reading to add to the first number. The result of adding 10 mm and 0.50 mm is a measurement of 10.50 mm.

Micrometers

A micrometer is an instrument designed for linear measurement using the decimal divisions of the inch or meter (**Figure 27**). While there are many types and styles of micrometers, most of the procedures in this manual require an outside micrometer. The outside micrometer is used to measure the outside diameter of cylindrical forms and the thickness of materials.

A micrometer's size indicates the minimum and maximum size of a part that it can measure. The usual sizes (**Figure 28**) are 0-1 in. (0-25 mm), 1-2 in. (25-50 mm), 2-3 in. (50-75 mm) and 3-4 in. (75-100 mm).

Micrometers that cover a wider range of measurement are available. These use a large frame with interchangeable anvils of various lengths. This type

DECIMAL PLACE VALUES*

0.1	Indicates 1/10 (one tenth of an inch or millimeter)
0.010	Indicates 1/100 (one one-hundreth of an inch or millimeter)
0.001	Indicates 1/1,000 (one one-thousandth of an inch or millimeter)

*This chart represents the values of figures placed to the right of the decimal point. Use it when reading decimals from one-tenth to one one-thousandth of an inch or millimeter. It is not a conversion chart (for example: 0.001 in. is not equal to 0.001 mm).

of micrometer offers a cost savings; however, its overall size may make it less convenient.

Reading a Micrometer

When reading a micrometer, numbers are taken from different scales and added together. The following sections describe how to read the measurements of various types of outside micrometers.

For accurate results, properly maintain the measuring surfaces of the micrometer. There cannot be any dirt or burrs between the tool and the measured object. Never force the micrometer closed around an object. Close the micrometer around the highest point so it can be removed with a slight drag. **Figure 29** shows the markings and parts of a standard inch micrometer. Be familiar with these terms before using a micrometer in the following sections.

Standard inch micrometer

The standard inch micrometer is accurate to one-thousandth of an inch or 0.001. The sleeve is marked in 0.025 in. increments. Every fourth sleeve mark is numbered 1, 2, 3, 4, 5, 6, 7, 8, 9. These numbers indicate 0.100, 0.200, 0.300, and so on.

The tapered end of the thimble has twenty-five lines marked around it. Each mark equals 0.001 in. One complete turn of the thimble will align its zero mark with the first mark on the sleeve or 0.025 in.

When reading a standard inch micrometer, perform the following steps while referring to **Figure 30**.
1. Read the sleeve and find the largest number visible. Each sleeve number equals 0.100 in.

2. Count the number of lines between the numbered sleeve mark and the edge of the thimble. Each sleeve mark equals 0.025 in.
3. Read the thimble mark that aligns with the sleeve line. Each thimble mark equals 0.001 in.

NOTE
If a thimble mark does not align exactly with the sleeve line, estimate the amount between the lines. For accurate readings in ten-thousandths of an inch (0.0001 in.), use a vernier inch micrometer.

4. Add the readings from Steps 1-3.

Vernier inch micrometer

A vernier inch micrometer is accurate to one ten-thousandth of an inch or 0.0001 in. It has the same marking as a standard inch micrometer with an additional vernier scale on the sleeve (**Figure 31**).

1

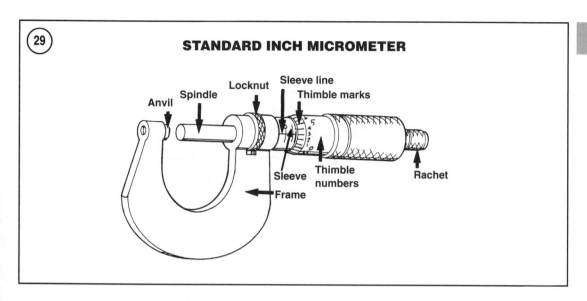

STANDARD INCH MICROMETER

Anvil · Spindle · Locknut · Sleeve line · Thimble marks · Sleeve · Thimble numbers · Frame · Rachet

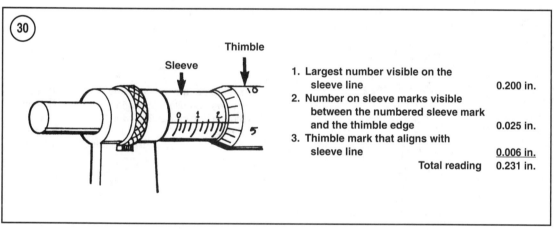

Sleeve · Thimble

1. Largest number visible on the sleeve line — 0.200 in.
2. Number on sleeve marks visible between the numbered sleeve mark and the thimble edge — 0.025 in.
3. Thimble mark that aligns with sleeve line — 0.006 in.

Total reading — 0.231 in.

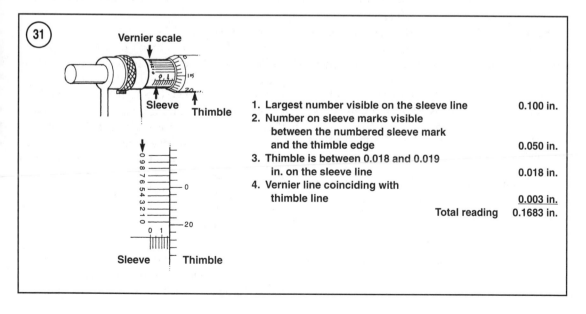

Vernier scale · Sleeve · Thimble · Sleeve · Thimble

1. Largest number visible on the sleeve line — 0.100 in.
2. Number on sleeve marks visible between the numbered sleeve mark and the thimble edge — 0.050 in.
3. Thimble is between 0.018 and 0.019 in. on the sleeve line — 0.018 in.
4. Vernier line coinciding with thimble line — 0.003 in.

Total reading — 0.1683 in.

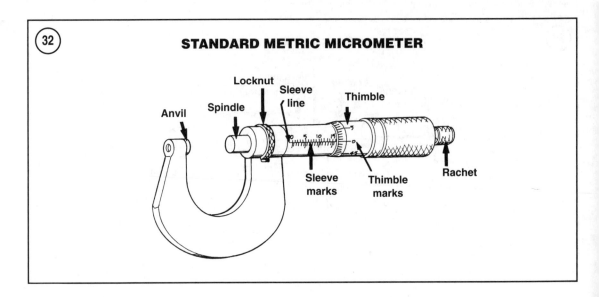

STANDARD METRIC MICROMETER

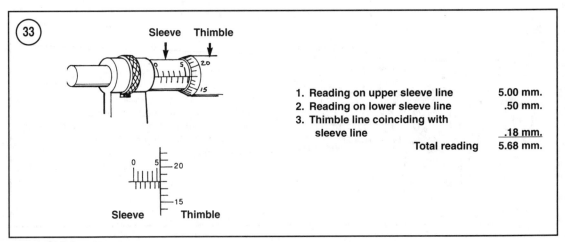

1. Reading on upper sleeve line   5.00 mm.
2. Reading on lower sleeve line   .50 mm.
3. Thimble line coinciding with
    sleeve line   .18 mm.
               Total reading   5.68 mm.

The vernier scale consists of 11 lines marked 1-9 with a 0 on each end. These lines run parallel to the thimble lines and represent 0.0001 in. increments.

When reading a vernier inch micrometer, perform the following steps while referring to **Figure 31**.

1. Read the micrometer in the same way as a standard micrometer. This is the initial reading.

2. If a thimble mark aligns exactly with the sleeve line, reading the vernier scale is not necessary. If they do not align, read the vernier scale in Step 3.

3. Determine which vernier scale mark aligns with one thimble mark. The vernier scale number is the amount in ten-thousandths of an inch to add to the initial reading from Step 1.

Metric micrometer

The standard metric micrometer (**Figure 32**) is accurate to one one-hundredth of a millimeter (0.01-mm). The sleeve line is graduated in millimeter and half millimeter increments. The marks on the upper half of the sleeve line equal 1.00 mm. Every fifth mark above the sleeve line is identified with a number. The number sequence depends on the size of the micrometer. A 0-25 mm micrometer, for example, will have sleeve marks numbered 0 through 25 in 5 mm increments. This numbering sequence continues with larger micrometers. On all metric micrometers, each mark on the lower half of the sleeve equals 0.50 mm.

The tapered end of the thimble has fifty lines marked around it. Each mark equals 0.01 mm.

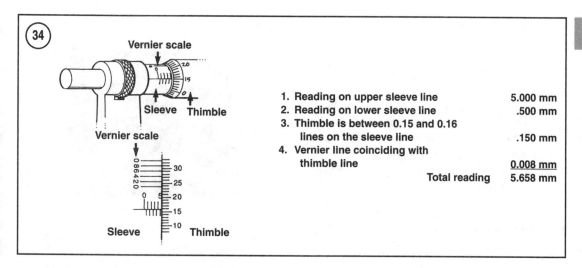

1. Reading on upper sleeve line   5.000 mm
2. Reading on lower sleeve line   .500 mm
3. Thimble is between 0.15 and 0.16
   lines on the sleeve line   .150 mm
4. Vernier line coinciding with
   thimble line   0.008 mm
                          Total reading   5.658 mm

One complete turn of the thimble aligns its 0 mark with the first line on the lower half of the sleeve line or 0.50 mm.

When reading a metric micrometer, add the number of millimeters and half-millimeters on the sleeve line to the number of one one-hundredth millimeters on the thimble. Perform the following steps while referring to **Figure 33**.
1. Read the upper half of the sleeve line and count the number of lines visible. Each upper line equals 1 mm.
2. See if the half-millimeter line is visible on the lower sleeve line. If so, add 0.50 to the reading in Step 1.
3. Read the thimble mark that aligns with the sleeve line. Each thimble mark equals 0.01 mm.

NOTE
If a thimble mark does not align exactly with the sleeve line, estimate the amount between the lines. For accurate readings in two-thousandths of a millimeter (0.002 mm), use a metric vernier micrometer.

4. Add the readings from Steps 1-3.

Metric vernier micrometer

A metric vernier micrometer (**Figure 34**) is accurate to two-thousandths of a millimeter (0.002-mm). It has the same markings as a standard metric micrometer with the addition of a vernier scale on the sleeve. The vernier scale consists of five lines marked 0, 2, 4, 6, and 8. These lines run parallel to the thimble lines and represent 0.002-mm increments.

When reading a metric vernier micrometer, perform the following steps and refer to **Figure 34**.
1. Read the micrometer in the same way as a standard metric micrometer. This is the initial reading.
2. If a thimble mark aligns exactly with the sleeve line, reading the vernier scale is not necessary. If they do not align, read the vernier scale in Step 3.
3. Determine which vernier scale mark aligns exactly with one thimble mark. The vernier scale number is the amount in two-thousandths of a millimeter to add to the initial reading from Step 1.

Micrometer Adjustment

Before using a micrometer, check its adjustment as follows.
1. Clean the anvil and spindle faces.
2A. To check a 0-1 in. or 0-25 mm micrometer:
   a. Turn the thimble until the spindle contacts the anvil. If the micrometer has a ratchet stop, use it to ensure that the proper amount of pressure is applied.
   b. If the adjustment is correct, the 0 mark on the thimble will align exactly with the 0 mark on the sleeve line. If the marks do not align, the micrometer is out of adjustment.
   c. Follow the manufacturer's instructions to adjust the micrometer.
2B. To check a micrometer larger than 1 in. or 25 mm use the standard gauge supplied by the manufacturer. A standard gauge is a steel block, disc or rod that is machined to an exact size.

a. Place the standard gauge between the spindle and anvil, and measure its outside diameter or length. If the micrometer has a ratchet stop, use it to ensure that the proper amount of pressure is applied.
b. If the adjustment is correct, the 0 mark on the thimble will align exactly with the 0 mark on the sleeve line. If the marks do not align, the micrometer requires adjustment.
c. Follow the manufacturer's instructions to adjust the micrometer.

Micrometer Care

Micrometers are precision instruments. They must be used and maintained with great care.

Note the following:

1. Store micrometers in protective cases or separate padded drawers in a toolbox.

2. When in storage, make sure the spindle and anvil faces do not contact each other or another object. If they do, temperature changes and corrosion may damage the contact faces.

3. Do not clean a micrometer with compressed air. Dirt forced into the tool will cause wear.

4. Lubricate micrometers with WD-40 to prevent corrosion.

Telescoping and Small Bore Gauges

Use telescoping gauges (**Figure 35**) and small hole gauges (**Figure 36**) to measure bores. Neither gauge has a scale for direct readings. An outside micrometer must be used to determine the reading.

To use a telescoping gauge, select the correct size gauge for the bore. Compress the movable post and carefully insert the gauge into the bore. Carefully move the gauge in the bore to make sure it is centered. Tighten the knurled end of the gauge to hold the movable post in position. Remove the gauge and measure the length of the posts. Telescoping gauges are typically used to measure cylinder bores.

To use a small-bore gauge, select the correct size gauge for the bore. Carefully insert the gauge into the bore. Tighten the knurled end of the gauge to carefully expand the gauge fingers to the limit within the bore. Do not overtighten the gauge, as there is no built-in release. Excessive tightening can damage the bore surface and damage the tool. Remove the gauge and measure the outside dimension

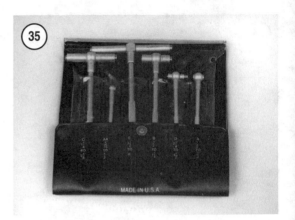

(**Figure 37**). Small hole gauges are typically used to measure valve guides.

Dial Indicator

A dial indicator (A, **Figure 38**) is a gauge with a dial face and needle used to measure variations in dimensions and movements. Measuring brake rotor runout is a typical use for a dial indicator.

Dial indicators are available in various ranges and graduations and with three basic types of mounting bases: magnetic, clamp, or screw-in stud. When

1

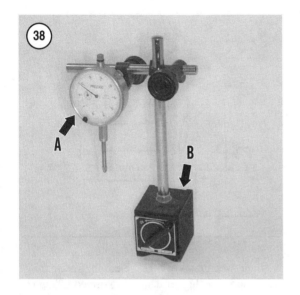

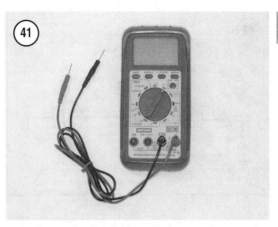

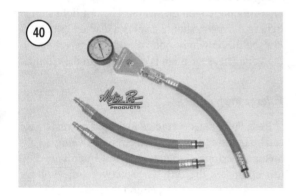

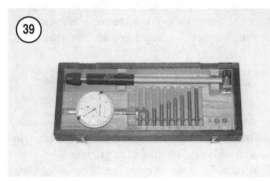

(anvils) to fit the gauge to various bore sizes. The bore gauge is used to measure bore size, taper and out-of-round. When using a bore gauge, follow the manufacturer's instructions.

Compression Gauge

A compression gauge (**Figure 40**) measures combustion chamber (cylinder) pressure, usually in psi or kg/cm^2. The gauge adapter is either inserted or screwed into the spark plug hole to obtain the reading. Disable the engine so it will not start and hold the throttle in the wide-open position when performing a compression test. An engine that does not have adequate compression cannot be properly tuned. See Chapter Three.

Multimeter

A multimeter (**Figure 41**) is an essential tool for electrical system diagnosis. The voltage function indicates the voltage applied or available to various electrical components. The ohmmeter function tests circuits for continuity, or lack of continuity, and measures the resistance of a circuit.

Some manufacturers'specifications for electrical components are based on results using a specific test meter. Results may vary if using a meter not recommend by the manufacturer. Such requirements are noted when applicable.

Ohmmeter (analog) calibration

Each time an analog ohmmeter is used or if the scale is changed, the ohmmeter must be calibrated.

purchasing a dial indicator, select the magnetic stand type (B, **Figure 38**) with a continuous dial.

Cylinder Bore Gauge

A cylinder bore gauge is similar to a dial indicator. The gauge set shown in **Figure 39** consists of a dial indicator, handle, and different length adapters

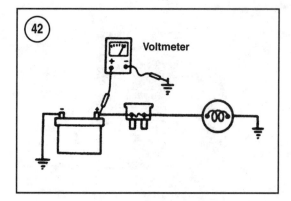

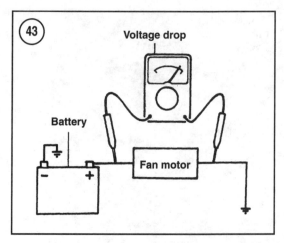

Digital ohmmeters do not require calibration.
1. Make sure the meter battery is in good condition.
2. Make sure the meter probes are in good condition.
3. Touch the two probes together and observe the needle location on the ohms scale. The needle must align with the 0 mark to obtain accurate measurements.
4. If necessary, rotate the meter ohms adjust knob until the needle and 0 mark align.

ELECTRICAL SYSTEM FUNDAMENTALS

A thorough study of the many types of electrical systems used in today's vehicles is beyond the scope of this manual. However, a basic understanding of electrical basics is necessary to perform simple diagnostic tests.

Voltage

Voltage is the electrical potential or pressure in an electrical circuit and is expressed in volts. The more pressure (voltage) in a circuit, the more work that can be performed.

Direct current (DC) voltage means the electricity flows in one direction. All circuits powered by a battery are DC circuits.

Alternating current (AC) means that the electricity flows in one direction momentarily then switches to the opposite direction. Alternator output is an example of AC voltage. This voltage must be changed or rectified to direct current to operate in a battery powered system.

Measuring voltage

Unless otherwise specified, perform all voltage tests with the electrical connectors attached.

When measuring voltage, select the meter range that is one scale higher than the expected voltage of the circuit to prevent damage to the meter. To determine the actual voltage in a circuit, use a voltmeter. To simply check if voltage is present, use a test light.

NOTE
When using a test light, either lead can be attached to ground.

1. Attach the negative meter test lead to a good ground (bare metal). Make sure the ground is not insulated with a rubber gasket or grommet.
2. Attach the positive meter test lead to the point being checked for voltage (**Figure 42**).
3. Turn on the ignition switch. The test light should light or the meter should display a reading. The reading should be within one volt of battery voltage. If the voltage is less, there is a problem in the circuit.

Voltage drop test

Resistance causes voltage to drop. This resistance can be measured in an active circuit by using a voltmeter to perform a voltage drop test. A voltage drop test compares the difference between the voltage available at the start of a circuit to the voltage at the end of the circuit while the circuit is operational. If the circuit has no resistance, there will be no voltage drop. The greater the resistance, the greater the voltage drop will be. A voltage drop of one volt or more indicates excessive resistance in the circuit.

1. Connect the positive meter test lead to the electrical source (where electricity is coming from).
2. Connect the negative meter test lead to the electrical load (where electricity is going). See **Figure 43**.

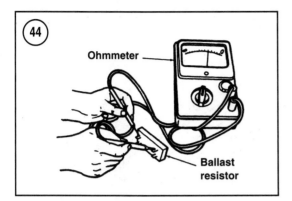

Ohmmeter

Ballast
resistor

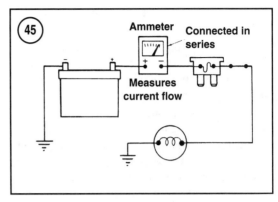

Ammeter Connected in
series

Measures
current flow

3. If necessary, activate the component(s) in the circuit.

4. A voltage reading of 1 volt or more indicates excessive resistance in the circuit. A reading equal to battery voltage indicates an open circuit.

Resistance

Resistance is the opposition to the flow of electricity within a circuit or component and is measured in ohms. Resistance causes a reduction in available current and voltage.

Resistance is measured in a inactive circuit with an ohmmeter. The ohmmeter sends a small amount of current into the circuit and measures how difficult it is to push the current through the circuit.

An ohmmeter, although useful, is not always a good indicator of a circuit's actual ability under operating conditions. This is due to the low voltage (6-9 volts) that the meter uses to test the circuit. The voltage in an ignition coil secondary winding can be several thousand volts. Such high voltage can cause the coil to malfunction, even though it tests acceptable during a resistance test.

Resistance generally increases with temperature. Perform all testing with the component or circuit at room temperature. Resistance tests performed at high temperatures may indicate high resistance readings and result in the unnecessary replacement of a component.

Measuring resistance and continuity testing

CAUTION
*Only use an ohmmeter on a circuit that has no voltage present. The meter will be damaged if it is connected to a live circuit. An analog meter must be calibrated each time it is used or the scale is changed. See **Multimeter** in this chapter.*

A continuity test can determine if the circuit is complete. Perform this type of test using an ohmmeter or a self-powered test lamp.

1. Disconnect the negative battery cable.

2. Attach one test lead (ohmmeter or test light) to one end of the component or circuit.

3. Attach the other test lead to the opposite end of the component or circuit (**Figure 44**).

4. A self-powered test light will come on if the circuit has continuity or is complete. An ohmmeter will indicate either low or no resistance if the circuit has continuity. An open circuit is indicated if the meter displays infinite resistance.

Amperage

Amperage is the unit of measure for the amount of current within a circuit. Current is the actual flow of electricity. The higher the current, the more work that can be performed up to a given point. If the current flow exceeds the circuit or component capacity, the system will be damaged.

Measuring amps

An ammeter measures the current flow or amps of a circuit (**Figure 45**). Amperage measurement requires that the circuit be disconnected and the ammeter be connected in series to the circuit. Always use an ammeter that can read higher than the anticipated current flow to prevent damage to the meter. Connect the red test lead to the electrical source and the black test lead to the electrical load.

SPECIAL TOOLS

Some of the procedures in this manual require special tools. These are described in the appropriate chapter and are available from either the manufacturer or a tool supplier.

In many cases, an acceptable substitute may be found in an existing tool kit. Another alternative is to make the tool. Many schools with a machine shop curriculum welcome outside work that can be used as practical shop applications for students.

BASIC SERVICE METHODS

Most of the procedures in this manual are straightforward and can be performed by anyone reasonably competent with tools. However, consider personal capabilities carefully before attempting any operation involving major disassembly of the engine.

1. Front, in this manual, refers to the front of the vehicle. The front of any component is the end closest to the front of the vehicle. The left and right sides refer to the position of the parts as viewed by the rider sitting on the seat facing forward.

2. Whenever servicing an engine or suspension component, secure the vehicle in a safe manner.

3. Tag all similar parts for location and mark all mating parts for position. Record the number and thickness of any shims as they are removed. Identify parts by placing them in sealed and labled plastic bags.

4. Tag disconnected wires and connectors with masking tape and a marking pen. Do not rely on memory alone.

5. Protect finished surfaces from physical damage or corrosion. Keep gasoline and other chemicals off painted surfaces.

6. Use penetrating oil on frozen or tight bolts. Avoid using heat where possible. Heat can warp, melt or affect the temper of parts. Heat also damages the finish of paint and plastics.

7. When a part is a press fit or requires a special tool for removal, the information or type of tool is identified in the text. Otherwise, if a part is difficult to remove or install, determine the cause before proceeding.

8. To prevent objects or debris from falling into the engine, cover all openings.

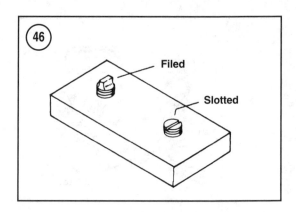

9. Read each procedure thoroughly and compare the illustrations to the actual components before starting the procedure. Perform the procedure in sequence.

10. Recommendations are occasionally made to refer service to a dealership or specialist. In these cases, the work can be performed more economically by the specialist than by the home mechanic.

11. The term *replace* means to discard a defective part and replace it with a new part. *Overhaul* means to remove, disassemble, inspect, measure, repair and/or replace parts as required to recondition an assembly.

12. Some operations require the use of a hydraulic press. If a press is not available, have these operations performed by a shop equipped with the necessary equipment. Do not use makeshift equipment that may damage the vehicle.

13. Repairs are much faster and easier if the vehicle is clean before starting work. Degrease the vehicle with a commercial degreaser; follow the directions on the container for the best results. Clean all parts with cleaning solvent as they are removed.

> *CAUTION*
> *Do not apply a chemical degreaser to an O-ring drive chain. These chemicals will damage the O-rings. Use kerosene to clean O-ring type chains.*

> *CAUTION*
> *Do not direct high-pressure water at steering bearings, carburetor hoses, wheel bearings, suspension and electrical components, or O-ring drive chains. The water will force the grease out of the bearings and possibly damage the seals.*

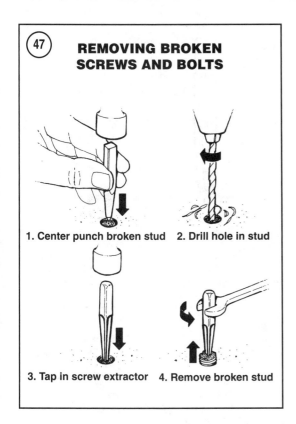

(47) REMOVING BROKEN SCREWS AND BOLTS

1. Center punch broken stud

2. Drill hole in stud

3. Tap in screw extractor

4. Remove broken stud

14. If special tools are required, have them available before starting the procedure. When special tools are required, they will be described at the beginning of the procedure.

15. Make diagrams of similar-appearing parts. For instance, crankcase bolts are often not the same lengths. Do not rely on memory alone. It is possible that carefully laid out parts will become disturbed, making it difficult to reassemble the components correctly without a diagram.

16. Make sure all shims and washers are reinstalled in the same location and position.

17. Whenever a rotating part contacts a stationary part, look for a shim or washer.

18. Use new gaskets if there is any doubt about the condition of old ones.

19. If self-locking fasteners are used, replace them with new ones. Do not install standard fasteners in place of self-locking ones.

20. Use grease to hold small parts in place if they tend to fall out during assembly. Do not apply grease to electrical or brake components.

Removing Frozen Fasteners

If a fastener cannot be removed, several methods may be used to loosen it. First, apply penetrating oil such as Liquid Wrench or WD-40. Apply it liberally and let it penetrate for 10-15 minutes. Rap the fastener several times with a small hammer. Do not hit it hard enough to cause damage. Reapply the penetrating oil if necessary.

For frozen screws, apply penetrating oil as described, then insert a screwdriver in the slot and rap the top of the screwdriver with a hammer. This loosens the rust so the screw can be removed in the normal way. If the screw head is too damaged to use this method, grip the head with locking pliers and twist the screw out.

Avoid applying heat unless specifically instructed, as it may melt, warp or remove the temper from parts.

Removing Broken Fasteners

If the head breaks off a screw or bolt, several methods are available for removing the remaining portion. If a large portion of the remainder projects out, try gripping it with locking pliers. If the projecting portion is too small, file it to fit a wrench or cut a slot in it to fit a screwdriver (**Figure 46**).

If the head breaks off flush, use a screw extractor. To do this, centerpunch the exact center of the remaining portion of the screw or bolt. Drill a small hole in the screw and tap the extractor into the hole. Back the screw out with a wrench on the extractor (**Figure 47**).

Repairing Damaged Threads

Occasionally, threads are stripped through carelessness or impact damage. Often the threads can be repaired by running a tap (for internal threads on nuts) or die (for external threads on bolts) through the threads (**Figure 48**). To clean or repair spark plug threads, use a spark plug tap.

If an internal thread is damaged, it may be necessary to install a Helicoil or some other type of thread insert. Follow the manufacturer's instructions when installing their insert.

If it is necessary to drill and tap a hole, refer to **Table 8** for metric tap and drill sizes.

Stud Removal/Installation

A stud removal tool is available from most tool suppliers. This tool makes the removal and installation of studs easier. If one is not available, thread two nuts onto the stud and tighten them against each other. Remove the stud by turning the lower nut (**Figure 49**).

1. Measure the height of the stud above the surface.
2. Thread the stud removal tool onto the stud and tighten it, or thread two nuts onto the stud.
3. Remove the stud by turning the stud remover or the lower nut.
4. Remove any threadlocking compound from the threaded hole. Clean the threads with an aerosol parts cleaner.
5. Install the stud removal tool onto the new stud or thread two nuts onto the stud.
6. Apply threadlocking compound to the threads of the stud.
7. Install the stud and tighten with the stud removal tool or the top nut.
8. Install the stud to the height noted in Step 1 or its torque specification.
9. Remove the stud removal tool or the two nuts.

Removing Hoses

When removing stubborn hoses, do not exert excessive force on the hose or fitting. Remove the hose clamp and carefully insert a small screwdriver or pick tool between the fitting and hose. Apply a spray lubricant under the hose and carefully twist the hose off the fitting. Clean the fitting of any corrosion or rubber hose material with a wire brush. Clean the inside of the hose thoroughly. Do not use any lubricant when installing the hose (new or old). The lubricant may allow the hose to come off the fitting, even with the clamp secure.

Bearings

Bearings are used in the engine and transmission assembly to reduce power loss, heat and noise resulting from friction. Because bearings are precision parts, they must be maintained by proper lubrication and maintenance. If a bearing is damaged, replace it immediately. When installing a new bearing, take care to prevent damaging it. Bearing replacement procedures are included in the individ-

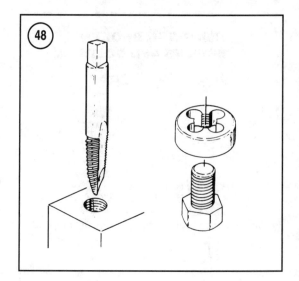

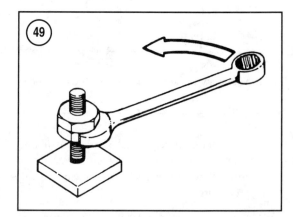

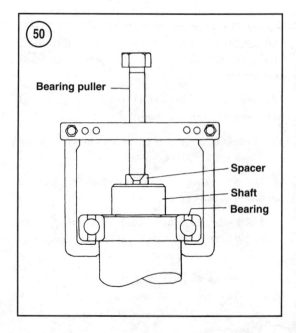

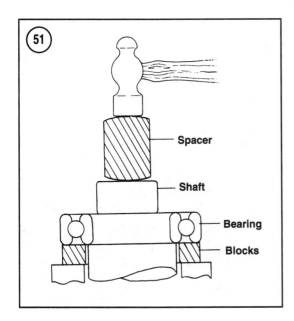

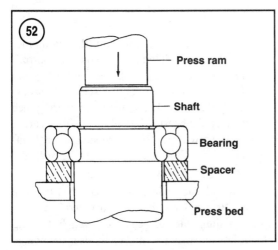

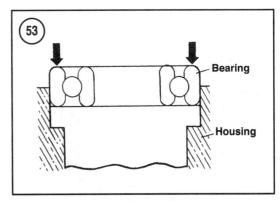

ual chapters where applicable; however, use the following sections as a guideline.

NOTE
Unless otherwise specified, install bearings with the manufacturer's mark or number facing outward.

Removal

While bearings are normally removed only when damaged, there may be times when it is necessary to remove a bearing that is in good condition. However, improper bearing removal will damage the bearing and maybe the shaft or case half. Note the following when removing bearings.

1. When using a puller to remove a bearing from a shaft, take care that shaft is not damaged. Always place a piece of metal between the end of the shaft and the puller screw. In addition, place the puller arms next to the inner bearing race. See **Figure 50**.

2. When using a hammer to remove a bearing from a shaft, do not strike the hammer directly against the shaft. Instead, use a brass or aluminum rod between the hammer and shaft (**Figure 51**) and make sure to support both bearing races with wooden blocks as shown.

3. The ideal method of bearing removal is with a hydraulic press. Note the following when using a press:

    a. Always support the inner and outer bearing races with a suitable size wooden or aluminum ring (**Figure 52**). If only the outer race is supported, pressure applied against the balls and/or the inner race will damage them.

    b. Always make sure the press arm (**Figure 52**) aligns with the center of the shaft. If the arm is not centered, it may damage the bearing and/or shaft.

    c. The moment the shaft is free of the bearing, it will drop to the floor. Secure or hold the shaft to prevent it from falling.

Installation

1. When installing a bearing in a housing, apply pressure to the *outer* bearing race (**Figure 53**). When installing a bearing on a shaft, apply pressure to the *inner* bearing race (**Figure 54**).

2. When installing a bearing as described in Step 1, some type of driver is required. Never strike the bearing directly with a hammer or the bearing will be damaged. When installing a bearing, use a piece

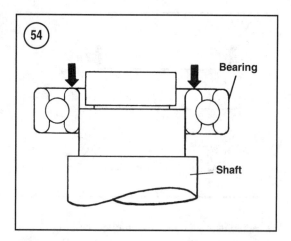

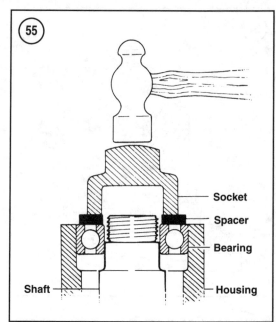

of pipe or a driver with a diameter that matches the bearing race. **Figure 55** shows the correct way to use a driver and hammer to install a bearing.

3. Step 1 describes how to install a bearing in a case half and over a shaft. However, when installing a bearing over a shaft and into a housing at the same time, a tight fit will be required for both outer and inner bearing races. In this situation, install a spacer underneath the driver tool so that pressure is applied evenly across both races. See **Figure 55**. If the outer race is not supported as shown in **Figure 55**, the balls will push against the outer bearing race and damage it.

Interference Fit

1. Follow this procedure when installing a bearing over a shaft. When a tight fit is required, the bearing inside diameter will be smaller than the shaft. In this case, driving the bearing on the shaft using normal methods may cause bearing damage. Instead, heat the bearing before installation. Note the following:
   a. Secure the shaft so it is ready for bearing installation.
   b. Clean all residues from the bearing surface of the shaft. Remove burrs with a file or sandpaper.
   c. Fill a suitable pot or beaker with clean mineral oil. Place a thermometer rated above 120° C (248° F) in the oil. Support the thermometer so that it does not rest on the bottom or side of the pot.
   d. Remove the bearing from its wrapper and secure it with a piece of heavy wire bent to hold it in the pot. Hang the bearing in the pot so it does not touch the bottom or sides of the pot.

   e. Turn the heat on and monitor the thermometer. When the oil temperature rises to approximately 120° C (248° F), remove the bearing from the pot and quickly install it. If necessary, place a socket on the inner bearing race and tap the bearing into place. As the bearing chills, it will tighten on the shaft so installation must be done quickly. Make sure the bearing is installed completely.

2. Follow this step when installing a bearing in a housing. Bearings are generally installed in a housing with a slight interference fit. Driving the bearing into the housing using normal methods may damage the housing or cause bearing damage. Instead, heat the housing before the bearing is installed. Note the following:

> *CAUTION*
> *Before heating the housing in this procedure, wash the housing thoroughly with detergent and water. Rinse and rewash the cases as required to remove all traces of oil and other chemical deposits.*

   a. Heat the housing to approximately 212° F (100° C) in an oven or on a hot plate. An easy way to check that it is at the proper temperature is to place tiny drops of water on the housing; if they sizzle and evaporate immedi-

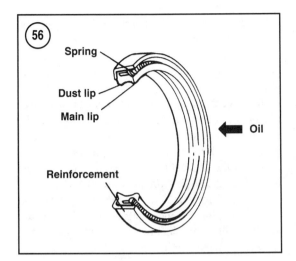

Spring
Dust lip
Main lip
← Oil
Reinforcement

ately, the temperature is correct. Heat only one housing at a time.

CAUTION
Do not heat the housing with a propane or acetylene torch. Never bring a flame into contact with the bearing or housing. The direct heat will destroy the case hardening of the bearing and will likely warp the housing.

b. Remove the housing from the oven or hot plate, and hold onto the housing with a kitchen potholder, heavy gloves or heavy shop cloth. It is hot!

NOTE
Remove and install the bearings with a suitable size socket and extension.

c. Hold the housing with the bearing side down and tap the bearing out. Repeat for all bearings in the housing.

d. Before heating the bearing housing, place the new bearing in a freezer if possible. Chilling a bearing slightly reduces its outside diameter while the heated bearing housing assembly is slightly larger due to heat expansion. This will make bearing installation easier.

NOTE
Always install bearings with the manufacturer's mark or number facing outward.

e. While the housing is still hot, install the new bearing(s) into the housing. Install the bearings by hand, if possible. If necessary, lightly tap the bearing(s) into the housing with a socket placed on the outer bearing race (**Figure 53**). Do not install new bearings by driving on the inner-bearing race. Install the bearing(s) until it seats completely.

Seal Replacement

Seals (**Figure 56**) are used to contain oil, water, grease or combustion gasses in a housing or shaft. Improper removal of a seal can damage the housing or shaft. Improper installation of the seal can damage the seal. Note the following:
1. Prying is generally the easiest and most effective method of removing a seal from a housing. However, always place a rag underneath the pry tool (**Figure 57**) to prevent damage to the housing.
2. Pack waterproof grease in the seal lips before the seal is installed.
3. In most cases, install seals with the manufacturer's numbers or marks facing out.
4. Install seals with a socket placed on the outside of the seal as shown in **Figure 58**. Drive the seal squarely into the housing. Never install a seal by hitting against the top of the seal with a hammer.

STORAGE

Several months of non-use can cause a general deterioration of the vehicle. This is especially true in areas of extreme temperature variations. This deterioration can be minimized with careful preparation for storage. A properly stored vehicle will be much easier to return to service.

Storage Area Selection

When selecting a storage area, consider the following:
1. The storage area must be dry. A heated area is best, but not necessary. It should be insulated to minimize extreme temperature variations.
2. If the building has large window areas, mask them to keep sunlight off the vehicle.
3. Avoid buildings in industrial areas where corrosive emissions may be present. Avoid areas close to saltwater.
4. Consider the area's risk of fire, theft or vandalism. Check with an insurer regarding vehicle coverage while in storage.

Preparing the Vehicle for Storage

The amount of preparation a vehicle should undergo before storage depends on the expected length of non-use, storage area conditions and personal preference. Consider the following list the minimum requirement:
1. Wash the vehicle thoroughly. Make sure all dirt, mud and road debris are removed.
2. Start the engine and allow it to reach operating temperature. Drain the engine oil regardless of the riding time since the last service. Fill the engine with the recommended type of oil.
3. Drain all fuel from the fuel tank, run the engine until all the fuel is consumed from the lines and carburetor(s).
4. Remove the spark plug(s) and pour a teaspoon of engine oil into the cylinder(s). Place a rag over the opening(s) and slowly turn the engine over to distribute the oil. Reinstall the spark plug(s).
5. Cover the exhaust and intake openings.
6. Reduce the normal tire pressure by 20%.
7. Apply a protective substance to the plastic and rubber components, including the tires. Make sure to follow the manufacturer's instructions for each type of product being used.
8. Place the vehicle on a stand or wooden blocks, so the wheels are off the ground. If this is not possible, place a piece of plywood between the tires and the ground. Inflate the tires to the recommended pressure if the vehicle can not be elevated.
9. Cover the vehicle with old bed sheets or something similar. Do not cover it with any plastic material that will trap moisture.

Returning the Vehicle to Service

The amount of service required when returning a vehicle to service after storage depends on the length of non-use and storage conditions. In addition to performing the reverse of the above procedure, make sure the brakes, clutch, throttle and engine stop switch work properly before operating the vehicle. Refer to Chapter Three and evaluate the service intervals to determine which areas require service.

Table 1 FRAME IDENTIFICATION NUMBERS

Model	Starting Frame Serial Number
1996	JH2NE030*TM0000001-on
1997	JH2NE030*VM100001-on
1998	JH2NE030*WM200001-WM201585
1998	
49-state	JH2NE030*WK300001-on
California	JH2NE031*WM200001-WM200528
California	JH2NE031*WK300001-on
1999	
49-state	JH2NE030*XK400001-on
California	JH2NE031*XK400001-on
2000	
49-state	JH2NE030*YK500001-on
California	JH2NE031*YK500001-on

Table 2 VEHICLE DIMENSIONS

	mm	in.
Overall length	2130	83.9
Overall width	840	33.1
Overall height	1240	48.8
Wheelbase	1425	56.1
Seat height	930	36.6

Table 3 VEHICLE WEIGHT SPECIFICATIONS

	kg	lb.
Dry weight	116.5	257
Curb weight	125	276
Maximum weight capacity	100	220

Table 4 DECIMAL AND METRIC EQUIVALENTS

Fractions	Decimal in.	Metric mm	Fractions	Decimal in.	Metric mm
1/64	0.015625	0.39688	33/64	0.515625	13.09687
1/32	0.03125	0.79375	17/32	0.53125	13.49375
3/64	0.046875	1.19062	35/64	0.546875	13.89062
1/16	0.0625	1.58750	9/16	0.5625	14.28750
5/64	0.078125	1.98437	37/64	0.578125	14.68437
3/32	0.09375	2.38125	19/32	0.59375	15.08125
7/64	0.109375	2.77812	39/64	0.609375	15.47812
1/8	0.125	3.1750	5/8	0.625	15.87500
9/64	0.140625	3.57187	41/64	0.640625	16.27187
5/32	0.15625	3.96875	21/32	0.65625	16.66875
11/64	0.171875	4.36562	43/64	0.671875	17.06562
3/16	0.1875	4.76250	11/16	0.6875	17.46250
13/64	0.203125	5.15937	45/64	0.703125	17.85937
7/32	0.21875	5.55625	23/32	0.71875	18.25625
15/64	0.234375	5.95312	47/64	0.734375	18.65312
1/4	0.250	6.35000	3/4	0.750	19.05000
17/64	0.265625	6.74687	49/64	0.765625	19.44687
9/32	0.28125	7.14375	25/32	0.78125	19.84375
19/64	0.296875	7.54062	51/64	0.796875	20.24062
5/16	0.3125	7.93750	13/16	0.8125	20.63750
21/64	0.328125	8.33437	53/64	0.828125	21.03437
11/32	0.34375	8.73125	27/32	0.84375	21.43125
23/64	0.359375	9.12812	55/64	0.859375	22.82812
3/8	0.375	9.52500	7/8	0.875	22.22500
25/64	0.390625	9.92187	57/64	0.890625	22.62187
13/32	0.40625	10.31875	29/32	0.90625	23.01875
27/64	0.421875	10.71562	59/64	0.921875	23.41562
7/16	0.4375	11.11250	15/16	0.9375	23.81250
29/64	0.453125	11.50937	61/64	0.953125	24.20937
15/32	0.46875	11.90625	31/32	0.96875	24.60625
31/64	0.484375	12.30312	63/64	0.984375	25.00312
1/2	0.500	12.70000	1	1.00	25.40000

Table 5 CONVERSION TABLES

Multiply	By	To get equivalent of
Length		
Inches	25.4	Millimeter
Inches	2.54	Centimeter
Miles	1.609	Kilometer
Feet	0.3048	Meter
Millimeter	0.03937	Inches
Centimeter	0.3937	Inches
Kilometer	0.6214	Mile
Meter	3.281	Mile
Fluid volume		
U.S. quarts	0.9463	Liters
U.S. gallons	3.785	Liters
U.S. ounces	29.573529	Milliliters
Imperial gallons	4.54609	Liters
Imperial quarts	1.1365	Liters
Liters	0.2641721	U.S. gallons
Liters	1.0566882	U.S. quarts
Liters	33.814023	U.S. ounces
Liters	0.22	Imperial gallons
Liters	0.8799	Imperial quarts
Milliliters	0.033814	U.S. ounces
Milliliters	1.0	Cubic centimeters
Milliliters	0.001	Liters
Torque		
Foot-pounds	1.3558	Newton-meters
Foot-pounds	0.138255	Meters-kilograms
Inch-pounds	0.11299	Newton-meters
Newton-meters	0.7375622	Foot-pounds
Newton-meters	8.8507	Inch-pounds
Meters-kilograms	7.2330139	Foot-pounds
Volume		
Cubic inches	16.387064	Cubic centimeters
Cubic centimeters	0.0610237	Cubic inches
Temperature		
Fahrenheit	(F − 32) 0.556	Centigrade
Centigrade	(C × 1.8)	Fahrenheit
Weight		
Ounces	28.3495	Grams
Pounds	0.4535924	Kilograms
Grams	0.035274	Ounces
Kilograms	2.2046224	Pounds
Pressure		
Pounds per square inch	0.070307	Kilograms per square centimeter
Kilograms per square centimeter	14.223343	Pounds per square inch
Kilopascals	0.1450	Pounds per square inch
Pounds per square inch	6.895	Kilopascals
Speed		
Miles per hour	1.609344	Kilometers per hour
Kilometers per hour	0.6213712	Miles per hour

Table 6 HONDA GENERAL TORQUE SPECIFICATIONS*

Thread diameter	N•m	in.-lb.	ft.-lb.
5 mm bolt and nut	5	44	–
6 mm bolt and nut	10	88	–
8 mm bolt and nut	22	–	16
10 mm bolt and nut	34	–	25
12 mm bolt and nut	54	–	40
5 mm screw	4	35	–
6 mm screw	9	80	–
6 mm flange bolt with 8 mm head (small flange surface)	9	80	–
6 mm flange bolt with 8 mm head (large flange surface)	12	106	–
6 mm flange bolt with 10 mm head and nut	12	106	–
8 mm flange bolt and nut	26	–	20
10 mm flange bolt and nut	39	–	29

*This table lists general torque specifications for metric fasteners found on Honda motorcycles. Use this table when a specific torque specification is not listed for a fastener at the end of the appropriate chapter. The torque specifications listed in this table are for threads that are clean and dry.

Table 7 TECHNICAL ABBREVIATIONS

ABDC	After bottom dead center
ATDC	After top dead center
BBDC	Before bottom dead center
BDC	Bottom dead center
BTDC	Before top dead center
C	Celsius (Centigrade)
cc	Cubic centimeters
cid	Cubic inch displacement
CDI	Capacitor discharge ignition
cu. in.	Cubic inches
F	Fahrenheit
ft.	Feet
ft.-lb.	Foot-pounds
gal.	Gallons
H/A	High altitude
hp	Horsepower
in.	Inches
in.-lb.	Inch-pounds
I.D.	Inside diameter
kg	Kilograms
kgm	Kilogram meters
km	Kilometer
kPa	Kilopascals
L	Liter
m	Meter
MAG	Magneto
ml	Milliliter
mm	Millimeter
N•m	Newton-meters
O.D.	Outside diameter
oz.	Ounces
psi	Pounds per square inch
PTO	Power take off
pt.	Pint
qt.	Quart
rpm	Revolutions per minute

Table 8 METRIC TAP AND DRILL SIZES

Metric size	Drill equivalent	Decimal fraction	Nearest(mm)
3 × 0.50	No. 39	0.0995	3/32
3 × 0.60	3/32	0.0937	3/32
4 × 0.70	No. 30	0.1285	1/8
4 × 0.75	1/8	0.125	1/8
5 × 0.80	No. 19	0.166	11/64
5 × 0.90	No. 20	0.161	5/32
6 × 1.00	No. 9	0.196	13/64
7 × 1.00	16/64	0.234	15/64
8 × 1.00	J	0.277	9/32
8 × 1.25	17/64	0.265	17/64
9 × 1.00	5/16	0.3125	5/16
9 × 1.25	5/16	0.3125	5/16
10 × 1.25	11/32	0.3437	11/32
10 × 1.50	R	0.339	11/32
11 × 1.50	3/8	0.375	3/8
12 × 1.50	13/32	0.406	13/32
12 × 1.75	13/32	0.406	13/32

CHAPTER TWO

TROUBLESHOOTING

Diagnosing mechanical problems is reasonably simple if orderly procedures are followed. The first step in any troubleshooting procedure is to define the symptoms as closely as possible. Then, localize the problem and test those areas that could cause the symptoms.

Proper lubrication, maintenance and periodic tune-ups as described in Chapter Three will reduce the necessity for troubleshooting. However, even with the best of care, the motorcycle may require troubleshooting.

Do not overlook the obvious. If the engine will not start, is the engine stop switch shorted out? Is the engine flooded with fuel?

If the engine suddenly quits, what sound did it make? Consider this and check the easiest, most accessible problem first. If the engine sounded like it ran out of fuel, make sure there is fuel in the tank. If there is fuel in the tank, is it reaching the carburetor? The fuel tank vent hose may be plugged, preventing fuel from flowing from the fuel tank to the carburetor.

Gather as many symptoms as possible to aid in diagnosis. Note whether the engine lost power gradually or all at once, what color smoke (if any) came from the exhaust and so on. Learning to recognize and describe symptoms will make repairs easier.

After the symptoms are defined, test and analyze areas which could cause problems. Fancy equip-

ment and complicated test gear are not needed to determine whether home repairs are possible. A few simple checks could avoid a large repair bill and lost time. On the other hand, be realistic and *do not attempt repairs that require professional attention*. Service departments tend to charge heavily for the reassembly of damaged or abused equipment. Use common sense and do not get in over your head.

OPERATING REQUIREMENTS

An engine needs three basics to run properly: correct air/fuel mixture, sufficient compression and a spark at the right time. If one basic requirement is missing, the engine will not run. If all of the basic requirements are present but one or more are not working or adjusted correctly, the engine may start and run but it will not run properly. Four-stroke engine operating principles are described under *Engine Operating Principles* in Chapter Four.

If the bike has been sitting for any length of time and refuses to start, check and clean the spark plug. If the plug is not fouled, then inspect the fuel delivery system, including the fuel tank, fuel shutoff valve, in-line fuel filter (if used) and fuel line. Gasoline deposits may have gummed up the carburetor's fuel valve and seat, jets and small air passages. Gasoline tends to lose its potency after standing for long periods, and as it evaporates the air/fuel mixture becomes richer. Condensation may also contaminate it with water. Drain the old gas and fill the tank with fresh gasoline.

STARTING THE ENGINE

If the engine refuses to start, use the following outline as a guide to basic starting procedures. In all cases, make sure that the tank has an adequate supply of fresh fuel. Then refer to the following section that best matches the prevailing air and engine temperatures.

> *WARNING*
> *Never operate the motorcycle in a closed area. Exhaust gases contain carbon monoxide, a colorless, odorless, poisonous gas. Carbon monoxide levels build quickly in a small closed area and can cause unconsciousness and death in a short time. Always start the engine outside.*

Choke Lever

A cold engine needs a rich air/fuel mixture to start. To richen the fuel mixture, a separate choke circuit is installed inside the carburetor. A hand-operated choke lever (A, **Figure 1**) mounted on the outside of the carburetor controls the choke circuit. Opening the choke lever increases the amount of fuel delivered to the engine. To *open* the choke circuit for starting a cold engine, pull the choke lever up all the way. To *close* the choke circuit after the engine has warmed up or when starting a warm or hot engine, push the choke lever all the way down. The choke lever also has a detent position, located halfway between its fully ON and fully OFF positions. The detent position is used just after starting a cold engine. Its use is explained further in the following sections.

Starting a Cold Engine
(Normal Air Temperature)

Normal air temperature is between 50-95° F (10-25° C).
1. Shift the transmission to NEUTRAL.
2. Turn the fuel valve on (B, **Figure 1**).
3. Pull the choke lever all the way up (A, **Figure 1**).

4. With the throttle completely *closed*, kick the engine over.
5. When the engine starts, push the choke lever (A, **Figure 1**) down to its detent position. Work the throttle slightly to keep the engine running.
6. After about 30 seconds, push the choke lever all the way down and continue to idle the engine by operating the throttle.

Starting a Cold Engine
(Cold Air Temperature)

Cold air temperature is 50° F (10° C) or below.
1. Shift the transmission to NEUTRAL.
2. Turn the fuel valve on (B, **Figure 1**).
3. Pull the choke lever all the way up (A, **Figure 1**).
4. With the throttle completely *closed*, kick the engine over.
5. When the engine starts, work the throttle slightly to keep the engine running.
6. Continue to work the throttle until the engine runs cleanly with the choke lever pushed all the way down.

Starting a Warm or Hot Engine

1. Shift the transmission into NEUTRAL.
2. Turn the fuel valve on (B, **Figure 1**).
3. Push the choke lever (A, **Figure 1**) down. Make sure the choke is closed.
4. Kick the engine over. When the engine starts, work the throttle to keep the engine running.
5. If the engine will not start, perform the following:
   a. Pull the starter decompressor lever (A, **Figure 2**) all the way in and press the engine stop button (B) in.
   b. Open the throttle all the way and operate the kickstarter lever several times to clear the en-

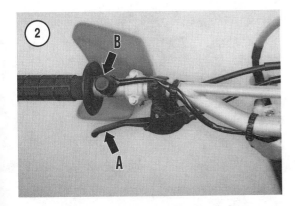

NOTE
If the engine refuses to start, check the carburetor overflow hose at the bottom of the float bowl. If fuel is running out of the overflow hose, the float valve is stuck open, allowing the carburetor to overfill. Tap the carburetor a few times to dislodge the material holding the float valve open. If fuel continues to run out of the hose, turn the fuel valve off and service the carburetor as described in Chapter Eight.

gine of fuel. Release the decompressor lever and the engine stop switch.

c. Close the throttle and kick the engine over. When the engine starts, work the throttle to keep the engine running.

d. If the engine still will not restart, it is probably flooded. Refer to *Starting a Flooded Engine* in this section.

Starting a Flooded Engine

If the engine is hard to start and there is a strong gasoline smell, the engine is probably flooded. Push the choke lever down (A, **Figure 1**) and shift the transmission into NEUTRAL. Pull the starter decompressor lever (A, **Figure 2**) all the way in and press the engine stop button (B, **Figure 2**). Then open the throttle all the way and kick the engine over several times to clear it of excess fuel. Release the starter decompressor lever and the engine stop switch and kick the engine over with the throttle closed. Depending on how badly the engine is flooded, it will generally start after a few hard kicks.

If the engine is flooded badly, it may be necessary to remove the spark plug and dry off its insulator, or install a new plug. When a flooded engine first starts to run, it will initially sputter and run slowly as it burns off the excess fuel. Then the engine will rev quickly and clear out. Release the throttle grip at this point and work it slowly to make sure the engine is running cleanly. Because a flooded engine smokes when it first starts to run, always start it outside and in a well-ventilated area with the bike's muffler pointing away from all objects. Do not start a flooded engine in a closed area.

Starter Decompressor Lever

The engine decompressor system is an automatic type that is interlocked with the kickstarter. There is also a manually operated starter decompressor lever mounted on the left side of the handlebar (A, **Figure 2**). If the engine is difficult to kick over, use the starter decompressor lever as follows:

1. With the throttle closed, push down on the kickstarter until it meets resistance.

2. Pull the starter decompressor lever (A, **Figure 2**) all the way in and push the kickstarter down approximately 1/4 to 1/2 the length of a full stroke.

3. Release the starter decompressor lever and kick the engine over following the appropriate starting procedure listed in this section.

STARTING DIFFICULTIES

When the engine turns over but is difficult to start, or will not start at all, first check for obvious problems. Go down the following list step by step, keeping in mind the three engine operating requirements described under *Operating Requirements* earlier in this chapter. If all three requirements are present, the engine should start and run. However, if one or more of the requirements are out of adjustment, or malfunctioning because of worn or damaged parts, the engine may start and run, but it will not run well.

NOTE
If the kickstarter is difficult to operate or if the engine made unusual noises when it quit running, the starting problem is probably due to mechanical damage. Refer to Step 10.

1. Make sure the choke lever (A, **Figure 1**) is in the correct position. Pull the choke lever *up* for a cold engine and push it *down* for a warm or hot engine. See *Starting The Engine* in this chapter.

2. Remove the spark plug and check to see if the insulator is wet. If the plug insulator is dry, fuel is not reaching the carburetor. Continue with Step 3.

NOTE
While the spark plug is out of the cylinder head, check it for external damage. Cracked porcelain can cause the engine to misfire or a no spark condition.

3. Make sure the fuel tank has an adequate supply of fresh fuel. If there is fuel in the tank, make sure the fuel tank vent tube (**Figure 3**) is not clogged. A plugged or pinched tube will prevent fuel from flowing to the carburetor. Remove the tube from the filler cap, wipe off one end and blow through it. Remove the filler cap and check that its hose nozzle is not plugged.

WARNING
Do not use an open flame to check in the tank. A serious explosion is certain to result.

4. Disconnect the fuel line at the carburetor and insert the end of the hose into a clear, plastic container. Turn the fuel valve on (B, **Figure 1**) and see if fuel flows freely. If fuel does not flow remove the fuel cap and try again. If the fuel now flows out of the fuel line, the vent hole in the cap is plugged. If fuel does not flow out of the line and there is a fuel filter installed in the fuel line, remove the filter and turn the fuel valve on again. If the fuel now starts to flow, the filter is clogged and must be replaced. If no fuel comes out, the fuel valve may be damaged or blocked by debris.

5. A strong smell of gasoline probably means the cylinder is flooded. Refer to *Starting a Flooded Engine* in this chapter.

6. Check the carburetor overflow hose on the bottom of the float bowl. If fuel runs out of the hose, the float valve is stuck open. Turn the fuel valve off and tap the carburetor a few times. Then turn the fuel valve back on. If fuel continues to run out the end of the hose, remove and service the carburetor as described in Chapter Eight. Check the carburetor vent hoses to make sure they are clear. Check the end of each hose for contamination.

NOTE
Even if fuel is reaching the carburetor, the fuel system could still be the problem. The jets (pilot and main) could be clogged or the air filter could be restricted. If the bike was recently washed or ridden in wet conditions, check for water in the fuel tank and carburetor. However, before removing the carburetor, continue with Step 7 to make sure the engine has spark.

7. Make sure the engine stop switch (B, **Figure 2**) is working properly. Disconnect the engine stop switch leads and try to restart the engine. If necessary, test the engine stop switch with a test light or ohmmeter as described in Chapter Nine.

WARNING
If the engine stop switch is defective, install a new switch as soon as possible. It is not safe to ride the motorcycle with a missing or disconnected engine stop switch.

8. Make sure the spark plug cap-to-spark plug connection is secure (**Figure 4**). Grasp the plug cap and remove it from the spark plug with a twisting/pulling motion. Inspect and clean the plug terminal and cap connection of any corrosion. It may be necessary to replace the plug cap if excessive corrosion is present. Install the plug cap onto the plug, it should snap firmly onto the plug terminal.

9. Perform the *Spark Test* as described in this chapter. If there is a strong spark, perform Step 10. If there is no spark or if the spark is very weak, test the ignition system as described under *Ignition System Troubleshooting* in this chapter.

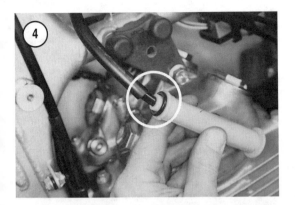

d. Operate the kickstarter. As the piston comes up on the compression stroke, rising pressure in the cylinder will force your finger off of the spark plug hole. This indicates that the cylinder probably has sufficient cylinder compression to start the engine.

11. Make sure air is able to enter the engine through the air box. Remove the seat and check the air box opening for an obstruction. Check inside the air box to make sure the air filter is not blocked, collapsed or damaged.

Spark Test

Perform the following spark test to determine if the ignition system is operating properly.

CAUTION
Before removing the spark plug in Step 1, clean all dirt and debris away from the plug base. Dirt that falls into the cylinder will cause rapid wear to the top end components.

1. Disconnect the plug wire and remove the spark plug. Examine the spark plug for any type of physical damage.

NOTE
*When performing a spark test, a spark tester (**Figure 5**) can be used in place of a spark plug. This tool (Motion Pro part No. 08-0122) allows the user to see and hear the intensity of the spark When using a spark tester, set the gap to 6 mm (1/4 in.).*

2. Insert the spark plug (or spark tester) into the plug cap and ground the spark plug base against the cylinder head and away from the plug hole (**Figure 6**). Position the spark plug or spark tester so the electrodes are visible.

WARNING
Mount the spark plug or spark tester away from the plug hole in the cylinder head. The spark made across the spark plug or spark tester terminals can ignite gasoline vapors in the cylinder.

WARNING
Do not hold the spark plug, wire or connector or a serious electrical shock may result.

NOTE
If the fuel and ignition system are working properly, the remaining area to check is the mechanical system. Unless the engine seized or there is some other type of mechanical problem, mechanical problems affecting the top end generally occur over a period of time. Isolate a mechanical problem to either the top or bottom end.

10. Check cylinder compression as follows:

NOTE
*The following test allows the compression to be checked away from the shop. However, the engine may have a compression problem even though it passes the following test. Check engine compression with a compression gauge as described under **Tune-up** in Chapter Three.*

a. Turn the fuel valve off.
b. Remove the spark plug and ground it against the cylinder head and away from the plug hole.
c. Place your finger over the spark plug hole.

3. Turn the engine over with the kickstarter. A fat blue spark should be evident across the spark plug electrodes or spark tester terminals. Note the following:

a. If the spark is intermittent, weak (white or yellow in color), or if there is no spark, continue with Step 4.

b. If the spark is good, go to Step 6.

4. Make sure the engine stop switch (B, **Figure 2**) is working properly. Disconnect the engine stop switch leads and check the spark.

a. If there is now spark, the engine stop switch is damaged. Replace the switch and retest.

b. If there is still no spark, test the engine stop switch with an ohmmeter (Chapter Nine) before reconnecting it into the wiring harness to make sure it is not a secondary problem. If the switch tests good, reconnect it back into the wiring harness and continue with Step 5.

> *WARNING*
> *If the engine stop switch is defective, install a new one as soon as possible. It is not safe to ride the motorcycle with a missing or disconnected engine stop switch.*

5. A loose, corroded or damaged spark plug cap terminal (**Figure 4**) is common source of ignition system problems, especially when the problem is intermittent. Perform the following:

a. Disconnect the spark plug cap from the spark plug. Then hold the plug wire and try to turn the cap. The cap must fit securely. If there is any looseness, the terminal inside the cap may have pulled away from the coil wire.

b. Install the spark plug into the plug cap. The terminal ring inside the plug cap must snap tightly onto the spark plug when connecting the parts together. If the connection is weak, replace the plug cap.

c. Unscrew and remove the plug cap (**Figure 4**) from the coil wire. If a plastic tie is used to hold the plug cap in place, cut it before removing the plug cap.

d. Check the metal terminal inside the plug cap for corrosion or other damage. Remove any corrosion with a file or sandpaper. Visually inspect the terminal connection for corrosion and damage.

e. Check the wire strands in the exposed end of the plug wire for corrosion and damage.

f. Check the coil wire where it attaches to the ignition coil for looseness or play which may indicate a weak or broken plug wire.

g. Hold the coil wire (without the spark plug cap and terminal) 6 mm (1/4 in.) from the cylinder head as shown in **Figure 7**. Have an assistant kick the engine over with the kickstarter. A fat blue spark should be evident at the end of the coil wire. If there is a good spark, either the spark plug cap terminal is faulty or its terminal is not making good contact with the coil wire.

h. Trim the end of the plug wire (approximately 6 mm/1/4 in.) to expose clean wire for the plug cap terminal to contact.

i. Pack the plug cap or the coil wire end with dielectric grease to prevent moisture from entering the plug cap and causing corrosion.

j. Screw the plug cap securely onto the end of the plug wire. Make sure there is good contact between the plug wire core and the plug cap terminal. Repeat the spark test. If there is still no spark, continue with Step 6.

6. If the spark plug cap is working properly, test the ignition system as described under *Ignition System Troubleshooting* in this chapter.

7. If the spark is good, perform the *Engine is Difficult to Start* procedure in this chapter.

Engine is Difficult to Start

If the engine has spark, good compression and fuel is reaching the carburetor, but it is difficult to start, check for one or more of the following possible malfunctions:

1. Incorrect air/fuel mixture:

a. Excessively dirty or blocked air filter element.

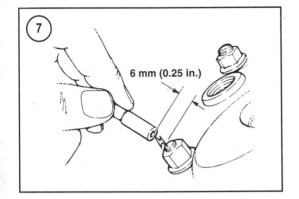

7

6 mm (0.25 in.)

b. Incorrect carburetor operation.
c. Incorrect choke operation.
d. Clogged pilot jet.
e. Clogged pilot passage.
f. Intake manifold air leak.
g. Flooded carburetor.
2. Engine flooded:
  a. Incorrect starting procedure.
  b. Fuel level too high.
  c. Worn float valve and seat assembly.
  d. Float valve stuck open.
  e. Damaged float.
3. No fuel flow:
  a. Clogged fuel line.
  b. Clogged fuel filter (if used).
  c. Clogged fuel valve.
  d. Clogged or restricted float valve.
  e. Clogged fuel tank cap vent hose (**Figure 3**) or cap.
  f. Fuel valve turned off.
  g. No fuel.
  h. Incorrect float adjustment.
  i. Damaged float.
4. Weak spark:
  a. Fouled or wet spark plug.
  b. Loose or damaged plug cap-to-plug connection.
  c. Loose or damaged plug wire-to-plug cap (**Figure 4**) connection.
  d. Defective ignition coil.
  e. Defective ignition control module.
  f. Damaged ignition pulse generator or exciter coil (at stator plate).
  g. Sheared flywheel key.
  h. Loose flywheel nut.
  i. Loose electrical connections.
  j. Dirty electrical connections.
  k. Damaged flywheel.
5. Low engine compression:

a. Loose spark plug or missing spark plug gasket.
b. Insufficient valve clearance.
c. Incorrect decompressor system adjustment.

NOTE
The decompressor system must be adjusted after adjusting the valve clearance. See Chapter Three.

d. Incorrect valve timing.

NOTE
*To check the valve timing, remove the cylinder head cover and bring the engine to TDC on its compression stroke. Refer to **Cylinder Head Cover** in Chapter Four.*

e. Stuck or damaged piston rings.
f. Excessive piston ring wear.
g. Excessively worn piston and/or cylinder.
h. Loose cylinder head fasteners.
i. Incorrect cylinder head installation.
j. Warped cylinder head.
k. Blown head gasket.
l. Stuck valve(s).

Engine Starts But Stops Immediately

If the engine starts but then stops, check for one or more of the following conditions:
  a. Contaminated fuel.
  b. Fuel tank vent tube partially restricted (**Figure 3**).
  c. Incorrect decompressor system adjustment or operation.
  d. Air leaks. Check for a loose or damaged intake manifold.
  e. Pilot screw closed.
  f. Incorrect ignition timing due to a defective ignition system component.

Engine Will Not Turn Over

If the engine will not turn over because of a mechanical problem, check for one or more of the following possible malfunctions:

NOTE
*After referring to the following list, refer to **Drive Train Noise** in this chapter for additional information.*

2

1. Kickstarter:
   a. Defective kick shaft or kick gear.
   b. Broken kickstarter return spring.
   c. Damaged kickstarter ratchet gear.
   d. Seized or damaged idler gear.
   e. Incorrect ratchet gear installation. See *Kickstarter and Idle Gear* in Chapter Six.
2. Engine:
   a. Broken valve(s).
   b. Seized piston.
   c. Broken piston skirt.
   d. Seized crankshaft bearings.
   e. Seized connecting rod bearing.
   f. Broken connecting rod.
   g. Seized primary drive gear/clutch assembly.
   h. Seized transmission gear or bearing.

ENGINE PERFORMANCE

In the following check list, it is assumed that the engine runs, but is not operating at peak performance. Use this list to isolate a performance malfunction.

Throttle Sticks

1. Damaged throttle cable(s).
2. Damaged throttle grip.
3. No operating clearance between the end of the throttle grip and handlebar.
4. Incorrect throttle cable routing.
5. Debris between the carburetor throttle valve and bore.
6. Excessively worn throttle valve and/or bore.
7. Stuck or damaged linkage at carburetor.

Engine Will Not Idle

If the engine will not idle as described in Chapter Three, check for the following problems:
1. Incorrect valve clearance.
2. Incorrect ignition timing.
3. Incorrect carburetor adjustment.
4. Plugged pilot jet.

NOTE
If the engine starts with the choke on but cuts out when the choke is off, or will not idle unless the choke is on, disas-

semble the carburetor (Chapter Eight) and check for a plugged pilot jet.

5. Obstructed fuel line or fuel shutoff valve.
6. Fouled or improperly gapped spark plug.
7. Leaking head gasket.
8. Loose carburetor clamp screws.
9. Leaking intake manifold.
10. Incorrect float adjustment.
11. Fuel tank cap vent hose partially restricted (**Figure 3**).

Poor Low Speed Performance

Check for one or more of the following possible malfunctions:
1. Incorrect air/fuel mixture:
   a. Restricted air filter intake.
   b. Incorrect carburetor adjustment.
   c. Clogged pilot jet.
   d. Clogged air passage.
   e. Loose or cracked air box boot.
   f. Loose carburetor hose clamps.
   g. Clogged fuel tank cap vent hose (**Figure 3**).
   h. Choke stuck in the on or detent position.
   i. Incorrect float adjustment.
2. Weak spark:
   a. Fouled or wet spark plug.
   b. Incorrect spark plug heat range.
   c. Loose or damaged spark plug cap connection.
   d. Loose or damaged plug wire-to-plug cap connection.
   e. Defective ignition coil.
   f. Defective ignition control module.
   g. Defective ignition pulse generator or exciter coil (at stator).
   h. Loose electrical connections.
   i. Dirty electrical connections.
   j. Incorrect ignition timing, indicating a faulty ignition system component.
3. Low engine compression:
   a. Loose spark plug or missing spark plug gasket.
   b. Excessive valve guide clearance.
   c. Damaged valve(s).
   d. Stuck piston rings.
   e. Excessive piston ring wear.
   f. Excessively worn piston and/or cylinder.
   g. Loose cylinder head fasteners.
   h. Incorrect cylinder head installation.
   i. Warped cylinder head.

j. Damaged cylinder head gasket.

k. Damaged base gasket.

4. Dragging brakes. Refer to *Brakes* in this chapter for additional information.

Poor High Speed Performance

Check for one or more of the following possible malfunctions:

1. Incorrect air/fuel mixture:
   a. Clogged air filter element.
   b. Clogged carburetor air vent tubes.
   c. Incorrect jet needle clip position.
   d. Incorrect main jet.
   e. Clogged main jet.
   f. Worn jet needle and/or needle jet.
   g. Clogged air jet or air passage.
   h. Loose or cracked air box boot.
   i. Loose carburetor holder clamps.
   j. Partially restricted fuel tank cap vent hose (**Figure 3**).
   k. Worn float valve and seat.
   l. Fuel level too high or too low.

NOTE
*Check the fuel flow closely when troubleshooting this type of problem. While there may be sufficient fuel flow for low speed operation, a partial restriction in the fuel tank vent hose (**Figure 3**) can reduce the flow needed for high speed operation.*

   m. Clogged fuel line.
   n. Clogged fuel filter.
   o. Clogged fuel valve.
   p. The fuel mixture is contaminated with water.

2. If the engine speed drops or cuts out abruptly:
   a. Restricted air intake.
   b. Restricted muffler.
   c. Clutch slipping.

NOTE
If the engine speed does not increase after releasing the clutch, the clutch is probably slipping.

   e. Clogged main jet.
   f. Fuel level too high or too low.
   g. Choke valve partially stuck.
   h. Throttle valve does not open all the way.
   i. Brake dragging.

j. Engine overheating.

k. Contaminated fuel.

l. Damaged ignition system.

3. Low engine compression:
   a. Loose spark plug or missing spark plug gasket.
   b. Excessive valve guide clearance.
   c. Damaged valve(s).
   d. Stuck piston rings.
   e. Excessive piston ring wear.
   f. Excessively worn piston and/or cylinder.
   g. Loose cylinder head fasteners.
   h. Incorrect cylinder head installation.
   i. Warped cylinder head.
   j. Damaged cylinder head gasket.
   k. Damaged base gasket.

4. Engine:
   a. Incorrect valve clearance.
   b. Incorrect valve timing.

Engine Knocking

If the engine knocks under acceleration, check for the following:

1. Excessive carbon buildup in the combustion chamber.

2. Excessive piston-to-cylinder clearance.

3. Incorrect spark plug heat range (hot). Refer to *Spark Plug* in Chapter Three.

4. Defective ignition system component, resulting in overly advanced timing.

NOTE
A damaged ignition control module or system component can change the ignition timing. If the engine accelerates to a higher rpm than before, the ignition control module unit may be damaged. If the condition is allowed to continue, higher engine temperatures, resulting from overadvanced ignition timing, will burn a hole in the piston. To confirm this condition, check the ignition timing as described in Chapter Nine.

5. Poor quality fuel.

CAUTION
All Honda XR400R models require 92 octane fuel or higher.

Engine Overheating

Check for one or more of the following possible malfunctions:
1. Excessive carbon buildup in the combustion chamber (cylinder head and piston).
2. Incorrect air/fuel mixture.
3. Incorrect spark plug heat range (hot). Refer to *Spark Plug* in Chapter Three.
4. Clutch slipping.
5. Brakes dragging.
6. Damaged cylinder head cooling fins.
7. Defective ignition system component, resulting in overly advanced timing.

Black Exhaust and Engine Runs Roughly

1. Restricted air filter intake.
2. Carburetor adjustment too rich.
3. Carburetor floats damaged or incorrectly adjusted.
4. Choke not operating correctly.
5. Contaminated fuel.
6. Excessive piston-to-cylinder clearance.
7. Restricted exhaust system.

Engine Loses Power

1. Incorrect carburetor adjustment.
2. Engine overheating.
3. Defective ignition system component, resulting in overly advanced timing.
4. Incorrect spark plug gap.
5. Restricted exhaust system.
6. Brakes dragging.

Engine Lacks Acceleration

1. Clogged air filter.
2. Incorrect carburetor adjustment.
3. Clogged fuel line.
4. Defective ignition system component, resulting in overly advanced timing.
5. Brakes dragging.

Engine Backfires Under Acceleration

1. Defective ignition system component, resulting in overly advanced timing.
2. Sheared flywheel key.
3. Incorrect carburetor adjustment (lean).

Engine Backfires During Engine Braking

1. Defective carburetor air cut-off valve.
2. Lean pilot jet.

Rich Operating Condition

1. Restricted air intake.
2. Float level too high.
3. Damaged float valve and seat.
4. Incorrect choke operation.
5. Clogged air jets.
6. Flooded carburetor.
7. Damaged float.

Lean Operating Condition

1. Leaking air filter seal.
2. Float level too low.
3. Damaged float valve and seat.
4. Partially restricted fuel hose.
5. Clogged carburetor air vent hose.
6. Intake manifold air leak.

TOP END COMPONENTS

Worn or damaged top end components will lower compression, cause a rough idle, and affect performance. The first signs of problems may be from excessive exhaust smoke and unusual engine noises (piston slap). To isolate engine problems related to the cylinder head and other top end components, perform the leak-down test described in this chapter. Check engine compression as described in Chapter Three.

Reduce wear and damage to the engine top end by changing the engine oil and filter at regular intervals, cleaning the air filter often and making sure the carburetor jetting is correct.

Low Engine Compression

If engine compression is low, check for one or more of the following conditions:
1. Decompressor system out of adjustment.
2. Worn or damaged valves:
   a. Valve stuck open.
   b. Incorrect valve timing.
   c. Bent or burned valves.
   d. Damaged valve seat.
   e. Damaged valve spring(s).
3. Cylinder head:
   a. Loose spark plug.
   b. Leaking cylinder head gasket.
   c. Warped cylinder head gasket surface.
   d. Cracked cylinder head.
4. Cylinder:
   a. Worn, stuck or broken piston ring(s).
   b. Worn or damaged piston and cylinder.

Compression Too High

If the engine compression is too high, check for carbon build-up on the piston crown and combustion chamber surfaces. Excessive engine compression will cause overheating and detonation and result in engine damage. Remove all carbon deposits from the piston and combustion chamber surfaces. See Chapter Four.

Excessive Noise

1. Cylinder head and camshaft assembly:
   a. Worn or damaged cam chain tensioner.
   b. Loose, worn or damaged cam chain.
   c. Worn or damaged cam sprocket teeth.
   d. Worn or damaged camshaft.
   e. Worn or damaged rocker arm.
   f. Worn or damaged rocker arm shaft.
   g. Worn or damaged valve stem end.
2. Valves:
   a. Incorrect valve adjustment.
   b. Burned valve face.
   c. Stuck or bent valve.
   d. Damaged valve seat.

   e. Damaged valve spring.

Excessive Smoke

Excessive exhaust smoke is usually a sign of wear or damage to the valve stems, guides or seals. Black or blue exhaust smoke is a sign of excessive piston, piston ring and cylinder bore wear. White smoke coming out of the crankcase breather tube (**Figure 8**) indicates a seized piston ring. If the engine smokes after reassembling the top end, check for incorrectly installed or broken piston rings.

Piston Slap

Piston slap is an audible slapping or rattling noise resulting from excessive piston-to-cylinder clearance. When allowed to continue, piston slap will eventually cause the piston skirt to shatter. In some cases, a shattered piston may cause secondary engine damage. This damage can be prevented by servicing the air filter at specified intervals (see Chapter Three), and by close visual inspection of all top end components, checking each part for scuff marks, scoring, cracks and other signs of abnormal wear. Replace parts that exceed service limits or show damage.

Other noises may be caused by a worn or damaged piston pin bore, piston pin or a worn connecting rod bore.

Piston Seizure

Possible causes of piston seizure are incorrect cylinder bore clearance, piston rings with an improper end gap, compression leak, incorrect engine oil, spark plug of the wrong heat range, incorrect ignition timing, a lean air/fuel mixture or a defective engine lubricating system. Overheating from any cause may result in piston seizure.

PREIGNITION

Preignition is the premature burning of fuel and is caused by hot spots in the combustion chamber. The fuel actually ignites before it is supposed to. Glowing deposits in the combustion chamber, inadequate cooling or an overheated spark plug can all cause preignition. Power loss is the first symptom,

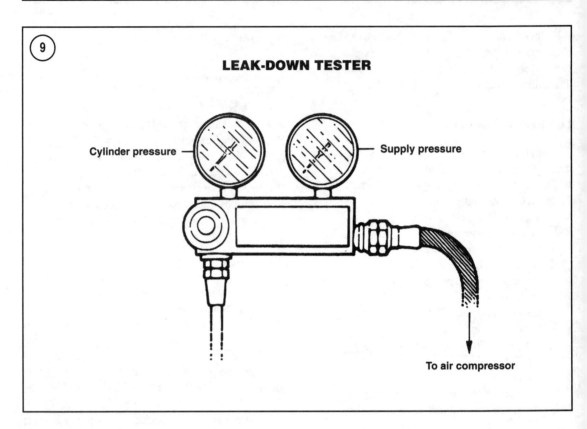

⑨

LEAK-DOWN TESTER

Cylinder pressure —   — Supply pressure

To air compressor

but this problem will eventually result in damage to the internal parts of the engine because of higher combustion chamber temperatures.

DETONATION

Commonly called "spark knock" or "fuel knock," detonation is the violent explosion of fuel in the combustion chamber prior to the proper time of combustion. Damage can result. Use of low octane gasoline is a common cause of detonation.

Even when high octane gasoline is used, detonation can still occur if the engine is improperly timed. Other causes are a lean fuel mixture at or near full throttle, inadequate engine cooling, or the excessive accumulation of deposits within the combustion chamber.

ENGINE NOISES

Often the first evidence of an internal engine problem is a strange noise. An unusual knocking, clicking or tapping sound may be a warning of impending trouble.

1. *Clicking or tapping noises*— These usually come from the valve train and indicate excessive valve clearance. A sticking valve may also sound like a valve with excessive clearance. Excessive wear in valve train components can cause similar engine noises.

2. *Knocking or pinging during acceleration*— Caused by using a lower octane fuel than recommended. Pinging can also be caused by a spark plug of the wrong heat range and lean carburetor jetting. Refer to *Spark Plug* in Chapter Three. Check also for excessive carbon buildup in the combustion chamber or a defective ignition control module.

3. *Slapping or rattling noises at low speed or during acceleration*— May be caused by piston slap (excessive piston-to-cylinder wall clearance). Check also for a bent connecting rod or excessive piston pin-to- piston clearance. Piston slap will always be louder when the engine is cold.

4. *Knocking or rapping while decelerating*— Usually caused by excessive rod bearing clearance.

5. *Persistent knocking and vibration or other noise*— Usually caused by excessive main bearing clearance. If the clearance is within specification, consider the following:

a. Loose engine mounts.
b. Cracked frame.
c. Leaking cylinder head gasket.
d. Exhaust pipe leakage at cylinder head.
e. Stuck piston ring.
f. Broken piston ring.
g. Partial engine seizure.
h. Excessive piston pin clearance.
i. Excessive crankpin clearance.
j. Excessive crankshaft runout.
k. Worn or damaged primary drive gear.

6. *Rapid on-off squeal*— Compression leak around cylinder head gasket or spark plug.

ENGINE LEAK DOWN TEST

An engine leak down test can identify engine problems from leaking valves, a blown head gasket or broken, worn or stuck piston rings. A cylinder leakage test is performed by applying compressed air to the cylinder through a special tester and then measuring the percent of leakage. A cylinder leakage tester and an air compressor are needed to perform this test (**Figure 9**).

Follow the manufacturer's directions along with the following information when performing a cylinder leakage test.

1. Remove the air filter assembly. Open and secure the throttle in the wide-open position.
2. Set the piston to TDC on its compression stroke. See *Valve Adjustment* in Chapter Three.
3. Remove the spark plug.
4. Install the cylinder leakage tester (**Figure 10**) in the spark plug hole according to the manufacturer's instructions.

NOTE
To prevent the engine from turning over when you apply air pressure to the cylinder, shift the transmission into fifth gear and have an assistant apply the rear brake.

5. Perform a cylinder leakage test by applying air pressure to the combustion chamber. Follow the manufacturer's instructions. Listen for air leaking and note the following:

NOTE
If a large amount of air escapes from the exhaust pipe or through the carburetor, the air may be leaking through an open valve. Make sure the engine is at TDC on the compression stroke.

a. Air escaping through the exhaust pipe indicates a leaking exhaust valve.
b. Air escaping through the carburetor indicates a leaking intake valve.
c. Air escaping through the crankcase breather tube suggests worn piston rings. Check by disconnecting the breather tube at the air box. See **Figure 8**, typical.

6. If the cylinder leak down is 10 per cent or higher, further service is required.
7. Disconnect the test equipment and install all of the parts previously removed.

FUEL SYSTEM

Many riders automatically assume that the carburetor is at fault when the engine does not run properly. While fuel system problems are not uncommon, carburetor adjustment is seldom the answer. In many cases, adjusting the carburetor only compounds the problem.

When troubleshooting the fuel system, start at the gas tank and work through the system, reserving the carburetor as the final point. Most fuel system problems result from an empty fuel tank, a plugged fuel filter or fuel valve, or old fuel. Fuel system troubleshooting is covered thoroughly under *Starting Difficulties* and *Engine Performance* in this chapter.

A malfunctioning carburetor choke (**Figure 11**) can also cause engine starting and operating problems. Check the choke by opening and closing the choke lever at the carburetor (A, **Figure 1**).

ELECTRICAL TROUBLESHOOTING

Electrical troubleshooting can be very time consuming and frustrating without proper knowledge, tools and a suitable plan. Refer to the wiring diagrams at the end of this book to determine how the circuit works. Trace current paths from the power source through the circuit components to ground.

As with all troubleshooting procedures, analyze typical symptoms in a systematic procedure. Never assume anything and do not overlook the obvious, such as an electrical connector that has separated. Test the simplest and most obvious cause first and try to make tests at easily accessible points on the bike.

Preliminary Checks and Precautions

Prior to beginning any electrical troubleshooting procedure perform the following:

a. Disconnect each electrical connector in the suspect circuit and make sure there are no bent metal pins on the male side of the electrical connector.

b. Check each female end of the connector. Make sure that the metal connector on the end of each wire is pushed all the way into the plastic connector.

c. Check all electrical wires where they enter the individual metal connector in both the male and female plastic connector.

d. Make sure all electrical connectors within the connector are clean and free of corrosion. Clean and then pack the connectors with a dielectric grease.

e. After servicing the connectors, reconnect them and make sure they are fully engaged and locked together.

f. Never pull on the wires when separating a connector—pull only on the connector housing.

TEST EQUIPMENT

Ohmmeter

An ohmmeter measures the resistance to current flow within a circuit. When troubleshooting, use an ohmmeter to check the following:
1. Wire continuity.
2. Engine stop switch operation.
3. Lighting coil resistance.

4. Bulbs.

When measuring resistance with an ohmmeter, low resistance indicates that the circuit is complete or has continuity. Before using an analog ohmmeter, calibrate it by touching the leads together and turning the ohm calibration knob until the meter reads zero.

Continuity Test

A continuity test will determine if the circuit is complete with no opens in either the electrical wires or components within that circuit.

Unless otherwise specified, all continuity tests are made with the electrical connector still connected. Insert the test leads into the backside of the connector and make sure the test lead touches the electrical wire or metal connector within the connector. If the test lead only touches the wire insulation a false reading will result.

Always check both sides of the connectors as one side may be loose or corroded, thus preventing electrical flow through the connector. This test can be performed with a self-powered test light or an ohmmeter. An ohmmeter will give the best results.

1. Attach one test lead to one end of the part of the circuit to be tested.

2. Attach the other test lead to the other end of the part of the circuit to be tested.

3. Read the ohmmeter scale. The ohmmeter will indicate either low or no resistance (indicating a complete circuit) or infinite resistance (indicating an open circuit). When measuring the resistance of an electrical component, compare the actual reading to the service specification listed in the correct table (Chapter Nine).

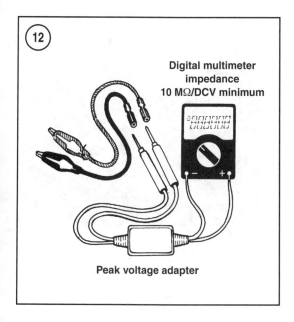

Digital multimeter
impedance
10 MΩ/DCV minimum

Peak voltage adapter

Voltmeter

A voltmeter is required to measure the voltage regulator output. Refer to Chapter Nine for test procedures.

Peak Voltage Tester

Refer to *Peak Voltage Tester* in Chapter Nine.

IGNITION SYSTEM

All models are equipped with a capacitor discharge ignition (CDI) system. This solid state system uses no contact breaker point to trigger the ignition, so problems with the capacitor discharge system are relatively few. However, if an ignition problem does occur, it generally causes a weak or no spark condition or changes the ignition timing. Ignition timing cannot be adjusted on the XR400R. If the timing is incorrect, a component in the ignition system is defective and must be replaced.

Honda does not provide resistance specifications for testing the ignition system components of the XR400R. Instead, they base ignition system troubleshooting on peak voltage and the required peak voltage readings. Peak voltage tests check the voltage output of the ignition coil, exciter coil and ignition pulse generator at normal cranking speed, allowing the tester to identify ignition system problems quickly and accurately. To make these tests, a peak voltage tester or adapter is required (**Figure 12**). See *Peak Voltage Tester* in Chapter Nine.

NOTE
*All peak voltage specifications in the test are **minimum** values. As long as the measured voltage meets or exceeds the specification, consider the test results satisfactory. On some components, the voltage may greatly exceed the minimum specification.*

Ignition System Troubleshooting

If there is no spark or if the spark is intermittent, perform the following steps in order.

NOTE
If the spark is intermittent, perform the tests with the engine cold, then hot.

1. Remove the seat (Chapter Fifteen).
2. Remove the fuel tank (Chapter Eight).
3. Perform the spark test using a new spark plug or spark tester as described under *Spark Test* in this chapter. If there is no spark, continue with Step 4.
4. Check the spark plug cap and coil wire connection (**Figure 4**) as described under *Spark Test* in this chapter. Note the following:
    a. If there was a spark with the plug cap removed, replace the plug cap and retest.
    b. If there is no spark, continue with Step 5.
5. Check the spark plug wire connections at the ignition coil (**Figure 13**). Inspect the wires for cracks or brittle insulation. Make sure the ignition coil's ground connection is tight and free of all corrosion. Inspect the ignition coil for cracks, carbon tracks or other damage. If there is still no spark, continue with Step 6.
6. Make sure the engine stop switch (B, **Figure 2**) is not stuck or working improperly. Disconnect the engine stop switch leads and recheck the spark. Note the following:
    a. If there is now spark, the engine stop switch is damaged. Replace the switch and retest.
    b. If there is still no spark, test the engine stop switch with an ohmmeter (Chapter Nine) before reconnecting it into the wiring harness to make sure it is not a secondary problem. If the switch tests good, reconnect it and continue with Step 7.

WARNING
If the engine stop switch is defective, install a new one as soon as possible.

It is not safe to ride the motorcycle with a missing or disconnected engine stop switch.

NOTE
The following steps require the use of a peak voltage tester. If a peak voltage tester is not available, refer all testing to a Honda dealership.

7. Perform the *Ignition Coil Primary Peak Voltage Test* in Chapter Nine. After recording the test results, note the following:
   a. If the peak voltage is lower than 100 volts, go to Step 8.
   b. If there is no peak voltage reading, go to Step 9.
   c. If the peak voltage reading is normal, but there is no spark, go to Step 10.

NOTE
For a description and location of the electrical components in the following steps, refer to the appropriate section in Chapter Nine and the wiring diagram at the end of the book.

8. If the peak voltage is less than 100 volts, check for one or more of the following conditions in the order given:
   a. Incorrect peak voltage adapter connections. Check connections and retest.
   b. The multimeter impedance is below 10 M ohms/DCV.
   c. The engine cranking speed is slow. The engine must be kicked over forcefully to ensure a high enough cranking speed. If the kickstarter is damaged, repair it before continuing with the test.
   d. Loose or dirty electrical connectors or an open circuit in the ignition circuit.
   e. Damaged exciter coil. Test the exciter coil peak voltage as described in Chapter Nine.
   f. Damaged ignition coil. Replace the ignition coil and retest.
   g. If none of the above listed items has a problem, the ignition control module may be defective.

9. If there was no peak voltage reading in Step 7, check for one or more of the following conditions in the order given:
   a. Incorrect peak voltage adapter connections. Check connections and retest.

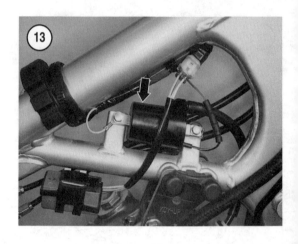

   b. Short circuit in the engine stop switch wire or switch. Test the switch as described in Chapter Nine.
   c. Loose or damaged ignition control module connector.
   d. Loose or damaged ground connection in the ignition control module. If the ignition control module connector is good, check all of the ground wires and connectors leading to it.
   e. Damaged peak voltage tester.
   f. Damaged exciter coil. Test the exciter coil peak voltage as described in Chapter Nine.
   g. Damaged ignition pulse generator. Test the ignition pulse generator peak voltage as described in Chapter Nine.
   h. If none of the above listed items has a problem, the ignition control module may be defective.

10. If the peak voltage readings are correct, but there is no spark, check for one or more of the following conditions in the order given:
   a. Damaged spark plug. Replace the spark plug and retest.
   b. Damaged spark plug wire or cap.
   c. Damaged ignition coil.

11. Perform the *Exciter Coil Peak Voltage Test* in Chapter Nine. After recording the test results, note the following before continuing with the diagnosis:
   a. If the peak voltage reading is lower than 100 volts, go to Step 12.
   b. If there is no peak voltage reading, go to Step 13.

12. If the peak voltage reading was lower than 100 volts, check for one or more of the following conditions in the order given:

a. Incorrect peak voltage adapter connections. Check connections and retest.

b. The multimeter impedance is below 10 M ohms/DCV.

c. The engine cranking speed is slow. The engine must be kicked over forcefully to ensure a high enough cranking speed. If the kickstarter is damaged, repair it before continuing with the test.

d. If none of the above listed items has a problem, the exciter coil may be defective. Test the exciter coil as described in Chapter Nine.

13. If there was no peak voltage reading in Step 11, check for one or more of the following conditions in the order given:

a. Damaged peak voltage tester.

b. Damaged exciter coil.

14. Perform the *Ignition Pulse Generator Peak Voltage Test* in Chapter Nine. After recording the test results, note the following before continuing with the diagnosis:

a. If the peak voltage reading is lower than 100 volts, go to Step 15.

b. If there is no peak voltage reading, go to Step 16.

15. If the peak voltage reading was lower than 100 volts, check for one or more of the following conditions in the order given:

a. Incorrect peak voltage adapter connections. Check connections and retest.

b. The multimeter impedance is below 10 M ohms/DCV.

c. The engine cranking speed is slow. The engine must be kicked over forcefully to ensure a high enough cranking speed. If the kickstarter is damaged, repair it before continuing with the test.

d. If none of the above listed items has a problem, the ignition pulse generator may be defective.

16. If there was no peak voltage reading in Step 14, check for one or more of the following conditions in the order given:

a. Damaged peak voltage adapter or tester.

b. Damaged ignition pulse generator.

NOTE
If the test results (Steps 3-16) obtained are accurate, the ignition control module can be considered defective by a process of elimination. However,

if any step was performed incorrectly, replacing the ignition control module may not fix the problem. It is more likely that a poor connection is at fault, as opposed to the ignition control module. Make sure that all other possibilities are eliminated before replacing the ignition control module. Most dealers will not accept returns on electrical components.

17. Install all parts previously removed.

AC LIGHTING SYSTEM TROUBLESHOOTING

If the headlight or taillight bulb keeps burning out, troubleshoot the lighting circuit as follows:

1. Make sure the bulb wattage is correct. See Chapter Nine.

2. Perform the *Regulated Voltage Test* in Chapter Nine. Note the following:

a. If the voltage reading is low, perform the *Lighting Coil Resistance Test* in Chapter Nine. If the resistance reading is incorrect, replace the stator coil as described under *Left Crankcase Cover and Stator Coil* in Chapter Nine. If the resistance reading is good, go to Step 3.

b. If the voltage reading is high, check the ground circuit as described under *Wiring Harness Test* in Chapter Nine. If the reading is good, continue with Step 3. If the reading is incorrect, check the ground wire for an open circuit.

3. Check the AC regulator connector halves (**Figure 14**) for a loose, damaged or dirty connection. If the connector halves are good, replace the AC regulator.

CLUTCH

The two main clutch problems are clutch slip (clutch does not engage fully) and clutch drag (clutch does not disengage fully). Problems associated with clutch noise will be discussed at the end of this section.

The main cause of clutch slip or drag is incorrect clutch adjustment or a rough operating clutch lever or clutch release lever at the engine. Before removing the clutch for inspection, perform the following checks:

1. Check the clutch cable routing from the handlebar to the engine. Make sure the cable is routed properly and both cable ends are mounted correctly.

2. With the engine turned off and the transmission in NEUTRAL, pull and release the clutch lever. If the clutch lever is hard to pull or its movement is rough, check for the following:

    a. Damaged clutch cable.

    b. Incorrect clutch cable routing (see Step 1).

    c. Dry clutch cable.

    d. Damaged clutch lever and perch assembly at the handlebar.

    e. Damaged clutch release lever assembly at the engine.

    f. Damaged clutch lifter plate bearing.

3. If the items in Step 1 and 2 are good, and the clutch lever moves without any excessive roughness or binding, check the clutch adjustment as described in Chapter Three. Note the following:

    a. If the clutch can not be adjusted within the limits specified in Chapter Three, check for a stretched or damaged clutch cable.

    b. If the clutch cable and its adjustment are good, check the friction plates for excessive wear.

4. If these steps do not locate the problem, refer to the *Clutch Slipping* or *Clutch Dragging* procedure that follows in this section.

Clutch Slipping

When the clutch slips, the engine sounds like it is accelerating faster than what the actual forward speed indicates. Because the clutch plates are spinning against each other and not engaging, an excessive amount of heat accumulates in the clutch. This heat causes rapid and excessive clutch plate wear, warpage, and clutch spring fatigue.

If the clutch slips, check for one or more of the following possible malfunctions:

1. *Clutch wear or damage*:

    a. Incorrect clutch adjustment.

    b. Weak or damaged clutch springs.

NOTE
If the clutch springs are worn and the friction plates are within specifications, check the plates for glaze buildup before reassembling the

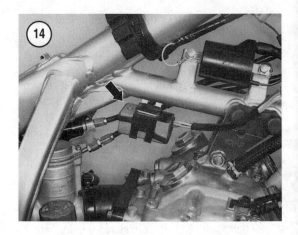

clutch. Remove and deglaze the clutch plates as described in Chapter Six.

    c. Loose clutch springs.

    d. Worn friction plates.

    e. Warped steel plates.

    f. Incorrectly assembled clutch.

    g. Clutch release mechanism wear or damage.

    h. Damaged clutch housing (at clutch lifter).

2. *Clutch/Transmission oil*:

    a. Low oil level.

    b. Oil additives.

    c. Low viscosity oil.

Clutch Dragging

Clutch drag occurs when the clutch does not slip enough. When in gear and releasing the clutch, the bike will creep or jump forward. Once underway, the transmission is difficult to shift. If this condition is not repaired, transmission gear and shift fork wear and damage will occur from the grinding of the transmission gears.

If the clutch drags, check for one or more of the following possible malfunctions:

1. *Clutch wear or damage*:

    a. Excessive free play measurement at the clutch lever.

    b. Clutch release mechanism wear or damage.

    c. Incorrect spindle and lifter piece engagement inside the clutch cover.

    d. Warped steel plates.

    e. Swollen friction plates.

    f. Warped pressure plate.

    g. Incorrect clutch spring tension.

    h. Incorrectly assembled clutch.

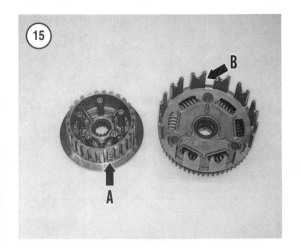

i. Loose clutch nut.

j. Notched clutch boss splines (A, **Figure 15**).

k. Notched clutch housing grooves (B, **Figure 15**).

> *NOTE*
> *The wear described in substeps j and k are a common cause of clutch drag on high-use engines.*

l. Damaged clutch lifter.

2. *Clutch/transmission oil*:

a. Oil level too high.

b. High viscosity oil.

Clutch Noise

Worn or damaged clutch components usually cause excessive clutch noise. If the clutch starts to exhibit more noise than normal, refer to Chapter Six and check for the following conditions:

1. Excessive clutch housing inside diameter and outer guide wear (**Figure 16**).

> *NOTE*
> *Excessive clutch housing bore wear is usually accompanied by a rattling noise in the right crankcase cover that is more noticeable at idle. The noise is reduced or eliminated when the clutch housing is placed under a load.*

2. Excessive friction disc-to-clutch housing clearance.

3. Excessive clutch housing-to-primary drive gear backlash.

EXTERNAL SHIFT MECHANISM AND TRANSMISSION

The XR400R engine is equipped with a 5-speed constant mesh transmission. Because some transmission symptoms are hard to distinguish from clutch symptoms, investigate the easiest and most accessible areas first. For example, if the gears grind during shifting, the problem may be caused by a dragging clutch instead of worn or damaged transmission gears. However, if the clutch drag problem is not repaired, transmission damage will eventually occur. An incorrectly assembled or damaged external shift mechanism assembly will also cause shifting problems. To prevent an incorrect diagnosis, perform the following inspection procedure to troubleshoot the external shift mechanism and transmission. At the same time, refer to the troubleshooting chart in **Figure 17** for a list of common transmission symptoms and possible causes.

The external shift mechanism assembly consists of the stopper lever (A, **Figure 18**), shift cam (B) and shift shaft. The shift shaft (**Figure 19**) is installed inside the crankcase.

> *NOTE*
> *When trying to shift a constant mesh transmission by hand, one of the transmission shafts must be turning. Have an assistant turn the rear wheel (with the drive chain installed) while you operate the shift pedal or shift cam by hand.*

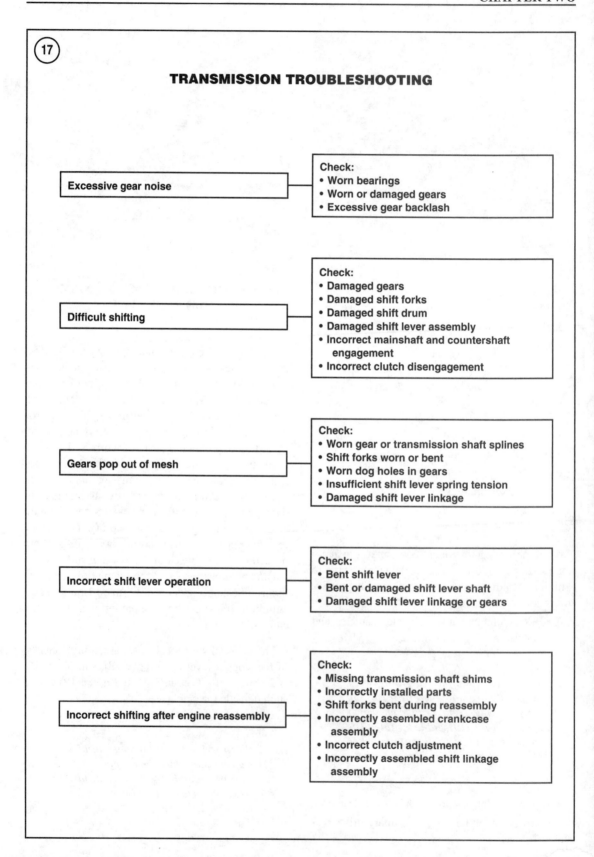

(17)

TRANSMISSION TROUBLESHOOTING

Excessive gear noise

Check:
- Worn bearings
- Worn or damaged gears
- Excessive gear backlash

Difficult shifting

Check:
- Damaged gears
- Damaged shift forks
- Damaged shift drum
- Damaged shift lever assembly
- Incorrect mainshaft and countershaft engagement
- Incorrect clutch disengagement

Gears pop out of mesh

Check:
- Worn gear or transmission shaft splines
- Shift forks worn or bent
- Worn dog holes in gears
- Insufficient shift lever spring tension
- Damaged shift lever linkage

Incorrect shift lever operation

Check:
- Bent shift lever
- Bent or damaged shift lever shaft
- Damaged shift lever linkage or gears

Incorrect shifting after engine reassembly

Check:
- Missing transmission shaft shims
- Incorrectly installed parts
- Shift forks bent during reassembly
- Incorrectly assembled crankcase assembly
- Incorrect clutch adjustment
- Incorrectly assembled shift linkage assembly

1. Make sure that the clutch is properly adjusted. Eliminate any clutch drag or slipping problem. If the clutch is good, continue with Step 2.

2. Support the bike with the rear wheel off the ground.

3. Remove the clutch as described in Chapter Six.

4. Change gears with the shift pedal, while an assistant rotates the rear wheel. Watch the movement of the stopper lever assembly (A, **Figure 18**). When the shift cam turns during each gear change, the stopper lever roller should move in and out of the shift cam detents. Each detent position represents a different gear position. The raised detent position on the shift cam is the NEUTRAL position (B, **Figure 18**). The stopper lever assembly is held under tight spring tension. When the shift cam turns and moves the stopper lever roller out of a detent, spring tension forces the stopper lever to stay in contact with the shift cam and to move into the next detent position. If this is not happening, try to pry the stopper lever away from the shift cam with a screwdriver (**Figure 20**). If the stopper lever will not move, it was installed incorrectly or it has seized on its pivot bolt. Reinstall it and try shifting the transmission again. If the installation was not the problem, remove the stopper lever assembly (Chapter Six) and check it for damage. If the stopper lever assembly is acceptable, continue with Step 5.

> *NOTE*
> *If the transmission overshifts, check for a broken shift shaft return spring (**Figure 21**) or a weak or damaged stopper lever spring (**Figure 22**).*

5. Check the shift drum as follows:
   a. Shift the transmission into NEUTRAL (if possible), and make a mark on the crankcase that aligns with the shift drum NEUTRAL detent position. **Figure 18** shows the shift cam in its NEUTRAL position.
   b. While turning the rear wheel or the mainshaft, turn the shift cam to change gears. Each time the shift drum moves and a new detent position aligns with the mark made in sub-step a, the transmission should change gear.
   c. The transmission should shift into each gear. If the shift drum cannot be turned, or if it locks into a particular gear position, the shift shaft (**Figure 19**) or transmission is damaged.

A locked shift drum indicates a damaged shift fork, a seized transmission gear or bearing, or a damaged shift drum.

6. To service the shift shaft and transmission, disassemble the engine and remove the transmission as described in Chapter Five. Then service the transmission as described in Chapter Seven.

7. Install all parts previously removed.

KICKSTARTER

If the kick pedal sticks or slips, the problem is usually easy to find once the right crankcase cover is removed. The kickstarter assembly can be serviced with the engine mounted in the frame.

Refer to the following troubleshooting information for a list of common kickstarter symptoms and possible causes. To service the kickstarter assembly, refer to *Kickstarter* in Chapter Six.

NOTE
*A good way to inspect the kickstarter is to remove the clutch (Chapter Six) and then reinstall the kick pedal (**Figure 23**) onto the kickstarter. Hold the return spring (**Figure 23**) by hand to prevent it from slipping out and operate the kick pedal by hand while watching the movement of the ratchet gear when it engages the teeth on the kick gear.*

Kickstarter Lever or Shaft Slips

1. Worn or damaged kick shaft.
2. Worn or damaged kick gear.
3. Worn or damaged idle gear and bushing.
4. Ratchet gear not engaging with kick gear.
5. Damaged kick shaft circlip groove or circlip.

Kickstarter Does Not Return

1. Kickstarter incorrectly installed.
2. Return spring is not indexed properly.
3. Damaged return spring.
4. Kick gear seized on shaft.
5. Damaged return spring.
6. Incorrectly assembled kickstarter assembly. If the kickstarter does not operate after reassembling it, the ratchet may not be properly indexed with the kick shaft. Check the ratchet alignment as described under *Kickstarter* in Chapter Six.

Kickstarter is Hard to Kick Over

1. Kickstarter axle—check the following:
   a. Seized kick gear.
   b. Seized kick idler gear and bushing.
   c. Stripped kick pedal and/or kickstarter shaft splines.
   d. Kickstarter incorrectly installed.
2. Engine—check the following:
   a. Seized piston and cylinder.
   b. Broken piston.
   c. Damaged crankcase assembly.
   d. Damaged right crankcase cover.
   e. Seized or broken crankshaft.
   f. Seized crankshaft main bearings.
3. Transmission oil—check the following:
   a. Low viscosity gear oil.
   b. Deteriorated gear oil.

DRIVE TRAIN NOISE

This section covers drive train assembly noises: drive chain, clutch and transmission. Abnormal noises are a good indicator of a developing problem. The problem is recognizing the difference between a normal and abnormal noise. Investigate any new noise, no matter how minor.

1. *Drive chain noise*— Normal drive chain noise can be considered a low-pitched, continuous whining sound. The noise will vary, depending on the speed of the bike, the riding terrain, proper lubrication, chain and sprocket wear, and alignment. When checking abnormal drive chain noise, consider the following:
   a. Inadequate lubrication—A dry chain will give off a loud whining sound. Clean and lu-

bricate the drive chain at regular intervals (Chapter Three).
b. Incorrect chain adjustment—Check and adjust the drive chain as described in Chapter Three.
c. Worn chain—Check chain wear at regular intervals, and replace it when its overall length exceeds the wear limit specified in Chapter Three.
d. Worn or damaged sprockets—Worn or damaged sprockets accelerate chain wear. Inspect the sprockets carefully as described in Chapter Three.
e. Worn, damaged or missing drive chain sliders and rollers—Chain sliders and rollers are in constant contact with the chain. Check them often for loose, damaged or missing parts. A missing chain slider or roller will increase chain slack and may cause rapid chain wear against the frame or swing arm.

2. *Clutch noise*— Investigate any noise that develops in the clutch. Drain the engine oil (Chapter Three) and check for bits of metal or clutch plate material in the oil. If the oil looks and smells normal, remove the clutch (Chapter Six) and check for the following:
a. Worn or damaged clutch housing and primary drive gear teeth.
b. Excessive clutch housing-to-friction plate clearance.
c. Loose clutch nut.
d. Clutch damage.

3. *Transmission noise*— Like the clutch, any new noise in the transmission must be investigated. Drain the engine oil (Chapter Three). Wipe a small amount of oil on a finger and rub the finger and

thumb together. Check for the presence of metallic particles. Some transmission associated noises are caused by:
a. Low engine oil level.
b. Worn or seized transmission gear(s).
c. Chipped or broken transmission gear(s).
d. Excessive gear side play.
e. Worn or damaged transmission bearing(s).

NOTE
If metallic particles are found in Step 2 or Step 3, remove and inspect the clutch. If necessary, disassemble the engine and inspect the transmission.

FRONT SUSPENSION AND STEERING

1. Handlebar vibration:
a. Loose or damaged handlebar clamps.
b. Incorrect handlebar clamp installation.
c. Bent or cracked handlebar.
d. Worn handlebar rubber dampers, if so equipped.
e. Loose steering stem nut.
f. Worn or damaged front wheel bearings.
g. Bent axle.
h. Dry rotted tire.
i. Excessively worn front tire.
j. Damaged rim.
k. Loose, missing or broken engine mount bolts and mounts.
l. Cracked frame, especially at the steering head.
m. Incorrect tire pressure for riding conditions.

2. Difficult steering (handlebar is hard to turn):
a. Low front tire air pressure.
b. Incorrect throttle cable routing.
c. Incorrect clutch cable routing.
d. Steering stem adjustment is tight.
e. Bent steering stem.
f. Improperly lubricated steering bearings.
g. Damaged steering bearings and races.

3. Front wheel wobble:
a. Loose front axle fasteners.
b. Worn or damaged front wheel bearings.
c. Damaged hub.
d. Loose or broken spokes.
e. Bent rim.
f. Front wheel incorrectly installed.

g. Loose front fork fasteners.
4. Hard front suspension:
   a. High fork oil level.
   b. Incorrect fork oil viscosity (thick).
   c. Incorrect fork adjustment.
   d. Bent or damaged fork tubes.
   e. Clogged or damaged internal fork components.
5. Soft front suspension:
   a. Weak fork springs.
   b. Low fork oil level.
   c. Incorrect fork oil viscosity (thin).
   d. Incorrect fork adjustment.
   e. Low front tire pressure.

REAR SUSPENSION

1. Soft rear suspension:
   a. Incorrect shock absorber adjustment.
   b. Leaking shock absorber.
   c. Weak shock spring.
   d. Low nitrogen pressure in shock absorber.
   e. Incorrect shock spring preload adjustment.
2. Hard rear suspension:
   a. Incorrect shock absorber adjustment.
   b. High rear tire pressure.
   c. Damaged shock absorber.
   d. Incorrect shock spring (hard).
   e. Incorrect shock spring preload adjustment.
   f. Damaged swing arm and linkage bearings.
3. Rear wheel wobble:
   a. Loose rear axle fasteners.
   b. Worn or damaged rear wheel bearings.
   c. Damaged hub.
   d. Loose or broken spokes.
   e. Bent rim.
   f. Rear wheel incorrectly installed.
   g. Damaged swing arm.
   h. Damaged swing arm and linkage bearings.

FRAME NOISE

Frame or suspension noises are usually caused by loose, worn or damaged parts. Various noises that are related to the frame are listed below:

1. *Disc brake noise*— A screeching sound during braking is the most common disc brake noise. Some other disc brake noises can be caused by:
   a. Glazed brake pad surface.
   b. Worn brake pads.
   c. Warped brake disc.
   d. Loose brake disc mounting bolts.
   e. Loose or missing brake caliper mounting bolts.
   f. Damaged caliper.
   g. Cracked wheel hub at the brake disc mounts.
2. *Front fork noise*— Check for the following:
   a. Contaminated fork oil.
   b. Low fork oil level.
   c. Broken fork spring.
   d. Worn or damaged front fork bushings.
3. *Rear shock absorber noise*— Check for the following:
   a. Loose shock absorber mounting bolts.
   b. Cracked or broken shock spring.
   c. Damaged shock absorber.
4. Some other frame associated noises are caused by:
   a. Broken frame.
   b. Broken swing arm.
   c. Loose engine mounting bolts.
   d. Dry or damaged steering bearings.
   e. Loose mounting bracket(s).

BRAKES

The disc brakes are critical to riding performance and safety. Inspect the front and rear brake frequently and replace any excessively worn or damaged parts immediately. When replacing or refilling the brake fluid, use only DOT 4 brake fluid from a closed and sealed container. See Chapter Thirteen for additional information on brake fluid and disc brake service. Use the troubleshooting procedures in **Figure 24** to help isolate disc brake problems.

When checking brake pad wear, make sure the brake pads in each caliper contact the disc squarely. If one of the brake pads is wearing unevenly, suspect a warped or bent brake disc, a damaged caliper or damaged caliper bracket pins.

(24)

DISC BRAKE TROUBLESHOOTING

2

Disc brake fluid leakage	Check: • Loose or damaged line fittings • Worn caliper piston seals • Scored caliper piston and/or bore • Loose banjo bolts • Damaged washers • Leaking master cylinder diaphragm • Leaking master cylinder secondary seal • Cracked master cylinder housing • Brake fluid level too high • Loose master cylinder cover
Brake overheating	Check: • Warped brake disc • Incorrect brake fluid • Caliper piston and/or brake pads binding • Riding brakes during riding
Brake chatter	Check: • Warped brake disc • Loose brake disc • Incorrect caliper alignment • Loose caliper mounting bolts • Loose front axle and/or clamps • Worn wheel bearings • Damaged front hub • Restricted brake hydraulic line • Contaminated brake pads
Brake locking	Check: • Incorrect brake fluid • Plugged passages in master cylinder • Incorrect front brake adjustment • Caliper piston and/or brake pads binding • Warped brake disc
Insufficient brakes	Check: • Air in brake lines • Worn brake pads • Low brake fluid level • Incorrect brake fluid • Worn brake disc • Worn caliper piston seals • Glazed brake pads • Leaking primary cup seal in master cylinder • Contaminated brake pads and/or disc
Brake squeal	Check: • Contaminated brake pads and/or disc • Dust or dirt collected behind brake pads • Loose parts

LUBRICATION, MAINTENANCE, AND TUNE-UP

This chapter covers all of the required periodic service procedures that do not require major disassembly. Regular, careful maintenance is the best guarantee for a trouble-free, long lasting motorcycle. All motorcycles designed for off-road use require proper lubrication, maintenance and tune-up to maintain a high level of performance and extend engine, suspension and chassis life.

When performing lubrication, maintenance and tune-ups, use common sense and follow the correct procedures. Remember that damage can result from improper tuning and adjustment. In addition, where special tools or testers are called for during a particular maintenance or adjustment procedure, use the correct tool or refer service to a qualified motorcycle service shop or Honda dealership.

Tables 1-12 are at the end of this chapter.

SERVICE INTERVALS

The service intervals in **Table 1** and **Table 2** are based on time and mileage intervals. Check the items described in **Table 3** before using the

XR400R in competition. Strict adherence to these recommendations will ensure long service from the motorcycle.

TORQUE SPECIFICATIONS

A torque wrench is required to perform many of the maintenance and service procedures in this chapter. The maintenance and service torque specifications are in **Table 4**.

TUNE-UP

A tune-up is a general adjustment and maintenance to insure peak engine and suspension performance. Follow the service intervals listed in **Table 1** and **Table 2** or **Table 3** (competition) to keep the engine, steering, suspension and brakes in order.

Tune-up procedures are listed in a logical sequence. Some procedures should be done with the engine cold and others with the engine hot. For example, check the valve adjustment when the engine is cold and adjust the carburetor and drain the en-

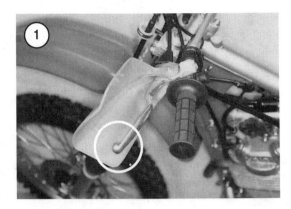

gine oil when the engine is hot. Make sure the spark plug and air filter are in good condition before adjusting the carburetor.

After completing a tune-up, record the date, the motorcycle operating time interval, mileage or number of races completed, and the type of service performed at the back of this book. This information will provide an accurate record on the type of service performed. This record can also be used to schedule future service procedures at the correct time.

Engine Tune-Up Procedure

1. Tighten cylinder head nuts (Chapter Four).
2. Check exhaust pipe fasteners for tightness (Chapter Four).
3. Clean and re-oil air filter.
4. Check and service spark plug.
5. Check valve clearance.
6. Check decompressor system.
7. Check engine compression.
8. Check throttle operation and cable.
9. Check clutch operation and cable.
10. Clean spark arrestor.
11. Start engine and allow to warm to normal operating temperature.
12. Adjust carburetor.
13. Change engine oil and filter.
14. Check all exposed engine nuts and bolts for tightness.

Chassis Tune-Up Procedure

1. Clean and lubricate drive chain.
2. Check drive chain tension and alignment.
3. Check brake operation and cable adjustment.
4. Check rims, hubs and tires.

5. Check operation of front and rear suspension.
6. Check steering play.
7. Check all exposed steering and suspension nuts and bolts for tightness.

Test Ride

The test ride is an important part of the tune-up or service procedure. When test riding a motorcycle, always start slowly and ride in a safe place away from all other vehicles and people. Concentrate on the areas that were serviced. If the brakes were worked on, never apply full brake pressure at high speeds (emergencies excepted). It is safer to check the brakes at slower speeds and with moderate pressure. Do not continue to ride the motorcycle if the engine, brakes or any suspension or steering component is not working correctly.

PRE-RIDE INSPECTION

Perform the following checks before each race or before the first ride of the day. All of these checks, unless noted otherwise, are described in this chapter. If a component requires service, refer to the appropriate section.

1. Inspect the fuel hose and fittings for wetness. Check that each hose end is secured with a hose clamp.
2. Make sure the fuel tank is full and secure.
3. Remove the spark plug and check its firing tip. Regap the plug, if necessary. Install the spark plug and tighten securely.
4. Check the spark plug cap and high tension lead for tightness.
5. Make sure the air filter is clean and the air box and carburetor boots are secure.
6. Check the engine oil level.
7. Check the front and rear sprockets for excessive wear.
8. Check the clutch and brake levers and replace damaged levers.

> *WARNING*
> *If the ball is broken off the end of the brake or clutch lever, replace the damaged lever immediately. The lever ball (**Figure 1**) is designed to prevent the lever from puncturing your hand or arm during a crash.*

9. Check the throttle operation. Open the throttle all the way and release it. The throttle must close quickly with no binding or roughness. Repeat this step with the handlebar facing straight ahead and at both full lock positions. Then start the engine and open and release the throttle. It must open and close smoothly.

10. Check the clutch free play adjustment. Start the engine and check the clutch operation by pulling the clutch lever in and shifting the transmission into gear. If the engine stalls or if the bike creeps forward, adjust the clutch as described in this chapter.

11. Check the brake reservoir fluid levels. Add DOT 4 brake fluid to bring the levels to the FULL mark.

12. Make sure the front and rear brakes work properly.

13. Check the front fork and rear shock absorber for oil leaks.

14. Check the front and rear suspension adjustments, and if necessary, adjust as described in Chapter Eleven or Chapter Twelve.

15. Place the bike on a stand with the front wheel off the ground and check steering play.

16. With the front wheel off the ground, turn the handlebar from side to side. Make sure the control cables do not interfere with the handlebar or the handlebar controls.

17. Check the tires for damage.

18. Check each wheel for loose or damaged spokes. Make sure the rim locks are tight.

19. Check the tire pressure.

20. Check for worn, damaged or missing drive chain sliders and rollers.

21. Lubricate the drive chain.

22. Check the drive chain alignment and adjustment.

23. Check the tightness of all exposed fasteners. Make sure the sub-frame mounting bolts are tight.

24. Start the engine and make sure the engine stop switch works.

25. Before trail riding, make sure to have the necessary tools and spares on hand.

ENGINE LUBRICATION

WARNING
A serious fire hazard always exists around gasoline and other petroleum products. Do not allow any smoking

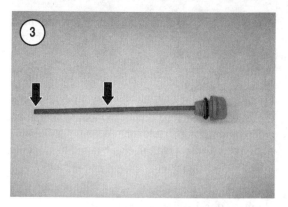

while refueling the machine or servicing the fuel system. Always have a fire extinguisher, rated for gasoline and electrical fires, on hand.

Engine Oil Level Check

The XR400 engine is a dry-sump design. The majority of the oil is stored in the frame, while the remainder is stored in the crankcase. During normal operation the oil level is checked with the dipstick on the frame. The crankcase oil level can be check to determine if the lubrication system is maintaining the correct oil level in the crankcase. If an inspection of the crankcase oil level indicates a problem, do not operate the motorcycle until the cause has been determined.

CAUTION
Before checking the oil level, the engine must operate at idle speed to allow the oil to circulate throughout the system and reach sufficient temperature. If this is not done, the level will register low on the dipstick. Do not

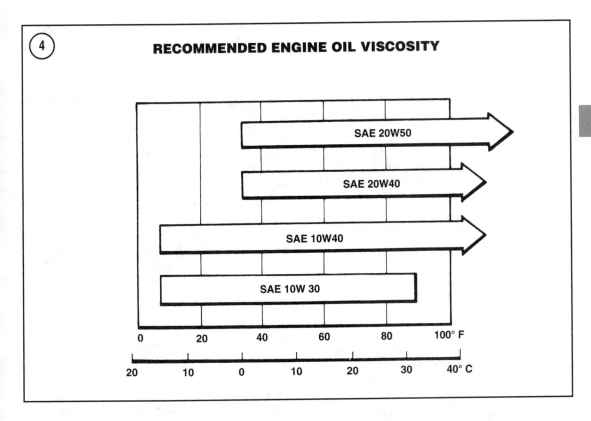

④ **RECOMMENDED ENGINE OIL VISCOSITY**

3

rev the engine as this will result in an inaccurate reading also.

WARNING
Because the engine must be warmed up before checking the oil level, do not start and run the motorcycle in a closed area. The exhaust gases contain carbon monoxide, a colorless, odorless, poisonous gas. Carbon monoxide levels build quickly in a closed area and can cause unconsciousness and death in a short time. When running the engine in the following sections, always do so in an area with adequate ventilation.

Dipstick

1. Support the motorcycle upright on level ground.
2. Start the engine and allow to idle for 5 minutes. If the ambient temperature is below 50° F (10° C), allow the engine to idle for an additional 5 minutes.
3. Clean the area around the dipstick.
4. Turn the engine off and immediately unscrew the dipstick (**Figure 2**) from the frame between the steering head and fuel tank.

5. Wipe the dipstick clean and reinsert it into the filler hole until it rests on top of the threads; do *not* screw it in.
6. Remove the dipstick and check the oil level. The level should be between the two lines (**Figure 3**). If necessary add the recommended type of oil (**Table 5**) through the dipstick hole to correct the level. See **Figure 4** for the recommended oil viscosity based on anticipated ambient temperatures (not engine oil emperature). Install and tighten the dipstick.

Crankcase oil level check bolt

Do not check the crankcase oil level immediately after operating the engine at high speed or the reading will be inaccurate.
1. Support the motorcycle upright on level ground.
2. Check the oil level with the dipstick as described in this chapter. Make sure the oil level on the dipstick is correct before removing the oil check bolt.

NOTE
Perform Step 3 to allow the engine oil level to stabilize the crankcase oil level. This is especially important if oil was just added to the oil tank.

3. Restart the engine and allow it to idle for a few minutes.

4. Turn the engine off.

5. Remove the crankcase oil level check bolt (A, **Figure 5**). The crankcase oil level is correct if the oil is up to the bottom surface of the threads in the hole.

6. If the oil level is correct on the dipstick but the crankcase oil level is too low, some part of the lubrication system is not operating correctly. Troubleshoot the lubrication system as described in Chapter Two.

7. Reinstall the crankcase oil level check bolt (A, **Figure 5**) and tighten.

Engine Oil and Filter Change

Table 1 and **Table 2** list the recommended oil and filter change intervals. This assumes the motorcycle is operated in moderate climates. If the motorcycle is operated under dusty conditions, the oil will get dirty more quickly and will require more frequent oil changes.

Use only a high quality detergent motor oil with an API classification of SF or SG. The classification is stamped or printed on top of the can or label on plastic bottles. Try to use the same brand of oil at each oil change. Refer to **Figure 4** for the recommended oil viscosity based on anticipated ambient temperatures (not engine oil temperature).

To change the engine oil and filter you will need the following:

    a. Drain pan.

    b. Funnel.

    c. Can opener or pour spout.

    d. Wrench and sockets

    e. Approximately two quarts of oil.

    f. New oil filter.

NOTE
Never dispose of motor oil in the trash, on the ground, or down a storm drain. Many service stations accept used motor oil and waste haulers provide curbside used motor oil collection. Do not combine other fluids with motor oil to be recycled. To locate a recycler, contact the American Petroleum Institute (API) at www.recycleoil.org.

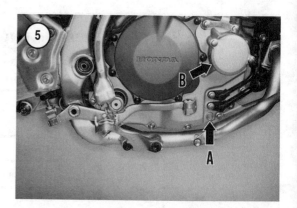

NOTE
Warming the engine allows the oil to heat up; thus it flows freely and carries contamination and any sludge buildup out with it.

1. Start the engine and let it warm to normal operating temperature.

2. Shut the engine off and prop the motorcycle on its sidestand.

3. Remove the dipstick (**Figure 2**).

NOTE
The motorcycle must be resting on its sidestand to ensure complete oil draining.

4. Place a large drain pan underneath the frame down tube (**Figure 6**) and crankcase (**Figure 7**) drain bolts. Remove both oil drain bolts and washers and drain the engine oil.

5. Inspect the drain bolts for head or thread damage. Check the washers for damage. Replace if necessary.

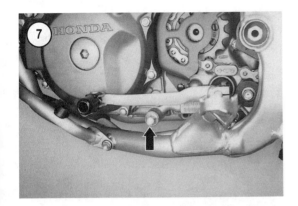

6. If the engine oil strainer screen requires cleaning, do so now as described under *Engine Oil Strainer Screen* in this chapter.

NOTE
An oil strainer is mounted behind the right crankcase cover. Although no service interval is specified for servicing the oil strainer, remove and clean the strainer after the engine has experienced some type of lubrication problem or when you notice contaminants in the engine oil. If the engine has not experienced these types of problems, it is a good idea to clean the oil strainer at least once a year. Refer to **Oil Strainer** *in this chapter.*

7. Replace the engine oil filter as described under *Engine Oil Filter Replacement.*

CAUTION
There are two separate torque requirements for the oil drain bolts. Refer to **Table 4** *for the correct torque specification. Overtightening the*

crankcase oil drain bolt may damage the crankcase.

8. Install the washer on the down tube oil drain bolt. Install the bolt (**Figure 6**) and tighten as specified in **Table 4**.
9. Install the washer on the crankcase oil drain bolt. Install the bolt (**Figure 7**) and tighten as specified in **Table 4**.
10. Wipe up any spilled oil from the frame tube and engine guard surfaces.

CAUTION
Due to the engine's dry sump design, it is necessary to add oil in two steps to achieve the correct oil level.

NOTE
The oil refill capacity varies with the type of service performed. Refer to **Table 6** *for the correct capacity.*

11. Support the motorcycle in an upright position.
12. Pour some of the recommended oil (**Table 5**) into the oil tank. Check the oil level with the dipstick. Continue to add oil until it aligns with the upper level mark (**Figure 3**) on the dipstick.
13. Install the dipstick (**Figure 2**) and tighten.
14. Start the engine and run at idle speed for 5 minutes.
15. Turn the engine off and remove the dipstick. Add oil until it aligns with the upper level mark (**Figure 3**) on the dipstick.
16. Install the dipstick and tighten.
17. Start the engine and check the oil level as described under *Engine Oil Level Check* in this section.
18. Check both engine oil drain bolts for leaks.

WARNING
Prolonged contact with oil may cause skin cancer. Wash your hands with soap and water after handling or coming in contact with motor oil.

Engine Oil Filter Replacement

1. Drain the engine oil as described in this section.
2. Remove the oil filter cover mounting bolts and remove the cover (B, **Figure 5**).
3. Remove and discard the oil filter (**Figure 8**).
4. Remove the spring (**Figure 9**) from the filter cavity.

5. Thoroughly clean the filter cavity in the right crankcase cover.

6. Remove the O-ring (A, **Figure 10**) from the oil filter cover groove. Discard the O-ring if leaking or damaged. Inspect the filter cover oil passage (B, **Figure 10**) for contamination.

7. Clean and dry the spring and oil filter cover.

8. Lubricate the O-ring with oil and install it into the oil filter cover groove.

9. Install the spring (**Figure 9**) into the guide inside the filter cavity.

CAUTION
Installing the oil filter backward will re-strict oil flow and cause engine damage.

10. Install the new oil filter with the OUT-SIDE mark facing out (**Figure 8**) and hold in position against the spring. Align the bore in the oil filter cover (**Figure 11**) with the hole in the oil filter and install the cover. Secure the oil filter cover with the two mounting bolts and tighten securely.

11. Refill the engine with oil as described in this section.

12. Check the oil filter cover for leaks.

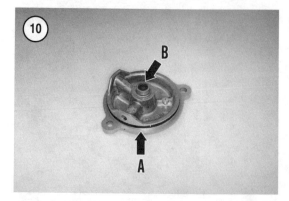

Engine Oil Strainer Screen
Removal/Cleaning/Installation

An engine oil strainer screen is located in the bottom of the frame down tube. Remove and clean the strainer screen at the intervals specified in **Table 1** or **Table 2**.

1. Remove the engine guard (Chapter Fifteen).

2. Drain the engine oil as described in this section.

3. Remove the banjo bolt and washers (A, **Figure 12**) securing the oil pump inlet hose to the oil strainer screen. Discard the washers.

4. Loosen and remove the oil strainer screen (B, **Figure 12**) and its O-ring. See **Figure 13**.

5. Remove the O-ring from the oil strainer screen. Discard the O-ring if leaking or damaged.

6. Clean the banjo bolt and oil strainer screen in solvent. Replace the oil strainer screen if it cannot be thoroughly cleaned.

7. Inspect the oil strainer screen (**Figure 14**) and replace if torn or damaged.

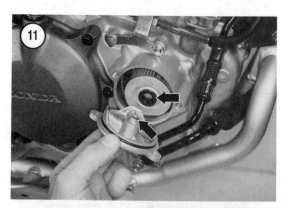

CAUTION
A damaged oil strainer screen allows unfiltered oil from the oil tank to enter the oil pump. Any debris that enters

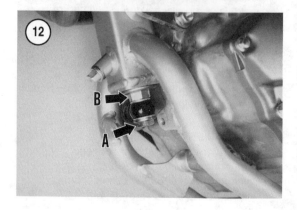

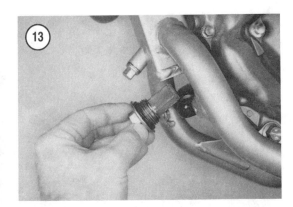

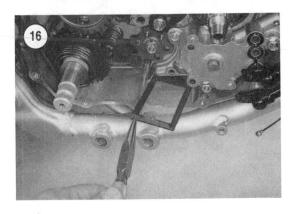

the oil pump can cause pump wear and damage and eventual loss of oil pressure.

8. Lubricate the O-ring with engine oil and install it onto the oil strainer screen (**Figure 13**).

> *NOTE*
> *Do not install the oil strainer screen until all solvent in the screen has either been blown off or evaporated. Solvent left in the screen wil contaminate the engine oil.*

9. Install the oil strainer screen (B, **Figure 12**) and tighten to the specification in **Table 4**.
10. Install the banjo bolt (A, **Figure 12**) and two new washers. Install a washer on each side of the oil pump inlet hose fitting. Tighten the banjo bolt to the specification in **Table 4**.
11. Refill the engine with oil as described in this chapter.
12. Install the engine guard (Chapter Fifteen).

Crankcase Oil Strainer
Removal/Cleaning/Installation

An oil strainer (**Figure 15**) is located in the crankcase behind the right crankcase cover. Servicing the crankcase oil strainer is not part of the periodic maintenance schedule. However, it is a good idea to remove and clean it on a yearly basis. If the lubrication system requires troubleshooting due to a malfunction, remove and inspect the oil strainer.

1. Remove the right crankcase cover (Chapter Six).
2. Unbolt and remove the oil strainer (**Figure 16**).
3. Clean and dry the oil strainer. Replace the oil strainer if the screen is damaged or if it cannot be thoroughly cleaned.
4. Reverse these steps to install the oil strainer.

AIR FILTER

An air filter traps dirt and other abrasive particles before they enter the engine. Even though the air filter is one of the least expensive service parts, it is often neglected at the expense of engine performance and wear. Never run the engine without a properly oiled and installed air filter element. Likewise, running the engine with a dry or damaged air filter element will allow unfiltered air to enter the engine. A well-oiled but dirty or clogged air filter will reduce the amount of air that enters the engine and cause a rich air/fuel mixture, resulting in poor engine starting, spark plug fouling and reduced engine performance. Frequent air filter inspection and cleaning is a critical part of minimizing engine wear and maintaining engine performance. **Figure 17** shows dirt that passed through an improperly installed or damaged air filter.

    Table 1 and **Table 2** list intervals for cleaning the air filter. Clean the air filter more often after riding in dusty, sandy, or muddy conditions.

1. Turn the air filter cover screws (A, **Figure 18**) counterclockwise and open the cover (B, **Figure 18**).

2. Release the air filter wire retainer (**Figure 19**) and remove the air filter (A, **Figure 20**) and its frame from the air box.

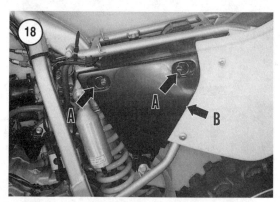

3. Use a flashlight and check inside the air box and carburetor boot for dirt and other debris that may have passed through the air filter.

4. Wipe the inside of the air box with a clean rag. If the air box cannot be cleaned while it is mounted on the bike, remove and clean the air box thoroughly.

5. Cover the air box opening with a clean shop rag.

6. Inspect all air box fittings for damage.

7. Pull the air filter off its frame (**Figure 21**).

8. Clean and dry the filter frame. Check the screen for tearing and other damage. Replace the filter frame if damaged or if the screen cannot be thoroughly cleaned.

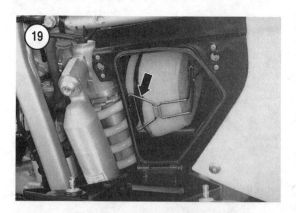

9. Before cleaning the air filter, check it for brittleness, separation or other damage. Replace the air filter if excessively worn or damaged. If there is no visible damage, clean the air filter as described below.

> *WARNING*
> *Do not clean the air filter element with gasoline or any type of low flash point solvent.*

10. Soak the air filter in a container filled with kerosene or an air filter cleaner. Gently squeeze the filter to dislodge and remove the oil and dirt from the filter pores. Repeat this step a few times, while swishing the filter around in the cleaner, then remove the air filter and set aside to air-dry.

11. Fill a clean pan with warm soapy water.

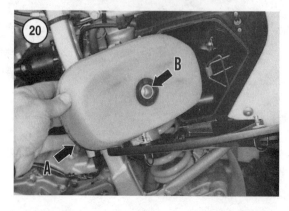

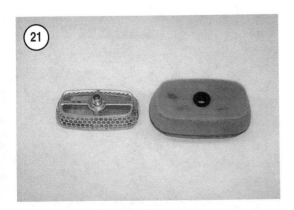

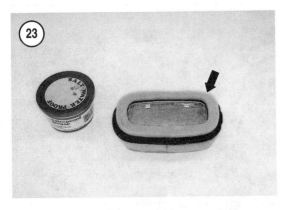

12. Submerge the air filter into the soapy water and gently work the solution into the filter pores. Soak and gently squeeze the filter to clean it.

CAUTION
Do not wring or twist the air filter when cleaning it. This could damage a filter pore or tear the filter loose at a seam.

13. Rinse the air filter in clear water while gently squeezing it.

14. Repeat these steps until there are no signs of dirt being rinsed from the filter.

15. After cleaning the air filter, inspect it carefully and replace if torn or damaged.

CAUTION
Do not run the engine with a damaged air filter as it will allow dirt to enter and damage the engine.

16. Set the air filter aside and allow it to dry thoroughly.

CAUTION
A damp air filter will not trap fine dust. Make sure the filter is dry before oiling it.

17. Properly oiling an air filter is a messy job. Wear a pair of disposable rubber gloves when performing this procedure. Oil the filter as follows:

a. Place the air filter into a plastic storage bag (**Figure 22**).

NOTE
Do not use motor oils to lubricate foam air filters. Foam air filter oil is specifically formulated for easy and thorough application into the filter pores and provides a tacky viscous medium to filter air borne contaminants. Motor oils are too thin to remain suspended in the filter; the oil will be drawn into the engine and allow dirt to pass through the filter.

b. Pour foam air filter oil onto the filter until the filter is soaked with oil.

c. Gently squeeze and release the filter to disperse the filter oil into the filter pores. Repeat until all the pores are saturated.

d. Remove the filter from the bag and check the pores for uneven oiling. Light or dark areas on the filter indicate this. If necessary, soak the filter and squeeze it again.

e. When the filter oiling is even, squeeze the filter a final time to remove any excess oil.

f. Remove the air filter from the bag.

18. Install the air filter onto its frame, aligning the nozzle on the frame with the rubber mounting hole in the filter (B, **Figure 20**).

19. Apply a coat of grease to the filter's sealing surface (**Figure 23**).

20. Install the air filter into the air box, inserting the knob (**Figure 24**) on the wire retainer into the mounting hole in the filter (B, **Figure 20**). Hook the wire retainer onto the bracket in the air box (**Figure 19**) to secure the air filter. Check that the air filter seats evenly against the air box.

> *CAUTION*
> *If the air filter is not installed correctly, dirt may enter the engine and damage it.*

21. Close the air filter cover (B, **Figure 18**) and turn the screws (A, **Figure 18**) clockwise to lock them.

22. Pour the remaining filter oil from the plastic bag back into the bottle for reuse.

SPARK PLUG

Correct Spark Plug Heat Range

Spark plugs are available in various heat ranges, hotter or colder than the plug originally installed by the manufacturer. See **Table 7** for recommended standard and colder heat range spark plugs. Honda does not provide a hotter heat range recommendation for the XR400R.

Select a spark plug of the heat range designed for the loads and conditions the motorcycle will be operating under. The incorrect heat range can cause the engine to overheat and damage the pistons.

In general, use a hot plug for low speeds and low temperatures. Use a cold plug for high speeds, high engine loads and high temperatures. The plug must operate hot enough to burn off deposits, but not so hot that it causes engine overheating and preignition. A spark plug of the correct heat range will have a light tan colored insulator tip after the plug has been in service. See *Reading Spark Plugs* in this section.

The reach (length) of a plug is also important. A too short plug will cause excessive carbon buildup, hard starting and plug fouling (**Figure 25**).

Spark Plug Removal

1. Grasp the spark plug cap as near the plug as possible and pull it off the plug (**Figure 26**). If it is stuck to the plug, twist it slightly to break it loose.

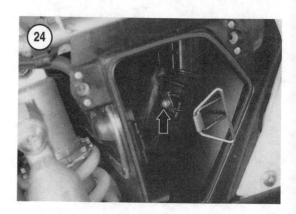

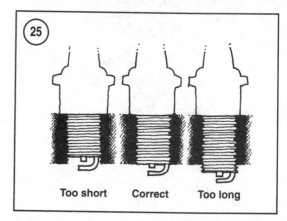

Too short   Correct   Too long

2. Blow any dirt and other debris away from the spark plug and spark plug hole in the cylinder head.

> *CAUTION*
> *The spark plug hole is recessed deeply inside the cylinder head and difficult to look into. Make sure to blow any debris out of the hole before removing the spark plug. Debris that falls through the spark plug hole will cause engine wear and damage.*

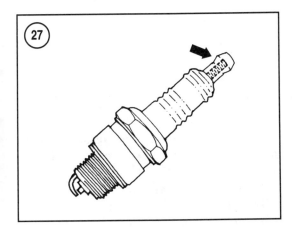

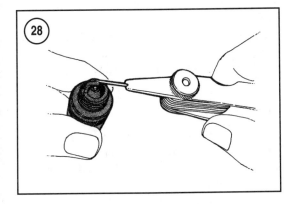

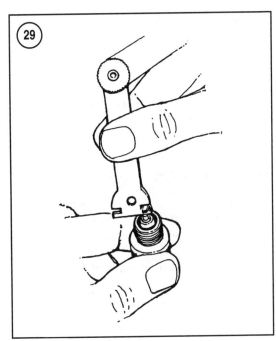

3

3. Remove the spark plug with a 14 mm spark plug wrench.

NOTE
If the plug is difficult to remove, apply penetrating oil, like WD-40 or Liquid Wrench, around the base of the plug and let it soak in about 10-20 minutes.

4. Inspect the plug carefully. Look for a broken center porcelain, eroded electrode, and carbon or oil fouling. See *Reading Spark Plugs* in this section.

Gapping and Installing the Plug

Gap used and new spark plugs to ensure a reliable, consistent spark. Use a spark plug gapping tool and a wire feeler gauge as described in this procedure.

1. Remove the new spark plug from the box. The small cap adapter (**Figure 27**) is not required with the original equipment spark plug cap.

2. Refer to the spark plug gap listed in **Table 7**. Insert a wire feeler gauge between the center and side electrode (**Figure 28**). When the gap is correct, a slight drag will be felt as the wire is pulled through. If there is no drag, or the gauge will not pass through, bend the side electrode with a gapping tool (**Figure 29**) to set the proper gap.

NOTE
Do not use a flat feeler gauge to check the spark plug gap on a used spark plug or the resulting gap will be too wide

3. Apply an anti-seize lubricant to the plug threads before installing the spark plug. Do not use engine oil.

4. Screw the spark plug in by hand until it seats. Very little effort is required. If force is necessary, the plug may be cross-threaded. Unscrew it and try again.

5. Tighten the spark plug as specified in **Table 4** or use a spark plug wrench and tighten a new plug an additional 1/4 to 1/2 turn after the gasket makes contact with the head. Tighten an old plug only an additional 1/4 turn after the gasket makes contact.

NOTE
Do not overtighten the spark plug. This may crush the gasket and cause a

compression leak or damage the threads in the cylinder head.

6. Install the spark plug cap (A, **Figure 26**) onto the spark plug. Make sure it is on tight.

CAUTION
Route the spark plug wire away from the exhaust pipe.

Reading Spark Plugs

Careful examination of the spark plug can determine valuable engine and spark plug information. This information is more accurate after performing the following steps.

1. Ride the motorcycle at full throttle in a suitable area.

NOTE
Operate the motorcycle long enough to obtain an accurate reading or color on the spark plug. If the original plug was fouled, use a new plug.

2. Push the engine stop switch, close the throttle and coast to a stop.
3. Remove the spark plug and compare it to **Figure 30**. Note the following:

Normal condition

If the plug has a light tan- or gray-colored deposit and no abnormal gap wear or erosion, good engine, carburetion and ignition conditions are indicated. The plug in use is of the proper heat range and may be serviced and returned to use.

Carbon fouled

Soft, dry, sooty deposits covering the entire firing end of the plug are evidence of incomplete combustion. Even though the firing end of the plug is dry, the plug's insulation decreases. An electrical path is formed that lowers the voltage from the ignition system. Engine mis-firing is a sign of carbon fouling. One or more of the following conditions can cause carbon fouling:

1. Rich fuel mixture.
2. Spark plug heat range too cold.
3. Clogged air filter.
4. Retarded ignition timing.

5. Ignition component failure.
6. Low engine compression.
7. Prolonged idling.

Oil fouled

The tip of an oil fouled plug has a black insulator tip, a damp oily film over the firing end and a carbon layer over the entire nose. The electrodes will not be worn. Common causes for this condition are:

1. Incorrect carburetor jetting.
2. Low idle speed or prolonged idling.
3. Ignition component failure.
4. Spark plug heat range too cold.
5. Engine not broken in.

Oil fouled spark plugs may be cleaned in an emergency, but it is better to replace them. Correct the problem before returning the engine to service.

Gap bridging

Plugs with this condition exhibit gaps shorted out by combustion deposits between the electrodes. The engine can still run with a bridged spark plug, but it will misfire. Check for an improper oil type or excessive carbon in the combustion chamber. Find and correct the cause of this condition.

Overheating

Badly worn electrodes and premature gap wear are signs of overheating, along with a gray or white blistered porcelain insulator surface. The most common cause for this condition is using a spark plug of the wrong heat range (too hot). If the spark plug is the correct heat range and still overheats, consider the following causes:

1. Lean fuel mixture.
2. Advanced ignition timing.
3. Engine air leak.
4. Overtightened spark plug.
5. Spark plug gasket missing.

Worn out

Corrosive gases formed by combustion and high voltage sparks have eroded the electrodes. Spark plugs in this condition require more voltage to fire under hard acceleration. Replace the spark plug.

SPARK PLUG CONDITIONS

NORMAL USE

OIL FOULED

CARBON FOULED

OVERHEATED

GAP BRIDGED

SUSTAINED PREIGNITION

WORN OUT

Preignition

If the electrodes are melted, preignition is almost certainly the cause. Check for carburetor mounting or intake manifold leaks and advanced ignition timing. It is also possible that a plug of the wrong heat range (too hot) is being used. Find the cause of the preignition before returning the engine to service.

ENGINE COMPRESSION CHECK

A compression check is one of the quickest ways to check the internal condition of the engine: valves, piston rings, piston and cylinder bore. It is a good idea to check the compression at each tune-up, record it, and compare it with the reading at the next tune-up. This will help to identify any developing problems.
1. Remove the spark plug as described in this chapter.
2. Install a compression gauge (A, **Figure 31**) into the cylinder head spark plug hole. Make sure the gauge is seated properly.
3. Push the engine stop switch and hold it.
4. Hold the throttle wide open and kick the engine over until the gauge needle gives its highest reading. The compression reading should be within the range listed in **Table 8**. Note the following:
    a. If the compression reading is low, disassemble the engine top end and measure the parts. See Chapter Four.
    b. If the reading is too high, there may be a buildup of carbon deposits in the combustion chamber or on the piston crown. Disassemble the top end and clean the parts of carbon as described in Chapter Four.

> *NOTE*
> *If the compression is low, the engine cannot be tuned to maximum performance. The worn parts must be replaced and the engine rebuilt.*

5. Push the release button on the compression gauge and remove it from the cylinder head.
6. Reinstall the spark plug as described in this chapter.

VALVE ADJUSTMENT

Cam Chain Adjustment

An automatic cam chain tensioner assembly is used. No adjustment is required.

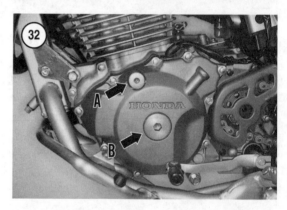

Valve Clearance
Inspection and Adjustment

Check and adjust the valve clearance with the engine cold. **Table 9** lists the correct valve clearance.

1. Remove the fuel tank, as described in Chapter Eight.

2. Remove the exhaust and intake valve covers (B, **Figure 31**).

3. Remove the timing mark hole cap (A, **Figure 32**) and O-ring.

4. Remove the crankshaft hole cap (B, **Figure 32**) and O-ring.

5. Remove the spark plug as described in this chapter. This will make it easier to rotate the engine in the following steps.

NOTE
The engine must be at top dead center (TDC) on its compression stroke before checking and adjusting the valve clearance.

CAUTION
*Do **not** align the flywheel mark by rotating the engine clockwise. If the timing marks are passed while rotating the engine, continue to rotate the engine counterclockwise until the correct alignment is achieved. Rotating the engine clockwise may cause the one-way decompression system to malfunction and result in an incorrect valve clearance.*

6. Using a socket on the flywheel bolt (**Figure 33**), turn the engine counterclockwise and align the T mark on the flywheel with the index mark on the left crankcase cover (**Figure 34**).

7. Make sure the sub-rocker arm is loose (**Figure 35**). If the sub-rocker arm is tight, the engine is not on its compression stroke. If so, turn the engine one full revolution counterclockwise and align the T mark on the flywheel with the index mark on the left crankcase cover (**Figure 34**).

8. Measure the intake and exhaust valve clearance by inserting a feeler gauge between the rocker arm pad and the valve stem as shown in **Figure 36**. When the clearance is correct (**Table 9**) a slight resistance will be felt as the gauge is inserted and withdrawn. If any clearance measurement is incorrect, continue with Step 9. If all the clearance measurements are correct, proceed to Step 10.

9. To adjust the clearance, perform the following:

   a. Use a 10 mm wrench and loosen the valve adjuster locknut (**Figure 37**).

   b. Use a regular screwdriver and turn the adjuster in or out until a slight resistance is felt on the feeler gauge (**Figure 37**).

   c. Hold the valve adjuster to prevent it from turning and tighten the locknut to the torque specification in **Table 4**.

d. Recheck the valve clearance to make sure the adjuster did not move when the locknut was tightened. Readjust the valve clearance if necessary.

10. Adjust the decompressor cable as described in *Decompression Cable Adjustment* in this chapter.

11. Inspect the valve cover O-rings and the hole caps. Replace cracked or damaged O-rings. Apply lithium grease to the O-rings.

12. Install the spark plug as described in this chapter.

13. Install the valve covers and O-rings (B, **Figure 31**) and torque to the specification in **Table 4**.

14. Install the timing mark hole cap (A, **Figure 32**) and O-ring and torque to the specification in **Table 4**.

15. Install the crankshaft hole cap (B, **Figure 32**) and O-ring and torque to the specification in **Table 4**.

16. Install the fuel tank as described in Chapter Eight.

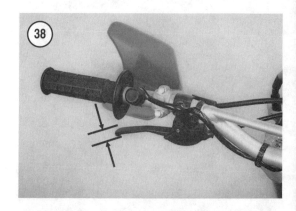

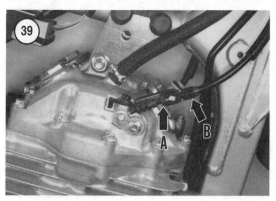

DECOMPRESSOR CABLE ADJUSTMENT

An incorrectly adjusted decompression cable can cause the engine to be difficult to start (loose) or idle erratically (tight). An extreme lack of cable free play could damage the valve, by not allowing it to seat.

NOTE
Always check the decompression cable adjustment after adjusting the valve clearance.

1. Set the engine at top dead center (TDC) on its compression stroke as described under *Valve Clearance Inspection and Adjustment* in this chapter.

2. Measure the free play at the tip of the decompression lever as shown in **Figure 38**. The free play specification is 5-8 mm (3/16-5/16 in.).

3. To adjust, loosen the locknut (A, **Figure 39**) and turn the adjust nut (B, **Figure 39**) to obtain the correct amount of free play. Tighten the locknut and recheck the free play adjustment.

CARBURETOR

This section describes service to the fuel hose, shutoff valve and steps on setting the engine idle

speed. Service these items at the intervals specified in **Table 1** or **Table 2**.

Fuel Hose Inspection

Inspect the fuel hose (A, **Figure 40**) for any leaks or damage. Make sure each end of the hose is secured with a hose clamp. Replace the fuel hose if it hardens or leaks. Replace weak and damaged hose clamps.

WARNING
A leaking fuel hose may cause an engine fire. Do not start the engine if the fuel hose or fuel shutoff valve is leaking or damaged.

Fuel Strainer Screen Cleaning

At the intervals specified in **Table 1** or **Table 2**, remove the fuel shutoff valve (B, **Figure 40**) and clean the fuel strainer screen. Refer to the service procedures in Chapter Eight. At the same time, in-

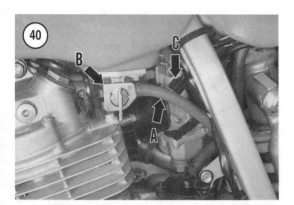

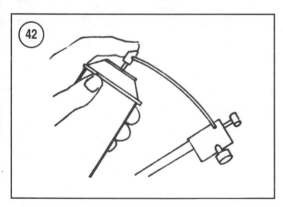

spect the O-ring installed in the fuel shutoff valve and replace if leaking or damaged.

Engine Idle Speed Adjustment

1. Start the engine and allow to warm up thoroughly.
2. Support the bike on its sidestand with the transmission in NEUTRAL.
3. Turn the idle stop screw (C, **Figure 40**) in or out to obtain the desired idle speed. When using a ta-

chometer, set the idle speed to the specification in **Table 10**.

CRANKCASE BREATHER (1998-ON CALIFORNIA MODELS)

Drain the crankcase breather tube at the intervals specified in **Table 2**. Drain the tube more frequently if riding in wet conditions.
1. Open the clamp and remove the drain plug (**Figure 41**) from the end of the tube to drain it.
2. Install the drain plug and secure it with it clamp.

IGNITION TIMING

Refer to Chapter Nine.

CONTROL CABLE LUBRICATION

This section describes lubrication procedures for the control cables and clutch cable lever assembly.

Control Cable Lubrication

Clean and lubricate the clutch, decompression and throttle cables at the intervals indicated in **Table 1** or **Table 2**. At the same time, check the cables for signs of wear and damage or fraying that could cause the cables to bind or break. The most effective method of control cable lubrication requires a cable lubricator (**Figure 42**) and a can of cable lube.

CAUTION
Do not use chain lube to lubricate the control cables unless it is also specified for control cable use.

1. Disconnect the clutch cable at the handlebar and at the engine.
2. Disconnect the throttle cables at the handlebar and at the carburetor. Refer to Chapter Eight for instructions and procedures.
3. Disconnect the decompression cable at the handlebar and at the cylinder head.
4. Attach a cable lubricator to the upper end of the cable following the manufacturer's instructions (**Figure 42**)
5. Insert the lubricant can nozzle into the hole in the lube tool, then press the button on the can and hold

down until the lubricant begins to flow out the other end of the cable.

NOTE
Place a shop cloth at the end of the cable to catch the lubricant as it runs out.

6. Disconnect the lubricator from the end of the cable.
7. Apply a light coat of grease to the upper cable ball before reconnecting it.
8. Reconnect the clutch cable at the engine and handlebar. Adjust the clutch cable as described in this chapter.
9. Lubricate the cable puller and slider (at the carburetor) with grease.
10. Reconnect the throttle cables at the carburetor and handlebar as described in Chapter Eight. Adjust the throttle cables as described in this chapter. Operate the throttle, checking that it opens and closes smoothly.
11. Reconnect the decompression cable at the handlebar and cylinder head. Adjust the decompression cable as described in this chapter.

Clutch Lever
Pivot Bolt Lubrication

Periodically, remove the clutch lever pivot bolt at the handlebar and lubricate the bolt with 10W-30 motor oil. Replace the pivot bolt if damaged.

Decompression Lever
Pivot Bolt Lubrication

Periodically, remove the decompression lever pivot bolt at the handlebar and lubricate the bolt with 10W-30 motor oil. Replace the pivot bolt if damaged.

THROTTLE CABLE ADJUSTMENT

The throttle cables will wear and stretch during use. This wear can be compensated for by adjusting the free play (amount the throttle grip moves before the throttle valve). Excessive free play will result in delayed throttle response, while insufficient free play may cause the idle speed to fluctuate when the handlebar is turned. The specified free play mea-

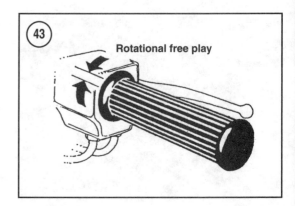
Rotational free play

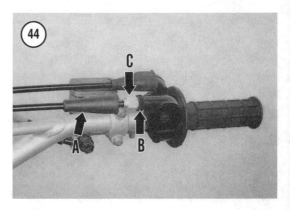

surement is 2-6 mm (1/8-1/4 in.). If it is not possible to achieve this measurement, replace the throttle cables.

Throttle Cable Adjustment
and Operation

Perform minor adjustments at the throttle grip and major adjustments at the cable adjuster on the carburetor cap.
1. Open and release the throttle grip with the handlebar pointed in various positions. In each position, the throttle must open and close smoothly. If the throttle cable binds or moves roughly, inspect the cable for kinks, bends or other damage. Replace a damaged cable. If the cable moves smoothly and is not damaged, continue with Step 2.
2. Slowly open the throttle and measure the free play at the throttle grip flange (**Figure 43**) until resistance is felt. If resistance is felt as soon as the throttle grip is turned, there is no cable free play.
3. If adjustment is necessary, slide the upper rubber cover (A, **Figure 44**) away from the cable adjuster. Loosen the locknut (B, **Figure 44**) and turn the ca-

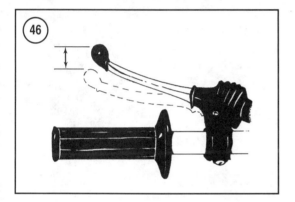

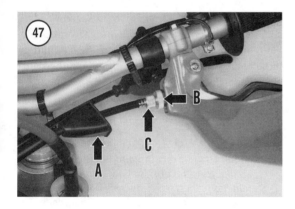

locknut. If necessary, fine-tune the adjustment at the upper throttle cable adjuster and tighten the locknut.

    c. Make sure both adjuster locknuts are securely tightened.

    d. Slide the upper rubber cover (A, **Figure 44**) over throttle housing at the handlebar.

5. If this adjustment procedure cannot correct the amount of free play, the throttle cable has stretched and needs to be replaced. Replace both throttle cables as described in Chapter Eight.

6. Make sure the throttle grip rotates freely from a fully closed to fully open position.

7. Start the engine and allow it to idle in NEUTRAL. Turn the handlebar from side-to-side. If the idle increases, the throttle cables are routed incorrectly or there is not enough throttle cable free play.

> *WARNING*
> *Before riding the motorcycle make sure the throttle cable operation and adjustment is correct. A damaged or incorrectly adjusted throttle cable can cause loss of control while riding.*

CLUTCH CABLE ADJUSTMENT

The clutch cable adjustment removes free play caused by cable stretch and clutch disc wear. Free play is the distance the clutch lever moves before disengaging the clutch. Maintain the clutch cable free play within the listed specification. Insufficient free play will cause clutch slippage and rapid clutch disc wear. Excessive free play will prevent the clutch from disengaging or cause the clutch to drag.

1. Pull the clutch lever toward the handlebar until resistance is felt and measure the free play at the end of the clutch lever (**Figure 46**). The correct free play measurement is 10-20 mm (3/8-3/4 in.). If resistance is felt as soon as the clutch lever is pulled, there is no cable free play.

2. At the hand lever pull the rubber cover (A, **Figure 47**) away from the clutch adjuster. Loosen the locknut (B, **Figure 47**) and turn the clutch cable adjuster (C, **Figure 47**) in or out to obtain the correct amount of free play. Tighten the locknut.

3. If the proper amount of free play cannot be achieved at the clutch lever adjuster, perform the following:

ble adjuster (C, **Figure 44**) in or out to achieve the correct free play measurement. Tighten the locknut.

4. If the correct amount of free play cannot be achieved at the throttle grip flange, perform the following:

    a. Loosen the locknut (B, **Figure 44**) and turn the throttle cable adjuster (C, **Figure 44**) in all the way.

    b. At the carburetor, loosen the cable adjuster locknut (A, **Figure 45**) and turn the adjuster (B, **Figure 45**) as required. Tighten the

a. At the clutch lever, loosen the locknut and turn the adjuster (B, **Figure 47**) in all the way, then back it out one turn. Tighten the locknut (C, **Figure 47**).

b. At the clutch arm, loosen the cable adjuster locknut (A, **Figure 48**) and turn the adjuster (B, **Figure 48**) to correct the amount of cable free play. Tighten the locknut. If necessary, fine-tune the adjustment at the clutch lever adjuster (C, **Figure 47**).

4. If this procedure cannot correct the amount of cable free play, either the cable has stretched to the point that it needs to be replaced or the clutch friction discs are worn and need replacing. Refer to Chapter Six for clutch cable and clutch service.

5. Slide the rubber cover (A, **Figure 47**) over the clutch cable adjuster.

6. Start the engine and check the clutch operation.

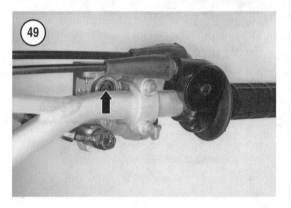

BRAKES

This section describes routine service procedures for the front and rear disc brakes. Refer to **Table 1** or **Table 2** for service intervals.

Brake Fluid Selection

Use new DOT 4 brake fluid from a sealed container.

WARNING
Do not use silicone based (DOT 5) brake fluid as it can cause brake component damage leading to brake system failure.

Brake Fluid Replacement

Replace the brake fluid at the intervals specified in **Table 1** or **Table 2**. Follow the brake bleeding procedure in Chapter Thirteen.

Brake Fluid Level Check

The brake fluid levels in the reservoirs must be kept above their minimum level lines. If the fluid level is low in any reservoir, check for loose or damaged hoses or loose banjo bolts. If there are no visible fluid leaks, check the brake pads for excessive wear. As the brake pads wear, the caliper piston(s) moves farther out of its bore, causing the brake fluid level to drop in the reservoir. Also, check the master cylinder bore and the brake caliper piston areas for signs of leaking brake fluid. If there is a noticeable fluid leak, replace the damaged part. Check the brake pads for wear as described in this chapter. Refer to Chapter Thirteen for brake service.

WARNING
If any reservoir is empty, or if the brake fluid level is so low that air is entering the brake system, bleed the brake system as described in Chapter Thirteen. Simply adding brake fluid to the reservoir will not restore the brake system to its full effectiveness.

1. Park the bike on level ground.

2. Clean any dirt from the master cylinder cover prior to removing it.

WARNING
Use only DOT 4 brake fluid. Do not use silicone based (DOT 5) brake fluid as it can cause brake component damage leading to brake system failure.

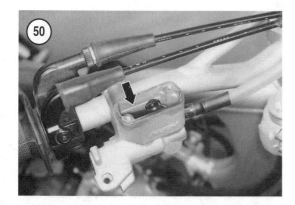

CAUTION
Handle brake fluid carefully. Do not spill it on painted or plastic surfaces as it will destroy the surface. Wash the area immediately with soapy water and thoroughly rinse.

3A. *Front*—Perform the following:
    a. Turn the handlebar so the master cylinder reservoir is level.
    b. Observe the brake fluid level through the inspection window (**Figure 49**) on the master cylinder reservoir. The brake fluid should be above the lower level line. If the brake fluid level is low, add brake fluid as described in the following steps.
    c. Remove the cover screws and remove the cover and diaphragm.
    d. Add DOT 4 brake fluid to bring the level to the upper level mark inside the reservoir (**Figure 50**).
    e. Inspect the cover and diaphragm and replace if damaged.
    f. Install the diaphragm and cover and tighten the screws securely.

3B. *Rear*—Perform the following:
    a. Make sure the brake fluid is above the lower level mark on the reservoir (**Figure 51**). To add brake fluid, continue with the following steps.
    b. Remove the master cylinder cap and diaphragm (**Figure 51**).
    c. Add DOT 4 brake fluid to bring the level to the upper level mark on the reservoir.
    d. Inspect the cap and diaphragm and replace if damaged.
    e. Install the diaphragm and cap. Tighten the cap securely.

Disc Brake Pad Wear

Inspecting the brake pads with the brake caliper in place only provides an indication of pad wear. To check for glazing and surface damage, remove and inspect the brake pads as described in Chapter Thirteen. Inspect the brake pads for uneven wear, scoring, grease or oil contamination. See **Figure 52** (front) and **Figure 53** (rear). Replace both brake pads as a set (in each caliper) if any pad is worn down to its wear limit groove or damaged. Refer to Chapter Thirteen for brake pad service.

Front Brake Lever Adjustment

Front brake pad wear is automatically compensated for by the pistons moving outward in the caliper. However, the distance between the brake lever and the throttle grip can be adjusted. Adjust the lever to suit rider preference.

CAUTION
*Be sure to maintain some front brake lever free play (**Figure 54**) when adjusting the brake lever in these steps. If there is no brake lever free play, the front brakes will drag on the brake disc. This will cause rapid brake pad wear and overheating of the front brake disc.*

1. Adjust the front brake lever as follows:
   a. Loosen the locknut and turn the adjuster (**Figure 54**) in or out to position the brake lever closer to or farther away from the grip. Measure the free play as shown in **Figure 54**. If the free play exceeds 10-20 mm (0.4-0.8 in.), there may be air in the front brake system.
   b. Tighten the locknut and check the free play. Make sure there is a small clearance between the master cylinder piston end and the adjuster bolt tip when the brake lever is at rest.
   c. Apply a small amount of silicone brake grease onto the master cylinder piston end and adjuster bolt tip.
2. Support the bike with the front wheel off the ground. Rotate the front wheel and check for brake drag. Operate the front brake lever several times to make sure it returns to the at-rest position after being released.

Rear Brake Pedal Adjustment

Adjust the rear brake pedal height to suit rider preference.
1. Loosen the locknut (A, **Figure 55**) and turn the pushrod (B, **Figure 55**) to achieve the desired brake pedal height. Tighten the locknut.
2. Check the position of the pushrod in relation to the brake pedal joint as follows:
   a. Make sure there is at least 1 mm (0.04 in.) clearance between the end of the pushrod and the brake pedal joint (**Figure 56**).

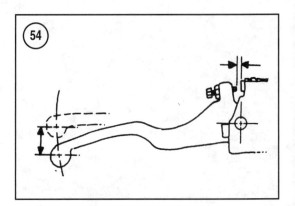

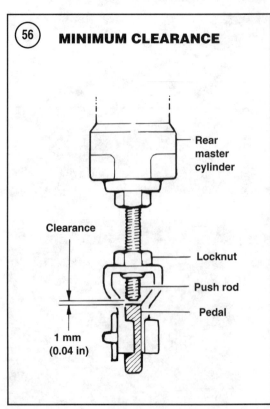

MINIMUM CLEARANCE

Rear master cylinder

Clearance

Locknut

Push rod

Pedal

1 mm (0.04 in)

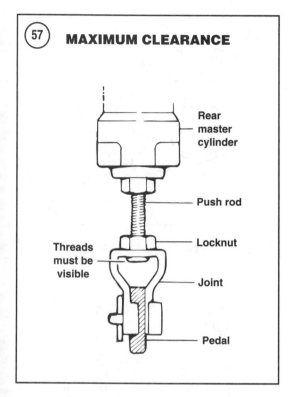

(57) **MAXIMUM CLEARANCE**

Rear master cylinder

Push rod

Threads must be visible

Locknut

Joint

Pedal

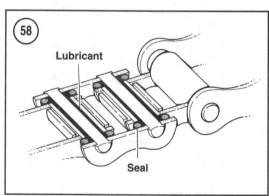

(58)

Lubricant

Seal

b. Make sure there are pushrod threads visible through the end of the brake pedal joint (**Figure 57**).

WARNING
Damage to the master cylinder pushrod or loss of rear brake can occur if the pushrod clearances are not maintained as described in Step 2.

3. Support the bike with the rear wheel off the ground. Rotate the rear wheel and check for brake drag. Operate the rear brake pedal several times to make sure it returns to the at-rest position after being released.

DRIVE CHAIN AND SPROCKETS

The XR400R comes equipped with an O-ring drive chain. **Table 1** and **Table 2** lists service intervals for the drive chain and sprockets.

Drive Chain
Cleaning

There is no maintenance interval for cleaning the drive chain. Clean the chain when it becomes caked with mud or after riding in sand.
1. Remove the drive chain as described in Chapter Ten.
2A. O-ring chain: Clean the drive chain in a plastic pan partially filled with kerosene. If necessary, remove dirt from the outside of the chain with a soft nylon brush. Do not use a brush with metal bristles as it will damage the O-rings.

CAUTION
Do not clean an O-ring drive chain with anything but kerosene. Gasoline and most solvents will cause the O-rings (Figure 58) to swell and deteriorate, permanently damaging the chain.

2B. Non-O-ring chain: Immerse the chain in a plastic pan containing a non-flammable or high flash point solvent. Allow the chain to soak for about a half hour. If necessary, remove dirt from the outside of the chain with a brush.
3. After cleaning the chain, hang it up to allow the cleaning solution to drip off. Lubricate the chain as described in this chapter.
4. Install the chain as described in Chapter Ten.

Drive Chain Lubrication
(O-Ring Chain)

NOTE
If the O-ring chain has been lubricated with a tacky chain lubricant, clean the chain (and sprockets) to remove all residue, dirt and grit as described in this chapter.

1. Support the bike with the rear wheel off the ground.
2. Shift the transmission into NEUTRAL.

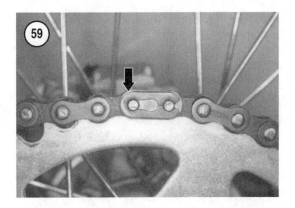

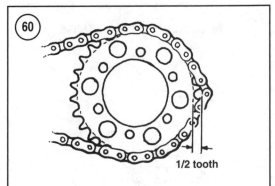

3. Lubricate the chain with SAE 50 weight motor oil or a non-tacky chain lubricant specifically formulated for O-ring chains.

> *CAUTION*
> *Do not use a tacky chain lubricant on O-ring chains. Dirt and other abrasive materials that stick to the chain will damage the O-rings. An O-ring chain is pre-lubricated during assembly by the manufacturer. External oiling is only required to prevent chain rust and to keep the O-rings pliable.*

4. Wipe off all excess oil from the chain, rear hub, wheel and tire.

5. Make sure the closed end (**Figure 59**) of the master link faces forward.

**Drive Chain Lubrication
(Non-O-ring Chain)**

Lubricate the drive chain before each ride and throughout the day as required. A properly maintained chain will provide maximum service life and reliability.

1. Support the bike on a workstand with the rear wheel off the ground.

2. Shift the transmission into NEUTRAL.

3. Turn the rear wheel and lubricate the chain with a chain spray. Do not overlubricate as this will cause dirt to collect on the chain and sprockets.

4. Wipe off all excess oil from the rear hub, wheel and tire.

5. Make sure the closed end (**Figure 59**) of the master link faces forward.

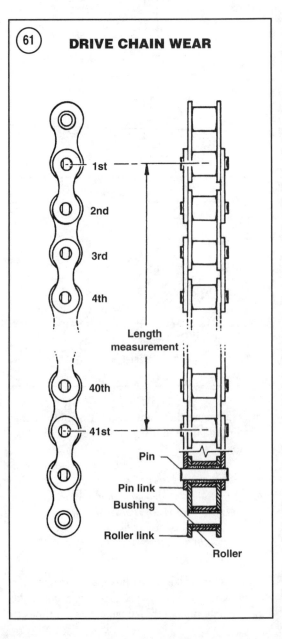

DRIVE CHAIN WEAR

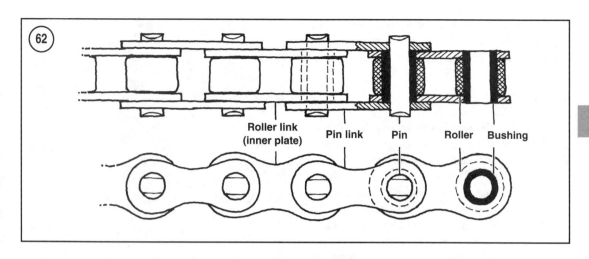

Roller link (inner plate)   Pin link   Pin   Roller   Bushing

3

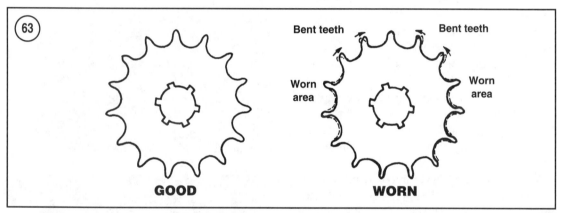

Bent teeth   Bent teeth

Worn area   Worn area

GOOD   WORN

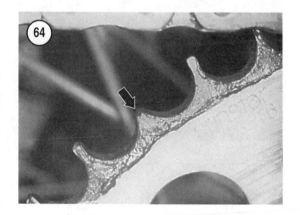

Drive Chain/Sprocket Wear Inspection

Check chain and sprocket wear frequently and re-place any parts that are excessively worn or dam-aged. At the rear sprocket, pull one of the links away from the sprocket. If the link pulls away more than 1/2 the height of a sprocket tooth, the chain is excessively worn (**Figure 60**). Check at different points around the chain.

To measure chain wear, perform the following:

1. Loosen the axle nut and tighten the chain adjust-ers to move the wheel rearward until the chain is tight (no slack).

2. Lay a scale along the chain run, and measure the length of any 40 links (41 pins) as shown in **Figure 61**. Replace the drive chain if the length measure-ment exceeds 638 mm (25.1 in.). Because chains wear and stretch unevenly, turn the rear wheel and measure at different points around the chain.

3. Check the inner chain plate faces (**Figure 62**). They must be lightly polished on both sides. If the chain shows considerable uneven wear on one side, the sprockets are not aligned. Excessive wear re-quires chain and sprocket replacement.

4. If the drive chain is worn, inspect the drive and driven sprockets for the following defects:

    a. Undercutting or sharp teeth (**Figure 63**).

    b. Broken teeth (**Figure 64**).

5. If wear or damage is evident, replace the chain and sprockets as a set. Rapid chain wear will occur if a new chain is installed on worn sprockets.

Drive Chain Adjustment

The drive chain must have adequate free play so the chain is not tight when the swing arm is horizontal. On the other hand, too much free play may cause the chain to jump off the sprockets, with potentially disastrous results. **Figure 65** shows an engine case damaged from a thrown chain.

Riding in mud and sand will make the chain tighter. Under these conditions, stop and check chain free play. If necessary, loosen the chain adjustment so that it is not too tight.

Check the drive chain free play before riding the bike. **Table 11** lists drive chain free play specifications.
1. Place the bike on a workstand with the rear wheel off the ground.
2. If the drive chain is stiff from dirt and sand, clean and lubricate it as described in this chapter.
3. Spin the wheel and check the chain at several spots. Check and adjust the chain at its tightest point (the chain wears unevenly).
4. Measure the drive chain free play midway between the sprockets on the lower chain run (**Figure 66**). Compare the drive chain free play with the specifications listed in **Table 11**. If necessary, adjust the drive chain as follows.

> *NOTE*
> *When adjusting the drive chain, you must also maintain rear wheel alignment. A misaligned rear wheel can cause poor handling and pulling to one side or the other, as well as increased chain and sprocket wear. All models have wheel alignment marks on the swing arm and chain adjusters.*

5. Loosen the axle nut (A, **Figure 67**).
6. Turn the chain adjusters (B, **Figure 67**) until the chain free play measurement is correct. Turn both chain adjusters (B, **Figure 67**) so the same number or scale mark on each adjuster aligns with the stopper pin on both sides of the swing arm.
7. When the chain free play is correct, check wheel alignment by sighting along the chain from the rear sprocket. The chain must leave the sprocket in a straight line (A, **Figure 68**). If it is turned to one side

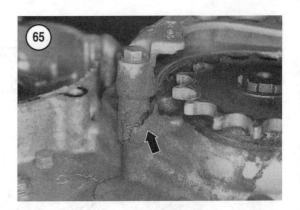

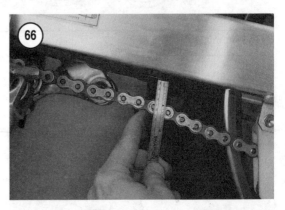

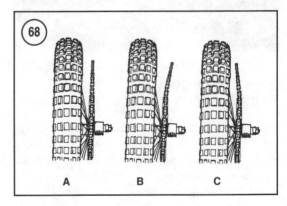

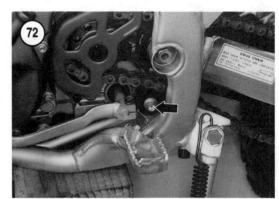

3

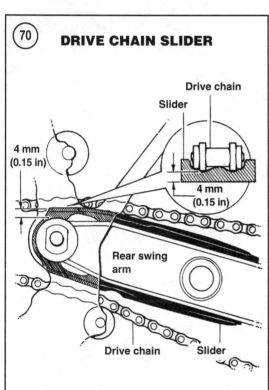

DRIVE CHAIN SLIDER

Drive chain

Slider

4 mm
(0.15 in)

4 mm
(0.15 in)

Rear swing
arm

Drive chain   Slider

or the other (B and C, **Figure 68**), first make sure the chain adjusters are set to the same number or scale mark. If the marks are correct, check the chain adjusters, stopper pins and swing arm for damage.

8. Tighten the rear axle nut (A, **Figure 67**) as specified in **Table 4**.

9. Spin the wheel several times and recheck the free play at its tightest point. Make sure the free play is within specification.

Drive Chain Slider Inspection

1. Remove the drive sprocket cover (A, **Figure 69**).

2. Inspect the chain slider (B, **Figure 69**) for excessive wear or damage.

3. Measure the chain slider wear grooves as shown in **Figure 70**. Replace the chain slider if the measurement is 4 mm (0.15 in.) or less from the upper surface. To replace the chain slider, remove the swing arm as described in Chapter Twelve.

4. Install the drive sprocket cover.

Chain Guide Slider Inspection

1. Inspect the chain guide (A, **Figure 71**) for loose mounting bolts or damage. Check the chain guide alignment.

2. If the drive chain is visible through the chain guide inspection window on the slider housing (B, **Figure 71**), replace the chain guide slider.

Drive Chain Rollers Inspection

Inspect the upper and lower drive chain rollers (**Figure 72**) for excessive wear, loose mounting bolts or excessively worn or damaged bushings. Replace if necessary.

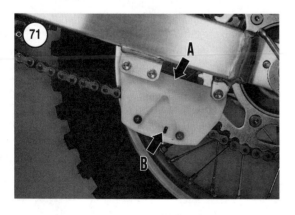

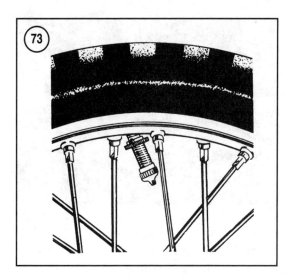

SIDESTAND

Service the sidestand as described in Chapter Fifteen.

HEADLIGHT AIM

Check and adjust the headlight aim as described in Chapter Nine.

TIRES AND WHEELS

Tire Pressure

Check and set the tire pressure to maintain good traction and handling and to prevent rim damage. **Table 12** lists the standard tire pressure for the front and rear wheels.

Tire Inspection

Inspect the tires for wear or damage before each ride. Check the valve stem alignment. If the valve is sideways (**Figure 73**), the tire and tube have slipped on the rim. To prevent the valve from separating from the tube, straighten the tube as described under *Tube Alignment* in this chapter.

Wheel Spoke Tension

NOTE
During break-in for a new or a respoked wheel, check the spoke tension every 15 minutes for the first

hour of riding. Most spoke seating takes place during initial use.

Check each spoke for tightness with a spoke wrench (**Figure 74**). If the spokes are loose, tighten them as described in Chapter Ten.

NOTE
Most spokes loosen as a group rather than individually. Tighten loose spokes carefully. Overtightening just a few spokes will exert uneven pressure on the rim. Never tighten spokes so tightly that the spoke wrench rounds off the nipple flats.

Rim Inspection and Runout

Inspect the rims for damage (**Figure 75**). Replace damaged rims.

To perform a quick inspection of wheel runout (wobble), support the bike with the wheel(s) off the ground. Hold a pointer against the fork leg or swing arm and rotate the wheel. If run out is excessive, true the wheel as described in Chapter Ten.

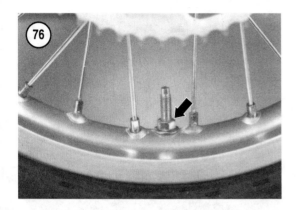

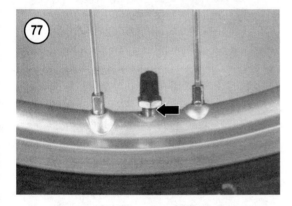

4. While an assistant steadies the bike, break the tire-to-rim seal all the way around the wheel on both sides.

5. After the tire seal is broken, place the bike on a stand with the wheel off the ground.

6. Spray some soapy water along the tire bead on both sides of the tire.

7. Have an assistant apply the brake.

8. By hand, turn the tire and the tube until the valve stem is straight up. See **Figure 77**.

9. When the valve stem is aligned, install the valve stem core and inflate the tire. If the soap and water solution dries, reapply it to help the tire seat on the rim. Check the tire to make sure it seats evenly all the way around the rim.

> *WARNING*
> *Do not overinflate the tire and tube. If the tire will not seat properly remove the valve stem core and lubricate the tire again.*

10. Tighten the rim lock(s) securely.

11. Adjust the tire pressure (**Table 12**) and install the valve stem nut and cap (**Figure 77**).

WHEEL BEARINGS

Inspection

The wheel bearings are sealed (**Figure 78**) and do not require periodic lubrication. Periodically check the condition of the seals and bearings. If the seals are reusable, wipe off their outer surface, then pack the lip of each seal with grease. To replace the seals and wheel bearings, refer to the service procedures in Chapter Ten.

STEERING

Steering Bearings

While there is no service interval for cleaning and lubricating the steering bearings (**Figure 79**), do so at least once a year. Remove the steering stem to clean and lubricate the bearings. Refer to Chapter Eleven for complete service procedures.

Steering Head Adjustment Check

The steering head on all models consists of upper and lower tapered roller bearings. Check the bear-

Tube Alignment

Check the valve stem-to-rim alignment. **Figure 73** shows a valve stem that has slipped with the tire. If the tube is not repositioned, the valve stem will eventually separate from the tube, causing a flat. To realign the tube and tire:

1. Wash the tire and rim.

2. Remove the valve stem core and release all air pressure from the tube.

3. Loosen the rim lock nut(s) (**Figure 76**).

ing play at the specified maintenance intervals (**Table 1** or **Table 2**) or whenever it feels loose. A loose bearing adjustment will hamper steering and cause premature bearing and race wear. In extreme conditions, a loose bearing adjustment can cause loss of control. Refer to *Steering Play Inspection and Adjustment* in Chapter Eleven.

Front Suspension Check

1. Apply the front brake and pump the fork vigorously up and down. Check fork movement, noting any abnormal noise or oil leaks.
2. Make sure the upper and lower fork tube pinch bolts are tight.
3. Make sure the handlebar holder bolts are tight.
4. Make sure the front axle and the axle holder fasteners are tight.

> *NOTE*
> *If any of the above mentioned fasteners are loose, refer to Chapter Eleven for correct procedures and torque specifications.*

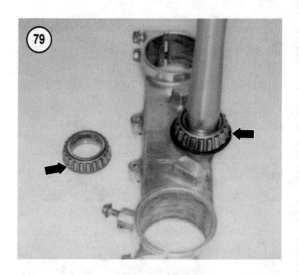

FRONT FORK

Oil Change

Periodically change the oil in the front fork. The cartridge-type fork on these models is not designed to have the fork oil drained and replaced while the fork is assembled or installed on the bike. Refer to Chapter Eleven for procedures to drain and refill the fork oil and to set the oil level.

REAR SHOCK ABSORBER

Oil Change

Periodically change the oil in the rear shock absorber. Refer this service to a Honda dealership.

REAR SWING ARM AND LINKAGE

Rear Suspension Check

1. Support the bike on a stand with the rear wheel off the ground.
2. Check swing arm bearing play as described in Chapter Twelve.

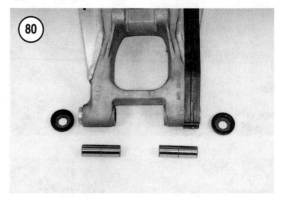

3. Check the tightness of all rear suspension mounting bolts.

4. Check that the rear axle nut is tight.

> *NOTE*
> *If any of the previously mentioned fasteners are tight, refer to Chapter Twelve for correct procedures and torque specifications.*

Swing Arm Bearing Assembly Lubrication

Periodically remove and lubricate the swing arm bearings, pivot collars and pivot bolts (**Figure 80**). The swing arm must be removed and partially disassembled to lubricate the bushings and bearings. Do not remove the needle bearings (**Figure 81**) for lubrication. Refer to Chapter Twelve for complete service procedures.

3

Shock Linkage Lubrication

Periodically service and lubricate the shock linkage assembly bearings, pivot collars and pivot bolts. Do not remove the needle bearing cages to lubricate them. Refer to Chapter Twelve for complete service procedures.

Rear Shock Absorber
Bearing and Pivot Bolt Lubrication

During shock linkage lubrication, lubricate the shock absorber pivot bolts, collar and needle bearing (**Figure 82**). Do not remove the bearing for lubrication. Refer to Chapter Twelve for service procedures.

SPARK ARRESTOR
CLEANING

At the service intervals in **Table 1** or **Table 2**, remove and clean the spark arrestor.

1. Unbolt and remove the spark arrestor and its gasket from the muffler housing.
2. Clean the spark arrestor with a stiff wire brush.
3. Inspect the spark arrestor and replace if the screen is torn or damaged.
4. Install the spark arrestor using a new gasket. Tighten the mounting bolts securely.

NUTS, BOLTS AND OTHER FASTENERS

Constant vibration can loosen many of the fasteners on the motorcycle. Check the tightness of all fasteners, especially the following:
1. Engine mounting hardware.
2. Cylinder head hanger bolts.
3. Engine crankcase covers.
4. Handlebar and front fork.
5. Shift pedal.
6. Kickstarter pedal.
7. Brake pedal and lever.
8. Exhaust system.

Tables 1-12 are on the following pages.

Table 1 NON-COMPETITION MAINTENANCE SCHEDULE (1996-1997)

Every 10 days or 300 miles (500 km)	Inspect and lubricate drive chain
After first week of operation (200 miles/350 km) **or when breaking in the engine or chassis**	Inspect valve clearance Replace engine oil and oil filter Inspect dececompressor system Inspect engine idle speed Inspect and lubricate drive chain Inspect drive chain slider Inspect brake system Inspect clutch adjustment and operation Check for loose, missing or damaged fasteners Inspect wheels and tires Inspect steering adjustment
Every 30 days of operation (1,000 miles/1,600 km)	Inspect fuel line Clean fuel strainer screen Inspect throttle operation and cable adjustment Clean air filter Inspect valve clearance Inspect spark plug condition Replace engine oil and filter Clean oil strainer screen (located in frame down tube) Inspect decompressor system Inspect engine idle speed Inspect and lubricate drive chain Inspect drive chain slider Inspect brake fluid level Inspect brake pads Inspect brake system Inspect headlight aim Inspect clutch system Inspect sidestand Inspect front and rear suspension Check for loose, missing or damaged fasteners Inspect wheels and tires Inspect steering adjustment
Every 100 hours (1,000 miles/1,600 km)	Clean spark arrestor
Every 2 years	Replace brake fluid

Table 2 NON-COMPETITION MAINTENANCE SCHEDULE (1998-ON)

Every 300 miles (500 km) or 3 months	Inspect and lubricate drive chain
Initial 100 miles (150 km) **or after engine or suspension break-in**	Inspect valve clearance Replace engine oil and filter Inspect decompressor system Check engine idle speed Inspect and lubricate drive chain Inspect brake system

(continued)

Table 2 NON-COMPETITION MAINTENANCE SCHEDULE (1998-ON) (continued)

	Inspect clutch system Check for loose, missing or damaged fasteners Inspect wheels and tires Inspect steering adjustment
Initial 600 miles (1,000 km) or 6 months	Clean air filter Inspect crankcase breather Inspect spark plug Check valve clearance Replace engine oil and filter Inspect decompressor system Check engine idle speed Inspect and lubricate drive chain Inspect drive chain slider Check brake fluid Inspect brake pads Inspect brake system Inspect clutch system Inspect wheels and tires
2,000 miles or 12 months	Inspect fuel line Clean fuel strainer screen Inspect throttle operation Clean air filter Inspect crankcase breather Inspect spark plug Check valve clearance Replace engine oil and filter Clean oil strainer screen (in frame down tube) Inspect decompressor system Check engine idle speed Inspect and lubricate drive chain Inspect drive chain slider Check brake fluid level Inspect brake pads Inspect brake system Check headlight aim Check clutch system Check sidestand Check front and rear suspension Check for loose, missing or damaged fasteners Inspect wheels and tires Inspect steering adjustment
3,000 miles or 18 months	Clean air filter Inspect crankcase breather Inspect spark plug Check valve clearance Replace engine oil and filter Inspect decompressor system Check engine idle speed Inspect and lubricate drive chain Inspect drive chain slider Check brake fluid Inspect brake pads Inspect brake system Inspect clutch system Inspect wheels and tires

(continued)

3

Table 2 NON-COMPETITION MAINTENANCE SCHEDULE (1998-ON) (continued)

4,000 miles or 24 months	Inspect fuel line Clean fuel strainer screen Inspect throttle operation Clean air filter Inspect crankcase breather Inspect spark plug Check valve clearance Replace engine oil and filter Clean oil strainer screen (in frame down tube) Inspect decompressor system Check engine idle speed Inspect and lubricate drive chain Inspect drive chain slider Check brake fluid level Inspect brake pads Inspect brake system Check headlight aim Check clutch system Check sidestand Check front and rear suspension Check for loose, missing or damaged fasteners Inspect wheels and tires Inspect steering adjustment
Every 1,000 miles (1,600 km) or 100 hours	Clean spark arrestor
Every 2 years	Replace brake fluid

Table 3 COMPETITION MAINTENANCE SCHEDULE (ALL MODELS)

Check the following items as described in this chapter:	Engine oil level Fuel tank Brake system Brake fluid Tires and wheels Drive chain Sprockets Seat Clutch Engine stop switch Fuel line Valve clearance Cam chain Engine idle speed Decompressor system Spark plug Steering head Front suspension Rear suspension Swing arm bearings Rear suspension linkage bearings Control cables Engine mounting bolts Other fasteners Spark arrestor

Table 4 MAINTENANCE TORQUE SPECIFICATIONS

	N·m	in.-lb.	ft.-lb.
Banjo bolt at oil strainer	37	–	27
Brake lever adjuster locknut	6	53	–
Crankcase oil drain bolt	25	–	18
Crankshaft hole cap	7	62	–
Down tube oil drain bolt	39	–	29
Driven sprocket	32	–	24
Fuel valve mounting bolt	9	80	–
Oil strainer screen	54	–	40
Rear axle nut	88	–	65
Rim lock	13	115	–
Spark plug	18	–	13
Timing mark hole cap	10	88	7
Valve adjusting locknut	24	–	18
Valve covers	15	–	11

Table 5 RECOMMENDED LUBRICANTS AND FUEL

Engine oil	Honda GN4 or HP4 10W-40 or 20W-50 API SF or SG
Air filter	Foam air filter oil
Drive chain[1]	Pro Honda Chain Lube or other non-tacky O-ring chain lubricant
Brake fluid	DOT 4
Steering and suspension lubricant	Multipurpose grease
Fuel	Pump gasoline with Octane rating of 92 or higher
Control cables[2]	Cable lube

1. Use kerosene to clean O-ring drive chain.
2. Do not use chain lube to clean and lubricate control cables.

Table 6 ENGINE OIL CAPACITY

	Liters	U.S. qt.	Imp. qt.
Oil change only	1.7	1.8	1.5
Oil and filter change	1.8	1.9	1.6
After engine disassembly	2.2	2.3	1.9

Table 7 SPARK PLUG TYPE AND GAP

Spark plug type	
Standard	NGK DPR8Z Denso X24GPR-U
Colder plug for high speed riding	NGK DPR9Z Denso X27GPR-U
Spark plug gap	0.6-0.7 mm (0.023-0.028 in.)

Table 8 ENGINE COMPRESSION

Engine compression	686-980 kPa (100-142 psi) @ 450 rpm

Table 9 VALVE CLEARANCE

Intake valve	0.081-0.121 mm (0.0032-0.0048 in.)
Exhaust valve	0.106-0.147 mm (0.0042-0.0058 in.)

Table 10 ENGINE IDLE SPEED

Engine idle speed	1200-1400 rpm

Table 11 DRIVE CHAIN SLIDER SPECIFICATIONS

Drive chain slack	35-45 mm (1 1/3-1 3/4 in.)
Drive chain size/link	DID 520V8/108
	RK 520MOZ6/108
Drive chain length at 41 pins/40 links service limit	638 mm (25.1 in.)

Table 12 TIRE INFLATION PRESSURE

	psi (kPa)
Front and rear tire	15 (103)

CHAPTER FOUR

ENGINE TOP END

The engine is an air-cooled single cylinder, with a chain driven overhead cam operating four valves.

This chapter provides complete service and overhaul procedures, including information for disassembly, removal, inspection, service and reassembly of the engine top end components

Table 1 lists general engine specifications. **Tables 2** and **3** list engine service specifications. **Tables 1-4** are at the end of the chapter.

ENGINE OPERATING PRINCIPLES

Figure 1 explains basic four-stroke engine operation. Use this information when troubleshooting or repairing the engine.

EXHAUST SYSTEM

Removal/Installation

Refer to **Figure 2**.

1. Remove the right side cover (Chapter Fifteen).

2. Loosen the muffler band bolt (A, **Figure 3**).

3. Remove the front (B, **Figure 3**) and rear muffler mounting bolts and muffler.

4. Remove the exhaust pipe joint nuts at the cylinder head (**Figure 4**), then remove the exhaust pipe.

5. Remove and discard the exhaust pipe gaskets from the cylinder head.

6. Install by reversing the removal steps, plus the following.

7. Install new exhaust pipe gaskets.

8. Install the pipe joints over the cylinder head studs with their punch marks facing in the direction shown in **Figure 2**.

9. Loosely install all of the exhaust pipe fasteners.

10. To reduce the chance of an exhaust leak at the cylinder head, tighten the bolts in the following order and to the torque specifications in **Table 4**:

   a. Exhaust pipe joint nuts.

   b. Front muffler mounting bolt

   c. Rear muffler mounting bolt.

   d. Muffler band bolt.

11. Start the engine and check for exhaust leaks.

① **FOUR-STROKE ENGINE PRINCIPLES**

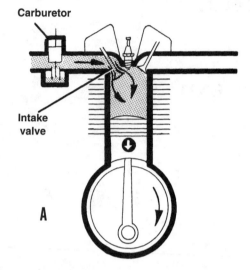

As the piston travels downward, the exhaust valve closes and the intake valve opens, drawing the new air-fuel mixture from the carburetor into the cylinder. When the piston reaches the bottom of its travel (BDC), the intake valve closes and remains closed for the next 1 1/2 revolutions of the crankshaft.

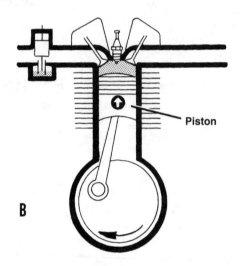

While the crankshaft continues to rotate, the piston moves upward, compressing the air-fuel mixture.

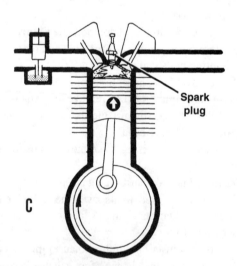

As the piston nears the top of its travel, the spark plug fires, igniting the compressed air-fuel mixture. This piston continues to top dead center (TDC) and is pushed downward by the expanding gasses.

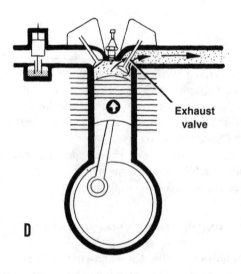

When the piston almost reaches BDC, the exhaust valve opens and remains open until the piston is near TDC. The upward travel of the piston forces the exhaust gases out of the cylinder. After the piston has reached TDC, the exhaust valve closes and the cycle repeats.

(2)

EXHAUST SYSTEM

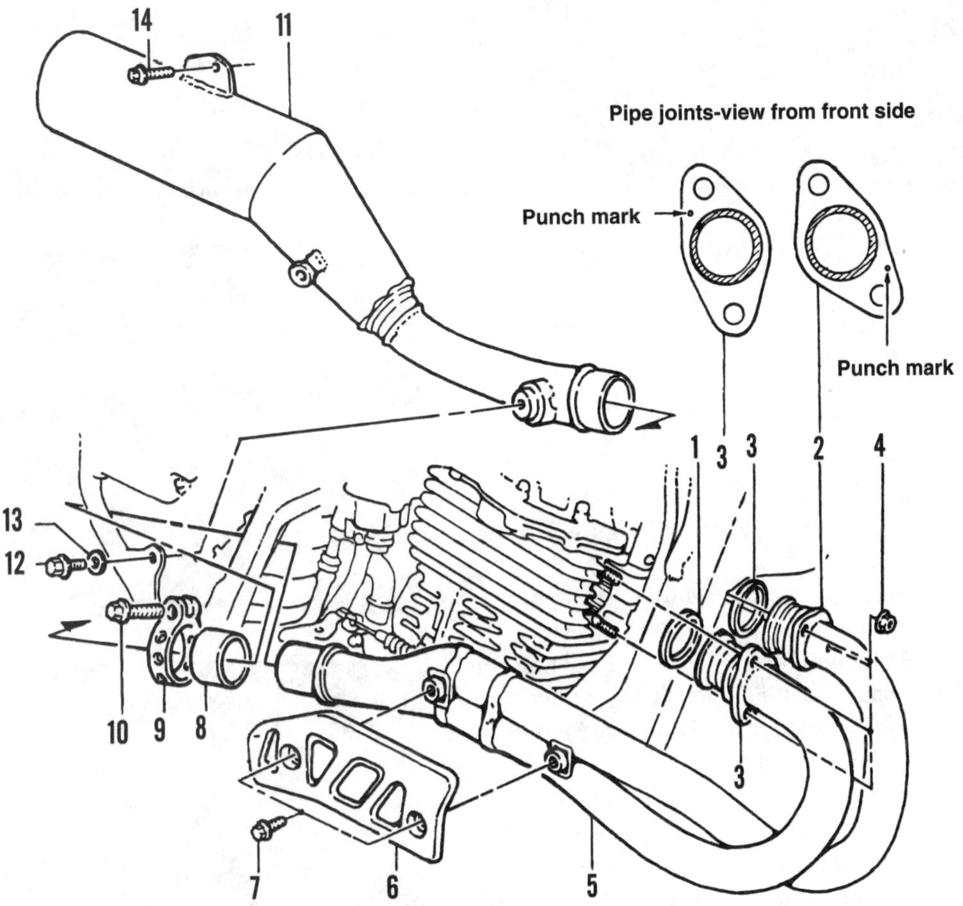
14
11
Pipe joints-view from front side
Punch mark
Punch mark
1
3
3
2
4
13
12
10
9
8
3
7
6
5

1. Gaskets
2. Left pipe joint
3. Right pipe joint
4. Joint nuts
5. Exhaust pipe
6. Heat shield
7. Screws
8. Gasket
9. Muffler band
10. Muffler band bolt
11. Muffler
12. Muffler mounting bolt (short)
13. Washer
14. Muffler mounting bolt (long)

CYLINDER HEAD COVER

The cylinder head cover can be serviced with the engine mounted in the frame.

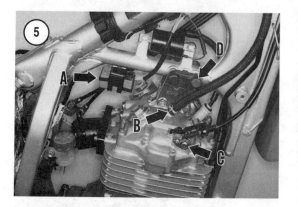

Removal

1. Remove the fuel tank (Chapter Eight).

2. Remove the AC regulator (A, **Figure 5**) as described in Chapter Nine.

3. Disconnect the breather tube (B, **Figure 5**).

4. Loosen the decompressor cable locknuts (C, **Figure 5**). Remove the cable holder mounting bolt and disconnect the cable from the valve lifter arm.

5. Remove the rubber caps (D, **Figure 5**) from the engine hanger nuts and bolts.

6. Disconnect the spark plug cap at the spark plug.

7. Unbolt and remove the upper engine hanger brackets (A, **Figure 6**).

8. Remove the intake and exhaust valve covers (B, **Figure 6**) and O-rings.

9. Remove the timing hole cap and crankshaft hole cap and O-rings (**Figure 7**) on the left crankcase cover.

10. Set the engine at TDC on its compression stroke as follows:

> *CAUTION*
> *Do **not** turn the crankshaft clockwise in the following steps.*

  a. Rotate the crankshaft with the nut on the crankshaft.

  b. Turn the crankshaft counterclockwise and align the T mark on the flywheel with the index notch in the crankcase cover (**Figure 8**) or the crankcase index mark (**Figure 9**).

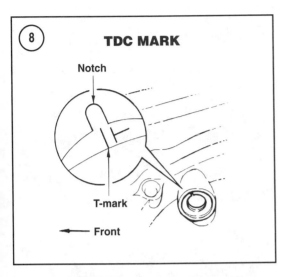

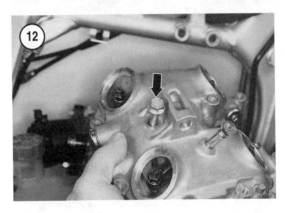

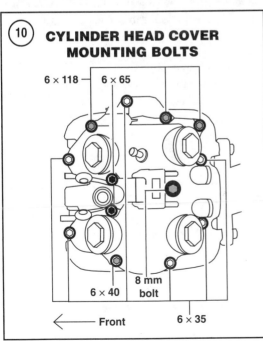

c. Check to see if the piston is at TDC on its compression stroke by trying to move the rocker arms by hand. When the piston is at TDC on its compression stroke, the rocker arms will have slack. If the rocker arms are tight (no slack), turn the crankshaft one full turn counterclockwise and realign the T mark. Recheck the rocker arm slack.

11. Loosen the cylinder head cover 6 mm bolts and the 8 mm bolt (**Figure 10**) in a crisscross pattern, starting with the center bolts and working outward.

12. Remove all of the 6 mm bolts. The 8 mm bolt (**Figure 11**) must be removed with the cylinder head cover.

NOTE
Two dowel pins align the cylinder head cover with the cylinder head. When removing the cylinder head cover, do not allow the dowel pins to fall into the cylinder head.

13. Lift the cylinder head cover and move it to the right, while at the same time lifting the 8 mm bolt (**Figure 12**).

14. Remove the gasket and two dowel pins (A, **Figure 13**).

Installation

1. Remove all gasket residue from the cylinder head cover and cylinder head mating surfaces.
2. Fill the two engine pockets with engine oil (**Figure 14**).
3. Lubricate the camshaft lobes with engine oil.
4. Install the two dowel pins (A, **Figure 13**) and a new gasket.
5. Set the engine at TDC on its compression stroke as follows:

> *CAUTION*
> *Do not turn the crankshaft clockwise in the following steps.*

    a. Rotate the crankshaft with the nut on the crankshaft.
    b. Turn the crankshaft counterclockwise and align the T mark on the flywheel with the index notch in the crankcase cover (**Figure 8**) or the crankcase index mark (**Figure 9**).
    c. Make sure the camshaft lobes (B, **Figure 13**) are facing down. If the camshaft lobes are facing up, turn the crankshaft one full turn counterclockwise and realign the T mark. Recheck the camshaft lobe position.

6. Install the 8 mm bolt into the cylinder head cover hole (**Figure 12**), and then install the cylinder head cover onto the engine while holding the 8 mm bolt up.
7. Refer to **Figure 10** and install the 6 mm bolts.
8. Tighten the 8 mm bolt and the 6 mm bolts finger-tight.
9. Tighten the cylinder head cover 6 mm mounting bolts securely in a crisscross pattern. Tighten the cylinder head cover 8 mm bolt to the specification in **Table 4**.
10. Install and tighten the timing hole cap and the crankshaft hole cap and O-rings (**Figure 7**) as specified in **Table 4**.
11. Install and tighten the intake (B, **Figure 6**) and exhaust valve covers and O-rings.
12. Install the upper engine hanger brackets (A, **Figure 6**), bolts and nuts. Tighten the nuts as specified in **Table 4**.
13. Reconnect the spark plug cap.

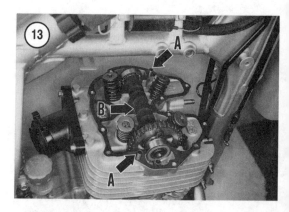

14. Install the rubber caps (D, **Figure 5**) onto the upper engine hanger nuts and bolts.
15. Reconnect the decompressor cable onto the valve lifter arm. Then install the cable holder. Adjust the decompressor cable (Chapter Three).
16. Reconnect the breather tube (B, **Figure 5**).
17. Install the AC regulator (A, **Figure 5**) as described in Chapter Nine.
18. Install the fuel tank (Chapter Eight).

Disassembly

Refer to **Figure 15**.
1. Remove the valve caps and O-rings.
2. If necessary, remove the valve lifter arm assembly (A, **Figure 16**) as follows:
    a. Remove the rocker arm shaft dowel pin (**Figure 17**) by filing a notch in the pin as shown in **Figure 18**. Orient the notch so it faces the valve cover hole.

> *CAUTION*
> *Be careful not to damage the cylinder head cover or rocker arms during the removal procedure.*

15

CYLINDER HEAD COVER

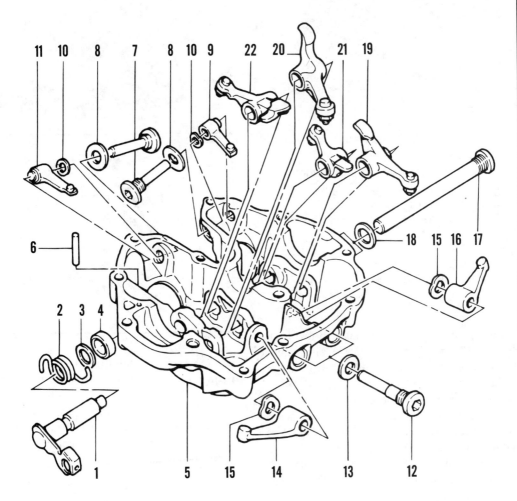

1. Valve lifter arm
2. Spring
3. Washer
4. Seal
5. Cylinder head cover
6. Dowel pin
7. Sub-rocker arm shafts
8. Sealing washers
9. Exhaust sub-rocker arm A
10. Wave washer
11. Exhaust sub-rocker arm B

12. Intake sub-rocker arm shafts
13. Sealing washer
14. Intake sub-rocker arm
15. Wave washer
16. Intake sub-rocker arm
17. Rocker arm shafts
18. Sealing washers
19. Left intake rocker arm
20. Right intake rocker arm
21. Left exhaust rocker arm
22. Right exhaust rocker arm

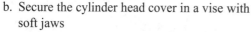

b. Secure the cylinder head cover in a vise with soft jaws

c. Insert a punch or screwdriver up through the valve cover hole and tap the dowel pin out of the cylinder head cover.

d. Remove the valve lifter arm, spring and washer.

NOTE
Label all of the rocker arm compo-nents so they can be reassembled cor-rectly.

3. Loosen and remove the exhaust sub-rocker arm shafts (7, **Figure 15**) and washers (8). Then remove the sub-rocker arms (9 and 11, **Figure 15**) and wave washers (10).

4. Loosen and remove the intake sub-rocker arm shafts (12, **Figure 15**) and washers (13). Then re-move the sub-rocker arms (14 and 16, **Figure 15**) and wave washers (15).

5. Loosen and remove the rocker arm shafts (17, **Figure 15**) and sealing washers (18). Then remove the following rocker arms:

a. Left side intake rocker arm shaft (19, **Figure 15**).

b. Right side intake rocker arm shaft (20).

c. Left side exhaust rocker arm shaft (21).

d. Right side exhaust rocker arm shaft (22).

Cylinder Head Cover Inspection

1. Clean the cylinder head cover gasket surface.

2. Clean and dry the cylinder head cover. Clean the oil passage with compressed air.

3. Inspect the camshaft bearing surfaces in the cyl-inder head cover for cracks or wear.

4. Replace the cylinder head cover if damaged.

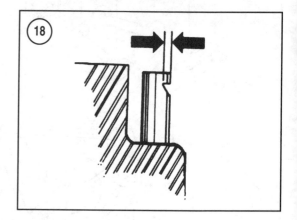

Rocker Arms and Shafts Inspection

When measuring the rocker arm components in this section, compare the actual measurements to the specifications in **Table 2**. Replace parts that are out of specification or show damage.

NOTE
Maintain the alignment of the rocker arm components during cleaning and inspection.

1. Clean and dry the parts.

2. Inspect the rocker arm pad where it contacts the cam lobe and where the adjuster contacts the valve stem. Look for scratches, flat spots, uneven wear and scoring.

3. Inspect the valve adjuster pads for flat spots, cracks or other damage. Inspect the locknuts for damage.

4. Inspect the rocker arm shafts for scoring, cracks or other damage.

5. Measure the rocker arm bore inside diameter.

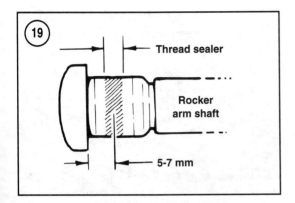

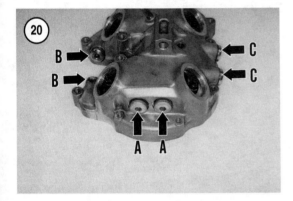

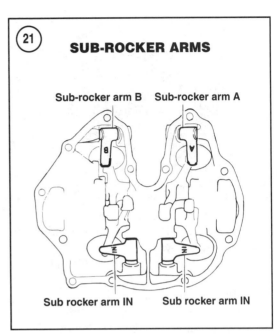

6. Measure the rocker arm shaft outside diameter.

7. Calculate the rocker arm-to-rocker arm shaft clearance as follows:

   a. Subtract the rocker arm shaft outside diameter (Step 6) from the rocker arm bore inside diameter (Step 5).

   b. Replace the rocker arm and/or the rocker arm shaft if the clearance is out of specification.

8. Repeat for each sub-rocker arm and shaft and each rocker arm and shaft assembly.

Valve Lifter Arm Inspection

Refer to **Figure 15**.

1. Clean and dry the parts.

2. Inspect the valve lifter arm and shaft assembly (1, **Figure 15**) for severe wear, deep scoring or other damage. Replace if damaged.

3. Replace the spring (2, **Figure 15**) if weak or damaged.

4. Replace the seal (4, **Figure 15**) in the cylinder head cover if leaking or damaged.

Assembly

Refer to **Figure 15**.

1. Remove all sealer residue from the rocker arm and cylinder head cover threads.

2. Lubricate the sub-rocker arm, rocker arms and rocker arm shafts with engine oil.

3. Install new washers onto the end of each rocker arm shaft.

NOTE
Make sure to install the sub-rocker arms, rocker arms and rocker arm shafts in their original positions.

4. Install the intake (19 and 20, **Figure 15**) and exhaust rocker arms (21 and 22), rocker arm shafts (17) and washers (18). Apply a threadlocking compound to the rocker arm shaft threads as shown in **Figure 19**. Tighten the rocker arm shafts (A, **Figure 20**) as specified in **Table 4**.

5. Install the sub-rocker arms (**Figure 21**) and wave washers into the cylinder head cover, then install the sub-rocker arm shafts. Apply a threadlocking compound to the sub-rocker arm shaft threads as shown in **Figure 19**. Tighten the intake and exhaust sub-rocker arm shafts (B and C, **Figure 20**) as specified in **Table 4**.

6. If removed, install the valve lifter arm assembly as follows:

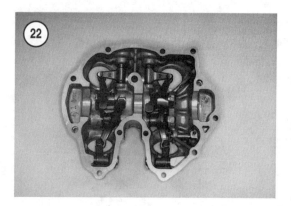

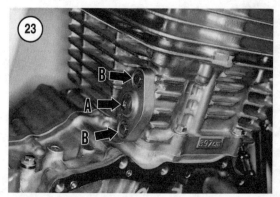

a. Pack the seal lips (4, **Figure 15**) with multi-purpose grease.

b. Install the spring (2, **Figure 15**) and washer (3) onto the valve lifter arm and install the arm into the cylinder head cover.

c. Hook the spring onto the valve lifter arm and cylinder head cover boss (B, **Figure 16**).

d. Align the groove in the valve lifter arm with the dowel pin hole.

e. Align a dowel pin with the groove in the valve lifter arm and press it into the cylinder head cover (**Figure 17**).

7. See **Figure 22** for an assembled view of the cylinder head cover assembly.

CAMSHAFT AND CAM CHAIN TENSIONER

The camshaft and cam chain tensioner can be removed with the engine mounted in the frame.

Removal

1. Remove the cylinder head cover as described in this chapter.

2. Remove the spark plug as described in this chapter.

3. Remove the cam chain tensioner as follows:

a. Loosen the screw (A, **Figure 23**) at the end of the tensioner housing.

b. Remove the two cam chain tensioner mounting bolts (B, **Figure 23**) and remove the tensioner assembly and gasket.

NOTE
Cover the area underneath the camshaft with a shop rag when removing the bolts in Steps 4 and 5.

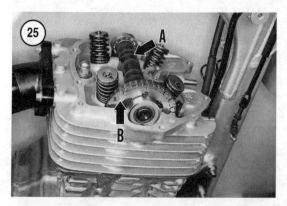

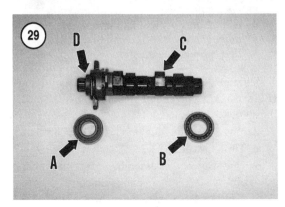

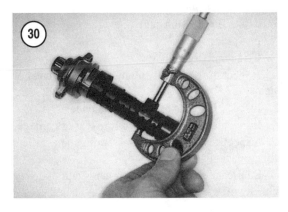

4. Remove the exposed camshaft sprocket bolt (**Figure 24**).

5. Using a socket on the flywheel bolt, turn the engine counterclockwise and remove the other camshaft sprocket bolt.

6. Attach a piece of wire to the camshaft chain.

7. Remove the camshaft (A, **Figure 25**) from the sprocket. Both bearings will come with the camshaft.

8. Remove the sprocket (B, **Figure 25**) from the cam chain.

NOTE
Cover the chain tunnel when removing the parts in Steps 9 and 10.

9. Remove the plunger (**Figure 26**) and spring (**Figure 27**).

10. Remove the two setting pins (**Figure 28**).

CAUTION
When rotating the crankshaft after removing the camshaft, pull up on the cam chain and keep it taut. Make sure the cam chain is meshing with the crankshaft timing sprocket, or the cam chain may kink and bind against the sprocket, causing chain and sprocket damage.

Camshaft Inspection

When measuring the camshaft in this section, compare the actual measurements to the specifications in **Table 2**. Replace the camshaft if out of specification or if it shows damage as described in this section.

1. Remove the bearings (A and B, **Figure 29**) from the camshaft ends. Both bearings are a slip fit.

2. Clean the camshaft sprocket mounting bolts and camshaft threads.

3. Clean and dry the camshaft and bearings.

4. Turn each camshaft bearing (A and B, **Figure 29**) by hand. The bearings must turn with no roughness, binding or excessive play. Replace damaged bearings. If the bearings are good, lubricate them with engine oil.

5. Check the cam lobes (C, **Figure 29**) for scoring or other damage.

6. Measure the cam lobe height with a micrometer (**Figure 30**).

7. To check camshaft runout, remove the decompression system (D, **Figure 29**) as described in this

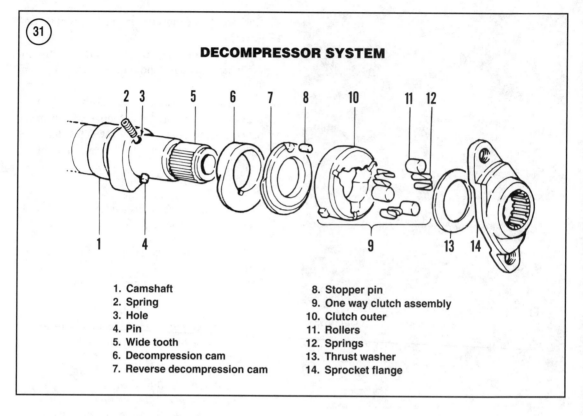

(31)

DECOMPRESSOR SYSTEM

1. Camshaft
2. Spring
3. Hole
4. Pin
5. Wide tooth
6. Decompression cam
7. Reverse decompression cam
8. Stopper pin
9. One way clutch assembly
10. Clutch outer
11. Rollers
12. Springs
13. Thrust washer
14. Sprocket flange

chapter. Support the camshaft ends across two V-blocks and measure runout with a dial indicator.

8. Inspect the camshaft bearing surfaces in the cylinder head for scoring, cracks or other damage.

9. Inspect the plunger (**Figure 26**) for scoring or other damage. Check the spring (**Figure 27**) for distortion or breakage.

10. Inspect the camshaft mounting bolts for damage. Replace the bolts as a set.

11. Inspect the setting pins (**Figure 28**) for scoring or other damage.

12. Inspect the decompression system as described in this chapter.

Camshaft Decompression Assembly Inspection/Disassembly/Reassembly

Refer to **Figure 31**.

CAUTION
When removing and installing the decompression assembly with a press, do not support the camshaft across its sprocket flange or allow the support blocks or press bed to contact the

camshaft lobes or decompression cam. Doing so will cause permanent damage to the camshaft and/or decompressor assembly.

1. Support the reverse decompression cam flange (**Figure 32**) in a press and press the camshaft out of the sprocket flange.

2. Remove the following parts from the camshaft:
   a. Thrust washer.
   b. One-way clutch assembly consisting of the clutch outer, rollers and springs.
   c. Reverse decompression cam.
   d. Stopper pin.
   e. Decompression cam.
   f. Spring.

3. Clean and dry all parts.

4. Inspect the camshaft sliding surface for wear or damage.

5. Inspect the cams for wear or damage.

6. Inspect the one-way clutch for wear or damage.

7. Inspect the one-way clutch springs and rollers for damage.

8. Lubricate the thrust washer, cams and one-way clutch with engine oil.

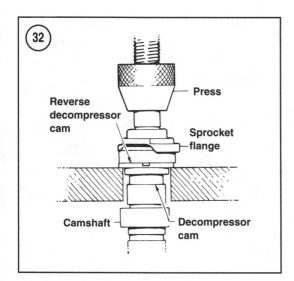

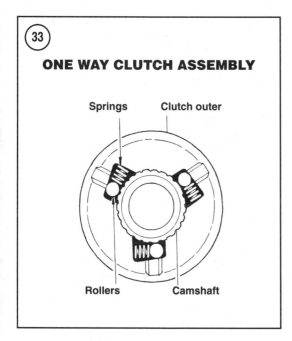

ONE WAY CLUTCH ASSEMBLY

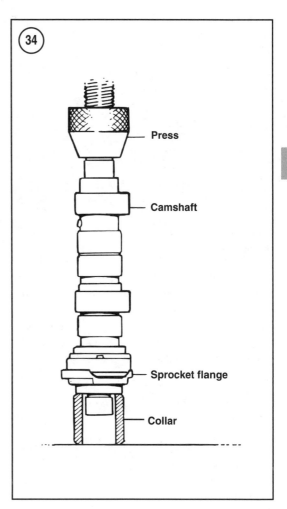

9. Install the spring (2, **Figure 31**) into the camshaft hole (3).

10. Hold the spring and install the decompression cam over it. Align the notch in the decompression cam with the pin (4, **Figure 31**) in the camshaft.

11. Install the reverse decompression cam over the camshaft. Then install the stopper pin (8, **Figure 31**) into the clutch outer (10). Assemble the clutch outer with the decompression cam (7), using the stopper pin to align both parts.

12. Install the springs and rollers into the clutch outer (**Figure 33**).

13. Install the thrust washer (13, **Figure 31**) and seat it against the clutch outer.

CAUTION
When pressing the sprocket flange onto the camshaft, do not support the sprocket flange by its extended bolt arms. Doing so will damage the sprocket flange. Support the sprocket flange as shown in ***Figure 34***.

14. Align the wide groove in the sprocket flange (14, **Figure 31**) with the wide tooth on the camshaft (5). Support the sprocket flange middle section with a suitable collar (**Figure 34**) and press the sprocket flange onto the camshaft.

15. Remove the camshaft from the press and inspect the decompression assembly.

Camshaft Sprocket Inspection

Inspect the camshaft sprocket for broken or chipped teeth. Check the bolt holes for cracks. If the camshaft sprocket is damaged or severely worn, inspect the crankshaft sprocket, cam chain, chain guides and chain tensioner for damage. Check the chain and guides as described in Chapter Five.

Cam Chain Tensioner Inspection

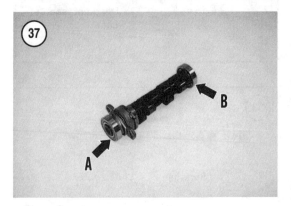

The cam chain tensioner (**Figure 35**) is a sealed unit. Do not disassemble it.
1. Clean the cam chain tensioner and cylinder block mating surfaces.
2. Check the tensioner shaft and housing for damage.
3. Turn the cam chain lifter shaft clockwise with a small screwdriver and release it. The shaft should move smoothly and under spring tension. The tensioner shaft should spring out of the housing when released. The tensioner shaft should not move into the tensioner housing when pushed by hand.

Camshaft Installation

NOTE
Cover the cam chain tunnel when installing parts in Steps 1 and 2.

1. Install the two setting pins (**Figure 28**).
2. Install the spring (**Figure 27**) and plunger (**Figure 26**). See **Figure 36**.
3. Lubricate the camshaft bearings (**Figure 29**) with engine oil.

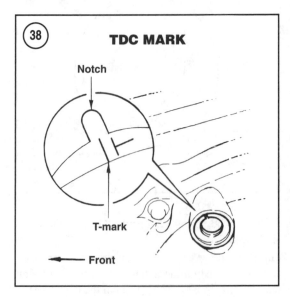

4. Install the sealed bearing onto the cam sprocket side of the camshaft with its sealed side facing out (A, **Figure 37**). Install the other bearing onto the opposite camshaft end (B, **Figure 37**).

5. Lubricate the camshaft lobes, journals and cylinder head journals with molybdenum oil.

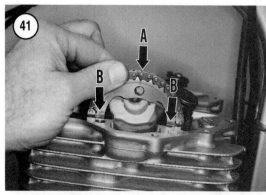

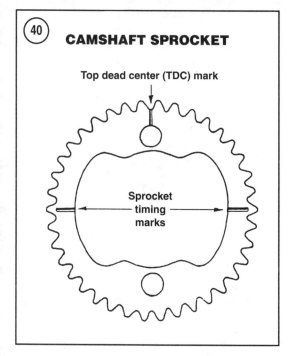

CAMSHAFT SPROCKET

Top dead center (TDC) mark

Sprocket timing marks

the crankcase cover (**Figure 38**) or the crankcase index mark (**Figure 39**).

NOTE
Figure 40 shows the camshaft sprocket and its timing marks.

7. Fit the camshaft sprocket into the cam chain with the top dead center mark (A, **Figure 41**) facing up and the sprocket timing marks (B, **Figure 41**) aligned with the cylinder head gasket surface.

8. Hold the camshaft sprocket and install the camshaft (**Figure 42**) through it. Position the camshaft so that the cam lobes face *down*. Install the camshaft sprocket onto the camshaft flange.

9. Apply a medium-strength threadlock to the threads on each camshaft sprocket bolt.

10. Turn the camshaft and align the exposed camshaft and sprocket bolt holes. Do not turn the cam chain, as doing so will change the flywheel timing mark alignment.

11. Install the first camshaft sprocket bolt (**Figure 43**) and finger tighten.

NOTE
The engine must be set at top dead center (TDC) on the compression stroke before installing and timing the camshaft.

CAUTION
When rotating the crankshaft in the following steps, keep the cam chain taut and meshed with the timing sprocket on the crankshaft.

6. Make sure the cam chain is meshing with the crankshaft sprocket. Using a socket on the flywheel bolt, turn the crankshaft counterclockwise and align the T mark on the flywheel with the index notch in

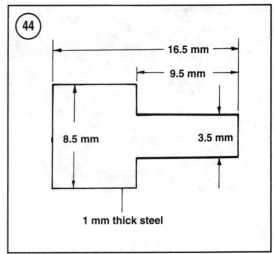

12. Turn the crankshaft counterclockwise and install the second camshaft sprocket bolt. Finger tighten the bolt.

13. Turn the crankshaft counterclockwise until the TDC mark (**Figure 40**) on the camshaft sprocket faces up. Tighten the exposed camshaft sprocket bolt (**Figure 43**) to the specification in **Table 4**. Turn the crankshaft counterclockwise and torque the other camshaft sprocket bolt.

14. Turn the crankshaft counterclockwise several times using the flywheel bolt. Align the T mark on the flywheel with the index notch in the crankcase cover (**Figure 38**) or the crankcase index mark (**Figure 39**). Make sure the camshaft sprocket timing marks align with the cylinder head gasket surface as shown in **Figure 41**. If these marks do not align as shown, the camshaft timing is incorrect.

> *NOTE*
> *Before installing the cam chain tensioner, make a stopper plate that will lock the tensioner in its retracted position. Use a piece of thin metal (1.0 mm/0.040 in.), to make a stopper plate of the dimensions shown in Figure 44.*

15. Install the cam chain tensioner (**Figure 35**) as follows:

   a. Remove the cam chain tensioner screw and O-ring from the end of the tensioner housing.

   b. Turn the tensioner shaft clockwise with the stopper plate until it fully retracts the shaft. Engage the outer stopper plate arms with two slots cut into the tensioner housing to lock the shaft. See **Figure 45**.

   c. Install the cam chain tensioner housing and a new gasket onto the cylinder block. Hold the

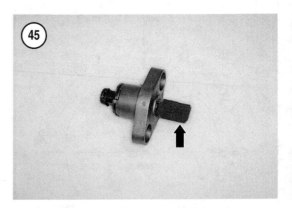

tensioner housing (A, **Figure 46**) in place and install the two mounting bolts. Tighten securely.

> *NOTE*
> *When the stopper plate is removed an audible click should be heard, indicating that the tensioner shaft has extended into position. If no click is heard, remove the cam chain tensioner housing and inspect the shaft operation.*

   d. Remove the stopper plate (B, **Figure 46**) to allow the tensioner shaft to extend fully.

   e. Install the cam chain tensioner screw and a new O-ring. Tighten the screw to the specification in **Table 4**.

16. Repeat Step 11 and check the camshaft timing marks.

17. Install the cylinder head cover as described in this chapter.

CYLINDER HEAD

Removal

> *CAUTION*
> *Do not remove the cylinder head until the engine is cool, or the head may warp.*

1. Remove the fuel tank (Chapter Eight).
2. Remove the carburetor (Chapter Eight).
3. Remove the exhaust pipe as described in this chapter.
4. Remove the camshaft as described in this chapter.
5. Loosen the cylinder head mounting nuts (**Figure 47**) in a crisscross pattern.
6. Remove the cylinder head nuts and washers.
7. Remove the cylinder head (**Figure 47**).
8. Remove and discard the cylinder head gasket.
9. Remove the two dowel pins (A, **Figure 48**).

Cylinder Head Inspection

1. Without removing the valves, remove all carbon deposits from the combustion chamber (**Figure 49**).

> *CAUTION*
> *Do not clean the combustion chamber after removing the valves. Doing so will damage the valve seat surfaces. A scratched or damaged valve seat will cause poor valve seating.*

2. Examine the spark plug threads in the cylinder head for damage. Clean with a spark plug tap. If damage is severe, repair the threads with a steel thread insert.
3. Clean the gasket mating surface.
4. Clean and dry the cylinder head.
5. Examine the piston crown for damage or aluminum deposits. If found, check the spark plug, valves and combustion chamber for damage. Aluminum deposits on these surfaces indicate that the damage is caused by a lean fuel mixture or preignition.
6. Inspect the intake manifold for cracks or other damage.
7. Inspect the intake manifold O-ring for cracks and other damage.
8. Check for cracks in the combustion chamber and exhaust port. Replace the cylinder head if it cannot be repaired.

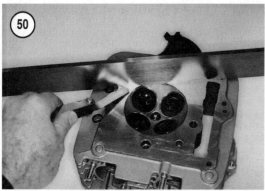

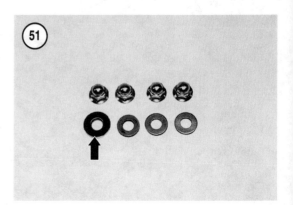

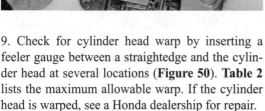

9. Check for cylinder head warp by inserting a feeler gauge between a straightedge and the cylinder head at several locations (**Figure 50**). **Table 2** lists the maximum allowable warp. If the cylinder head is warped, see a Honda dealership for repair.

10. Check the cylinder head studs and nuts for thread damage, cracks and twisting.

11. To service the valves, refer to *Valves and Valve Components* in this chapter.

Installation

1. Clean the cylinder head and cylinder mating surfaces.

2. Install the two cylinder head dowel pins (A, **Figure 48**).

3. Make sure the notches in the front cam chain guide seat into the cylinder block grooves (B, **Figure 48**).

4. Install a new cylinder head gasket.

5. Run the cam chain through the cylinder head chain tunnel. Then install the cylinder head onto the cylinder block and over the two dowel pins.

6. Install the cylinder head nuts (**Figure 47**) as follows:

     a. Install the large washer (**Figure 51**) over the front stud. Install the four remaining cylinder head washers and nuts over the studs.

     b. Lubricate the cylinder head nut threads and seating surfaces with engine oil.

     c. Install the cylinder head nuts and tighten finger-tight.

7. Tighten the cylinder head nuts (**Figure 47**) in 2-3 stages in a crisscross pattern to the specification in **Table 4**.

8. Install the camshaft as described in this chapter.

9. Install the carburetor (Chapter Eight).

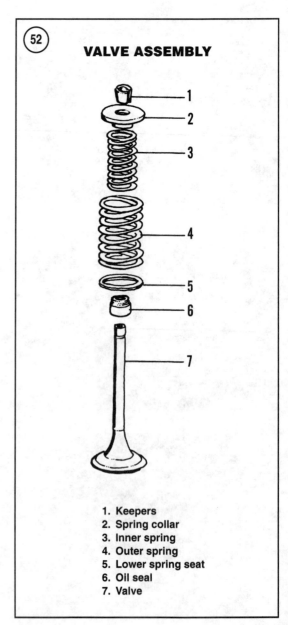

VALVE ASSEMBLY

1. Keepers
2. Spring collar
3. Inner spring
4. Outer spring
5. Lower spring seat
6. Oil seal
7. Valve

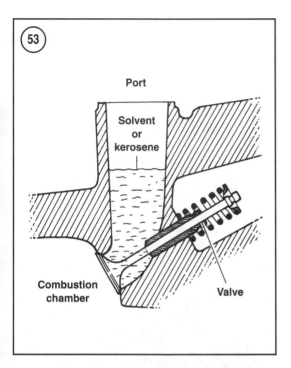

Port

Solvent
or
kerosene

Combustion
chamber

Valve

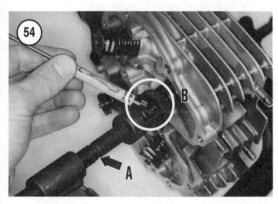

10. Install the exhaust pipe as described in this chapter.

11. Install the fuel tank (Chapter Eight).

VALVES AND VALVE COMPONENTS

The following procedures describe valve component inspection to determine the type of service required. The inspection requires a valve spring compressor. Complete valve service requires more specialized equipment. If these tools are not available, it is more cost effective to refer valve service to an experienced machine shop or Honda dealership.

Refer to **Figure 52** when servicing the valves in this section.

Solvent Test

Before removing the valves from the cylinder head, perform a solvent test to check the valve-to-valve seat seal.

1. Remove the cylinder head as described in this chapter.
2. Support the cylinder head with the exhaust port facing up (**Figure 53**). Pour solvent or kerosene into the port. Immediately check the combustion chamber for fluid leaking past the exhaust valves.
3. Repeat Step 2 for the intake port and intake valves.
4. If there is fluid leakage around one or both sets of valves, the valve(s) is not seating correctly. The following conditions will cause poor valve seating:
   a. A bent valve stem.
   b. A worn or damaged valve seat (in cylinder head).
   c. A worn or damaged valve face.
   d. A crack in the combustion chamber.

Valve Removal

1. Remove the cylinder head as described in this chapter.
2. Perform the solvent test as described in this chapter.

> *CAUTION*
> *Keep all component parts of each valve assembly together. Do not mix components from the different valves or excessive wear may result.*

3. Install a valve spring compressor (A, **Figure 54**) squarely over the valve spring collar and the valve head.
4. Tighten the valve spring compressor until the valve keepers separate. Remove valve keepers (B, **Figure 54**).
5. Gradually loosen the valve spring compressor and remove it from the head.
6. Remove the spring collar and both valve springs.

> *CAUTION*
> *Remove any burrs from the valve stem grooves before removing the valves*

(Figure 55); otherwise the valve guides may be damaged as the valve stems pass through them.

7. Remove the valve.

8. Remove the lower spring seat.

9. Pull the oil seal off the valve guide (**Figure 56**) and discard it.

10. Repeat Steps 3-9 for the other valves.

Inspection

Refer to the troubleshooting chart in **Figure 57** when performing valve inspection procedures in this section.

When measuring the valve components in this section, compare the actual measurements to the specifications in **Table 2**. Replace parts that are out of specification or show damage as described in this section.

1. Clean and dry each valve assembly. Do not gouge or damage the valve seating surfaces.

2. Inspect the contact surface (**Figure 58**) of each valve for burning. If necessary, lap the valves to remove minor roughness and pitting, as described in this chapter.

3. Inspect the valve stems for wear and roughness. Measure the valve stem outside diameter for wear using a micrometer (**Figure 59**).

4. Remove all carbon and varnish from the valve guides with a stiff spiral wire brush before measuring wear.

> *NOTE*
> *If the required measuring tools, are not available, go to Step 7.*

5. Measure each valve guide at the top, center and bottom positions.

6. Subtract the measurement made in Step 3 from the measurement made in Step 5. The difference is the valve stem-to-guide clearance. See **Table 2** for correct clearance. Replace any guide or valve that is out of specification. Refer to *Valve guide Replacement* in this chapter.

7. If measuring tools are not available, insert each valve in its guide. Hold the valve off its seat and rock it sideways. If the valve rocks more than slightly, the guide is probably worn. However, as a final check, take the cylinder head to a dealership or

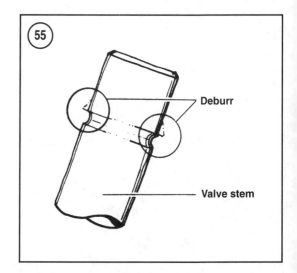

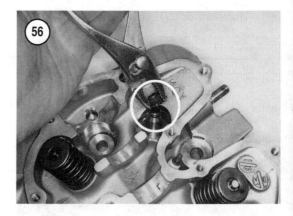

machine shop and have the valves and valve guides measured.

8. Check the inner and outer valve springs as follows:

   a. Check the valve spring for cracks or other damage.

   b. Check each spring for distortion or tilt (**Figure 60**) with a square.

   c. Measure the valve spring length with a vernier caliper (**Figure 61**). Compare the measurements to the length specified in **Table 2**.

   d. Replace defective springs as a set.

9. Check the spring collar, lower spring seat and valve keepers for damage.

10. Inspect the valve seats in the cylinder head (**Figure 62**). They should be smooth and even, and have a polished seating surface. Recondition worn or burned valve seats as described in this chapter. Check valve seats as follows:

(57)

VALVE TROUBLESHOOTING

4

Valve deposits

Check:
- Worn valve guide
- Carbon buildup from incorrect engine tuning
- Carbon buildup from incorrect carburetor adjustment
- Dirty or gummed fuel
- Dirty engine oil

Valve sticking

Check:
- Worn valve guide
- Bent valve stem
- Deposits collected on valve stem
- Valve burning or overheating

Valve burning

Check:
- Valve sticking
- Cylinder head warped
- Valve seat distorted
- Valve clearance incorrect
- Incorrect valve spring
- Valve spring worn
- Worn valve seat
- Carbon buildup in engine
- Engine ingnition and/or carburetor adjustments incorrect

Valve seat/face wear

Check:
- Valve burning
- Incorrect valve clearance
- Abrasive material on valve face and seat

Valve damage

Check:
- Valve burning
- Incorrectly installed or serviced valve guides
- Incorrect valve clearance
- Incorrect valve, spring seat and retainer assembly
- Detonation caused by incorrect ignition and/or carburetor adjustments

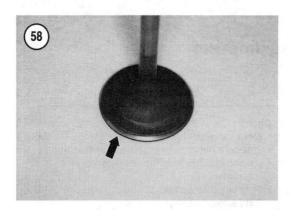

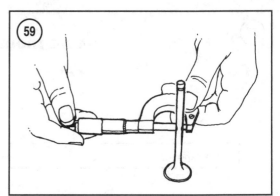

a. Clean the valve seat and valve mating areas with contact cleaner.

b. Coat the valve seat with Prussian Blue.

c. Install the valve into its guide and rotate it against its seat with a valve lapping tool. See *Valve Lapping* in this chapter.

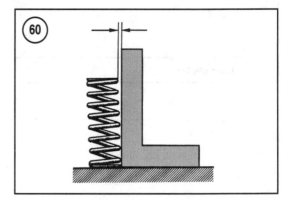

d. Lift the valve out of the guide and measure the seat width impression left on the valve or in the cylinder head (**Figure 63**) with a vernier caliper.

e. The seat width must measure within the specifications listed in **Table 2** all the way around the seat. If the seat width exceeds the service limit (**Table 2**), regrind the seats as described under *Valve Seat Reconditioning* in this chapter.

f. Clean the seat and valve contact surfaces.

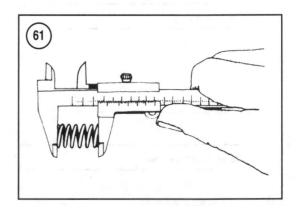

Valve Guide Replacement

If there is excessive valve stem-to-guide clearance, the valve guides must be replaced. This procedure requires specialized equipment. If the proper tools are not available, it is more cost effective to refer valve guide replacement to an experienced machine shop or Honda dealership. If a valve guide is replaced, the valve seat must be reconditioned.

Valve Seat Reconditioning

Special valve surfacing tools are required to properly recondition the valve seats in the cylinder head. If these tools are not available, refer this service to an experienced machine shop or Honda dealership.

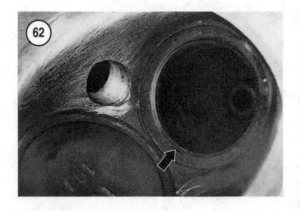

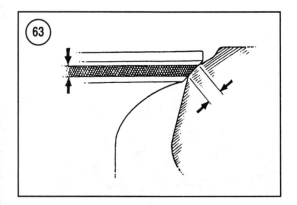

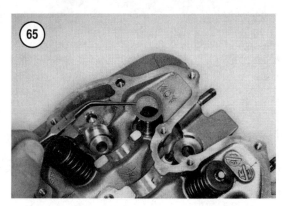

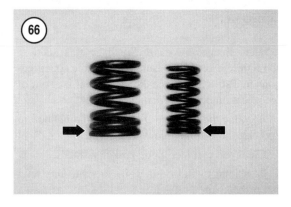

Valve Lapping

Valve lapping is a procedure where a fine grade valve grinding compound is placed between the valve face and its seat. The valve is then rotated against its seat with a lapping stick attached to the valve head. If the wear or distortion is not too great, lapping can restore the valve seal without machining.

Perform this procedure after determining that the valve seat width and outside diameter are within specifications.

1. Apply a light coating of fine grade valve lapping compound onto the valve face.
2. Insert the valve into the head.
3. Wet the suction cup of the lapping stick and stick it onto the head of the valve. Lap the valve to the seat by spinning the lapping stick in both directions. Every 5 to 10 seconds, rotate the valve 180° in the valve seat. Continue this action until the mating surfaces on the valve and seat are smooth and equal in size.
4. Examine the valve seat (**Figure 62**) in the cylinder head. It must be smooth and even with a polished seating ring.
5. Clean the valves and cylinder head in solvent to remove all grinding compound. Any compound left on the valves or cylinder head will cause wear and damage.
6. Install the lapped valve into the cylinder head.
7. Test the valve seal as described under *Solvent Test* in this chapter. If fluid leaks past any of the seats, remove that valve and repeat the lapping procedure until there is no leakage.

Installation

1. Lubricate a new seal with engine oil and push it onto the end of the valve guide (**Figure 64**).
2. Install the lower spring seat (**Figure 65**).

> *CAUTION*
> *To prevent the valve from damaging the seal, rotate the valve as it passes through the seal in Step 3.*

3. Coat a valve stem with molybdenum disulfide paste and install into its correct guide. Hold the valve in position.

> *NOTE*
> *Install the valve springs with their narrow pitch end (coils closest together) facing the cylinder head (**Figure 66**)*

4. Install the inner and outer valve springs (**Figure 67**).

5. Install the spring collar (**Figure 68**).

6. Place the valve spring compressor (**Figure 54**) over the spring collar and compress the spring.

7. Install the valve keepers (**Figure 69**). Release the compressor and ensure that the keepers are seated in the valve stem grooves (**Figure 69**) by tapping the end of the valve stem with a soft-faced hammer.

8. Repeat Steps 1-6 for the other valves.

9. Perform the *Solvent Test* in this chapter.

10. Install the cylinder head onto the engine, and adjust the valve clearance as described in Chapter Three.

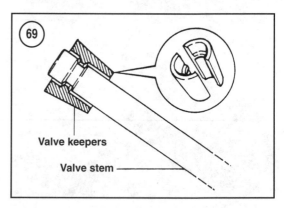

Valve keepers

Valve stem

CYLINDER

Removal

1. Remove the cylinder head as described in this chapter.

2. Remove the front cam chain guide (A, **Figure 70**).

3. Remove the two 6 mm bolts (B, **Figure 70**) and the four 10 mm bolts (C) and washers.

4. Loosen the cylinder by tapping around the perimeter with a soft-faced hammert.

5. Pull the cylinder straight up and off the crankcase. Remove the base gasket.

6. Remove the two dowel pins (**Figure 71**).

7. If necessary, remove the piston as described in this chapter.

8. Cover the crankcase opening.

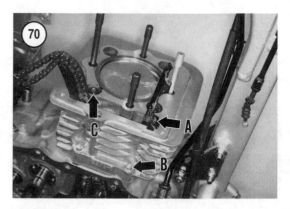

Inspection

When measuring the cylinder in this section, compare the actual measurements to the specifications in **Table 3**. Service the cylinder if it is out of specification or shows damage.

1. Remove the cylinder O-ring (**Figure 72**) before washing the cylinder block in solvent.

2. Clean the cylinder block gasket surfaces.

3. Wash the cylinder block in solvent. Dry with compressed air.

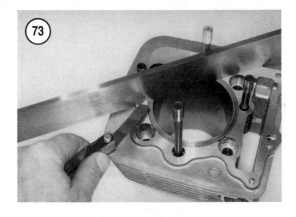

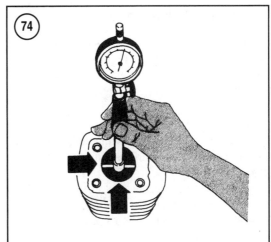

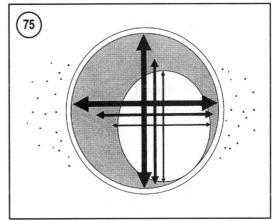

4. Check the dowel pin holes for cracks or other damage.

5. Inspect the cylinder block for warp by placing a straight edge across the upper cylinder block surface, and inserting a feeler gauge between the straight edge and cylinder block at different locations (**Figure 73**).

6. Measure the cylinder bore with a bore gauge or inside micrometer (**Figure 74**) at the points shown in **Figure 75**. Measure in line with the piston pin and at 90° to the pin. Use the largest measurement to determine cylinder bore. If the taper or out-of-round is greater than the specifications, bore the cylinder oversize and install a new piston and rings.

7. If the cylinder is not worn past the service limit, check the bore for scratches or gouges. The bore still may require boring and reconditioning.

8. After servicing the cylinder, wash the bore in hot soapy water. Wash the cylinder until a clean white cloth can be passed through the cylinder without becoming contaminated.

CAUTION
Any fine grit residue from the machining or boring operations that is not removed from the cylinder will cause rapid and excessive wear to the engine. Solvents cannot adequately remove this material. Use an abundant supply of soap and hot water to remove the fine grit residue.

Cylinder Stud Replacement

Three different length cylinder studs are used on the cylinder block. Refer to **Figure 76** and identify the studs as follows:
1. Stud A: 10 × 73 mm.
2. Stud B: 10 × 60 mm.
3. Stud C: 10 × 92 mm.

Install the studs to the following heights as measured from the cylinder surface to the top of the stud (**Figure 77**):
1. Stud A: 62-63 mm (2.44-2.48 in.).
2. Stud B: 49-50 mm (1.93-1.97 in.).
3. Stud C: 81-82 mm (3.19-3.23 in.).

Installation

1. Clean the cylinder block and crankcase mating surfaces.
2. Install the O-ring into the groove in the bottom of the cylinder (**Figure 72**).
3. Install the two dowel pins into the crankcase (**Figure 71**).
4. Install a *new* base gasket. Make sure all holes align.
5. If removed, install the piston as described in this chapter.

> *CAUTION*
> *Make sure to install and secure the piston pin circlips.*

6. Install a piston holding fixture under the piston.

> *NOTE*
> *To fabricate a wooden piston holding fixture from a piece of scrap wood, refer to the example in* ***Figure 78***.

7. Stagger the piston rings around the piston as shown in **Figure 79**.
8. Lubricate the cylinder wall, piston and rings with engine oil.
9. Align the cylinder with the piston and install the cylinder. Compress each ring by hand as it enters the cylinder.
10. Remove the piston holding fixture and slide the cylinder all the way down (**Figure 70**).
11. Pull the cam chain and wire up through the chain tunnel.
12. Slowly turn the engine over while holding the cylinder against the crankcase. The piston must

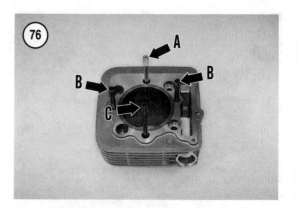

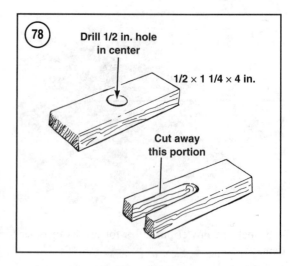

Drill 1/2 in. hole in center

1/2 × 1 1/4 × 4 in.

Cut away this portion

move within the bore without any binding or roughness.
13. Lubricate the 10 mm cylinder mounting bolt threads, seating surfaces and washers with engine oil.
14. Install the four 10 mm cylinder mounting bolts (C, **Figure 70**) and washers. Tighten in a crisscross pattern to the specification in **Table 4**.

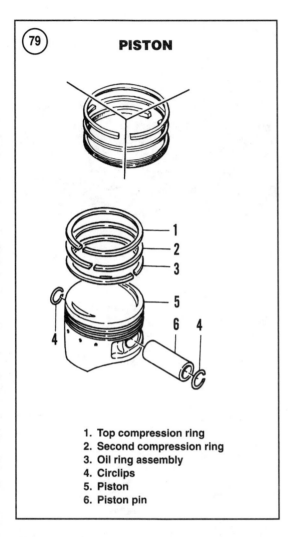

PISTON

1. Top compression ring
2. Second compression ring
3. Oil ring assembly
4. Circlips
5. Piston
6. Piston pin

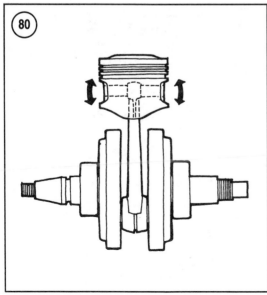

15. Install the two 6 mm cylinder mounting bolts (B, **Figure 70**) and tighten as specified in **Table 4**.
16. Install the front cam chain guide into the crankcase and set it into the cylinder grooves (A, **Figure 70**).
17. Install the cylinder head as described in this chapter.

PISTON AND PISTON RINGS

Refer to **Figure 79** when servicing the piston and rings in the following section.

Piston Removal/Installation

1. Remove the cylinder as described in this chapter.
2. Place towels below the piston to prevent the piston pin circlips from falling into the crankcase.
3. Before removing the piston, hold the rod and rock the piston (**Figure 80**). Any rocking motion (do not confuse with the normal sliding motion) indicates wear on the piston pin, rod bushing, pin bore, or a combination of all three.
4. Remove the piston circlips (**Figure 81**).

NOTE
Discard the piston circlips. New circlips must be installed during reassembly.

5. Push the piston pin (A, **Figure 82**) out of the piston by hand. If the pin is tight, use a homemade tool (**Figure 83**) to remove it. Do not drive the piston pin out as doing so may damage the piston pin, connecting rod or piston.
6. Lift the piston (B, **Figure 82**) off the connecting rod.
7. Inspect the piston as described in this chapter.

Piston Inspection

1. Remove the piston rings as described in this chapter.

2. Soak the piston in solvent to soften the carbon deposits.

3. Clean the carbon from the piston crown with a soft scraper or wire wheel mounted in a drill. A thick carbon buildup will reduce piston cooling and lead to detonation and piston damage.

CAUTION
Do not wire brush the piston skirt.

4. After cleaning the piston, examine the crown for signs of wear or damage. If the crown appears pecked or spongy-looking, also check the spark plug, valves and combustion chamber for aluminum deposits. If these deposits are found, the engine is overheating.

5. Examine each ring groove (**Figure 84**) for burrs, dented edges or other damage. Pay particular attention to the top compression ring groove as it usually wears more than the others. The oil ring groove and rings generally show less wear than the compression rings and grooves. If there is evidence of oil ring groove wear or if the oil ring is tight and difficult to remove, the piston skirt may have collapsed due to excessive heat. Replace the piston.

6. Check the oil control holes in the piston for carbon buildup. Clean the holes with wire.

7. Check the piston skirt (**Figure 85**) for cracks or other damage. If the piston shows signs of partial seizure (bits of aluminum built up on the piston skirt), replace the piston.

NOTE
If the piston skirt is worn or scuffed unevenly from side-to-side, the connecting rod may be bent or twisted.

8. Check the piston circlip grooves for wear, cracks or other damage.

9. Measure piston-to-cylinder clearance as described under *Piston Clearance* in this chapter.

Piston Pin Inspection

When measuring the piston pin in this section, compare the actual measurements to the specifications in **Table 3**. Replace the piston pin if it is out of specification or if it shows damage.

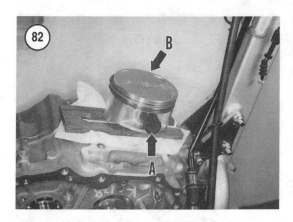

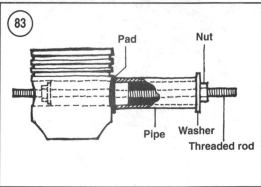

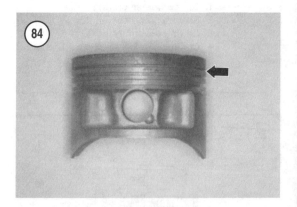

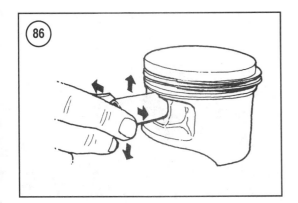

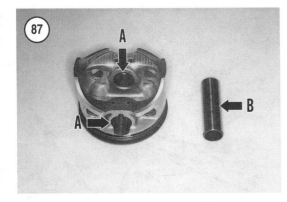

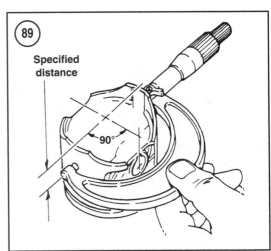

1. Clean and dry the piston pin.

2. Inspect the piston pin for chrome flaking or cracks.

3. Oil the piston pin and install it in the piston. Slowly rotate the piston pin and check for tightness and radial play (**Figure 86**). Confirm piston pin clearance by performing the following steps.

4. Measure the piston pin bore inside diameter (A, **Figure 87**.

5. Measure the piston pin outside diameter (B, **Figure 87**).

6. Subtract the measurement made in Step 4 from the measurement made in Step 5. The difference is the piston-to-piston pin clearance.

Connecting Rod Inspection

1. Inspect the connecting rod (**Figure 88**) for cracks or heat damage.

2. Measure the connecting rod piston pin bore diameter. Compare the measurement to the specification in **Table 3** and replace the connecting rod (Chapter 5) if it is not within specification.

Piston Clearance

1. Make sure the piston and cylinder walls are clean and dry.

2. Measure the cylinder bore with a bore gauge or inside micrometer (**Figure 74**) at the points shown in **Figure 75**. Measure in line with the piston pin and at 90° to the pin. Use the largest measurement to determine cylinder bore diameter. If the cylinder bore is out of specification, replace the piston and bore the cylinder oversize. If the cylinder bore is within specification, continue with Step 3.

3. Measure the piston diameter with a micrometer at a right angle to the piston pin bore (**Figure 89**). Measure 15 mm (0.6 in.) up from the edge of the piston skirt (**Figure 89**).

4. Subtract the piston diameter from the largest bore diameter. The difference is piston-to-cylinder clearance. If clearance exceeds the service limit in **Table 3**, replace the piston and bore the cylinder oversize.

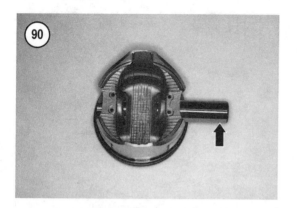

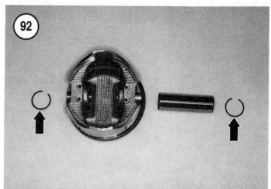

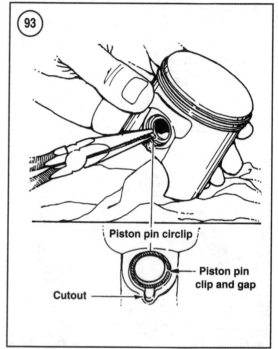

Piston Installation

1. Install the piston rings onto the piston as described in this chapter.

2. Coat the connecting rod pin bore, piston pin and piston with engine oil.

3. Slide the piston pin into the piston until its end is flush with the piston pin boss (**Figure 90**).

4. Place the piston over the connecting rod so the IN mark (**Figure 91**) on the piston crown faces toward the intake (rearward) side of the engine.

5. Line up the piston pin with the connecting rod. Push the piston pin (A, **Figure 82**) through the connecting rod and into the other side of the piston. Center the piston pin in the piston.

6. Install *new* piston pin clips (**Figure 92**) in both ends of the piston pin boss (**Figure 81**). Make sure they seat in the piston grooves completely.

CAUTION
Do not align the piston pin clip end gap with the cut out in the piston (Figure 93).

7. Install the cylinder as described in this chapter.

Piston pin circlip

Piston pin clip and gap

Cutout

**Piston Ring
Inspection and Removal**

The ring assembly (**Figure 94**) consists of the top and second compression rings and a lower oil control ring assembly (two ring rails and expander spacer). When measuring the piston rings in this section, compare the actual measurements to the specifications in **Table 3**. If the piston rings are out of specification or if they show damage, replace the piston rings as a set.

1. Measure the side clearance of each ring in its groove with a flat feeler gauge (**Figure 95**). If the clearance is greater than specified, replace the rings.

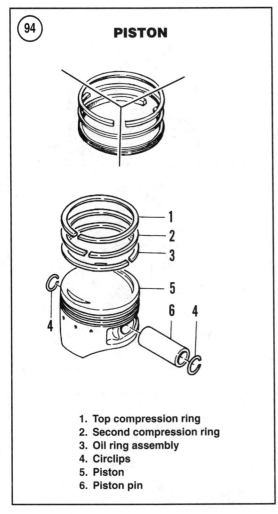

PISTON

1. Top compression ring
2. Second compression ring
3. Oil ring assembly
4. Circlips
5. Piston
6. Piston pin

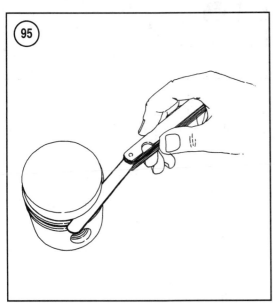

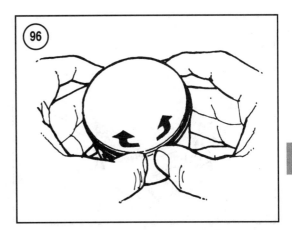

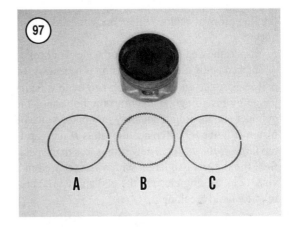

If the clearance is still excessive with new rings, replace the piston.

> *WARNING*
> *The edges of all piston rings are very sharp. Be careful when handling them to avoid cut fingers.*

> *NOTE*
> *Store the rings in order of removal, to avoid confusion during reassembly.*

2. Remove the compression rings with a ring expander tool, or spread the ring ends by hand, and lift the rings out of their grooves and up over the piston (**Figure 96**).

3. Remove the oil ring assembly by first removing the upper (A, **Figure 97**) and then the lower (B) ring rails. Then remove the expander spacer (C).

4. Remove carbon residue from the piston ring grooves (**Figure 98**) with a broken piston ring (if available). Do not remove aluminum material from

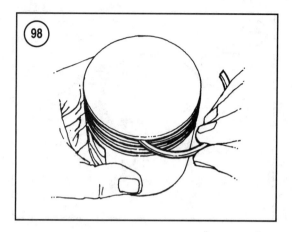

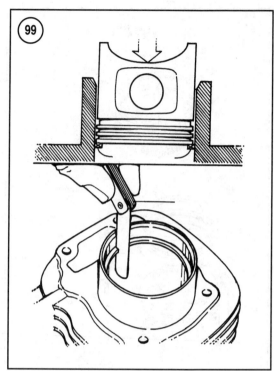

the ring grooves as this will increase the side clearance.

5. Inspect the ring grooves for burrs, nicks or broken or cracked lands. Replace the piston if necessary.

6. Measure the end gap of each ring with a feeler gauge by installing the ring into the bottom of the cylinder and tapping it squarely into place with the piston (**Figure 99**). Replace the rings if the gap is too large. If the gap on a new ring is less than specified, file the end gap larger with a file secured in a vise. Grip the ring close to the end and work carefully to avoid breaking it.

> *NOTE*
> *When measuring the oil control ring end gap, measure the upper and lower ring rail end gaps only. Do not measure the expander spacer (B, **Figure 97**).*

7. Roll each compression ring around its piston groove (**Figure 100**) to check for binding. Repair minor damage with a fine-cut file.

Piston Ring Installation

1. When installing new piston rings, hone or deglaze the cylinder wall. This will help the new rings to seat in the cylinder. After honing, measure the end gap of each ring and compare to the dimensions in **Table 3**.

> *CAUTION*
> *If the cylinder was honed or deglazed, clean the cylinder as described under **Cylinder Block Inspection** in this chapter.*

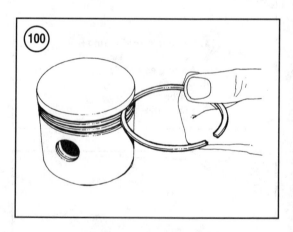

2. Clean and dry the piston and rings.

3. Install the piston rings as follows:

> *NOTE*
> *Install the piston rings with a ring expander tool or by hand (**Figure 96**). Make sure the manufacturer marks face up.*

a. Install the oil ring assembly (**Figure 101**) into the bottom ring groove. First install the expander spacer, then the bottom and top ring rails.

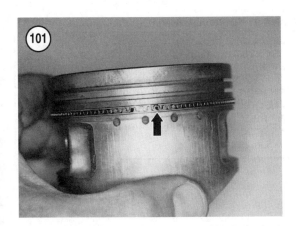

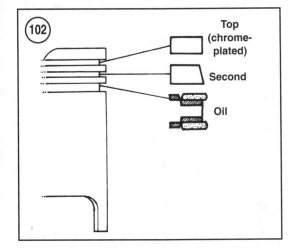

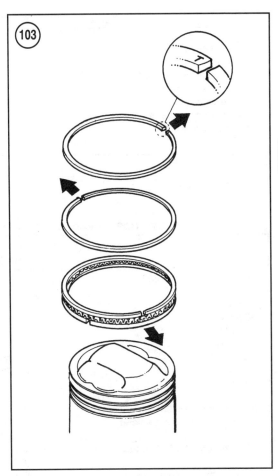

b. Install all rings with the manufacturer marks facing up.

c. Install the second compression ring (**Figure 102**).

d. Install the top compression ring (**Figure 102**).

4. Seat the rings in their grooves and position the end gaps around the piston as shown in **Figure 103**.

NOTE
Do not align the piston ring end gaps with each other when installing the

cylinder; or compression pressures may escape through the gaps.

ENGINE BREAK-IN

The performance and service life of the engine depends greatly on a careful and sensible break-in. For the first 15 miles, avoid full-throttle starts and hard acceleration.

Tables 1-4 are on the following pages.

Table 1 GENERAL ENGINE SPECIFICATIONS

Displacement	397 cc (24.2 cu. in.)
Bore and stroke	85.0 x 70.0 mm (3.35 x 2.76 in.)
Compression ratio	9.3:1
Valve timing (at 1 mm lift)	
Intake valve opens	11° BTDC
Intake valve closes	41.5° ABDC
Exhaust valve opens	40° BBDC
Exhaust valve closes	10° ATDC
Engine weight	38.5 kg (85 lb.)

Table 2 CYLINDER HEAD, CAMSHAFT AND VALVE SERVICE SPECIFICATIONS

	New mm (in.)	Service limit mm (in.)
Cylinder head warp limit	–	0.10 (0.004)
Camshaft		
Cam lobe height		
Intake	30.925-31.025 (1.2175-1.2215)	30.82 (1.213)
Exhaust	30.827-30.927 (1.2137-1.2176)	30.72 (1.209)
Runout	–	0.03 (0.001)
Rocker arms and shafts		
Rocker arm inside diameter	11.500-11.518 (0.4528-0.4535)	11.53 (0.454)
Rocker arm shaft outside diameter	11.466-11.484 (0.4514-0.4521)	11.41 (0.449)
Rocker arm-to-shaft clearance	0.016-0.052 (0.0006-0.0020)	0.10 (0.004)
Sub-rocker arms and shafts		
Sub-rocker arm inside diameter	7.000-7.015 (0.2756-0.2762)	7.05 (0.278)
Sub-rocker arm shaft outside diameter	6.972-6.987 (0.2745-0.2751)	6.92 (0.272)
Sub-rocker arm-to-shaft clearance	0.013-0.043 (0.0005-0.0017)	–
Valves		
Valve stem outside diameter		
Intake	5.475-5.490 (0.2156-0.2154)	5.46 (0.215)
Exhaust	5.455-5.470 (0.2148-0.2154)	5.44 (0.214)
Valve guide inside diameter		
Intake and exhaust	5.500-5.512 (0.2165-0.2170)	5.52 (0.217)
Valve stem-to-guide clearance		
Intake	0.010-0.037 (0.0004-0.0015)	0.12 (0.005)
Exhaust	0.030-0.057 (0.0012-0.0022)	0.14 (0.006)
Valve seat width	1.0-1.1 (0.039-0.043)	2.0 (0.08)

(continued)

Table 2 CYLINDER HEAD, CAMSHAFT AND VALVE SERVICE SPECIFICATIONS (continued)

	New mm (in.)	Service limit mm (in.)
Valve springs Free length		
Inner	37.19 (1.464)	36.3 (1.43)
Outer	44.20 (1.740)	43.1 (1.70)

4

Table 3 CYLINDER, PISTON AND PISTON RING SERVICE SPECIFICATIONS

	New mm (in.)	Service limit mm (in.)
Cylinder		
Inside diameter	85.000-85.010 (3.3465-3.3468)	85.10 (3.350)
Out-of-round	–	0.05 (0.002)
Taper	–	0.05 (0.002)
Warp	–	0.10 (0.004)
Piston		
Outside diameter	84.960-84.985 (3.3449-3.3459)	84.880 (3.3417)
Piston-to-cylinder clearance	0.015-0.050 (0.0006-0.0020)	0.10 (0.004)
Piston pin bore inside diameter	20.002-20.008 (0.7875-0.7877)	20.060 (0.7898)
Piston pin		
Outside diameter	19.994-20.000 (0.7872-0.7874)	19.964 (0.7860)
Piston-to-piston pin clearance	0.002-0.014 (0.0001-0.0006)	0.096 (0.0038)
Connecting rod		
Piston pin bore diameter	20.020-20.041 (0.7882-0.7890)	20.067 (0.7900)
Piston pin-to-connecting rod clearance	0.020-0.047 (0.0008-0.0019)	0.103 (0.0041)
Piston rings		
End gap		
Top	0.20-0.35 (0.008-0.014)	0.50 (0.020)
Second	0.35-0.50 (0.014-0.020)	0.65 (0.026)
Oil (side rails)	0.2-0.7 (0.00.03)	0.9 (0.04)
Piston ring-to-ring groove clearance		
Top	0.0.030-0.065 (0.0012-0.0026)	0.14 (0.006)
Second	0.015-0.050 (0.0006-0.0020)	0.12 (0.005)

Table 4 ENGINE TOP END TORQUE SPECIFICATIONS

	N•m	in.-lb.	ft.-lb.
Camshaft sprocket bolts[3]	20	–	15
Cam chain tensioner screw	4	35	–
Crankshaft hole cap	8	71	–
Cylinder mounting bolts			
6 mm	12	106	–
10 mm[2]	44	–	33
Cylinder head cover 8 mm bolt	26	–	19
Cylinder head nut[2]	44	–	32
Exhaust pipe joint nuts	18	–	13
Exhaust sub-rocker arm shaft[1]	27	–	20
Intake sub-rocker arm shaft[1]	27	–	20
Muffler			
Band bolt	20	–	15
Front and rear mounting bolts	32	–	24
Rocker arm shaft[1]	27	–	20
Spark plug	18	–	13
Sub-rocker arm shaft[1]	27	–	20
Timing hole cap	10	88	–
Upper engine hanger bracket nuts			
8 mm	26	–	19
10 mm	54	–	40
Valve adjust locknut	24	–	18
Valve hole cap	15	–	11

1. Apply a theadlock to the threads as described in the text.
2. Lubricate seating surfaces and threads with engine oil.
3. Apply a thread lock to the threads.

CHAPTER FIVE

ENGINE LOWER END

This chapter describes service procedures for the following lower end components:

1. Cam chain and tensioners.
2. Crankcase.
3. Crankshaft assembly.
4. Transmission (removal and installation).
5. Internal shift mechanism (removal and installation).

Throughout the text, mention of the left and right side of the engine refers to the engine as it sits in the vehicle's frame, not as it may sit on the workbench.

Table 1 lists crankshaft service specifications. **Table 2** lists torque specifications. **Tables 1** and **2** are at the end of the chapter.

ENGINE

Removal/Installation

When disassembling the engine, remove as many engine components as possible from the engine before removing the engine from the frame. This allows the use of the frame as a holding fixture.

1. Before disassembling the engine, perform a compression test (Chapter Three) and leak down test (Chapter Two). Record the readings for future use.
2. Drain the engine oil (Chapter Three).
3. Support the bike on a stand with the rear wheel off the ground.
4. Remove the following:
    a. Fuel tank (Chapter Eight).
    b. Carburetor (Chapter Eight).
    c. Exhaust pipe (Chapter Four).
    d. Under guard (Chapter Fifteen).
    e. Rear brake pedal (Chapter Thirteen).
5. Disconnect the oil pump outlet (A, **Figure 1**) and inlet (B) pipes at the right crankcase cover. Then remove the dowel pins and O-rings (**Figure 2**).
6. Disconnect the drive chain (Chapter Ten).
7. Remove the shift pedal.
8. Disconnect the spark plug cap.

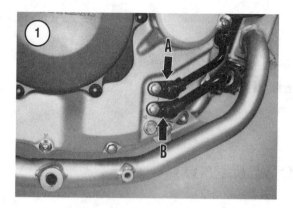

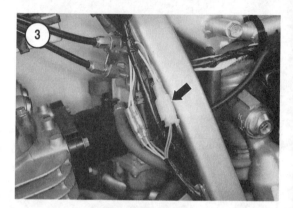

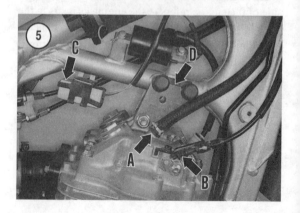

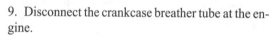

9. Disconnect the crankcase breather tube at the engine.

10. Disconnect the alternator connectors (**Figure 3**).

11. On 1998 and later California models, remove the breather separator (A, **Figure 4**) (Chapter Eight).

12. Remove the ignition control module (ICM) (B, **Figure 4**) as described in Chapter Nine.

13. Disconnect the breather tube (A, **Figure 5**) at the cylinder head.

14. Disconnect the decompression cable (B, **Figure 5**) from the valve lifter arm.

15. Remove the AC regulator (C, **Figure 5**) (Chapter Nine).

16. Disconnect the clutch cable (**Figure 6**) at the right crankcase cover.

17. If the engine is not going to be disassembled, perform the following:

   a. Unbolt the rear brake master cylinder reservoir (**Figure 7**). Reposition the reservoir when removing the engine, but do not disconnect the reservoir brake hose.

   b. Unbolt and remove the right footpeg (Chapter Fifteen).

   c. Remove the rubber caps, nuts, bolts, and the upper hanger plates (D, **Figure 5**).

18. If the engine is to be disassembled, remove the following components before removing the engine from the frame:

   a. Cylinder head (Chapter Four).

   b. Cylinder and piston (Chapter Four).

   c. Clutch (Chapter Six).

   d. Primary drive gear (Chapter Six).

   e. Kickstarter (Chapter Six).

   f. Oil pump (Chapter Six).

   g. External shift mechanism (Chapter Six).

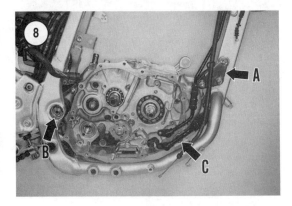

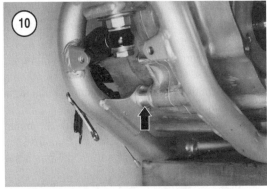

5

h. Flywheel and stator plate (Chapter Nine).

19. Remove the front engine hanger plate (A, **Figure 8**) nuts, bolts, cable guide and plates.

20. Remove the front lower mounting nut, bolt (A, **Figure 9**) and spacer (**Figure 10**).

21. Place a jack underneath the engine and support the engine with just enough tension to remove weight from the swing arm pivot shaft. Place a wooden block between the jack and engine to protect the crankcase.

22. Remove the swing arm pivot shaft nut (B, **Figure 8**) and pivot shaft (B, **Figure 9**).

CAUTION
Enlist the aid of an assistant to re-move the assembled engine from the frame. An assembled engine weighs approximately 38.5 kg (85 lbs.).

23. Pull the engine forward, then out the right side of the frame.

24. Reinstall the swing arm pivot shaft through the frame and swing arm to stabilize the swing arm.

25. Install the engine in the frame by reversing the preceding steps, and note the following:

26. Replace damaged engine mount fasteners.

27. Install the engine mounting bolts from the left side of the frame.

28. Install the swing arm pivot shaft (B, **Figure 9**) from the left side of the frame.

29. Tighten the following engine mount bolts and nuts to the specification in **Table 2**:

    a. Swing arm pivot shaft nut (B, **Figure 8**).

    b. Lower engine mounting nut (C, **Figure 8**).

    c. Front engine hanger plate nuts at engine and frame (A, **Figure 8**).

    d. Upper engine hanger plate nuts at engine and frame (D, **Figure 5**).

30. Make sure the electrical connectors are free of corrosion. Pack the connectors with a dielectric grease before reconnecting them.

31. Fill the engine with the recommended type and quantity of oil (Chapter Three).

32. Tighten the right footpeg mounting bolts to the specification in **Table 2**.

33. Install the shift pedal by aligning the punch mark on the pedal with the mark on the shift shaft (**Figure 11**). Tighten the gearshift pedal pinch bolt to the specification in **Table 2**.

34. Perform the following adjustments as described in Chapter Three:
   a. Decompression cable.
   b. Clutch cable.
   c. Throttle cables.
   d. Drive chain.

35. Make sure the front and rear brakes work properly.

36. Start the engine and check for the following:
   a. Engine leaks.
   b. Clutch operation.

37. If the engine top end, was rebuilt perform a compression test and a leak down test. Record the results and compare them to subsequent tests.

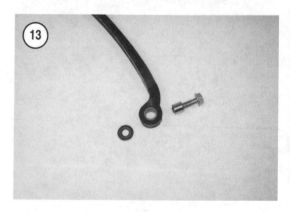

CAM CHAIN, DRIVE SPROCKET AND TENSIONER GUIDES

Removal/Installation

1. Remove the cylinder head (Chapter Four).

2. Remove the primary drive gear (Chapter Six).

3. Remove the front chain tensioner guide (A, **Figure 12**).

4. Remove the cam chain and drive sprocket (B, **Figure 12**).

5. Remove the pivot bolt, collar, rear chain tensioner guide (C, **Figure 12**) and washer.

6. Inspect the cam chain and both tensioner guides as described in this section.

7. Install the cam chain and tensioner guides by reversing these steps, and perform the following.

8. Install the rear chain tensioner guide (**Figure 13**) as follows:
   a. Install the collar and pivot bolt through the tensioner.
   b. Install the washer over the bolt on the backside of the tensioner (**Figure 13**).
   c. Apply a medium strength threadlock onto the pivot bolt threads and thread the pivot bolt into the crankcase (C, **Figure 12**). Tighten the pivot bolt securely.
   d. Pivot the rear tensioner guide by hand. It must move smoothly.

9. Install the cam chain drive sprocket by aligning the wide groove in the sprocket (A, **Figure 14**) with the short teeth on the crankshaft (B).

10. Install the front chain tensioner guide so its lower end seats into the crankcase bracket (A, **Fig-**

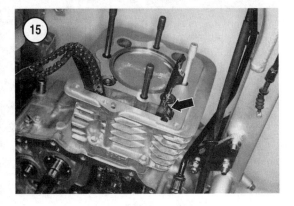

ure 12) and the top end seats into the cylinder notch (**Figure 15**).

Inspection

1. Clean and dry all parts.
2. Check the front tensioner for severe wear, cracks, hardness or other damage.
3. Check the rear tensioner assembly (**Figure 13**) for:
   a. Severely worn, cracked, hardened or damaged tensioner.
   b. Cracked or severely worn collar.
   c. Damaged washer.
   d. Damaged pivot bolt.
4. Check the cam chain for excessive wear, cracks, damaged pins or other damage.
5. Check the drive sprocket for cracks, missing teeth or other damage.
6. Replace worn or damaged parts as required.
7. If the cam chain and both tensioners are worn, check the chain tensioner for damage (Chapter Four).

CRANKCASE AND CRANKSHAFT

The crankcase consists of two halves of precision diecast aluminum alloy. The crankcase is easily damaged due to the thin walled construction. Do not hammer or pry on any interior or exterior surface. Do not pry or scrape on any machined surface. Pay particular attention to protecting the sealing surfaces from damage. The crankcase halves are available only as a matched set and are very expensive.

The crankshaft assembly consists of two full-circle flywheels pressed together on a crankpin. Two ball bearings in the crankcase support the crankshaft assembly.

The following procedure is presented as a complete, step-by-step major lower end overhaul. References to the left and right side of the engine refer to the engine as it sits in the frame, not as it may sit on the workbench.

Special Tools

A press is required to remove the crankshaft from the crankcase. Honda crankshaft installation tools (or equivalent) are required to install the crankshaft into the crankcase. These tools are described during the following service procedures.

Crankcase Disassembly

This procedure describes disassembly of the crankcase and removal of the transmission and internal shift mechanism. Crankshaft removal is covered in a separate procedure.

Chapter Seven describes transmission and internal shift mechanism service procedures.

1. Remove all exterior engine assemblies:
   a. Cylinder head, cylinder and piston (Chapter Four).
   b. Clutch, primary drive gear, oil pump, kickstarter and external shift linkage (Chapter Six).
   c. Alternator (Chapter Nine).
   d. Cam Chain, drive sprocket and tensioner guides (this chapter).

NOTE
To help ensure proper location of the crankcase bolts during assembly, draw the crankcase outline on cardboard and punch holes along the out-

5

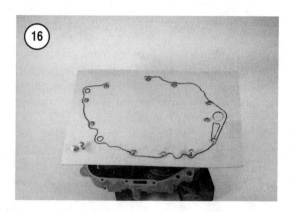

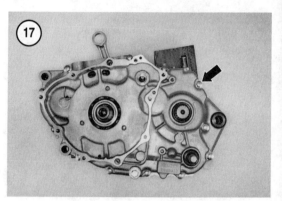

*line to correspond with the bolt
locations. As each bolt is removed
from the crankcase, insert it into its
appropriate location in the cardboard. (Figure 16).*

2. Loosen and remove the left crankcase bolts (**Figure 17**).

3. Turn the engine over and remove the right crankcase bolts (**Figure 18**).

4. Place the engine on wooden blocks with the right
side facing up.

> **CAUTION**
> *Perform this operation over the work-
> bench as the crankcase halves may
> easily separate. Do not hammer on
> the crankcase halves as doing so will
> damage them.*

> **CAUTION**
> *Force is not required when removing
> the right crankcase. Do not pry be-
> tween the crankcase mating surfaces.
> If the case will not come off, check for
> installed bolts or a damaged crank-
> shaft.*

5. Remove the right crankcase (**Figure 18**). Tap the
mainshaft if it is forced up with the crankcase.

6. Immediately check the bearings in the right
crankcase for shims stuck to them. If any are found,
install them on their respective shaft.

7. Remove the gasket and both dowel pins (**Figure
19**).

8. Pull the gearshift plate (A, **Figure 20**) off of the
shift drum, then remove the shift shaft (B) from the
engine.

9. Remove the shift fork shaft (**Figure 21**).

10. Remove the shift drum and shift forks (**Figure 22**).

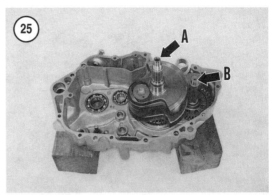

11. Remove the mainshaft and countershaft (**Figure 23**) together. See **Figure 24**.

12. If necessary, remove the crankshaft and balancer shaft as described in the following section.

Crankshaft/Balancer Shaft Removal

Remove the crankshaft (A, **Figure 25**) and balancer shaft (B, **Figure 25**) as follows.

1. Support the left crankcase in a press (**Figure 26**).

> *CAUTION*
> *When supporting the left crankcase in the press, make sure there is enough clearance to press the crankshaft out of the crankcase without the connecting rod contacting the press bed. Pressure on the connecting rod may bend it. Check the setup carefully before applying pressure to the crankshaft.*

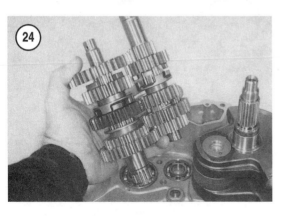

> *CAUTION*
> *Be sure to catch the crankshaft and balancer shaft once the crankshaft is free of the left crankcase. Do not al-*

low these parts to fall to the floor, which may cause damage.

2. Center the crankshaft under the press ram and press the crankshaft out of the crankcase.

3. Remove the crankshaft and balancer shaft (**Figure 27**).

4. Remove the left crankcase from the press.

Left Crankcase Bearing Removal

If the left crankcase bearing (**Figure 28**) came off with the crankshaft, remove it as follows. Do not assemble the engine with the left bearing installed on the crankshaft.

CAUTION
When supporting the bearing splitter in the press, make sure there is enough clearance to press the crankshaft out of the bearing without the connecting rod contacting the press bed. Pressure on the connecting rod may bend it. Check the setup carefully before applying pressure to the crankshaft.

CAUTION
Be sure to catch the crankshaft once it is free of the bearing. Do not allow the part to fall to the floor, which may damage it.

1. Remove the bearing with a bearing splitter and puller (**Figure 29**) or press (**Figure 30**).

2. Discard the bearing.

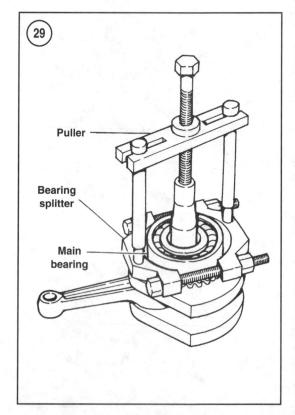

Puller

Bearing splitter

Main bearing

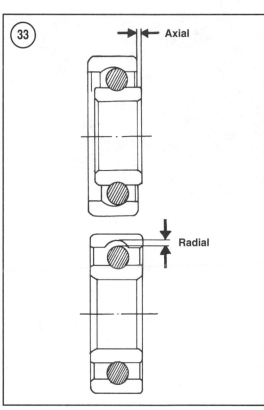

Crankcase Inspection

1. Remove the countershaft seal as described in this section.

2. Remove all sealer and gasket residue from the gasket surfaces.

> *CAUTION*
> *If compressed air is used to dry the crankcase bearings in Step 3, do not allow the bearing to rotate. The air jet can spin the bearing at extremely high speed, which will damage the bearing and may cause it to disintegrate, causing injury.*

3. Clean and dry the crankcase halves and bearings. See **Figure 31** and **Figure 32**.

4. Blow through each crankcase oil passage with compressed air.

5. Lightly oil the crankcase bearings with engine oil before checking the bearings in Step 6.

6. Check the bearings for roughness, pitting, galling and play by rotating them slowly by hand (**Figure 33**). Replace damaged bearings.

> *NOTE*
> *Always replace opposing bearings as a set.*

7. Replace damaged bearings as described under *Crankcase Bearing Replacement* in this chapter.

8. Carefully inspect the cases for cracks and fractures.

9. Check the areas around the stiffening ribs, around bearing bosses and threaded holes for damage. Refer crankcase repair to a shop specializing in the repair of precision aluminum castings.

10. Check the threaded holes in both crankcase halves for thread damage, dirt or oil buildup. If necessary, clean or repair the threads with the correct size metric tap.

11. Check the gearshift return spring pin (**Figure 34**) for looseness or damage. During installation, apply a medium strength thread lock to the pin threads and tighten to the specification in **Table 2**.

Countershaft and Shift shaft Seal Replacement

To replace the right countershaft seal, refer to *Crankcase Bearing Replacement* in this chapter.

Replace the left countershaft seal (A, **Figure 35**) and the shift shaft seal (B) as follows.

1. Pry the seal out of the crankcase with a wide-blade screwdriver (**Figure 36**) or a seal removal tool. Place a rag underneath the tool to protect the crankcase.

2. If necessary, replace the countershaft bearing before installing the new countershaft seal. Refer to *Crankcase Bearing Replacement* in this chapter.

3. Clean the seal bore.

4. Pack the lip of the new seal with a waterproof bearing grease.

5. Center the new seal into the crankcase with its closed side facing out.

6. Press or drive in the new seal until its outer surface is flush with or slightly below the seal bore inside surface (**Figure 35**).

Crankcase Bearing Replacement

1. Different size bearings are used in the left and right crankcase halves. Identify each bearing by referring to its size code mark.

2. Refer to *Bearing Replacement* in Chapter One for general information on bearing removal and installation.

3. Before removing the bearings, note and record which direction the bearing size codes face for proper reinstallation.

4. Use a hydraulic press (**Figure 37**) or a set of bearing drivers to remove and install the bearings. Use a blind bearing remover to remove bearings installed in blind holes (**Figure 38**).

5. To replace the right mainshaft bearing and seal, perform the following:

   a. Unbolt and remove the mainshaft bearing set plate (**Figure 39**).

   b. Press the bearing and seal (**Figure 40**) out of the right crankcase.

   c. Clean the bearing bore.

   d. Install the new seal with its closed side (**Figure 40**) facing out.

   e. Install the new bearing.

   f. Apply a medium strength threadlock to the set plate bolts. Install the mainshaft bearing set plate (**Figure 39**) and tighten the mounting bolts to the specification in **Table 2**.

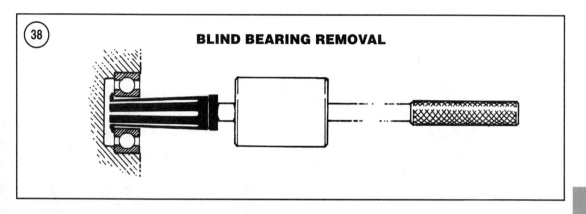

BLIND BEARING REMOVAL

5

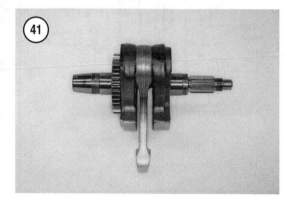

Crankshaft Inspection

When measuring the crankshaft and connecting rod in this section, compare the actual measurements to the specifications in **Table 1**. Replace the crankshaft as an assembly if any part is out of specification or shows damage. Individual crankshaft components are not available from Honda.

1. Clean the crankshaft (**Figure 41**) thoroughly with solvent. Clean the crankshaft oil passageway with compressed air. Dry the crankshaft with compressed air. Lubricate all bearing surfaces with a light coat of engine oil.

2. Check the crankshaft journals for scratches, heat discoloration or other defects.

3. Check the flywheel taper, threads and keyway for damage.

4. Check the crankshaft gear for damaged gear teeth (A, **Figure 42**).

5. Check the crank pin end of the connecting rod (B, **Figure 42**) for signs of excessive heat (blue coloration) or other damage.

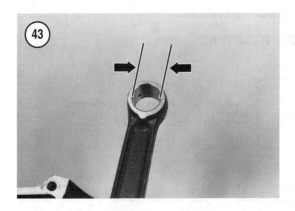

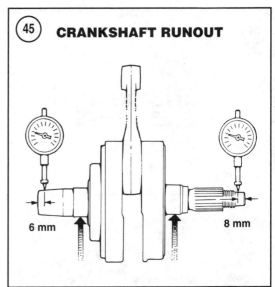

CRANKSHAFT RUNOUT

6 mm   8 mm

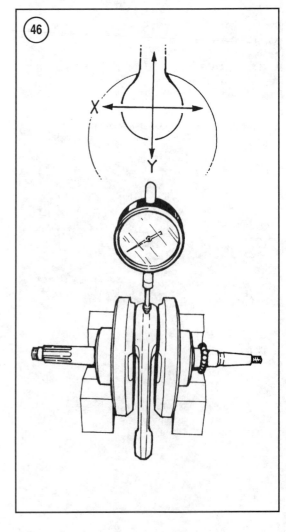

6. Check the piston pin end of the connecting rod for signs of excessive heat (blue coloration) or other damage.

7. Measure the connecting rod piston pin bore diameter (**Figure 43**).

8. Slide the connecting rod to one side and measure the connecting rod side clearance with a flat feeler gauge (**Figure 44**).

9. Place the crankshaft on a set of V-blocks or between lathe centers and measure runout with a dial indicator at the points shown in **Figure 45**.

10. Place the crankshaft on a set of V-blocks and measure the connecting rod radial clearance with a dial indicator. Measure in two directions as shown in **Figure 46**.

Balancer Shaft Inspection

1. Check the balancer shaft bearing journals (**Figure 47**) for deep scoring, excessive wear, heat discoloration or cracks.

2. Check the keyway in the end of the balancer shaft for cracks or excessive wear.

3. Check the balancer shaft gear teeth for cracks or other damage.

4. Replace the balancer shaft if damaged.

Shift Shaft Inspection

1. Clean and dry the shift shaft.
2. Check the shift shaft (**Figure 48**) for:
   a. Damaged splines.
   b. Bent shaft.
   c. Damaged return spring.
   d. Damaged reset spring.
3. Make sure both circlips seat in their grooves completely.

Transmission Assembly Inspection

Refer to Chapter Seven for all disassembly, inspection and reassembly procedures.

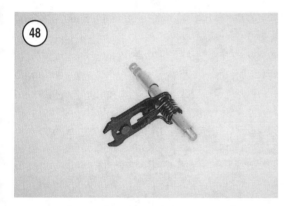

Crankshaft and Balancer Shaft Installation

The following Honda tools (or equivalent) are required to install the crankshaft and balancer shaft into the left crankcase:
   a. Threaded adapter (A, **Figure 49**).
   b. Shaft puller (B, **Figure 49**).
   c. Threaded adapter (C, **Figure 49**).
   d. Assembly collar (D, **Figure 49**).
1. Place the left crankcase on wooden blocks with its inner surface facing up.
2. Lubricate the crankshaft and balancer shaft bearings with oil.
3. Align the timing marks on the crankshaft and balancer shaft (**Figure 50**) and install both parts into the left crankcase (**Figure 51**). Recheck the timing by viewing the index marks on the crank weight and the balancer weight (**Figure 52**). Both index marks must align.

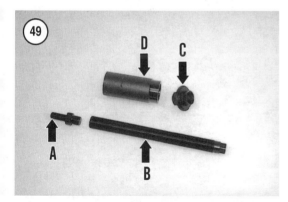

4. Install the threaded adapter into the crankshaft (**Figure 53**).

5. Install the assembly collar, shaft puller and threaded adapters onto the end of the crankshaft (A, **Figure 54**).

6. Secure the connecting rod at TDC with a large rubber band (B, **Figure 54**) to prevent it from contacting the crankcase as the crankshaft is pulled into its bearing.

7. Hold the threaded adapter and turn the shaft puller (**Figure 55**) to pull the crankshaft into the left main bearing. When installing the crankshaft, make sure it is pulled straight into the bearing.

8. Continue to turn the shaft puller until the crankshaft bottoms against the main bearing. Remove the crankshaft tools, rubber band and rotate the crankshaft. The crankshaft must rotate with no binding or roughness.

9. Recheck the crankshaft and balancer shaft index marks again to make sure they align (**Figure 52**).

> *CAUTION*
> *Severe engine damage will occur if the crankshaft and balancer shaft index marks do not align.*

Crankcase Assembly

1. Install the crankshaft and balancer shaft into the left crankcase.

2. If not previously performed, install a new countershaft seal and shift shaft seal.

3. Lubricate the crankcase bearings with engine oil.

4. Inspect the assembly of the following components as described in Chapter Seven. Make sure all washers and circlips are installed in their correct position.

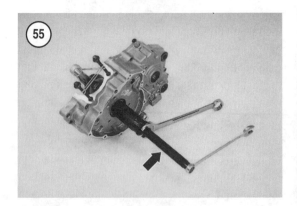

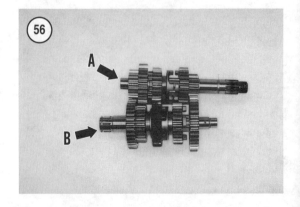

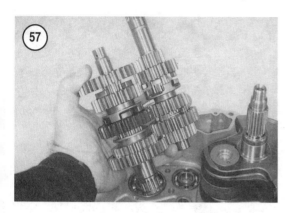

5

a. Mainshaft (A, **Figure 56**).
b. Countershaft (B, **Figure 56**).
5. Place the left crankcase on two wooden blocks.
6. Make sure both crankcase gasket surfaces are clean and dry.
7. Install the transmission shafts as follows:
   a. Mesh the countershaft and mainshaft together (**Figure 57**).
   b. Install the countershaft and mainshaft into the left crankcase (**Figure 58**). Make sure the left washer on each shaft is in place.

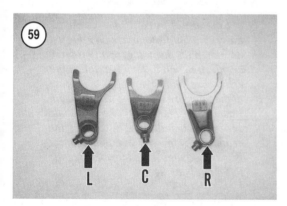

NOTE
To identify the shift forks when installing them in Step 8, refer to the letter mark on each shift fork: L (left-hand), C (center) or R (right-hand) (***Figure 59***).

8. Install the shift forks as follows:
   a. Install each shift fork with its letter mark (**Figure 59**) facing up (away from left crankcase).
   b. Install the L shift fork into the countershaft fifth gear groove (L, **Figure 60**).
   c. Install the C shift fork into the mainshaft third gear groove (C, **Figure 60**).
   d. Install the R shift fork into the countershaft fourth gear groove (R, **Figure 60**).
9. Install the shift drum into the left crankcase and engage the shift fork guide pins with the grooves in the drum (**Figure 61**).
10. Lubricate the shift fork shaft and the three shift fork shaft bores with engine oil.
11. Install the shift fork shaft (**Figure 62**) through the three shift forks. Make sure each shift fork engages with its respective gear and that its pin is in the correct shift drum groove.

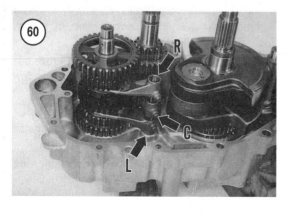

12. Install the shift shaft as follows:

   a. Lubricate the shift shaft spline end with grease.

   b. Pull the shift plate (**Figure 63**) back and hold in position.

   c. Install the shift shaft by aligning the return spring with the pin bolt (A, **Figure 64**) in the left crankcase, and release the shift plate (B).

13. Spin the transmission shafts and shift through the gears using the shift drum. Check the shifting into each gear. Make sure all parts are installed correctly *before* assembling the crankcase.

14. Shift the transmission assembly into NEUTRAL.

15. Install the two dowel pins (**Figure 65**) into the left crankcase.

16. Install a new crankcase gasket.

17. Lubricate all of the shafts and gears with engine oil.

18. Install the right crankcase over the left crankcase. Push it down squarely into place until it engages the dowel pins and seats completely against the opposite crankcase.

CAUTION
When the shafts line up properly, the right crankcase can be installed with-

out the use of force. If the crankcase halves do not fit together completely, do not pull them together with the crankcase bolts. Remove the right crankcase and investigate the cause of the interference. If the transmission was disassembled, make sure no gears are installed backward. If the crankshaft was removed, make sure it is installed and seated properly in the left main bearing.

19. Turn all of the exposed shafts, crankshaft and shift drum. Each component must turn freely with no binding. If everything operates correctly, continue with Step 20.

20. Remove the right crankcase bolts (**Figure 66**) from the cardboard guide and install them finger-tight.

21. Turn the engine over and install the left side mounting bolts (**Figure 67**) finger-tight. Then tighten securely in 2-3 stages and in a crisscross pattern.

22. Torque the right crankcase 6 mm mounting bolts to the general specification in **Table 6** of Chapter One.

23. Rotate the transmission shafts and crankshaft to ensure there is no binding. If there is any binding, remove the crankcase mounting bolts and the right crankcase and correct the problem.

24. Trim the crankcase gasket over the cylinder block opening.

25. Install all exterior engine assemblies as described in this chapter and other related chapters.

ENGINE BREAK-IN

If you replaced the piston rings, installed a new piston, bored or honed the cylinder or performed major lower end work, break-in the engine just as though it were new. The performance and service life of the engine depends greatly on a careful and sensible break-in. For the first 15 miles, avoid full-throttle starts and hard acceleration.

Table 1 CRANKSHAFT SERVICE SPECIFICATIONS

	New mm (in.)	Service limit mm (in.)
Crankshaft runout	–	0.12 (0.005)
Connecting rod		
Side clearance	0.05-0.45 (0.002-0.018)	0.6 (0.02)
Radial clearance	0.006-0.018 (0.0002-0.0007)	0.05 (0.005)
Piston pin bore diameter	20.020-20.041 (0.7882-0.7890)	20.067 (0.7900)

Table 2 ENGINE BOTTOM END TIGHTENING TORQUES

	N•m	in.-lb.	ft.-lb.
Front engine hanger plate nut			
At engine	54	–	40
At frame	26	–	19
Gearshift return spring pin	24		17
Gearshift pedal bolt	12	–	106
Lower engine mounting nut	54	–	40
Mainshaft bearing set plate bolt*	12	106	–
Swing arm pivot shaft nut	88	–	65
Upper engine hanger plate nut			
At engine	54	–	40
At frame	26	–	20
Right foot peg mounting bolts	42	–	31
*Apply a threadlocking compound.			

CHAPTER SIX

CLUTCH AND
EXTERNAL SHIFT MECHANISM

This chapter contains service procedures for the following components:

1. Right crankcase cover.
2. Clutch cover.
3. Clutch.
4. Primary drive gear.
5. Oil pump.
6. Kickstarter.
7. External shift mechanism.

Clutch specifications are listed in **Table 1**. **Tables 1-4** are at the end of the chapter.

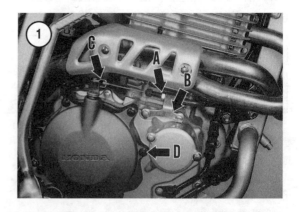

CLUTCH COVER
AND CLUTCH RELEASE ARM

The clutch cover is mounted on the right crankcase cover assembly and can be removed to service the clutch release arm and clutch assembly.

Removal/Installation

1. Drain the engine oil (Chapter Three).

2. Loosen the clutch cable locknuts (A, **Figure 1**). Unbolt and remove the clutch cable holder (B).

3. Disconnect the clutch cable (C, **Figure 1**) from the clutch arm.

4. Remove the clutch cover mounting bolts (D, **Figure 1**).

5. Turn the clutch release arm counterclockwise (**Figure 2**) to disconnect it from the clutch arm spindle, then remove the clutch cover.

6. Remove the two dowel pins.

7. If necessary, service the clutch release lever as described in this chapter.

8. Install the clutch cover by reversing the removal steps, and perform the following:

   a. Replace the clutch cover O-ring if leaking or damaged.

   b. Align the clutch cover with the right crankcase cover. Turn the clutch release arm clockwise (**Figure 3**) to engage its cutout (A, **Figure 4**) with the notch in the lifter piece flange (B, **Figure 4**).

   c. Tighten the clutch cover (B, **Figure 1**) mounting bolts securely.

   d. Fill the engine with the recommended type and quantity of oil (Chapter Three).

NOTE
Debris generated by burnt clutch plates contaminates the engine oil. After replacing damaged clutch plates, change the engine oil and filter. This step is important, even though the engine may be between oil changes, to remove contaminants from the lubrication system.

   e. Adjust the clutch (Chapter Three).

**Clutch Release Arm
Removal/Inspection/Installation**

1. Remove the clutch cover as described in this section.

2. Remove the clutch release arm (A, **Figure 5**) and spring (B) from the clutch cover.

3. Check the seal (A, **Figure 6**) and both needle bearings (B) for damage. Replace as described under *Seal and Needle Bearing Replacement* in this chapter.

4. Check the clutch release arm for damage.

5. Check the spring for cracks, stretched coils or other damage.

6. Lubricate the seal lips with grease.

7. Install the clutch release arm (A, **Figure 5**) and spring into the cover. Align the spring upper end with the hole in the clutch release arm and the spring lower end into the cover notch (B).

8. Install the clutch cover as described in this section.

Seal and Needle Bearing Replacement

1. Replace the seal (A, **Figure 6**) as follows:
   a. Carefully pry the seal out of the crankcase with a screwdriver.
   b. If necessary, replace the needle bearings before installing the new seal. Replace the bearings as described in Step 2.
   c. Pack the seal lips with a waterproof grease, then press the seal into the crankcase until it bottoms out. Install the seal with its closed side facing out.
2. Replace the needle bearings as follows:
   a. Remove the seal.
   b. Remove the upper bearings with a pilot bearing remover.
   c. Remove the lower bearing (B, **Figure 6**) with a pilot bearing remover.
   d. Press in the new lower bearing and then the new upper bearing.

RIGHT CRANKCASE COVER

Right Crankcase Cover
Removal

1. Drain the engine oil (Chapter Three).
2. Remove the rear brake pedal (Chapter Thirteen).
3. Remove the kickstarter pedal.
4. Disconnect the oil pump outlet (A, **Figure 7**) and inlet (B) pipes at the right crankcase cover. Remove the dowel pins and O-rings (**Figure 8**).
5. Loosen the clutch cable locknuts (A, **Figure 1**), then unbolt and remove the clutch cable holder (B).
6. Disconnect the clutch cable (C, **Figure 1**) from the clutch arm.
7. Remove the right crankcase cover nut (A, **Figure 9**) and bolts.
8. Turn the clutch release arm counterclockwise (**Figure 2**) to disconnect it from the clutch arm spindle, then remove the right crankcase cover (B, **Figure 9**) and gasket.
9. Locate the kickstarter shaft washer (A, **Figure 10**). Check the crankcase cover to see if the washer came off with the cover. If so, reinstall it onto the kickstarter shaft.
10. Remove the crankcase cover hollow (B, **Figure 10**) and solid (C) dowel pins.
11. Remove the oil pump O-ring (**Figure 11**).
12. Install the right crankcase cover by reversing these steps, and perform the following.

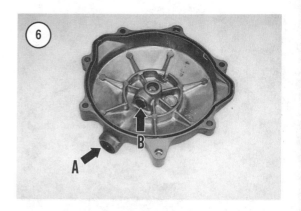

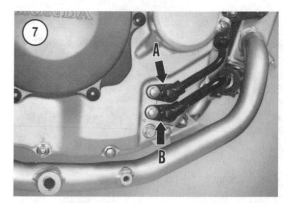

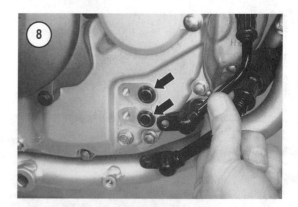

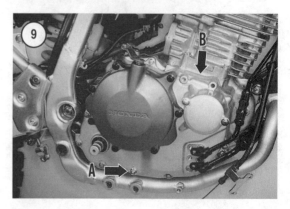

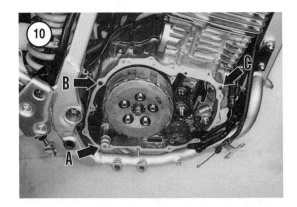

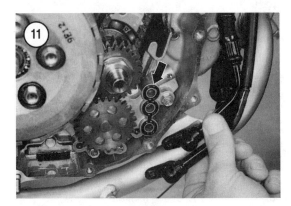

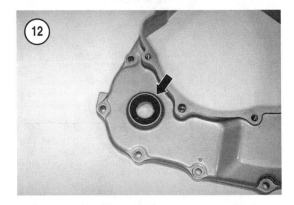

13. Lubricate a new oil pump O-ring and install it into the oil pump groove (**Figure 11**).

14. Align the clutch cover with the right crankcase cover. Turn the clutch release arm clockwise (**Figure 3**) to engage its cutout (A, **Figure 4**) with the notch in the lifter piece flange (B, **Figure 4**).

15. Tighten the right crankcase mounting bolts and nut (A, **Figure 9**) securely.

16. Lubricate the oil pipe O-rings (**Figure 8**) with engine oil before installing them.

17. Tighten the kickstarter pedal pinch bolt to the specification in **Table 4**.

18. Fill the engine with the recommended type and quantity of oil (Chapter Three).

NOTE
Debris generated by burnt clutch plates contaminates the engine oil. After replacing damaged clutch plates, change the engine oil and filter. This step is important, even though the engine may be between oil changes, to remove contaminants from the lubrication system.

19. Adjust the clutch (Chapter Three).

20. Adjust the rear brake (Chapter Three).

21. Start the engine and check for leaks at the right crankcase cover and both oil pipes.

Inspection

1. Clean the gasket surfaces.

2. Clean and dry the right crankcase cover.

3. Inspect the kickstarter (**Figure 12**) and crankshaft (**Figure 13**) seals for damage. Replace the seals if necessary.

4. Make sure the circlip (**Figure 13**) seats in the crankshaft seal bore completely.

Seal Replacement

1. To replace the crankshaft seal, first remove the circlip (**Figure 13**).

2. Pry the seal out of the cover with a wide-blade screwdriver. Pad the screwdriver to prevent damage to the cover.

2. Clean the seal bore.

3. Pack the lips of the new seal with grease.

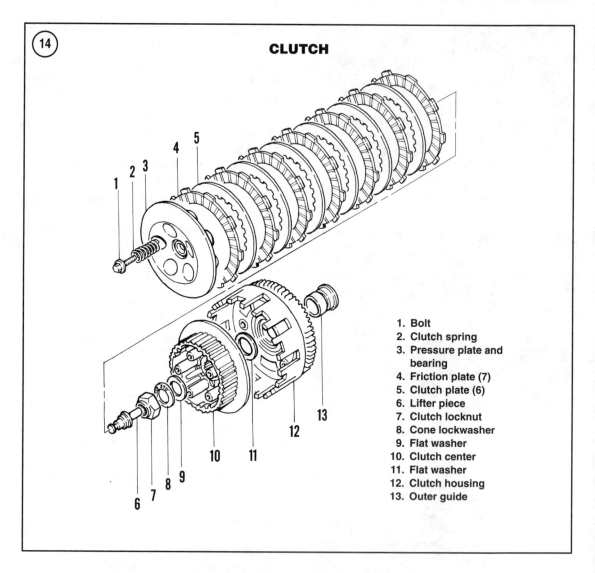

⑭   **CLUTCH**

1. Bolt
2. Clutch spring
3. Pressure plate and
   bearing
4. Friction plate (7)
5. Clutch plate (6)
6. Lifter piece
7. Clutch locknut
8. Cone lockwasher
9. Flat washer
10. Clutch center
11. Flat washer
12. Clutch housing
13. Outer guide

4. Drive the seal into its mounting bore with a hammer and socket or bearing driver until it bottoms out. Install the seal with its closed side facing out.

5. Install the circlip into the crankshaft seal bore, making sure it seats completely.

CLUTCH

Refer to **Figure 14**.

> *NOTE*
> *The clutch can be serviced through the clutch cover opening in the right crankcase cover. This section shows clutch service with the right crankcase cover removed for clarity.*

Removal

1. Drain the engine oil (Chapter Three).

2. Remove the clutch cover or right crankcase cover as described in this chapter.

3. Loosen the clutch spring bolts (A, **Figure 15**) in a crisscross pattern. Remove the bolts and springs.

4. Remove the pressure plate (B, **Figure 15**).

5. Remove the lifter piece (A, **Figure 16**).

6. Remove the friction plates (B, **Figure 16**) and clutch plates from the clutch housing.

7. Unstake the clutch locknut from the groove in the mainshaft (**Figure 17**).

8. Hold the clutch center with a clutch holder (A, **Figure 18**). Loosen and remove the clutch nut (B).

6

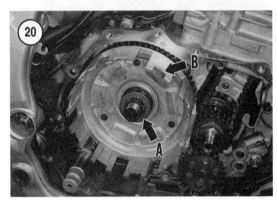

9. Remove the cone lock washer (A, **Figure 19**) and the flat washer (B).

10. Remove the clutch center (C, **Figure 19**).

11. Remove the flat washer (A, **Figure 20**).

12. Remove the clutch housing (B, **Figure 20**).

13. Remove the outer guide (**Figure 21**).

14. Inspect the clutch assembly as described under *Clutch Inspection* in this chapter.

Installation

1. Coat all clutch parts with engine oil before reassembly.

2. Install the outer guide (**Figure 21**).

3. Install the clutch housing (C, **Figure 19**). Make sure the clutch housing gears mesh with the idler and primary drive gears.

4. Install the flat washer (A, **Figure 20**).

5. Install the clutch center (C, **Figure 19**).

6. Install the flat washer (B, **Figure 19**).

7. Install the cone lock washer (A, **Figure 19**) with its OUT SIDE mark facing away from the clutch.

8. Lubricate the clutch locknut threads and seating surface with engine oil. Install the clutch locknut

with its shoulder (**Figure 22**) facing out and finger tighten.

9. Secure the clutch center with the holding tool (A, **Figure 18**) and tighten the clutch locknut (B, **Figure 18**) to the torque specified in **Table 4**. Remove the clutch holder tool.

10. Hold a punch against the clutch locknut nut (**Figure 23**) where it aligns with the flat on the end of the mainshaft. Strike the punch with a hammer to stake the nut into the mainshaft notch (**Figure 17**).

11. Install the friction plates and clutch plates as follows:

    a. Lubricate the friction plates and clutch plates with engine oil.

    b. Install a friction plate (**Figure 24**), then a clutch plate (**Figure 25**). Continue to alternately install the friction plates and clutch plates. The last plate installed must be a friction plate. Install the last friction plate so the tabs seat into the clutch housing grooves as shown in **Figure 26**.

12. Lubricate the lifter piece shoulder with oil and install it into the mainshaft (**Figure 27**).

13. Align the pressure plate and clutch center splines and install the pressure plate (B, **Figure 15**).

14. Install the clutch springs and clutch spring bolts (A, **Figure 15**). Tighten the clutch spring bolts securely in two or three steps, following a crisscross pattern.

15. Install the clutch cover or right crankcase cover as described in this chapter.

16. Refill the engine with the correct type and quantity of oil (Chapter Three).

17. Inspect and adjust the clutch (Chapter Three).

18. Shift the transmission into NEUTRAL and start the engine. After the engine warms up, pull the

6

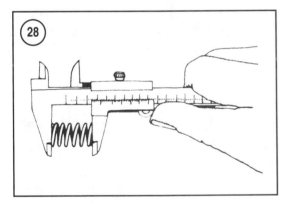

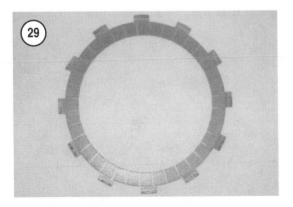

clutch in and shift the transmission into first gear. Note the following:

a. If the clutch makes a loud grinding and spinning noise immediately after the engine is started, either the engine is empty of oil or the new clutch plates were not lubricated with oil.

b. If the bike jumps forwards and stalls, or creeps with the transmission in gear and the clutch pulled in, recheck the clutch adjustment. If the clutch will not adjust properly, either the clutch cable or the friction plates are excessively worn. Replace them.

c. If the clutch adjustment is correct, operate the clutch lever while watching the clutch release lever (C, **Figure 1**) at the engine. The lever should move in and out as the clutch lever is operated by hand.

d. If the clutch adjustment, clutch cable and clutch release lever seem to be working correctly, the clutch may have been assembled incorrectly or there is a broken part in the clutch. Disassemble the clutch as described in this chapter and inspect the parts.

Clutch Inspection

When measuring the clutch and mainshaft components, compare the actual measurements to the specifications in **Table 1**. Replace parts that are out of specification or show damage as described in this section.

1. Clean and dry all parts.

2. Measure the free length of each clutch spring (**Figure 28**) with a vernier caliper. Replace the springs as a set if any one spring is too short.

3. Inspect the friction plates (**Figure 29**) as follows:

NOTE
If any friction plate is damaged or out of specification as described in the following steps, replace all of the friction plates as a set. Never replace only one or two plates.

a. The friction material used on the friction plates (**Figure 29**) is bonded onto an aluminum plate for warp resistance and durability. Inspect the friction material for excessive or uneven wear, cracks and other damage. Check the plate tangs for surface damage. The sides of the plate tangs where they contact the clutch housing fingers (A, **Figure 30**) must be smooth; otherwise, the plates cannot engage and disengage correctly.

NOTE
If the plate tangs are damaged, inspect the clutch housing fingers carefully as described in this chapter.

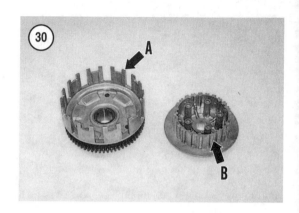

   b. Measure the thickness of each friction plate with a vernier caliper (**Figure 31**). Measure at several places around the plate.

4. Inspect the clutch plates (**Figure 32**) as follows:

   a. Inspect the clutch plates for cracks, damage or color change. Overheated clutch plates will have a blue discoloration.

   b. Check the clutch plates for an oil glaze buildup. Remove by lightly sanding both sides of each plate with 400 grit sandpaper placed on a surface plate or piece of glass.

   c. Place each clutch plate on a flat surface and check for warp with a feeler gauge (**Figure 33**).

   d. The clutch plate inner teeth mesh with the clutch center splines (B, **Figure 30**). Check the clutch plate teeth for any roughness or damage. The teeth contact surfaces must be smooth; otherwise, the plates cannot engage and disengage correctly.

NOTE
If the clutch plate teeth are damaged, inspect the clutch center splines carefully as described in this chapter.

5. Check the clutch housing (A, **Figure 30**) for the following conditions:

   a. Inspect the clutch housing grooves for cracks or galling. Repair minor damage with a file. If damage is excessive, replace the clutch housing. The grooves must be in good condition so the friction plates can slide within the housing.

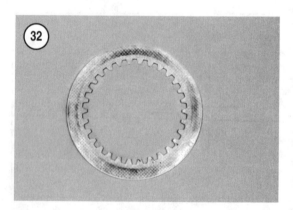

   b. Check the two clutch housing gears (**Figure 30**) for excessive wear, pitting, chipped gear teeth or other damage.

   c. Check the clutch housing bore (A, **Figure 34**) for cracks, pitting or other damage.

6. Measure the clutch housing bore (A, **Figure 34**).

7. Measure the outer guide inside diameter and outside diameter (B, **Figure 34**).

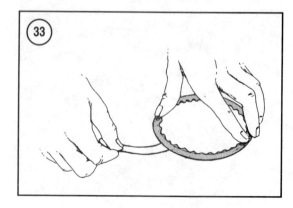

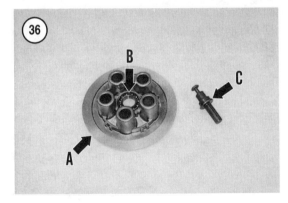

8. Measure the mainshaft outside diameter at the clutch outer guide operating area (**Figure 35**).

9. Inspect the clutch center (B, **Figure 30**) for the following conditions:

    a. Inspect the clutch center splines for rough spots, grooves or other damage. Repair minor damage with a file or oil stone. If the damage is excessive, replace the clutch center. The splines must be in good condition so the clutch plates can slide freely.

    b. Damaged spring towers and threads.

10. Check the pressure plate (A, **Figure 36**) for cracks or other damage. Check the bearing outer race fit in the pressure plate. The bearing must be a tight fit. If loose, replace the pressure plate.

11. Turn the pressure plate bearing (B, **Figure 36**) inner race by hand. If the bearing turns roughly or shows play, remove the bearing with a press and install a new bearing.

12. Inspect both ends of the lifter piece (C, **Figure 36**) for scoring or other damage.

13. Check each washer for nicks, burrs or damage.

OIL PUMP DRIVE GEAR AND PRIMARY DRIVE GEAR

Removal/Installation

1. Remove the right crankcase cover as described in this chapter.

2. Remove the clutch assembly, except for the clutch housing (A, **Figure 37**).

> *NOTE*
> *The primary drive gear and primary driven gear (clutch housing gear) must be locked together when loosening and tightening the primary drive gear nut. The easiest way to lock these gears is with a separate holding gear like the one shown in the following photographs. A large selection of gears, suitable for this purpose, can be found at a motorcycle wrecking yard.*

3. Lock the primary drive and driven gears with a holding gear (B, **Figure 37**).

4. Loosen and remove the primary drive gear nut (A, **Figure 38**) and washer (B).

5. Remove the holding gear (B, **Figure 37**) and the clutch housing (A).

6. Remove the oil pump drive gear (C, **Figure 38**) and the primary drive gear (D) from the crankshaft.

7. Inspect the gears as described under *Inspection* in this section.

8. Install the primary drive gear by aligning its wide groove (A, **Figure 39**) with the master tooth on the crankshaft (B).

9. Install the oil pump drive gear (**Figure 40**) with its OUT mark facing out and aligning its wide groove with the master tooth on the crankshaft.

10. Install the flat washer (B, **Figure 38**).

11. Lubricate the primary drive gear nut threads and seating surface (A, **Figure 38**) with engine oil. Install the nut and finger tighten.

12. Remove the oil pump (C, **Figure 37**) as described in this chapter.

13. Install the clutch housing (A, **Figure 37**).

14. Lock the primary drive and driven gears with a holding gear placed on the bottom side of the gears (B, **Figure 37**). Tighten the primary drive gear nut to the specification in **Table 4**.

15. Remove the holding gear and clutch housing from the engine.

16. Install the following components as described in this chapter:

    a. Oil pump.

    b. Clutch components.

    c. Right crankcase cover.

Inspection

1. Clean and dry all parts.

2. Check the oil pump drive gear and primary drive gear for:

    a. Broken or chipped teeth.

    b. Damaged splines.

3. Check the washer and nut for damage.

4. Replace parts with damage or excessive wear as described in this chapter.

OIL PUMP

Removal/Installation

1. Remove the right crankcase cover and clutch as described in this chapter.

2. Remove the oil pump driven gear (**Figure 41**).

3. Unbolt and remove the oil pump (**Figure 42**).

4. Remove the gasket (A, **Figure 43**) and two dowel pins (B).

5. If necessary, service the oil pump as described in this section.

6. If the oil pump is not going to be serviced, store it in a sealed plastic bag until reassembly.

7. Install the two dowel pins (B, **Figure 43**) and a new gasket (A).

8. Lubricate the oil pump rotors with engine oil.

9. Install the oil pump (**Figure 42**) and its mounting bolts. Tighten the bolts securely.

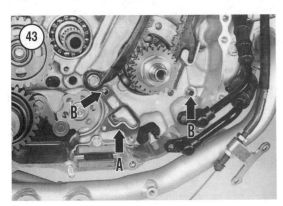

b. Stopper plate.
c. Spring.
d. Relief valve.
2. Clean and dry the parts.
3. Inspect the relief valve and the relief valve bore in the oil pump for scratches or other damage.
4. Inspect the spring for cracks, stretched coils or other damage.
5. Replace worn or damaged parts.
6. Lubricate the relief valve and its mounting bore with engine oil.
7. Install the relief valve (**Figure 46**) with its open side facing out.
8. Install the spring and stopper plate. Install a new cotter pin from the pump body side (**Figure 45**) and bend its arms over to lock it.

6

Oil Pump Disassembly

Refer to **Figure 44**.
1. If necessary, remove the relief valve assembly as described in this section.
2. Remove the two oil pump assembly bolts (A, **Figure 47**) and the pump base (B).
3. Remove the inner and outer rotors (**Figure 48**) from the pump base.
4. Remove the drive pin and shaft spacer (**Figure 49**).
5. Remove the pump spacer and the two dowel pins (**Figure 50**).
6. Remove the pump shaft and drive pin (**Figure 51**).
7. Remove the inner and outer rotors (**Figure 51**) from the body.

Inspection

When measuring the oil pump operating clearances, compare the actual measurements to the specifications in **Table 2**. Replace the oil pump as an assembly if any measurement is out of specification or if a part shows damage.
1. Clean and dry all parts.
2. Inspect the rotors for scratches, scoring or other damage.
3. Inspect the pump body and pump spacer rotor bores for scoring or other damage.
4. Inspect the pump shaft for damage. Check the drive pin holes for cracks.

10. Install the oil pump driven gear (**Figure 41**). Align the flat in the gear hole with the flat on the oil pump shaft.
11. Install the clutch and right crankcase cover as described in this chapter.

Relief Valve Removal/Inspection/Installation

Refer to **Figure 44**.
1. Remove the following:
   a. Cotter pin (**Figure 45**).

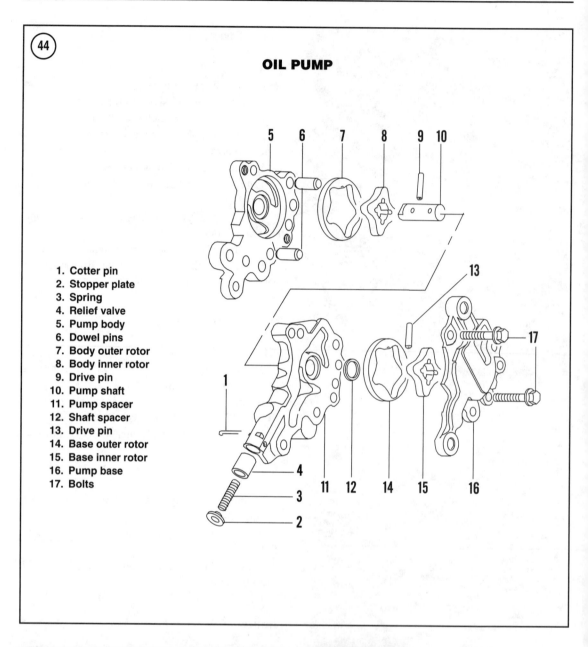

OIL PUMP

1. Cotter pin
2. Stopper plate
3. Spring
4. Relief valve
5. Pump body
6. Dowel pins
7. Body outer rotor
8. Body inner rotor
9. Drive pin
10. Pump shaft
11. Pump spacer
12. Shaft spacer
13. Drive pin
14. Base outer rotor
15. Base inner rotor
16. Pump base
17. Bolts

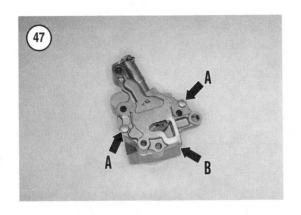

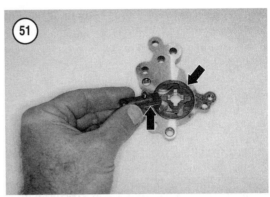

6

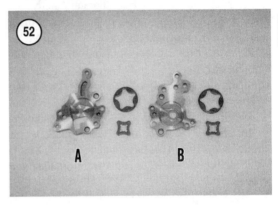

5. Inspect the drive pins and shaft spacer for damage.

> *NOTE*
> *Measure each oil pump operating clearance at several points and compare the largest reading to the service limit in* **Table 2**.

6. Refer to **Figure 52** to identify the rotor sets:
   a. Base rotor set (A).
   b. Body rotor set (B).

> *NOTE*
> *The body rotors (B,* **Figure 52***) are thicker than the base rotors (A).*

7. Install the inner and outer rotors into the pump base. Install the pump shaft and drive pin into the inner rotor (**Figure 53**).

8. Measure the body clearance with a feeler gauge (**Figure 53**).

9. Measure the tip clearance with a feeler gauge (**Figure 54**).

10. Measure the end clearance with a feeler gauge and straightedge (**Figure 55**).

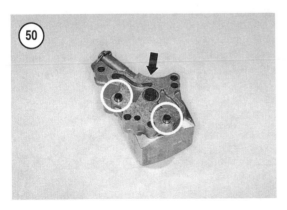

11. Repeat Steps 7-10 for the body rotor set (**Figure 56**).

Oil Pump Assembly

Refer to **Figure 44**.

1. Clean the parts thoroughly and place on a clean lint-free cloth.

2. Lubricate the rotors and rotor bores with engine oil.

3. Install the inner and outer rotors into the pump body. Install the outer rotor (7, **Figure 44**) with its punch mark facing away from the pump body.

4. Install the drive pin into the shoulder end of the pump shaft (**Figure 51**), then align the drive pin with the inner rotor slots and install the pump shaft (**Figure 56**).

5. Install the two dowel pins and the pump spacer (**Figure 50**).

6. Install the shaft spacer and drive pin (**Figure 49**).

7. Install the base inner rotor (15, **Figure 44**) over the drive pin. Install the base outer rotor (14, **Figure 44**) with its punch mark facing away from the pump spacer.

8. Install the pump base and secure it with the two oil pump assembly bolts (**Figure 47**). Tighten the bolts to the specification in **Table 4**.

9. Store the oil pump in a sealed plastic bag until installation.

KICKSTARTER AND IDLE GEAR

Refer to **Figure 57**.

Kickstarter Removal/Installation

> *NOTE*
> *If troubleshooting the kickstarter, examine its mounting position in the engine before removing it in the following steps. Make sure the return spring is mounted in the crankcase hole.*

1. Remove the right crankcase cover as described in this chapter.

2. Remove the washer (A, **Figure 58**) from the kick shaft.

> *WARNING*
> *Wear safety glasses when disconnecting the return spring in Step 3.*

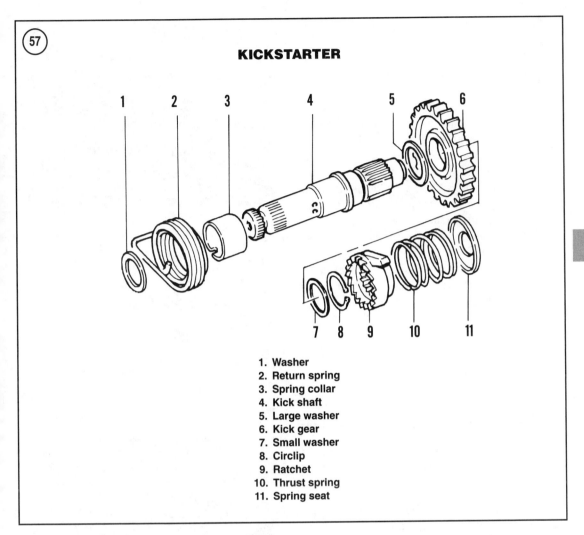

KICKSTARTER

1. Washer
2. Return spring
3. Spring collar
4. Kick shaft
5. Large washer
6. Kick gear
7. Small washer
8. Circlip
9. Ratchet
10. Thrust spring
11. Spring seat

3. Unhook the return spring (B, **Figure 58**) and allow the spring to unwind, then remove the kickstarter assembly.

4. Remove the thrust spring (10, **Figure 57**) and spring seat (11) if they are not on the shaft.

5. If necessary, service the kickstarter as described in this chapter.

NOTE
Steps 6-12 describe kickstarter installation.

6. Check the kickstarter to make sure the return spring end is installed through the hole (or slot) in the spring collar and into the hole in the kick shaft (**Figure 59**).

7. Lubricate both kick shaft ends with engine oil.

8. Install the thrust spring (10, **Figure 57**) and spring seat (11) onto the end of the kick shaft and compress them (A, **Figure 60**).

WARNING
Wear safety glasses when winding and connecting the return spring.

9. Install the kickstarter into the engine so the ratchet guide tab (B, **Figure 60**) seats against the stopper plate (C, **Figure 60**). See A, **Figure 61**.
10. Hold the kickstarter in place and turn the return spring (B, **Figure 61**) clockwise and insert its end into the crankcase hole (B, **Figure 58**).
11. Install the washer (A, **Figure 58**).

WARNING
Wear safety glasses when checking the kickstarter operation.

12. Check the kickstarter and idle gear operation as follows:

    a. Turn the idle gear (D, **Figure 58**) by hand. The idle gear and kick gear should turn freely.

    b. Install the kickstarter pedal. Apply pressure against the kickstarter and slowly operate the kickstarter pedal by hand. Make sure the ratchet operates correctly and engages the kick gear with the idle gear. Also make sure the return spring returns the kick shaft under sufficient spring tension and that the ratchet disengages from the kick gear.

    c. If the gears do not engage or disengage properly, remove the kickstarter and inspect the parts for correct assembly. If the kickstarter was disassembled, make sure the ratchet gear was properly indexed with the kick shaft. See the *Assembly* procedure in this chapter.

Kickstarter Disassembly

Refer to **Figure 57**.

1. Clean and dry the kickstarter assembly.

2. Disassemble the kickstarter assembly in the order shown in **Figure 57**.

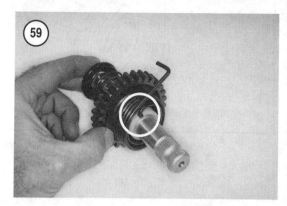

Kickstarter Inspection

When measuring the kickstarter components, compare the actual measurements to the specifications in **Table 3**. Replace parts that are out of specification or show damage as described in this section.

1. Check the kick shaft (A, **Figure 62**) for:

    a. Worn or damaged splines. Install the ratchet onto the kick shaft splines and slide it back and forth. The ratchet must slide freely.

    b. Elongation of the circlip groove.

    c. Elongation of the return spring hole.

    d. Scored or cracked operating surfaces. Install the kick gear onto the kick shaft and spin it by hand. The gear must turn freely.

2. Check the kick gear (B, **Figure 62**) for:

    a. Chipped or missing gear teeth.

    b. Worn, damaged or rounded-off ratchet teeth.

    c. Worn or damaged gear bore.

3. Measure the kick shaft outside diameter at the kick gear operating position (A, **Figure 62**).

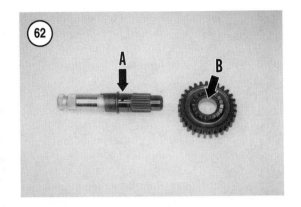

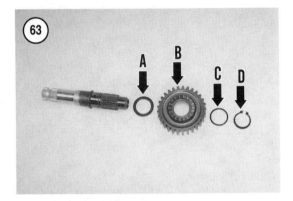

4. Measure the kick gear bore inside diameter (B, **Figure 62**).

5. Check the ratchet (9, **Figure 57**) for:

  a. Cracks or other damage.

  b. Worn, damaged or rounded-off ratchet teeth.

  c. Worn or damaged splines.

6. Inspect the return spring (2, **Figure 57**) and thrust spring (10) for cracks or other visible damage. Check both return spring ends for damage.

7. Check the spring collar (3, **Figure 57**) for excessive wear or damage.

8. Inspect the washers for burrs, excessive thrust wear and other damage.

6

Kickstarter Assembly

1. Lubricate all sliding surfaces with engine oil.

NOTE
Install the washers and circlip with their chamfered side facing toward the kick gear.

2. Install the large washer (A, **Figure 63**) and seat it against the kick shaft shoulder.

3. Install the kick gear (B, **Figure 63**) with its ratchet teeth facing away from the large washer.

4. Install the small washer (C, **Figure 63**) and a *new* circlip (D). Make sure the circlip seats completely in the kick shaft groove.

5. Align the index mark on the ratchet with the index mark on the kick shaft and install the ratchet (**Figure 64**).

NOTE
The kickstarter will not work if the index marks in Step 5 are not properly aligned.

6. Install the thrust spring and spring seat (**Figure 65**).

7. Install the spring collar. Align the hole (or slot) in the spring collar with the hole in the kick shaft (**Figure 66**).

8. Install the return spring end through the spring collar hole (or slot) and into the hole in the kick shaft (**Figure 59**).

Kick Pedal Disassembly/Reassembly

If the kick pedal fails to lock in place after returning it to its lock position, perform the following:

1. Remove the screw (A, **Figure 67**), ball and spring.
2. Remove the kick boss (B, **Figure 67**) from the kick pedal assembly.
3. Replace the seal if damaged.
4. Lubricate the kick boss shoulder with grease.
5. Lubricate the detent spring with grease.
6. Assemble the kick pedal by reversing these steps.

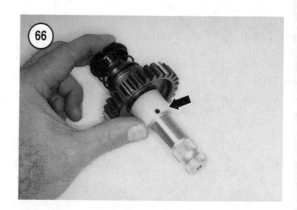

Idle Gear Removal/Installation

1. Remove the right crankcase cover and clutch as described in this chapter.
2. Remove the kickstarter as described in this chapter.
3. Unbolt and remove the stopper plate (A, **Figure 68**).
4. Remove the idle gear (B, **Figure 68**) and bushing (**Figure 69**).
5. Inspect the idle gear as described in this section.
6. Install the idle gear assembly by reversing these steps, and perform the following.
7. Install the idle gear and bushing with the bushing shoulder (**Figure 69**) facing toward the engine. See B, **Figure 68**.
8. Tighten the stopper plate (A, **Figure 68**) mounting bolts securely.

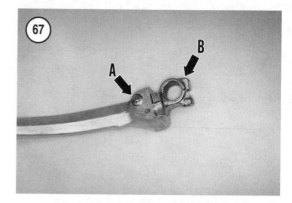

Inspection

When measuring the idle gear components, compare the actual measurements to the specifications in **Table 3**. Replace parts that are out of specification or show damage.

1. Inspect the idle gear (A, **Figure 70**) for:
    a. Broken or chipped teeth.
    b. Worn or scored gear bore.
2. Inspect the bushing inside and outside surfaces (B, **Figure 70**) for scoring, galling or other damage.
3. Measure the idle gear bore inside diameter (A, **Figure 70**).
4. Measure the idle gear bushing (B, **Figure 70**) inside diameter and outside diameter.
5. Measure the countershaft outside diameter at the idle gear bushing operating position (**Figure 71**).

NOTE
If the countershaft outside diameter is out of specification, replace the

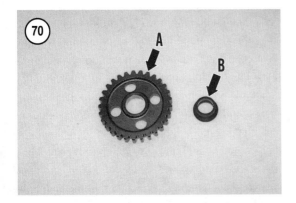

countershaft as described in Chapter Seven.

EXTERNAL SHIFT MECHANISM

The external shift mechanism consists of the stopper arm assembly and shift cam. These parts can be removed with the engine mounted in the frame. The shift shaft is installed inside the crankcase. To service the shift shaft, remove and disassemble the engine (Chapter Five).

Removal

1. Remove the right crankcase cover as described in this chapter.
2. Remove the kickstarter as described in this chapter.

NOTE
The stopper arm and shift cam can be removed with the oil pump and clutch installed. The following steps are shown with the clutch and oil pump removed to better illustrate the procedure.

3. Remove the stopper arm pivot bolt (A, **Figure 72**), stopper arm (B), washer and return spring.

NOTE
Before removing the shift cam and dowel pin (Step 4), place a shop cloth under the shift cam to prevent the dowel pin from falling into the crankcase.

4. Turn the shift cam (C, **Figure 72**) counterclockwise until it stops. Remove the shift cam bolt (C), shift cam (D) and dowel pin.

Inspection

Worn or damaged shift mechanism components will cause missed shifts and wear to the transmission gears, shift forks and shift drum. Replace parts that show excessive wear or damage.
1. Clean and dry the parts. Remove all threadlock residue from the shift cam mounting bolt threads.
2. Check the stopper arm (**Figure 73**) assembly for:
   a. Weak or damaged spring.
   b. Bent, cracked or damaged stopper arm.

c. Bent or damaged washer.
d. Damaged stopper arm pivot bolt.
3. Check the shift cam assembly for:
    a. Excessively worn or damaged mounting bolt.
    b. Excessively worn or damaged shift drum center ramps.
    c. Damaged dowel pin.

Installation

It is easier to install the stopper arm assembly first, then the shift cam.
1. Install the stopper arm assembly (**Figure 73**) as follows:
    a. Assemble the stopper arm as shown in **Figure 73** and **Figure 74**. Note in **Figure 74** that the stopper arm roller faces to the outside of the stopper arm.
    b. Install the stopper arm as shown in A, **Figure 75**. Finger-tighten the stopper arm pivot bolt.
    c. Using a screwdriver, push the stopper arm down and release it. When properly installed, the stopper arm will move and return under spring tension. If the stopper arm will not move, it is not centered properly on the pivot bolt. Loosen the bolt and reposition the stopper arm on the bolt shoulder. Retighten the bolt.
2. Install the dowel pin (B, **Figure 75**).
3. Apply a medium strength threadlock onto the shift cam mounting bolt threads. Set the bolt aside until it is to be installed.
4. Pry the stopper arm assembly away from the shift cam with a screwdriver (**Figure 76**). Install the shift cam by aligning the hole in the cam with the dowel pin (**Figure 76**). Install the shift cam with its raised side facing out.

5. Install the shift cam mounting bolt finger-tight. Remove the screwdriver so the stopper arm rests against the shift cam.
6. Turn the shift cam mounting bolt (C, **Figure 72**) clockwise until the shift cam locks in place, then tighten the bolt securely.
7. Tighten the stopper arm pivot bolt (A, **Figure 72**) to the specification in **Table 4**.
8. Raise the rear wheel off the ground. Check the shifting as follows:
    a. Slowly turn the rear wheel and shift the transmission into first gear, then shift to NEUTRAL and the remaining forward gears.
    b. If the transmission overshifts, the stopper arm assembly may not be installed correctly.
    c. If the transmission does not shift correctly, recheck the shift mechanism.
9. Install the kickstarter as described in this chapter.
10. Install the right crankcase cover as described in this chapter.

CLUTCH CABLE REPLACEMENT

1. Remove the fuel tank (Chapter Eight).
2. Loosen the clutch cable adjuster locknut and adjuster at the handlebar, then disconnect the clutch cable.
3. Disconnect the clutch cable at the clutch release lever.

NOTE
Prior to removing the cable, make a drawing of the cable routing through the frame. Replace the cable exactly as it was, avoiding any sharp turns.

4. Pull the cable out of any retaining clips on the frame.
5. Remove the cable.
6. Lubricate the new clutch cable before reconnecting it in the following steps. Refer to Chapter Three.
7. Install the new clutch cable by reversing these removal steps. Make sure it is correctly routed with no sharp turns. Adjust the clutch cable as described in Chapter Three.

6

Table 1 CLUTCH SERVICE SPECIFICATIONS

	New mm (in.)	Service limit mm (in.)
Clutch spring free length		
1996	45.5 (1.79)	44.4 (1.75)
1997-on	43.2 (1.70)	41.6 (1.64)
Friction plate thickness	2.92-3.08 (0.115-0.121)	2.69 (0.106)
Clutch plate (steel) warpage	–	0.30 (0.012)
Clutch housing bore diameter	28.000-28.021 (1.1024-1.1032)	28.04 (1.104)
Mainshaft outside diameter at		
clutch outer guide	21.959-21.980 (0.8645-0.8654)	21.91 (0.863)
Outer guide		
Inside diameter	22.010-22.035 (0.8665-0.8675)	22.05 (0.868)
Outside diameter	27.959-27.980 (1.1007-1.1016)	27.90 (1.098)

Table 2 OIL PUMP SERVICE SPECIFICATIONS

	New mm (in.)	Service limit mm (in.)
Body clearance	0.15-0.22 (0.006-0.009)	0.25 (0.010)
End clearance	0.02-0.09 (0.001-0.004)	0.12 (0.005)
Tip clearance	0.15 (0.006)	0.20 (0.008)

Table 3 KICKSTARTER SERVICE SPECIFICATIONS

	New mm (in.)	Service limit mm (in.)
Idle gear bore inside diameter	19.010-19.034 (0.7484-0.7494)	19.13 (0.753)
Idle gear bushing		
Inside diameter	14.000-14.018 (0.5512-0.5519)	14.05 (0.553)
Outside diameter	18.959-18.980 (0.7464-0.7472)	18.92 (0.745)
Kick gear bore inside diameter	22.020-22.041 (0.8669-0.8678)	22.12 (0.871)
Kick shaft outside diameter	21.959-21.980 (0.8645-0.8654)	21.91 (0.863)
Countershaft outside diameter at idle gear	13.966-13.984 (0.5498-0.5506)	13.93 (0.548)

Table 4 TIGHTENING TORQUES

	N•m	in.-lb.	ft.-lb.
Clutch locknut[1,2]	108	–	80
Kickstarter pedal pinch bolt	26	–	20
Oil pump assembly bolts	13	115	–
Primary drive gear nut[1]	88	–	65
Stopper arm pivot bolt	12	106	–

1. Lubricate fastener threads and seating surfaces with engine oil.
2. Stake nut as described in text.

CHAPTER SEVEN

TRANSMISSION AND INTERNAL SHIFT MECHANISM

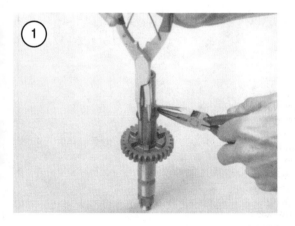

This chapter describes disassembly and reassembly of the transmission shafts and internal shift mechanism.

Table 1 lists transmission gear ratios. Service specifications are listed in **Table 2** and **Table 3**. **Tables 1-3** are at the end of the chapter.

TRANSMISSION TROUBLESHOOTING

Refer to *Transmission* in Chapter Two.

TRANSMISSION

Removal/Installation

Remove and install the transmission and internal shift mechanism as described under *Crankcase Disassembly/Reassembly* in Chapter Five.

TRANSMISSION OVERHAUL

Transmission Service Notes

1. Clean and dry the transmission shafts.
2. As the transmission shafts are disassembled, store the individual parts in a divided container so they can be reassembled in the correct order.
3. Replace all of the transmission circlips during reassembly.
4. To avoid damaging the new circlips during installation them, use the following technique:
   a. Open the new circlip with a pair of circlip pliers while holding the back of the circlip with a pair of pliers (**Figure 1**).
   b. Slide the circlip down the shaft and seat it into its correct transmission groove.

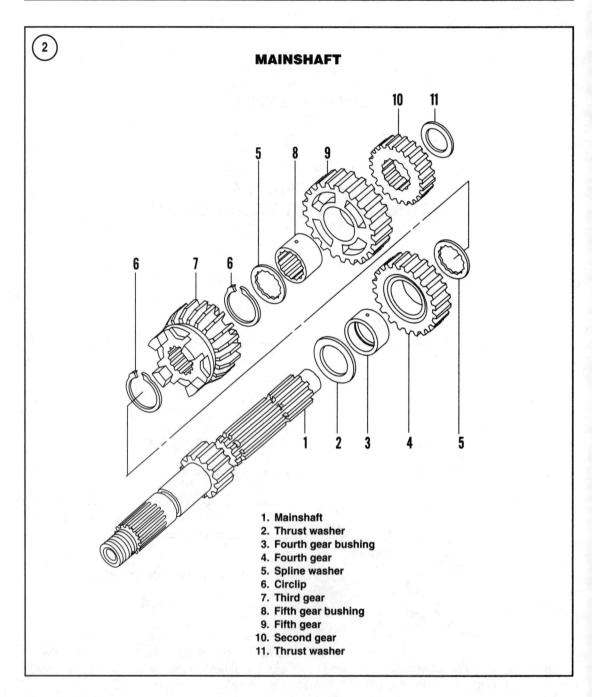

MAINSHAFT

1. Mainshaft
2. Thrust washer
3. Fourth gear bushing
4. Fourth gear
5. Spline washer
6. Circlip
7. Third gear
8. Fifth gear bushing
9. Fifth gear
10. Second gear
11. Thrust washer

Mainshaft Disassembly

Refer to **Figure 2**.

1. Disassemble the mainshaft in the order shown in **Figure 2**.

> *NOTE*
> *First gear is an integral part of the mainshaft.*

2. Inspect the mainshaft (**Figure 3**) assembly as described under *Transmission Inspection* in this chapter.

Mainshaft Assembly

1. Before assembling the mainshaft, note the following:

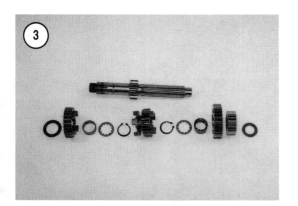

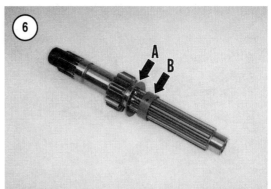

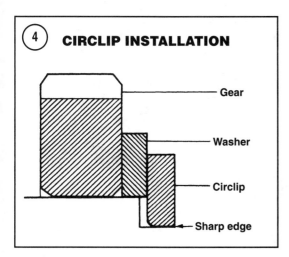

CIRCLIP INSTALLATION

Gear

Washer

Circlip

Sharp edge

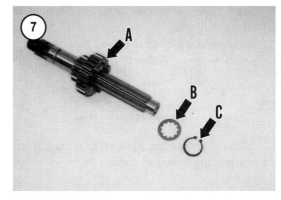

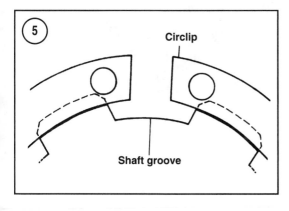

Circlip

Shaft groove

a. Install new circlips.

b. Install the circlips with their chamfered edge facing *away* from the thrust load (**Figure 4**).

c. Align the circlip end gaps with the transmission shaft grooves (**Figure 5**).

d. Lubricate all sliding surfaces with engine oil.

2. Install the thrust washer (A, **Figure 6**).

3. Install the fourth gear bushing (B, **Figure 6**).

4. Install fourth gear (A, **Figure 7**) with its gear dogs facing away from first gear.

5. Install the spline washer (B, **Figure 7**).

6. Install the circlip (C, **Figure 7**) into the groove next to fourth gear. See **Figure 8**.

7. Install third gear (**Figure 9**) with its shift fork groove toward fourth gear.

8. Install the circlip (A, **Figure 10**) into the groove next to third gear.

9. Install the spline washer (B, **Figure 10**).

10. Install the fifth gear bushing (A, **Figure 11**).

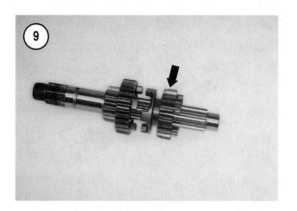

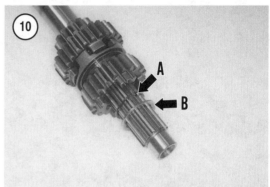

11. Install fifth gear with its dog slots (B, **Figure 11**) toward third gear.
12. Install second gear (A, **Figure 12**).
13. Install the thrust washer (B, **Figure 12**).

NOTE
The gear teeth on both sides of second gear are symmetrical (same shape).

14. Refer to **Figure 2** and **Figure 13** for the correct placement of the mainshaft gears.

Countershaft Disassembly

Refer to **Figure 14**.
1. Disassemble the countershaft in the order shown in **Figure 14**.
2. Inspect the countershaft assembly (**Figure 15**) as described under *Transmission Inspection* in this chapter.

Countershaft Assembly

Refer to **Figure 14**.
1. Before assembling the countershaft assembly, perform the following:
   a. Install new circlips.
   b. Install the circlips with their chamfered edge facing *away* from the thrust load (**Figure 4**).
   c. Align the circlip end gaps with the transmission shaft grooves (**Figure 5**).
   d. Lubricate all sliding surfaces with engine oil.

NOTE
Steps 2-11 assemble the countershaft's right side.

2. Install the thrust washer (A, **Figure 16**).

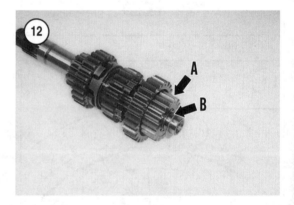

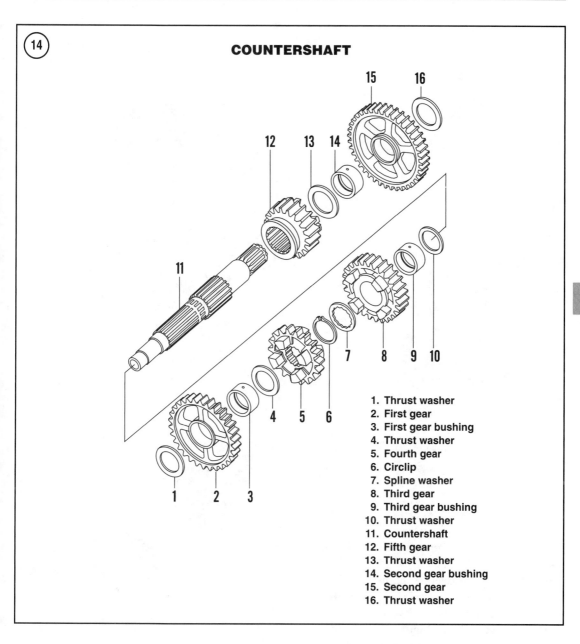

COUNTERSHAFT

1. Thrust washer
2. First gear
3. First gear bushing
4. Thrust washer
5. Fourth gear
6. Circlip
7. Spline washer
8. Third gear
9. Third gear bushing
10. Thrust washer
11. Countershaft
12. Fifth gear
13. Thrust washer
14. Second gear bushing
15. Second gear
16. Thrust washer

7

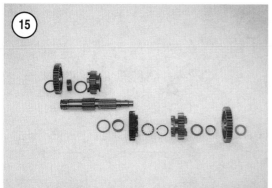

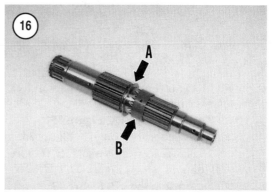

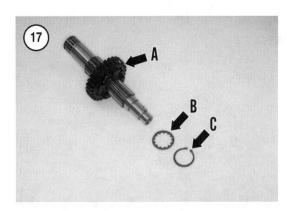

3. Install the third gear bushing (B, **Figure 16**).

4. Install third gear with its gear dogs facing toward the shaft's right side (A, **Figure 17**).

5. Install the spline washer (B, **Figure 17**).

6. Install the circlip (C, **Figure 17**) into the groove next to third gear. See **Figure 18**.

7. Install fourth gear (**Figure 19**) with its shift fork groove toward third gear.

8. Install the thrust washer (A, **Figure 20**).

9. Install the first gear bushing (B, **Figure 20**).

10. Install first gear with its shoulder (**Figure 21**) toward fourth gear. See A, **Figure 22**.

11. Install the thrust washer (B, **Figure 22**).

NOTE
*Steps 12-16 assemble the countershaft's left side (**Figure 23**).*

12. Install fifth gear (**Figure 24**) with its shift fork groove toward third gear.

13. Install the thrust washer (A, **Figure 25**).

14. Install the second gear bushing (B, **Figure 25**).

15. Install second gear with its shoulder (**Figure 26**) toward fifth gear. See A, **Figure 27**.

16. Install the thrust washer (B, **Figure 27**).

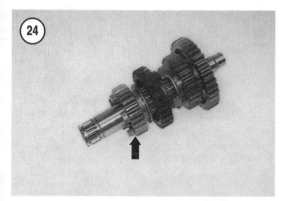

7

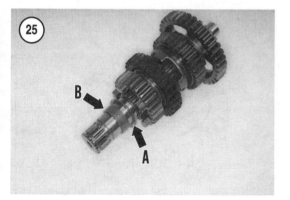

17. Refer to **Figure 14** and **Figure 28** for the correct placement of the countershaft gears.

TRANSMISSION INSPECTION

When measuring the transmission components in this section, compare the actual measurements to the specifications in **Table 2**. Replace parts that are out of specification or damaged.

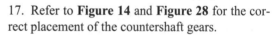

NOTE
Maintain the alignment of the transmission components when cleaning and inspecting the parts in this section.

1. Clean and dry the mainshaft and gears.
2. Inspect the mainshaft (**Figure 29**) and countershaft (**Figure 30**) for:
   a. Worn or damaged splines.
   b. Missing, broken or chipped first gear teeth (mainshaft).
   c. Worn or damaged bearing surfaces.
   d. Cracked or rounded-off circlip grooves.

3. Measure the mainshaft (**Figure 29**) outside diameter at the fourth gear operating position.

4. Measure the countershaft (**Figure 30**) outside diameter at the following gear operating positions:

    a. First gear.

    b. Second gear.

    c. Third gear.

5. Check each gear for excessive wear, burrs, pitting, or chipped or missing teeth. Check the splines on sliding gears and the bore on stationary gears for excessive wear or damage.

6. To check stationary gears for wear, install them (and bushing if used) on their correct shaft and in their original operating position. If necessary, use the old circlips to secure them in place. Then spin the gear by hand. The gear should turn smoothly. A rough turning gear indicates heat damage. Check for a dark blue color or galling on the operating surfaces. Rocking indicates excessive wear, either to the gear, bushing (if used) or shaft.

7. To check the sliding gears, install them on their correct shaft and in their original operating position. The gear should slide back and forth without any binding or excessive play.

8. Check the dogs on the gears for excessive wear, rounding, cracks or other damage. When wear is noticeable, make sure it is consistent on each gear dog. If one dog is worn more than the others, the others will be overstressed during operation and will eventually crack and fail. Check engaging gears as described in Step 10.

9. Check each gear dog recess for cracks, rounding and other damage. Check engaging gears as described in Step 10.

10. Check engaging gears by installing both gears on their respective shafts and in their original operating position. Mesh the gears together. Twist one gear against the other and then check the dog engagement. Then reverse the thrust load to check in the other operating position. Make sure the engagement in both directions is positive and without any slippage. Make sure there is equal engagement across all of the engagement dogs.

NOTE
*If there is excessive or uneven wear to the gear engagement dogs, check the shift forks carefully for bending and other damage. Refer to **Internal Shift Mechanism** in this chapter.*

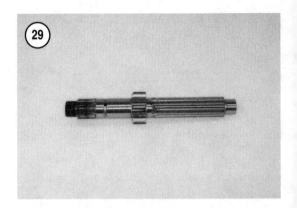

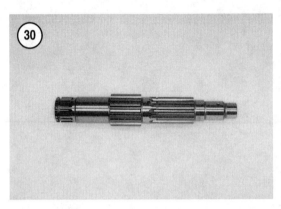

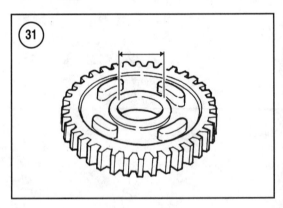

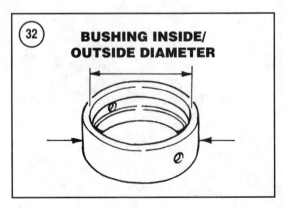

BUSHING INSIDE/ OUTSIDE DIAMETER

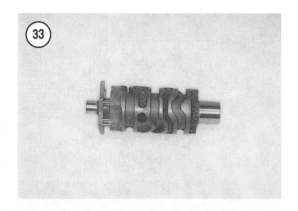

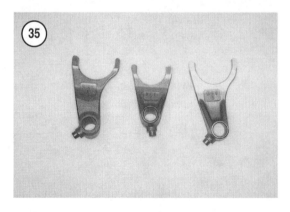

11. Measure the mainshaft fourth and fifth gear inside diameters (**Figure 31**).

12. Measure the countershaft first, second and third gear inside diameters (**Figure 31**).

13. Check the bushings for:

   a. Severely worn or damaged bearing surface.

   b. Worn or damaged splines.

   c. Cracked or scored gear bore.

14. Measure the mainshaft fourth and fifth gear bushing outside diameters (**Figure 32**).

15. Measure the mainshaft fourth gear bushing inside diameter (**Figure 32**).

16. Measure the countershaft first, second and third gear bushing inside and outside diameters (**Figure 32**).

17. Using the measurements recorded in the previous steps, determine the bushing-to-shaft and gear-to-bushing clearances specified in **Table 2**. Replace worn parts to correct any clearance not within specification.

NOTE
Replace defective gears and their mating gear at the same time, though they may not show equal wear or damage.

18. Check the washers for burns marks, excessive thrust wear or other damage.

19. Install *new* circlips.

INTERNAL SHIFT MECHANISM

Removal/Installation

Remove and install the transmission and internal shift mechanism as described in Chapter Five.

Shift Drum Inspection

1. Clean and dry the shift drum.
2. Check the shift drum (**Figure 33**) for:
   a. Scored or damaged bearing surfaces
   b. Worn or damaged grooves.
3. Measure the shift drum outside diameter at its right end (A, **Figure 34**) and compare to specifications in **Table 3**. Replace if out of specification.
4. Measure the shift drum journal inside diameter in the right crankcase (B, **Figure 34**) and compare to specifications in **Table 3**. Replace if out of specification.

Shift Fork and Shaft Inspection

Table 3 lists new and service limit specifications for the shift forks and shift fork shaft. Replace the shift forks and shaft if out of specification or if they show damage as described in this section.

1. Inspect each shift fork (**Figure 35**) for signs of wear or damage. Examine the shift forks where they contact the slider gear (A, **Figure 36**). These sur-

7

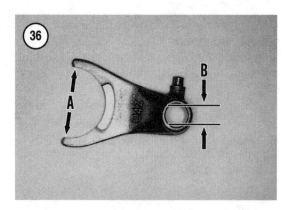

faces must be smooth with no signs of excessive wear, bending, cracks, heat discoloration or other damage.

2. Check each shift fork for arc-shaped wear or burn marks. These marks indicate a bent shift fork.

3. Check the shift fork shafts for bending or other damage. Install each shift fork on its shaft and slide it back and forth. Each shift fork must slide smoothly with no binding or tight spots. If any fork binds, check the shaft closely for bending.

4. Measure the thickness of each shift fork claw (**Figure 37**).

5. Measure the inside diameter (B, **Figure 36**) of each shift fork.

6. Measure the shift fork shaft outside diameter.

Table 1 TRANSMISSION GEAR RATIOS

Primary reduction system	
Type	Gear
Reduction ratio	2.826 (65/23)
Transmission	
Type	5-speed constant mesh
Gear ratios	
First	2.615 (34/13)
Second	1.842 (35/19)
Third	1.400 (28/20)
Fourth	1.120 (28/25)
Fifth	0.926 (25/27)
Final reduction ratio	3.000 (45/15)

Table 2 TRANSMISSION SERVICE SPECIFICATIONS

	Standard mm (in.)	Service limit mm (in.)
Countershaft outside diameter		
At first gear position	19.979-20.000 (0.7866-0.7874)	19.94 (0.785)
At second and third gear positions	24.959-24.980 (0.9826-0.9835)	24.92 (0.981)
Mainshaft outside diameter		
At fourth gear position	21.959-21.980 (0.8645-0.8654)	21.92 (0.863)
Gear inside diameter		
Countershaft first gear	23.000-23.021 (0.9055-0.9063)	23.07 (0.908)
Countershaft second and third gears	28.020-28.041 (1.1031-1.1040)	28.08 (1.106)
Mainshaft fourth gear	25.020-25.041 (0.9850-0.9859)	25.08 (0.987)
Mainshaft fifth gear	25.000-25.021 (0.9843-0.9851)	25.06 (0.986)
Gear bushing outside diameter		
At countershaft first gear position	22.959-22.980 (0.9039-0.9047)	22.90 (0.902)
At countershaft second and third gear positions	27.979-28.000 (1.1015-1.1024)	27.94 (1.100)
At mainshaft fourth gear position	24.979-25.000 (0.9834-0.9843)	25.90 (0.980)
At mainshaft fifth gear position	24.959-24.980 (0.9826-0.9835)	24.90 (0.980)
Gear bushing inside diameter		
Countershaft first gear	20.020-20.041 (0.7882-0.7890)	20.08 (0.791)
Countershaft second and third gears	25.000-25.021 (0.9843-0.9851)	25.06 (0.987)
Mainshaft fourth gear	22.000-22.021 (0.8661-0.8670)	22.10 (0.870)
Gear-to-bushing clearance	0.020-0.062 (0.0008-0.0022)	0.10 (0.004)
Gear bushing-to-shaft clearance	0.020-0.062 (0.0008-0.0022)	0.10 (0.004)

7

Table 3 SHIFT FORK AND SHIFT DRUM SERVICE SPECIFICATIONS

	Standard mm (in.)	Service limit mm (in.)
Shift drum outside diameter at right end	19.959-19.980 (0.7858-0.7866)	19.90 (0.783)
Shift drum journal inside diameter at right crankcase	20.000-20.033 (0.7874-0.7887)	20.07 (0.790)
Shift fork inside diameter	13.000-13.021 (0.5118-0.5126)	13.05 (0.514)
Shift fork claw thickness	5.93-6.00 (0.233-0.236)	5.5 (0.22)
Shift fork shaft outside diameter	12.966-12.984 (0.5105-0.5112)	12.90 (0.508)

CHAPTER EIGHT

FUEL AND EMISSION CONTROL SYSTEMS

The fuel system consists of the fuel tank, fuel shutoff valve, carburetor and air filter. On 1998 and later models sold in California, the emission control system consists of a breather separator and connecting hoses.

This chapter includes service procedures for all parts of the fuel system. Air filter service is covered in Chapter Three.

Table 1 lists carburetor specifications. **Table 2** lists fuel tank capacity. **Tables 1-3** are at the end of the chapter.

CARBURETOR

Removal

1. Place the bike on its sidestand.
2. Remove the subframe (Chapter Fifteen).
3. Turn the fuel valve off and disconnect the fuel hose at the carburetor or fuel tank.

4. Place a fuel container underneath the carburetor drain tube (A, **Figure 1**). Loosen the drain screw (B, **Figure 1**) and drain the float bowl through the drain tube. Tighten the drain screw securely and remove the fuel container. Discard the fuel into a fuel storage can.

5. Disconnect the drain and air vent tubes at the carburetor.

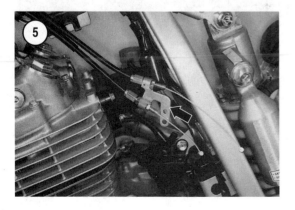

6. Loosen the hose clamp screw (C, **Figure 1**) at the carburetor.

7. Remove the cable holder screw (A, **Figure 2**) and cable holder (B) from the carburetor.

8. Pull the carburetor back and disconnect the throttle cables from the throttle drum (**Figure 3**). Remove the carburetor (**Figure 4**) between the shock absorber and the rear part of the frame.

9. If there is fuel in the carburetor, drain it into a suitable container and then dispose of it properly.

10. Cover the intake manifold and air box openings.

Installation

1. If removed, install the throttle cables onto the cable holder (**Figure 5**).

2. Connect the throttle cable ends onto the throttle drum (**Figure 3**).

3. Install the cable holder (B, **Figure 2**) onto the carburetor by aligning the hole in the cable holder with the fixed pin on the carburetor. Install and tighten the cable holder screw (A, **Figure 2**) securely.

4. Remove the cover from the intake manifold.

5. Align the lug on the carburetor with the groove in the intake manifold (C, **Figure 1**), then push the carburetor into the manifold. Tighten the hose clamp screw securely.

6. Connect the drain and air vent tubes onto the carburetor.

7. Install the fuel hose onto the carburetor or fuel tank.

8. Turn the fuel valve on and check for fuel leaks.

9. Check the throttle cable operation and adjustment (Chapter Three).

10. Install the subframe (Chapter Fifteen).

> *NOTE*
> *If the engine runs roughly after reinstalling the carburetor (seems to run out of gas), check the condition and routing of the carburetor air vent tube. Because the float bowl is externally vented, a pinched air vent tube will reduce the pressure inside the float bowl and slow the flow of fuel.*

Throttle Valve Removal

This section describes removal of the throttle valve assembly (15, **Figure 6**).

⑥ **CARBURETOR**

1. Top cover
2. Screw
3. O-ring
4. Carburetor body
5. Screw
6. Lockwasher
7. Link arm
8. Plastic washer
9. Spring
10. Connect arm
11. Washer
12. Pivot arm
13. E-clip
14. Jet needle
15. Throttle valve
16. Throttle drum
17. Return spring
18. Screw
19. Choke lever setting plate
20. Choke lever
21. Screw
22. Diaphragm cover
23. O-ring
24. Spring
25. Diaphragm
26. Throttle stop screw
27. Knob
28. Washer
29. Spring
30. Pilot screw
31. Spring
32. Washer
33. O-ring
34. Pilot jet
35. Baffle
36. Main jet
37. Needle jet holder
38. Needle jet
39. Float valve
40. Float
41. Pivot pin
42. Drain screw
43. O-ring
44. O-ring
45. Float bowl
46. Screw
47. O-ring
48. Drain bolt
49. Clip
50. Hose
51. Hose
52. Hose

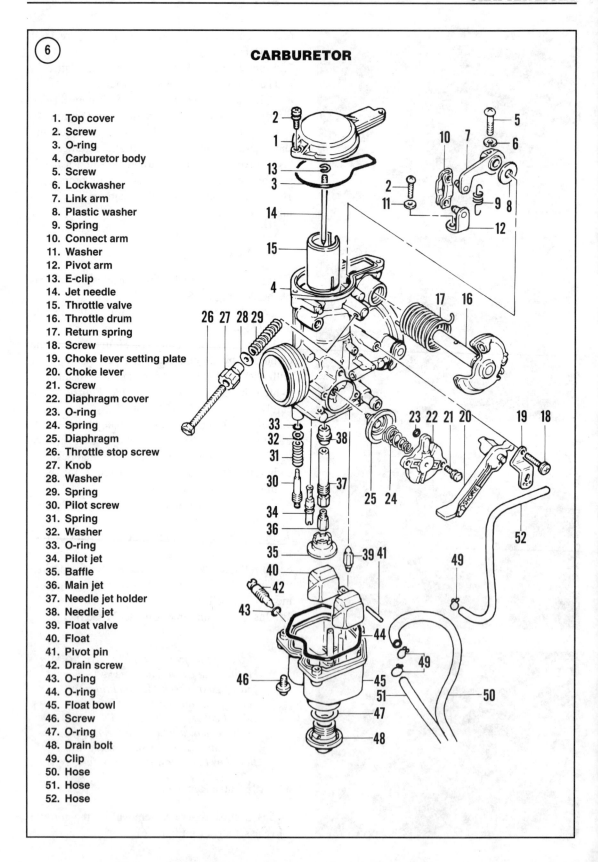

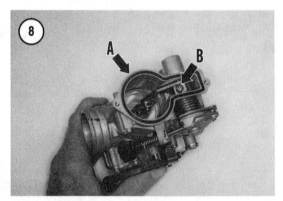

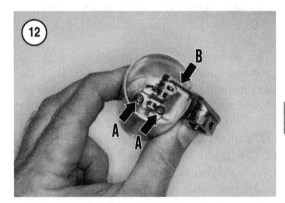

8

1. Remove the carburetor as described in this chapter.

2. Unscrew and remove the top cover (**Figure 7**) and O-ring (A, **Figure 8**).

3. Remove the link arm screw (B, **Figure 8**) and washer.

4. Remove the throttle drum and return spring (**Figure 9**).

5. Remove the plastic washer (**Figure 10**) installed between the link arm and carburetor bore.

6. Remove the throttle valve assembly (**Figure 11**). Do not damage the jet needle when handling the throttle valve.

7. To remove the jet needle:

    a. Remove the two screws (A, **Figure 12**) and remove the link arm (B) from the throttle valve.

    b. Remove the jet needle (**Figure 13**) from the throttle valve.

8. Check the throttle valve and carburetor bore for scoring and other damage.

9. Inspect the link arm for any binding or damage.

10. Inspect the jet needle for wear or other damage.

Throttle Valve Installation

1. If removed, install the e-clip (**Figure 14**) onto the jet needle. See **Table 1** for the jet needle clip position.

2. To install the jet needle:

   a. Install the jet needle into the throttle valve.

   b. Install the link arm (B, **Figure 12**) into the throttle valve and secure it with its two mounting screws (A).

3. Install the throttle valve assembly into the carburetor bore as shown in **Figure 11**, while at the same time making sure the jet needle enters the needle jet.

4. Hook the return spring (**Figure 15**) onto the throttle drum.

5. Install the throttle drum (**Figure 9**) through the carburetor, plastic washer and link arm. Hook the return spring end against the carburetor stopper pin (**Figure 16**).

6. Align the link arm and throttle drum shaft holes and install the screw and lockwasher (B, **Figure 8**). Tighten the screw securely.

7. Turn the throttle drum (**Figure 17**) by hand, making sure the throttle valve moves smoothly.

8. Install the O-ring (A, **Figure 8**).

9. Install the top cover (**Figure 7**) and tighten its two mounting screws.

10. Install the carburetor as described in this chapter.

Air Cut-Off Valve
Removal/Inspection/Installation

   The air cut-off valve enrichens the air/fuel mixture during engine deceleration to prevent engine back-firing. If backfiring occurs during braking and deceleration, check the air cut-off valve and its air passages for blockage or damage.

   Refer to **Figure 6**.

1. Remove the carburetor as described in this section.

2. Remove the screw (A, **Figure 18**), setting plate (B) and choke lever (C).

> *NOTE*
> *The air cut-off valve cover (D, **Figure** 18) is under spring pressure.*

3. Unscrew and remove the diaphragm cover (A, **Figure 19**) and spring (B).

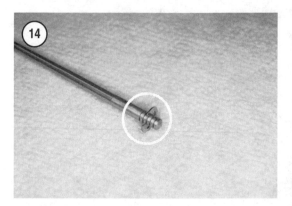

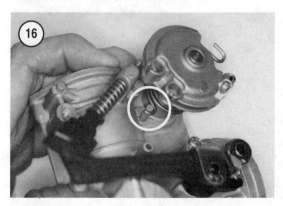

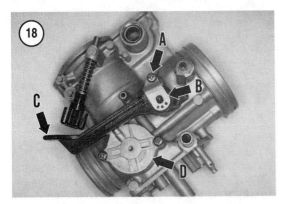

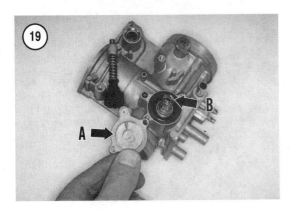

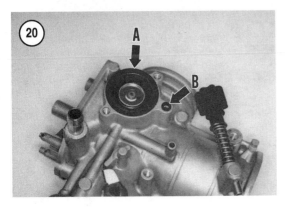

4. Remove the diaphragm (A, **Figure 20**) and O-ring (B).

5. Inspect the air cut-off valve assembly for:
   a. Damaged or deteriorated diaphragm. Check the metal parts for corrosion buildup and damage.
   b. Diaphragm tip wear.
   c. Damaged or stretched spring coils.
   d. Damaged O-ring.
   e. Blocked cover passage holes.

NOTE
If there is corrosion or other contamination in the air cut-off valve chamber, disassemble the carburetor and clean the air passages.

6. Install the O-ring (B, **Figure 20**) with its *flat* side facing the carburetor body.

7. Install the diaphragm (A, **Figure 20**) with its tip side facing down. Make sure the outer diaphragm edge seats in the housing groove completely.

8. Install the spring (B, **Figure 19**) with its tapered side facing away from diaphragm.

9. Install the cover (A, **Figure 19**) and hold in place. Make sure it is not pinching the diaphragm or O-ring. Install and tighten the cover mounting screws.

10. Install the choke lever (C, **Figure 18**) against the choke arm and secure with the setting plate (B) and screw (A). Make sure the plate holes seat over the choke lever balls as shown in **Figure 18**.

11. Operate the choke lever by hand. Make sure the lever moves smoothly and engages in the three different position stops.

12. Install the carburetor as described in this chapter.

Disassembly

Refer to **Figure 6**.

1. Remove the carburetor as described in this chapter.

2. Label and disconnect the hoses from the nozzles on the carburetor body and float bowl.

3. Remove the throttle valve as described in this chapter.

4. Remove the air cut-off valve as described in this chapter.

5. Remove the screws, hose guide (A, **Figure 21**), float bowl (B) and O-ring.

6. Remove the baffle (A, **Figure 22**).

> *CAUTION*
> *The float pin removed in Step 7 should be a slip fit. However, burrs on the pin or pedestal holes may make pin removal difficult. If the pin is tight, be careful not to damage the pedestals during removal. Doing so would require replacement of the of the carburetor body.*

7. Remove the float pin (**Figure 23**), float and float valve (**Figure 24**).
8. Unscrew and remove the main jet (B, **Figure 22**).
9. Unscrew and remove the needle jet holder (**Figure 25**).
10. Remove the needle jet (38, **Figure 6**).
11. Unscrew and remove the pilot jet (**Figure 26**).

> *CAUTION*
> *The pilot screw tip is easily damaged. Do not overtighten the pilot screw when seating it in Step 12. If the pilot screw tip breaks off, removal from the pilot screw bore may be impossible.*

12. Lightly seat the pilot screw, recording the number of turns required for reassembly reference, then remove the screw, spring, washer and O-ring (**Figure 27**). Remove the O-ring (**Figure 28**) if it stayed in the pilot screw bore.
13. Clean and inspect all parts.

Cleaning and Inspection

The O-rings used in the carburetor are not available separately, except the pilot screw O-ring, which is also available in a pilot screw kit. O-rings become hardened after prolonged use and heat, and loose their ability to seal properly. Purchase a gasket kit when overhauling the carburetor.

1. Thoroughly clean and dry all parts. Do not use a caustic carburetor cleaning solvent. Instead, use a petroleum-based solvent and rinse in clean hot water.
2. Dry the carburetor and jets with compressed air.

> *CAUTION*
> *Do **not** use wire or drill bits to clean the jets as minor gouges in a jet can alter flow rate and change the air/fuel mixture.*

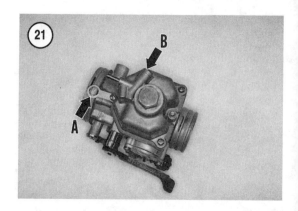

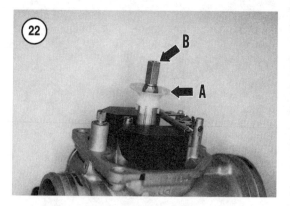

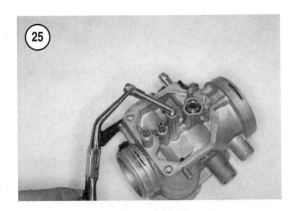

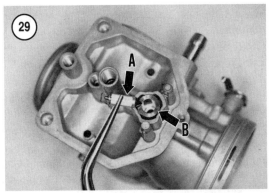

3. Clean all of the vacuum and overflow tubes with compressed air.

4. Replace the float bowl O-ring if leaking or damaged.

5. Inspect the float valve assembly as follows:

a. Check the end of the float valve (A, **Figure 29**) for steps, excessive wear or damage.

b. Push and release the spring loaded pin in the end of the float valve. The pin should compress and return under spring tension. Replace the float valve if the pin is stuck or returns slowly.

CAUTION
*The float valve seat (B, **Figure 29**) is an integral part of the carburetor body. Any attempt to remove or repair the seat will permanently damage the carburetor body.*

c. Check the float valve seat in the carburetor (B, **Figure 29**) for steps, uneven wear or other damage. If the seat is damaged, the float valve is probably damaged also. Replace the carburetor body if the float valve seat is worn or damaged to the point where the float valve cannot shut off the fuel flow when closed.

d. Inspect the float valve seat for dirt or grit that would prevent the float valve from closing. Clean with compressed air.

NOTE
A damaged float valve, float valve seat or a particle of dirt in the valve assembly will cause the carburetor to flood and overflow with fuel.

6. Inspect the float for deterioration or damage. Check the float by submersing it in a container of

water. If the float absorbs water and bubbles appear, replace it.

7. Remove the O-ring, washer and spring from the pilot screw assembly (**Figure 30**) and perform the following:

    a. Insect the pilot screw tip for scoring or damage.

    b. Check the spring for stretched coils or other damage.

    c. Install a new O-ring during installation.

    d. Assemble the pilot screw assembly in the order shown in **Figure 31**.

8. Inspect the choke valve (**Figure 32**) for damage. Replace the carburetor body if the choke valve is stuck or damaged. Do not attempt to remove the choke valve as it is an integral part of the carburetor body.

9. Make sure all openings in the carburetor body are clear. Clean with compressed air.

10. Check the float bowl for fuel sediment and other debris. Clean thoroughly.

Assembly

Refer to **Figure 6**.

1. Install the pilot screw (**Figure 27**) and lightly seat it, then back the screw out the number of turns recorded during removal. When installing a new pilot screw, install and adjust the pilot screw as described under *Pilot Screw Adjustment* in this chapter.

2. Install and tighten the pilot jet (**Figure 26**).

3. Install the needle jet (38, **Figure 6**).

4. Install and tighten the needle jet holder (**Figure 25**).

5. Install and tighten the main jet (B, **Figure 22**).

6. Hook the float valve onto the float (**Figure 33**). Install the float valve into the float valve seat (**Figure 24**).

7. Install the float pin through both carburetor pedestal arms and the float (**Figure 23**). Make sure the float valve is still attached to the float arm.

8. Check the float level as described under *Float Level Adjustment* in this chapter.

9. Install the baffle (A, **Figure 22**) by aligning its grooves with the raised lugs on the carburetor body.

10. Install the float bowl (B, **Figure 21**) and O-ring and tighten the mounting screws securely. Install the hose guide as shown in A, **Figure 21**.

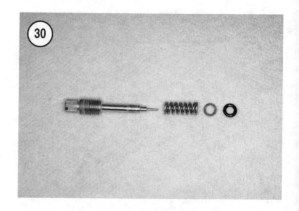

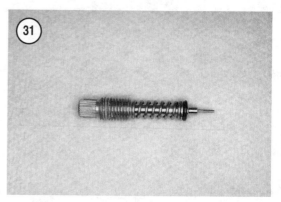

11. Install the cut-off valve as described in this chapter.

12. Install the throttle valve as described in this chapter.

13. Reconnect the hoses onto the carburetor body and float bowl nozzles.

14. Install the carburetor as described in this section.

15. Perform the *Pilot Screw Adjustment* in this chapter if a new pilot screw was installed.

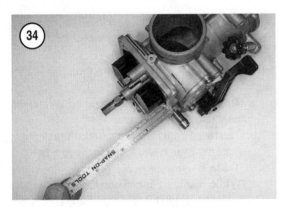

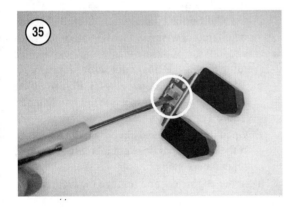

FLOAT LEVEL ADJUSTMENT

The float valve and float maintain a constant fuel level in the carburetor float bowl. Because the float level affects the fuel mixture throughout the engine's operating range, maintain the level within specifications.

1. Remove the carburetor as described in this chapter.

2. Remove the screws, hose guide (A, **Figure 21**), float bowl (B) and O-ring.

3. Remove the baffle (A, **Figure 22**).

NOTE
If the float valve does not seat fully in the float valve seat (Step 4), remove the float valve and check for dirt and other debris in the valve seat. Also check the float valve and seat for damage.

4. Hold the carburetor so the float arm tang just closes the float valve without compressing the spring-loaded pin in the end of the float valve. Measure the distance from the carburetor body gasket surface to the float (**Figure 34**) using a float level gauge, ruler or vernier caliper. See **Table 1** for the float level specification. Note the following:

   a. If the float level is incorrect, perform Step 5.
   b. If the float level is correct, go to Step 6.

CAUTION
The float pin removed in Step 5 should be a slip fit. However, burrs on the pin or pedestal holes may make pin removal difficult. If the pin is tight, be careful not to damage the pedestals during removal. Doing so would require replacement of the of the carburetor body.

5. Adjust the float level as follows:

   a. Remove the float pin (**Figure 23**), float and float valve (**Figure 24**).
   b. Remove the float valve from the bottom of the float (**Figure 33**).
   c. Adjust the float by bending the float arm tang toward or away from the float valve with a screwdriver (**Figure 35**).
   d. Hook the float valve onto the float (**Figure 33**) and install the float valve (**Figure 24**) into the float valve seat.
   e. Install the float pin through both carburetor pedestal arms and float (**Figure 23**).
   f. Check the float level (Step 4) and readjust if necessary. Repeat until the float level is correct.

NOTE
Replace the float if the float arm tang is damaged or misaligned to the point where it cannot be adjusted properly.

6. Install the baffle (A, **Figure 22**) by aligning its grooves with the raised lugs on the carburetor body.

7. Install the float bowl (B, **Figure 21**) and O-ring
and tighten its mounting screws securely. Install the
hose guide as shown in A, **Figure 21**.
8. Install the carburetor as described in this chapter.

PILOT SCREW ADJUSTMENT

The pilot screw (A, **Figure 36**) is preset by the
manufacturer. Adjustment is not necessary except
when the pilot screw is replaced.

WARNING
*Do not run the engine in an enclosed
area when adjusting the pilot screw.
Carbon monoxide gas emissions will
cause loss of consciousness and pos-
sibly death.*

1. Clean the air filter (Chapter Three).
2. Connect a tachometer to the engine following
the manufacturer's instructions.

NOTE
*To detect engine speed variation ac-
curately during this adjustment, use a
tachometer with graduations of 50
rpm or smaller.*

CAUTION
*The pilot screw tip is small (Figure
31) and easily damaged. Do not
overtighten the pilot screw when seating it in Step 3. If the pilot screw tip
breaks off, removal from the pilot
screw bore my be impossible.*

3. Turn the pilot screw (A, **Figure 36**) clockwise
until it lightly seats, then back out the number of
turns listed in **Table 1**.
4. Start the engine and warm to normal operating
temperature.
5. Open and release the throttle a few times, making sure it returns to its closed position. If necessary,
adjust the throttle cable (Chapter Three).
6. With the engine idling, turn the throttle stop
screw (B, **Figure 36**) to set the engine idle speed to
the rpm listed in **Table 1**.
7A. On 1996-1997 models, perform the following:
    a. Turn the pilot screw (A, **Figure 36**) in or out
      to obtain the highest engine idle speed.
    b. Turn the throttle stop screw (B, **Figure 36**) to
      reset the engine idle speed to the rpm listed in
      Table 1.

    c. Open the throttle and check throttle response.
      If the engine rpm does not increase smoothly,
      repeat these steps.
7B. On 1998 and later models, perform the following:
    a. Turn the pilot screw (A, **Figure 36**) in or out
      to obtain the highest engine idle speed.
    b. Turn the throttle stop screw (B, **Figure 36**) to
      reset the engine idle speed to the rpm listed in
      Table 1.
    c. While reading the tachometer, turn the pilot
      screw (A, **Figure 36**) in until the engine speed
      drops 100 rpm.
    d. On California models, turn the pilot screw
      counterclockwise 1/4 turn. On all other mod-
      els, turn the pilot screw counterclockwise 1/2
      turn. This is the final pilot screw adjustment.
    e. Turn the throttle stop screw (B, **Figure 36**) to
      reset the engine idle speed to the rpm listed in
      Table 1.
    f. Open the throttle and check throttle response.
      If the engine rpm does not increase smoothly,
      repeat these steps.
8. Turn the engine off and remove the tachometer.

CARBURETOR REJETTING

Changes in altitude, temperature and humidity
can affect engine performance, as can changes that
affect the engine's ability to breathe: jetting
changes, different exhaust pipes or air filters. To obtain maximum performance from the motorcycle,
jetting changes may be necessary. However, before
changing the jetting, make sure the engine is in
good running condition. For example, if the bike is
now running poorly under the altitude and weather
conditions where it once ran properly, it is unlikely

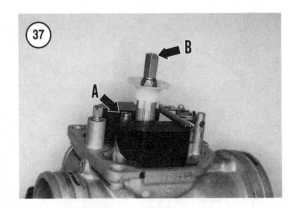

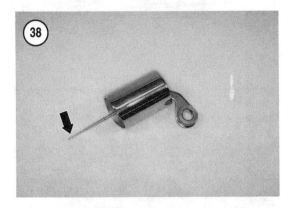

the carburetor jetting is at fault. Attempting to tune the engine by rejetting the carburetor would only complicate matters.

If the bike shows evidence of one of the following conditions, rejetting may be necessary:

1. Poor acceleration (too rich).
2. Excessive exhaust smoke (too rich).
3. Fouling spark plugs (too rich).
4. Engine misfires at low speeds (too rich).
5. Erratic acceleration (too lean).
6. Ping or rattle (too lean).

NOTE
Old gasoline can also cause engine pinging, as can using a gasoline with a low octane rating.

7. Running hot (too lean).
8. The engine accelerates properly but misfires at high speed.

Performance Variables

Before suspecting the carburetor as the cause for any of the previously listed operating conditions,

consider the following conditions, modifications and adjustments:

1. A dirty or nonstandard air filter element can effect carburetor performance; a dirty filter will cause a rich fuel mixture.
2. Incorrect ignition timing will effect engine performance.
3. A plugged or nonstandard exhaust system; a plugged silencer will result in poor acceleration.
4. Modified engine top end components.
5. Intake air leaks will cause the engine to run lean. Inspect the intake manifold, spark plug and cylinder head gasket surfaces.
6. Motorcycle operating in significantly different altitude, temperature and humidity conditions.
7. Fuel is old or contaminated. Old fuel looses its volatility.

Carburetor Variables

The following carburetor parts may be changed when rejetting the carburetor. See **Table 1** for the original carburetor jetting and jet needle clip specifications.

Pilot jet

The pilot jet (A, **Figure 37**) and pilot screw (A, **Figure 36**) setting controls the fuel mixture from 0 to about 1/8 throttle. Note the following:

1. Increasing the pilot jet number provides more fuel.

NOTE
Honda pilot jet sizes are numbered in increments of two or three. When using aftermarket jets, make sure the jet numbers correspond to Honda jet increments.

2. To adjust the idle mixture, refer to *Pilot Screw Adjustment* in this chapter.

Jet needle

The jet needle (**Figure 38**) controls the mixture, from a point just past idle speed to the point just short of full throttle. At full throttle, the jet needle is raised all the way up and the main jet controls fuel flow. While the jet needle is fixed in position by the clip, fuel cannot flow through the space between the needle jet and jet needle until the throttle valve is

8

raised. As the throttle valve is raised, the jet needle's tapered portion moves out of the needle jet. The grooves permit adjustment of the air/fuel mixture. If the clip is raised (thus dropping the needle deeper into the jet), the mixture will be leaner; lowering the clip (raising the needle) will result in a richer mixture. See **Figure 39**.

Main jet

The main jet (B, **Figure 37**) controls the mixture from 3/4 to full throttle, and has some effect at lesser throttle openings. Each main jet is stamped with a number. Larger numbers provide more fuel; smaller numbers provide less fuel. The main jet can be replaced through the bolt in the bottom of the float bowl.

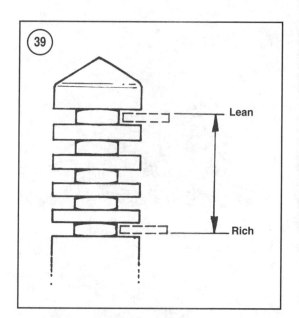

FUEL TANK

Table 2 lists fuel tank capacity for XR400R fuel tanks.

Removal/Installation

> **WARNING**
> *Some fuel may spill from the fuel tank and hose when performing this procedure. Because gasoline is extremely flammable, perform this procedure outside and away from all open flames (including pilot lights) and sparks. Do not smoke or allow anyone to smoke in the work area. Always work in a well-ventilated area. Wipe up spills immediately.*

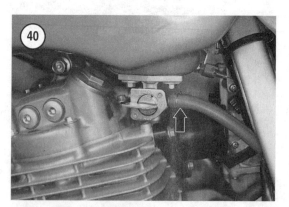

1. Support the bike securely.
2. Remove the seat (Chapter Fifteen).
3. Turn the fuel valve off and disconnect the fuel line (**Figure 40**) at the fuel tank.
4. Disconnect the mounting strap (**Figure 41**).
5. Pull the fuel tank vent tube (A, **Figure 42**) free from inside the steering stem.
6. Remove the fuel tank mounting bolts (B, **Figure 42**) and remove the fuel tank (C).
7. Check for loose, missing or damaged fuel tank brackets and rubber dampers. Tighten or replace parts as required.
8. Replace the heat cover (**Figure 43**) if damaged.

9. Reverse these steps to install the fuel tank, and perform the following:
   a. Check the throttle cables and wiring harness for proper routing.
   b. Secure each fuel hose end with a clamp.

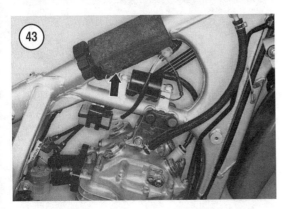

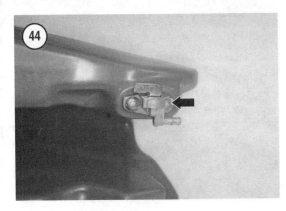

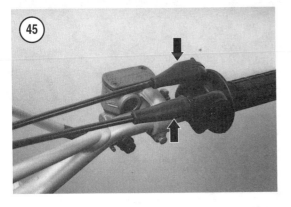

c. Insert the fuel tank vent tube end into the steering stem.

d. After reconnecting the fuel hose, turn the fuel valve on and check for leaks.

FUEL SHUTOFF VALVE

Removal/Installation

WARNING
Some fuel may spill from the fuel tank and hose when performing this procedure. Because gasoline is extremely flammable, perform this procedure outside and away from all open flames (including pilot lights) and sparks. Do not smoke or allow anyone to smoke in the work area. Always work in a well-ventilated area. Wipe up spills immediately.

1. Remove the fuel tank as described in this chapter.

2. Drain the fuel into a fuel storage container.

3. Remove the bolts and washers and remove the fuel shutoff valve (**Figure 44**).

4. Inspect the fuel screen for contamination, tearing or other damage. Replace the screen if it cannot be cleaned or if it is damaged. Use a new O-ring when installing the screen.

5. Reassemble the valve and install it on the tank. Remember to install the O-ring between the valve and tank.

6. Install the fuel tank as described in this chapter.

7. Add a small amount of fuel to the tank and check for leaks.

THROTTLE CABLE REPLACEMENT

The XR400 is equipped with a dual throttle cable arrangement. Replace both cables at the same time.

1. Support the bike on a workstand.

2. Remove the fuel tank as described in this chapter.

3. Make a drawing of the throttle cable routing from the throttle housing to the carburetor. Note the positions of any cable clips or guides.

4. Identify the two throttle cables at the throttle housing (**Figure 45**) and carburetor ends (**Figure 46**).

5. Pull the rubber cover away from the cable adjusters at the handlebar (**Figure 45**).

6. Unscrew and remove the lower throttle housing cover (A, **Figure 47**).

7. Unscrew and remove the front cable cover (B, **Figure 47**).

8. Unscrew and remove the rear cable cover and throttle wheel (**Figure 48**).

9. Loosen the throttle cable adjusters at the throttle housing (**Figure 49**). Disconnect the cables at the throttle (**Figure 50**) and carburetor.

10. Disconnect the throttle cables from any cable clips or guides.

11. Unscrew the throttle cable adjusters (**Figure 49**) at the throttle housing and remove the throttle cables.

12. Lubricate the new cables as described in Chapter Three. Wipe up any excessive cable lube from the bottom of the cables.

13. Install the new throttle cables through the frame, routing them from the handlebar to carburetor. Secure the cable with any frame clips or guides.

14. Refer to your notes to identify the front and rear cables and connect the cables at the carburetor.

15. Apply grease to the groove in the throttle (**Figure 50**).

16. Reconnect the throttle cables to the throttle (**Figure 50**). Thread the cable adjusters into the throttle housing (**Figure 49**).

17. Install the throttle wheel, rear cable cover (**Figure 48**) and tighten the mounting screw.

18. Install the front cable cover (B, **Figure 47**) and tighten the mounting screw.

19. Install the lower throttle housing cover (A, **Figure 47**) and mounting screws. Align the slit in the housing cover with the punch mark on the handlebar (**Figure 51**). Tighten the front mounting screw, then the rear mounting screw.

20. Check the throttle operation and adjust the throttle cable free play as described in Chapter Three. Tighten the cable adjuster locknuts.

21. Slide the rubber covers over the cable adjusters (**Figure 45**).

22. Install the fuel tank as described in this chapter.

23. Operate the throttle lever and make sure the carburetor cables, twist grip and throttle valve are operating correctly. If throttle operation is sluggish, check the cable routing, mounting and adjustment.

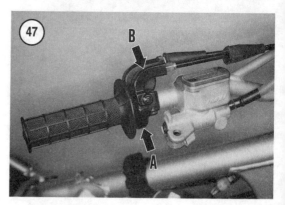

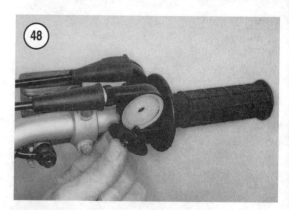

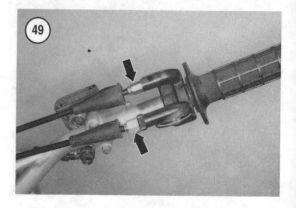

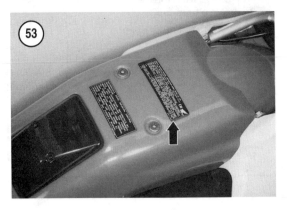

AIR BOX

Removal/Installation

1. Support the bike on its sidestand.

2. Disconnect the subframe from the frame and pivot it rearward (Chapter Fifteen).

3. Remove the bolts securing the air box to the subframe. Remove the air box (**Figure 52**).

4. Inspect the air boot to make sure it is sealing properly and no dirt is passing through the air filter. If there is dirt inside the air boot, check the boot and air filter for damage. If necessary, remove the air filter (Chapter Three) and clean the air box and boot thoroughly.

5. Inspect the air boot where it attached to the air box for loose mounting nuts, a damaged clamp or damaged hose.

6. Install the air box by reversing these removal steps.

EMISSION CONTROL
(1998-ON CALIFORNIA MODELS)

These models are equipped with an exhaust emission control system and a crankcase emission control system.

The exhaust emission control system consists of a lean pilot screw carburetor setting. The pilot screw adjustment position is preset and should not be adjusted unless the pilot screw is replaced. Refer to *Pilot Screw Adjustment* in this chapter.

The crankcase emission control system is a closed system that prevents crankcase vapors from discharging into the atmosphere. Blow-by gas that enters the crankcase is returned to the carburetor through a breather separator and air cleaner connecting tube.

Emission Control Label

An emission control label (**Figure 53**) is mounted on the rear fender.

Breather Separator
Removal/Installation

1. Disconnect the crankcase breather tube (A, **Figure 54**) at the breather separator.

2. Disconnect the breather separator drain tube (B, **Figure 54**) at the breather separator.

3. Disconnect the crankcase breather tube at the crankcase.

4. Unbolt and remove the breather separator (C, **Figure 54**).

5. Install by reversing these removal steps. Secure each hose end with a clamp.

Inspection

1. Inspect the breather separator housing and replace if cracked or damaged.

2. Replace damaged hoses.

Table 1   CARBURETOR SPECIFICATIONS

Carburetor	Keihin
Carburetor identification number	
1998-1997	PDK 1A
1998	
49-state	PDK 1C
California	PDK 1E
Main jet	
1996-1997	
Standard setting	162
Suggested jet for trail riding with noise suppressor and exhaust diffuser installed	158
1998-on	142
Pilot jet	
1996-1997	
Standard setting	62
Suggested jet for trail riding with noise suppressor and exhaust diffuser installed	60
1998-on	52
Jet needle clip position	
1996-1997	
Standard setting	3rd groove from top
Suggested clip position for trail riding with noise suppressor and exhaust diffuser installed	2nd groove from top
1998-on	3rd groove from top
Float level	14.5 mm (0.57 in.)
Idle speed	1,200-1,400 rpm
Pilot screw adjustment*	
1996-1997	
Initial opening	2 1/4 turns out
1998-on	
Initial opening	
California models	1 5/8 turns out
All other models	1 1/2 turns out
Final opening	
California models	1/4 turn out
All other models	1/2 turn out
*See text for adjustment procedure.	

Table 2 FUEL TANK CAPACITY

	Liters	U.S. gal	Imp gal.
Full	9.5	2.5	2.1
Reserve	1.5	0.4	0.3

Table 3 TIGHTENING TORQUES

	N•m	in.-lb.	ft.-lb.
Fuel valve mounting bolt	9	80	–
Sub-frame mounting bolts			
Upper	26	–	19
Lower	42	–	31

8

ELECTRICAL SYSTEM

This chapter describes component testing and service procedures for the electrical system. To troubleshoot the electrical system, refer to Chapter Two.

Electrical system specifications are found in **Table 1**. Headlight and taillight bulb types are listed in **Table 2**. **Tables 1-3** are found at the end of the chapter.

COMPONENT TESTING

Resistance Testing

Resistance tests are performed after disconnecting the component from the main wiring harness. It is not necessary to remove the part to test it. Instead, locate and disconnect the part's wiring connectors.

When using an ohmmeter, follow the manufacturer's instruction manual, while keeping the following guidelines in mind:

1. Make sure the test leads are connected properly.

2. Take all ohmmeter readings when the engine is cold (ambient temperature of 68° F/20° C). Readings taken on a hot engine will show increased resistance caused by engine heat and may lead to unnecessary parts replacement.

NOTE
With the exception of certain semiconductors, the resistance of a conductor increases as its temperature increases. In general, the resistance of a conductor rises 10 ohms per each degree of temperature change. The opposite is true if the temperature drops. To ensure accurate testing, Honda performs their tests at a controlled temperature of 68° F/20° C and bases their specifications on tests performed at this temperature.

3. When using an analog ohmmeter and switching between ohmmeter scales, always cross the test leads and zero the needle to assure a correct reading.

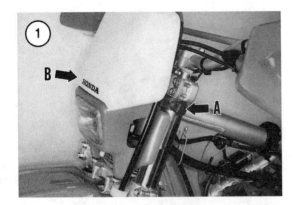

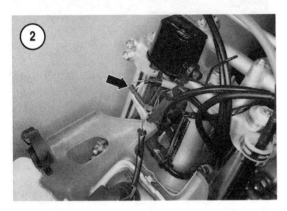

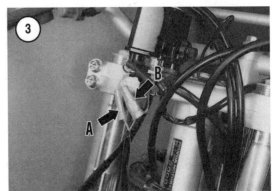

AC LIGHTING SYSTEM TESTING

An AC regulator controls the lighting system current. This system controls the alternator output to provide a consistent voltage. See *AC Regulator* in this chapter.

Troubleshooting

To troubleshoot the AC lighting system, refer to *AC Lighting System Troubleshooting* in Chapter Two and perform the test in this chapter.

Regulated Voltage Test

This section tests the integrity of the AC lighting system and requires a tachometer and voltmeter.
1. Start the engine and warm up to normal operating temperature, then shut the engine off.
2. Disconnect the front visor straps (A, **Figure 1**) and pivot the front visor (B, **Figure 1**) forward. Leave the electrical connectors attached (**Figure 2**).
3. Connect a positive voltmeter lead to the blue wire connector (A, **Figure 3**). Connect the negative lead to the green connector (B, **Figure 3**). Switch the voltmeter to its AC range. Make sure the meter leads do not touch or short across the other wires.
4. Connect a tachometer to the engine following the manufacturer's instructions.
5. Start the engine and slowly increase the engine speed to 3,000 rpm. The correct regulated voltage reading is 12.5-13.5 volts at 3,000 rpm. At this speed, the AC regulator should prevent any increase in voltage. Turn the engine off and interpret the results as specified in Steps 6-9.
6. If the regulated voltage reading is correct, the lighting circuit is working correctly.
7. If the regulated voltage reading is too low, check the lighting coil resistance as described under *Wiring Harness Test* and *Lighting Coil Resistance Test* in this chapter.
8. If the regulated voltage reading is too high, test the ground circuit as described under *Wiring Harness Test* in this section.
9. If all of the items tested in Step 7 and Step 8 are good, replace the AC regulator as described in this chapter.
10. Disconnect the tachometer.
11. Disconnect the voltmeter leads from the connectors. Check the wiring harness connectors to make sure they are clean and connected properly.
12. Install the front visor and secure it with its straps (A, **Figure 1**).
13. Start the engine and check the headlight operation.

Wiring Harness Test

This section tests the continuity of the lighting system wiring harness.
1. Remove the fuel tank (Chapter Eight).

9

2. Disconnect the AC regulator 4-pin connector (**Figure 4**).

3. Check the AC regulator connectors for loose or corroded connector pins and sockets.

> *NOTE*
> *Wait 10 minutes after engine shut-off before measuring the resistance in the following steps.*

4. *Lighting coil line test*: Use an ohmmeter set at R×1 and measure resistance between the pink and yellow connectors (**Figure 5**) on the wiring harness connector side. The correct resistance reading is 0.1-1.0 ohms. Note the following:

   a. If the resistance reading is good, the pink and yellow wires and connectors are in good condition.

   b. If there is no continuity (infinite resistance), perform the *Lighting Coil Resistance Test* in this chapter. If the lighting coil resistance reading is correct (0.1-1.0 ohms), check the pink and yellow wires and connectors installed between the AC regulator 4-pin connector and the alternator connectors (**Figure 6**) for damage or an open circuit.

5. *Ground circuit test*: Use an ohmmeter set at R×1 and check for continuity between the green connector pin in the wiring harness connector and ground. The ohmmeter should read continuity. If there is no continuity, check the green wire for damage.

6. Clean the connectors and reconnect them (**Figure 4**).

7. Install the fuel tank (Chapter Eight).

Lighting Coil Resistance Test

Test the lighting coil with the stator mounted on the engine.

1. Locate the alternator wiring harness connectors on the left side of the bike. Disconnect the pink and yellow connectors (**Figure 6**).

> *NOTE*
> *Wait 10 minutes after engine shut-off before measuring the lighting coil resistance in the following steps.*

2. Use an ohmmeter set at R × 1 and measure resistance between the pink and yellow connectors (**Figure 6**) on the alternator side of the connectors

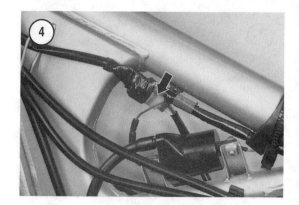

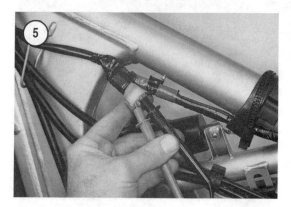

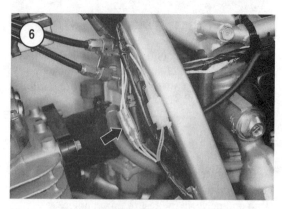

(**Figure 7**). The correct resistance reading is 0.1-1.0 ohms. Note the following:

   a. If the resistance reading is correct, the lighting coil is good.

   b. If there is no continuity (infinite resistance), the lighting coil is defective and the stator assembly must be replaced. The lighting coil cannot be replaced separately. Refer to *Left Crankcase Cover and Stator Coil* in this chapter.

3. Clean and reconnect the pink and yellow connectors (**Figure 6**).

AC REGULATOR

The AC regulator maintains system current to prevent the headlight and taillight bulbs from having reduced intensity. At higher engine speeds, the AC regulator reduces current levels to prevent the overloading of the circuit, which would damage the bulbs.

Testing

There are no test procedures for the AC regulator (**Figure 8**). If the regulator is suspect, first refer to *AC Lighting System Troubleshooting* in Chapter Two and test the system output, lighting coil resistance and wiring harness condition as described in this chapter. If all of these test are good, consider the AC regulator defective by a process of elimination. Make sure that nothing has been overlooked before purchasing a new regulator. Most parts suppliers will not accept returns on electrical components.

AC Regulator Removal/Installation

The AC regulator (**Figure 8**) is mounted beneath the fuel tank.
1. Remove the fuel tank (Chapter Eight).
2. Disconnect the AC regulator 4-pin connector (**Figure 4**).
3. Remove the AC regulator (**Figure 8**) from its frame mounting bracket.
4. Remove the rubber damper (**Figure 9**) from the AC regulator and install it onto the new unit.
5. Install the new AC regulator onto its frame mounting bracket.
6. Clean the wiring harness side connector, then connect the AC regulator 4-pin connector.
7. Install the fuel tank (Chapter Eight).

LEFT CRANKCASE COVER AND STATOR COIL

The stator and ignition pulse generator units are mounted inside the left crankcase cover. The stator coil is a subassembly consisting of the lighting coil and exciter coil.

Left Crankcase Cover Removal/Installation

1. Drain the engine oil (Chapter Three).
2. Disconnect the alternator connectors (**Figure 6**).
3. Disconnect the alternator wiring harness from the clamp (A, **Figure 10**).
4. Unbolt and remove the shift pedal (B, **Figure 10**).
5. Remove the left crankcase cover mounting bolts and washers and remove the cover (C, **Figure 10**).

6. Remove the 2 dowel pins (A, **Figure 11**) and gasket.

7. Remove the oil transfer dowel pin (B, **Figure 11**), if necessary.

8. Install the left crankcase cover by reversing these removal steps, while noting the following.

9. Before installing the left crankcase cover, remove any nuts, bolt or other magnetic debris from the flywheel.

10. Install a new left crankcase cover gasket.

11. Install the dowel pins (A and B, **Figure 11**).

CAUTION
The magnetic pull on the left crankcase cover is strong. Do not place your fingers behind the cover when installing it over the flywheel.

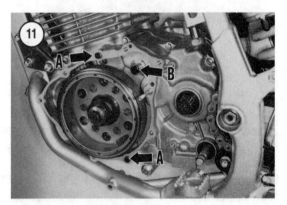

12. Install the left crankcase cover (C, **Figure 10**) and tighten its mounting bolts.

13. Fill the engine with the recommended type and quantity of oil (Chapter Three).

14. Install the shift pedal and secure it with its pinch bolt.

15. Secure the alternator wiring harness to its clamp (A, **Figure 10**).

16. Reconnect the alternator connectors (**Figure 6**).

17. Start the engine and check for leaks.

Stator Coil and Pulse Generator Removal/Installation

1. Remove the left crankcase cover as described in this section.

2. Unbolt and remove the clamp (A, **Figure 12**).

3. Remove the two pulse generator mounting bolts (B, **Figure 12**).

3. Remove the three stator coil mounting bolts (C, **Figure 12**).

4. Lift the wiring harness grommet out of the left crankcase cover and remove the stator coil and pulse generator coil assembly.

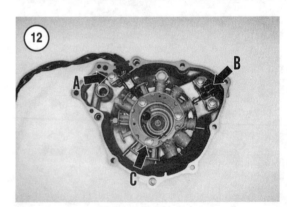

NOTE
Do not cut or unsolder the stator coil or pulse generator coil wires. If a coil is damaged, replace both coils as an assembly.

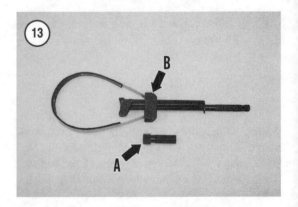

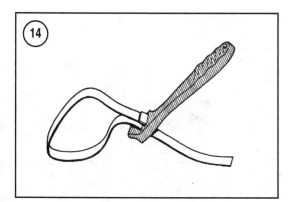

5. Clean the left crankcase cover in solvent and dry with compressed air. Remove all sealer residue from the wire grommet sealing surface.

6. Apply a medium strength threadlock onto the clamp and stator coil mounting bolt threads.

7. Install the stator coil (C, **Figure 12**) and tighten the mounting bolts securely.

8. Route the stator coil wiring harness in the cover and push the grommet into place.

9. Install the pulse generator coil and tighten the mounting bolts securely.

10. Apply an RTV or similar liquid sealant onto the wire grommet surface and push the grommet into the cover groove. Install the clamp and tighten its mounting bolt securely.

FLYWHEEL

Special Tools

A flywheel puller and flywheel holder are needed to remove and install the flywheel. Note the following suggested tools and part numbers:

    a. Honda flywheel puller (part No. 07933-3950000).

    b. Motion Pro flywheel puller (part No. 08-086 [A, **Figure 13**]).

    c. Honda flywheel holder (part No. 07725-0040000 [B, **Figure 13**]) or an equivalent type strap wrench. See **Figure 14**.

Removal/Installation

1. Remove the left crankcase cover as described in this chapter.

2. Hold the flywheel with a strap wrench (A, **Figure 15**) and remove the flywheel bolt and washer (B, **Figure 15**). See **Figure 16**.

3. Screw the flywheel puller (**Figure 17**) into the flywheel.

CAUTION
Do not try to remove the flywheel without a puller. Any attempt to do so can damage the flywheel and crankshaft.

CAUTION
If normal flywheel removal attempts fail, do not force the puller. Excessive force will strip the flywheel threads,

9

causing expensive damage. Take the engine to a dealer and have them remove the flywheel.

4. Hold the flywheel with the flywheel holder and gradually tighten the flywheel puller until the flywheel pops off the crankshaft taper.
5. Remove the flywheel and strap wrench.
6. Remove the Woodruff key (A, **Figure 18**) from the crankshaft groove.
7. Clean the flywheel and crankshaft tapers with an aerosol parts cleaner. There must be no oil or grease residue left on either taper.
8. Align the flywheel groove (B, **Figure 18**) with the Woodruff key (A, **Figure 18**) and install the flywheel.
9. Lubricate the flywheel bolt threads and its head seating surface with engine oil. Install the flywheel bolt and washer (**Figure 16**) and tighten finger-tight.
10. Hold the flywheel with the flywheel holder and tighten the flywheel bolt as specified in **Table 3**. Remove the flywheel holder.
11. Install the left crankcase cover as described in this chapter.

Inspection

1. Clean the flywheel in solvent and dry with compressed air.
2. Inspect the flywheel (**Figure 19**) for cracks or breaks.

> *WARNING*
> *Always replace a cracked or chipped flywheel. A damaged flywheel can fly apart at high rpm, throwing metal fragments into the engine. Do not repair a damaged flywheel.*

3. Inspect the flywheel tapered bore and the crankshaft taper for damage.
4. Inspect the flywheel bolt and washer for damage.

IGNITION SYSTEM TESTING

All models are equipped with a solid state capacitor discharge ignition (CDI) system.

Alternating current from the magneto is rectified and used to charge the capacitor. As the piston ap-

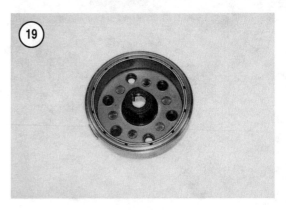

proaches the firing position, a pulse from the ignition pulse generator triggers the silicon controlled rectifier. This causes the capacitor to discharge into the primary side of the high-voltage ignition coil where the charge is amplified to a high enough voltage to jump the spark plug gap.

CDI Precautions

When servicing the CDI system, note the following:
1. Keep all electrical connections clean and secure.
2. Never disconnect any of the electrical connections while the engine is running, or excessive voltage may damage the ignition control module.
3. When kicking the engine over with the spark plug removed, make sure the spark plug is installed in the plug cap and grounded against the cylinder head. If not, excessive resistance may damage the ignition control module.
4. The ignition control module is mounted inside a thick rubber damper. Make sure the ignition control module is mounted correctly. Handle the ignition control module carefully when removing and in-

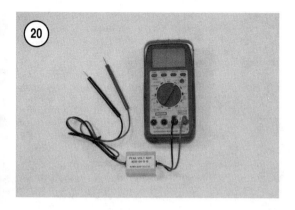

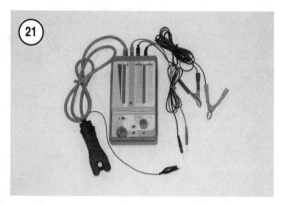

stalling it in the frame. The ignition control module unit is a sealed unit. Do not attempt to open it as this will cause permanent damage.

Troubleshooting

Refer to Chapter Two.

Peak Voltage Tests

The following tests describe ignition system troubleshooting using a peak voltage tester. Peak voltage tests are designed to check the voltage output of the ignition coil, exciter coil and pulse generator coil at normal cranking speed. This test makes it possible to identify ignition system problems quickly and accurately. To make these tests, a peak voltage tester is required; see *Peak Voltage Tester* in this section.

NOTE
*All peak voltage specifications in the following tests are **minimum** values. As long as the measured voltage meets or exceeds the minimum speci-*

fication, consider the test results satisfactory. On some components, the voltage may greatly exceed the minimum specification.

WARNING
High voltage is present during ignition system operation. Do not touch ignition system components, wires or test leads while cranking or running the engine.

Peak Voltage Tester

Honda does not provide resistance specifications for testing the ignition system components on the XR400R. All ignition test specifications are based on peak voltage readings, which require a peak voltage tester. It is impossible to determine peak voltage readings without the correct type of test equipment and the knowledge to use it. If a peak voltage tester is not available, your troubleshooting will be limited to making a spark test, checking ignition timing and visual inspection of the components, wiring and connectors. Use the following tools to test peak voltage:

1. Honda Peak Voltage Adapter (part No. 07HGJ-0020100) and digital multimeter with an input impedance of 10M ohms (10-megaohm). See **Figure 20**.

NOTE
The input impedance of a digital multimeter is usually given as a specification. Do not use a digital multimeter with an input impedance of less than 10M ohms. Using a meter with a lower input impedance may cause the circuit in the meter to give incorrect results. When selecting a digital multimeter for peak voltage and other ignition system testing, refer to the manufacturer's literature and determine the input impedance specification.

2. IgnitionMate peak-voltage ignition tester (Motion Pro part No. 08-0193). See **Figure 21**.

NOTE
An important part of ignition system troubleshooting, especially when using a peak voltage tester, is correct understanding and operation of the

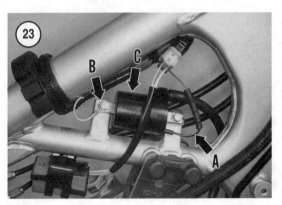

test equipment. To make accurate de-cisions based on the meter readings, make sure the equipment is in good working order and all test connec-tions are properly made and secure.

NOTE
Refer to the manufacturer's instruc-tions when using these tools.

Ignition Coil Primary Peak Voltage Test

1. Remove the fuel tank (Chapter Eight).

2. Check engine compression as described in Chapter Three. If the compression is low, the fol-lowing test results will be inaccurate.

3. Check all of the ignition component electrical connectors and wiring harnesses. Make sure the connectors are clean and properly connected.

4. Remove the spark plug cap and make sure the spark plug is tight.

5. Connect a known good spark plug to the spark plug cap and ground it against the cylinder head cover (**Figure 22**).

6. If a peak voltage adapter is used (**Figure 20**), connect it to the multimeter.

NOTE
When using the IgnitionMate tester or a similar peak voltage tester, follow the manufacturer's instructions for con-necting the tester to the ignition coil.

NOTE
*Do not disconnect the ignition coil primary wires (**Figure 23**) when per-forming Step 7.*

7. Connect the peak voltage adapter to the ignition coil. Connect the positive lead to the black/yellow terminal (A, **Figure 23**) and the negative lead to a ground (B, **Figure 23**).

WARNING
High voltage is present during igni-tion system testing. To prevent an electric shock, do not touch the spark plug or tester leads while cranking the engine.

8. Kick the kickstarter over firmly, while at the same time noting the peak voltage reading. Note the following:

NOTE
*All peak voltage specifications in the text and **Table 1** are **minimum** volt-ages. As long as the measured voltage meets or exceeds the minimum volt-age, consider the test results satisfac-tory. On some components, the voltage may greatly exceed the mini-mum specification.*

a. The minimum peak voltage reading is 100 volts.

b. If the peak voltage reading is less than 100 volts, there is a problem in the ignition system. The problem could be a defective component or damaged wiring. To isolate the problem, follow the procedures listed under *Ignition System Troubleshooting* in Chapter Two.

9. Disconnect the test leads.

10. Remove the spark plug from the plug cap and reconnect the plug cap onto the spark plug.

11. Install the fuel tank (Chapter Eight).

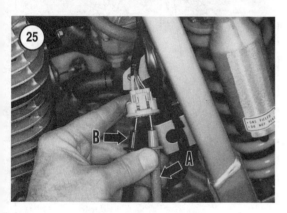

Exciter Coil Peak Voltage Test

1. Check all of the ignition component electrical connectors and wiring harnesses. Make sure the connectors are clean and properly connected.

2. If a peak voltage adapter is used (**Figure 20**), connect it to the multimeter.

3. Shift the transmission into NEUTRAL.

WARNING
High voltage is present during ignition system operation. Do not touch the spark plug, ignition components, connectors or test leads while cranking the engine.

4. Remove the ignition control module from the frame and disconnect its electrical connector (**Figure 24**) as described in this chapter.

NOTE
When using the IgnitionMate tester, follow the manufacturer's instructions for connecting the tester to the exciter coil terminals.

5. Perform the following:
   a. Connect the peak voltage adapter's positive lead to the black/red terminal (A, **Figure 25**) and the negative lead to the brown terminal (B, **Figure 25**) on the ignition control module wiring harness connector.
   b. Kick the kickstarter over firmly, while at the same time reading the peak voltage on the meter.

NOTE
*All peak voltage specifications in the text and **Table 1** are **minimum** voltages. As long as the measured voltage meets or exceeds the specification, consider the test results satisfactory. On some components, the voltage may greatly exceed the minimum specification.*

   c. If peak voltage reading is 100 volts minimum, the exciter coil is working correctly. Go to Step 8.
   d. If the peak voltage reading is less than 100 volts, perform Step 6.

6. Perform the following:
   a. Disconnect the test leads (**Figure 25**) at the ignition control module connector.
   b. Disconnect the exciter coil black/red and brown bullet connectors (**Figure 26**).
   c. Connect the positive test lead to the black/red connector (A, **Figure 26**) and the negative lead to the brown connector (B, **Figure 26**). Connect both leads on the exciter coil connector side, not on the wiring harness connector side.
   d. Kick the kickstarter over firmly, while at the same time reading the peak voltage on the meter.

9

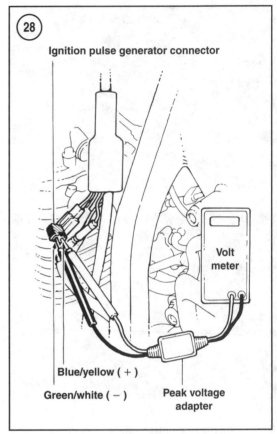

Ignition pulse generator connector

Volt meter

Blue/yellow (+)

Green/white (−)

Peak voltage adapter

7. If the peak voltage reading in Step 6 was 100 volts minimum but the reading in Step 5 is less than 100 volts, check the wire harness for an open circuit or loose connector. If both peak voltage readings (Step 5 and Step 6) are less than 100 volts, perform the ignition system troubleshooting procedures in Chapter Two.

8. Disconnect the test leads and install all parts removed.

Ignition Pulse Generator Peak Voltage Test

1. Check all of the ignition component electrical connectors and wiring harnesses. Make sure the connectors are clean and properly connected.

2. If a peak voltage adapter is used (**Figure 20**), connect it to the multimeter.

3. Shift the transmission into NEUTRAL.

> *WARNING*
> *High voltage is present during ignition system operation. Do not touch the spark plug, ignition components, connectors or test leads while cranking the engine.*

4. Remove the ignition control module from the frame and disconnect its electrical connector (**Figure 24**) as described in this chapter.

> *NOTE*
> *When using the IgnitionMate tester, follow the manufacturer's instructions for connecting the tester to the exciter coil terminals.*

5. Perform the following:

    a. Connect the peak voltage adapter's positive lead to the blue/yellow terminal (A, **Figure**

25) and the negative lead to the green terminal (B, **Figure 25**) on the ignition control module wiring harness connector.

    b. Kick the kickstarter over firmly, while at the same time reading the peak voltage on the meter.

> *NOTE*
> *All peak voltage specifications in the text and **Table 1** are **minimum** voltages. As long as the measured voltage meets or exceeds the specification, consider the test results satisfactory. On some components, the voltage may greatly exceed the minimum specification.*

    c. If peak voltage reading is 0.7 volts minimum, the ignition pulse generator coil is working correctly. Go to Step 9.

    d. If the peak voltage reading is less than 0.7 volts, perform Step 6.

6. Perform the following:

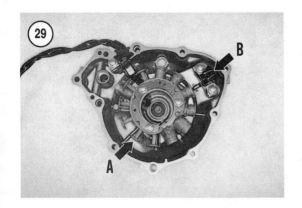

a. Disconnect the test leads (**Figure 25**) at the ignition control module connector.

b. Disconnect the ignition pulse generator connectors (**Figure 27**).

c. Connect the positive test lead to the blue/yellow connector (**Figure 28**) and the negative lead to the green connector (**Figure 28**). Connect both test leads on the ignition pulse generator connector side, not on the wiring harness connector side.

d. Kick the engine over swiftly using the kickstarter, while at the same time reading the peak voltage on the meter.

7. If the peak voltage reading in Step 5 was 0.7 volts minimum but the reading in Step 6 is less than 0.7 volts, check the wire harness for an open circuit or loose connector. If both voltage readings (Step 5 and Step 6) are less than 0.7 volts, perform the ignition system troubleshooting procedures in Chapter Two.

8. Disconnect the test leads and reinstall all parts.

IGNITION SYSTEM
(COMPONENT REPLACEMENT)

This section describes procedures for replacing the ignition system components. To test the ignition system components, refer to *Ignition System Testing* in this chapter. To troubleshoot the ignition system, refer to *Ignition System Troubleshooting* in Chapter Two.

Ignition Coil
Removal/Installation

The ignition coil is mounted on an upper frame rail (C, **Figure 23**).

1. Place the bike on the sidestand.

2. Remove fuel tank (Chapter Eight).

3. Disconnect the spark plug lead at the spark plug.

4. Disconnect the ignition coil primary electrical connectors.

5. Remove the bolts securing the ignition coil to the frame and remove the coil.

6. Install by reversing these removal steps, and perform the following.

7. Make sure all electrical connectors are tight and free of corrosion. Make sure the ground wire connection point on the coil (B, **Figure 23**) is free of rust and corrosion.

8. Pack the electrical connectors with dielectric grease.

Exciter Coil
Removal/Installation

The exciter coil is an integral part of the stator coil (A, **Figure 29**). If the exciter coil is damaged, replace the stator coil as an assembly. Refer to *Left Crankcase Cover and Stator Coil* in this chapter.

Ignition Pulse Generator
Removal/Installation

The ignition pulse generator is permanently wired to the stator coil (B, **Figure 29**). If the ignition pulse generator is damaged, replace the stator coil and ignition pulse generator as an assembly. Refer to *Left Crankcase Cover and Stator Coil* in this chapter.

Ignition Control Module
Removal/Installation

The ignition control module (**Figure 30**) is mounted on the left side of the frame, beside the carburetor.

9

1. On 1998 and later California models, remove the breather separator (Chapter Eight).

2. Remove the ignition control module and its rubber damper from the frame mounting bracket (**Figure 24**).

3. Squeeze the connector clamps (**Figure 31**) and disconnect the connector from the ignition control module.

4. Remove the rubber damper (**Figure 32**) from the ignition control module and install it onto the new module.

5. Reverse these steps to install the ignition control module, and perform the following.

6. Clean the ignition control module unit connectors with contact cleaner and pack them with dielectric grease.

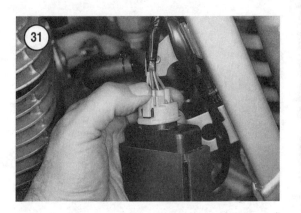

IGNITION TIMING

The XR400R is equipped with a capacitor discharge ignition (CDI), which has no moving parts or provision for adjusting the timing. However, the ignition timing can be checked as a troubleshooting aid. If the ignition timing is incorrect, there is a defective component in the ignition system.

> *WARNING*
> *Never start and run the motorcycle in a closed area. The exhaust gases contain carbon monoxide, a colorless, odorless, poisonous gas. Carbon monoxide levels build quickly in enclosed areas and can cause unconsciousness and death in a short time. When running the engine, always do so in a well-ventilated area.*

> *NOTE*
> *To check the timing, a separate 12-volt battery will be required to operate the timing light.*

1. Start the engine and warm to normal operating temperature. Turn the engine off.

2. Place the bike on the sidestand.

3. Remove the timing hole cap (**Figure 33**) from the left crankcase cover.

4. Connect the timing light battery leads to a separate 12 volt battery. Connect the timing light inductive lead to the spark plug wire.

5. Start and run the engine at idle speed (1200-1400 rpm).

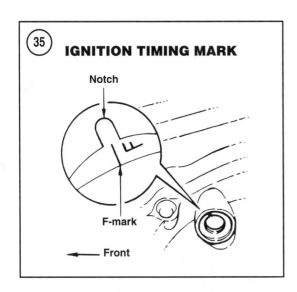

IGNITION TIMING MARK

Notch

F-mark

Front

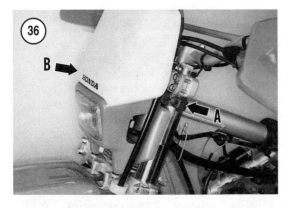

correct, one or more components in the ignition system are defective. To find the defective component(s), perform the *Ignition System Troubleshooting* procedure in Chapter Two.

8. Disconnect the timing light leads from the spark plug and battery.

9. Install the timing hole cap (**Figure 33**) and tighten to the specification in **Table 3**.

HEADLIGHT

See **Table 2** for the correct headlight bulb to use in the XR400R.

Bulb Replacement

1. Disconnect the front visor straps (A, **Figure 36**) and pivot the front visor (B, **Figure 36**) forward. Leave the electrical connectors attached.

2. Remove the dust cover (**Figure 37**).

3. Push the bulb socket in and turn it counterclockwise to remove it.

4. Remove the headlight bulb (**Figure 38**).

5. Reverse these steps to install a new headlight bulb, and perform the following.

6. Check the socket connectors for corrosion and clean if necessary.

7. Install the dust cover (**Figure 37**) so it seats tightly against the headlight housing. Check the wire harness routing from the headlight to make sure it will not pull and disconnect the connectors when the handlebar is turned.

8. Install the front visor and secure it with its straps (A, **Figure 36**).

9. Start the engine and check the headlight operation.

6. Point the timing light at the crankcase cover timing hole (**Figure 34**). The ignition timing is correct when the F mark on the flywheel aligns with the index notch on the crankcase cover (**Figure 35**). Turn the engine off.

7. If the ignition timing is correct, the ignition system is working correctly. If the ignition timing is in-

Headlight Adjustment

Adjust the headlight vertically by turning the adjust screw (**Figure 39**) mounted on the bottom of the headlight housing.

Headlight Housing
Disassembly/Reassembly

1. Remove the front visor and disconnect the headlight bulb connector as described under *Bulb Replacement* in this chapter.
2. Remove the two headlight housing mounting screws (A, **Figure 40**).
3. Remove the headlight adjust screw, nut and spring (B, **Figure 40**) and remove the headlight housing (C, **Figure 40**).
4. Reverse these steps to assemble the headlight housing.
5. After starting the engine, adjust the headlight as described in this chapter.

TAILLIGHT

See **Table 2** for taillight bulb specifications.

Bulb Replacement

1. Remove the two screws and the taillight lens (**Figure 41**).
2. Push the bulb in and turn it counterclockwise to remove it (**Figure 42**).
3. Reverse these steps to install a new bulb.
4. Start the engine and check the taillight operation.

Taillight Housing
Removal/Installation

1. Remove the seat (Chapter Fifteen).
2. Disconnect the headlight electrical connector (**Figure 43**) and release the wiring harness from the frame clips.
3. Remove the nuts, collars and the taillight housing assembly (**Figure 44**).
4. Reverse these steps to install the taillight housing.
5. Start the engine and check the taillight operation.

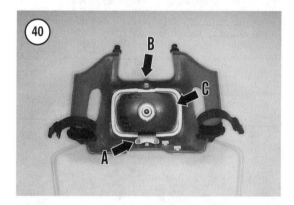

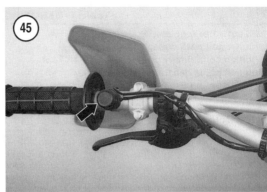

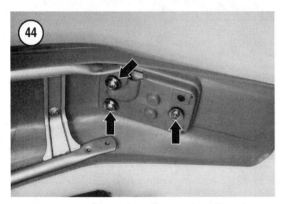

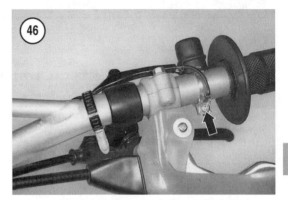

9

ENGINE STOP SWITCH

The engine stop switch (**Figure 45**) is mounted on the left side of the handlebar.

Testing

When troubleshooting the ignition system, isolate the engine stop switch by disconnecting the switch leads from the main wiring harness. If there is no spark with the leads connected and a spark after disconnecting them, the engine stop switch is the problem. See *Spark Test* in Chapter Two.

1. Remove the front visor as described under *Bulb Replacement* in this chapter.

2. Disconnect the engine stop switch connector terminals.

3. Use an ohmmeter set at R × 1 and connect the ohmmeter leads to the stop switch wires.

4. Push the stop switch button (**Figure 45**). There should be continuity.

5. If there is no continuity, the switch is defective.

6. Remove the screw (**Figure 46**) securing the switch to the handlebar and remove it.

7. Reverse these steps to install a new switch, making sure to route the switch wiring harness along its original path. Align the end of the switch bracket (**Figure 46**) with the punch mark on the handlebar.

WIRING DIAGRAM

The wiring diagram is located at the end of this book.

Tables 1-3 are on the following page.

Table 1 ELECTRICAL SPECIFICATIONS

AC regulator regulated voltage	12.5-13.5 volts @ 3000 rpm
Exciter coil peak voltage	100 volts minimum
Ignition coil primary peak voltage	100 volts minimum
Ignition pulse generator peak voltage	0.7 volts minimum
Ignition timing F mark	8 degrees BTDC at idle
Lighting coil resistance*	0.1-1.0 ohms

*Test temperature of 68° F (20° C).

Table 2 REPLACEMENT BULBS

Headlight	12 volt, 35 watt
Taillight	12 volt, 5 watt

Table 3 ELECTRICAL SYSTEM TORQUE SPECIFICATIONS

	N•m	in.-lb.	ft.-lb.
Crankshaft hole cap	8	71	–
Flywheel mounting bolt[1]	127	–	94
Left crankcase cover stud bolt[2]	10	88	–
Timing hole cap	10	88	–

1. Lubricate bolt seating surfaces and threads with engine oil.
2. Apply a theadlock onto threads.

CHAPTER TEN

WHEELS, TIRES AND DRIVE CHAIN

This chapter describes repair and maintenance for the front and rear wheels, wheel hubs, tires and the drive chain and sprockets.

Tire and wheel specifications are listed in **Table 1**. Drive chain and sprocket specifications are listed in **Table 2**. **Tables 1-3** are at the end of the chapter.

FRONT WHEEL

The front wheel can be removed with and without the front axle.

Removal
(Wheel With Axle)

To remove the front wheel without loosening the axle, perform the following:

1. Support the motorcycle with the front wheel off the ground.
2. Remove the odometer cable set screw (A, **Figure 1**) and remove the cable from the gear box.
3. Remove the nuts and axle holders (B, **Figure 1**) from both sides of the wheel.

4. Remove the front wheel and axle from the fork tubes (**Figure 2**).
5. Insert a plastic or wooden spacer block between the brake pads.

> *NOTE*
> *The spacer installed in Step 5 will prevent the piston from being forced out of the caliper if the brake lever is applied with the disc removed. If the piston is forced out, the caliper must be disassembled to reseat the piston.*

Removal
(Wheel Without Axle)

To remove the axle and front wheel separately, perform the following:

1. Support the motorcycle with the front wheel off the ground.
2. Remove the odometer cable set screw (A, **Figure 1**) and remove the cable from the gear box.
3. Loosen the axle holder nuts on the right side (B, **Figure 1**), then loosen the front axle (C, **Figure 1**).

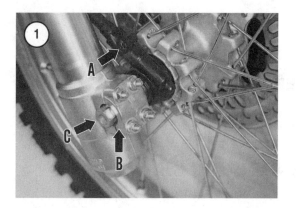

4. Remove the axle (A, **Figure 3**) and odometer gear box (B, **Figure 3**).

5. Remove the front wheel and the left collar (**Figure 4**).

6. Insert a plastic or wooden spacer block between the brake pads.

NOTE
The spacer installed in Step 6 will prevent the piston from being forced out of the caliper if the brake lever is applied with the disc removed. If the piston is forced out, the caliper must be disassembled to reseat the piston.

7. Remove both axle holders and the axle nut (**Figure 5**) from the fork tubes.

8. Inspect the front wheel as described in this section.

Installation

1. Clean the axle bearing surfaces on the fork tube and axle holders.

2. If the axle was removed from the front wheel, install it as follows:

   a. Lubricate the left seal lip with grease.

   b. Install the left collar into the seal (**Figure 4**) with its shoulder side facing out.

   c. Lubricate the odometer gear box gear teeth and gear retainer with grease.

   d. Align the two grooves in the odometer gear box gear teeth (A, **Figure 6**) with the gear retainer tabs (B, **Figure 6**) and install the odometer gear box (A, **Figure 7**).

   e. Lubricate the axle with grease.

   f. Install the axle (B, **Figure 7**) through the odometer box and install the axle nut (**Figure**

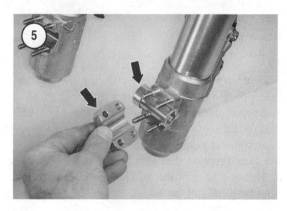

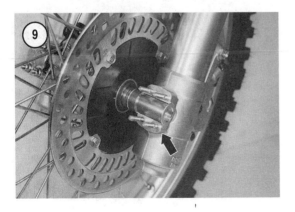

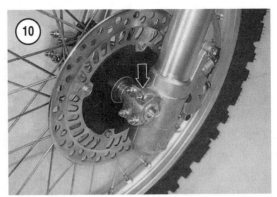

10

8) on the left side. Hold the axle and finger-tighten the axle nut.

3. Remove the spacer block from between the brake pads.

4. Carefully insert the disc between the brake pads while placing the front axle in the front fork axle holders. Make sure the axle nut is centered in the left axle holder as shown in **Figure 9**.

5. Position the odometer gear box (A, **Figure 1**) so the lug seats against the stopper on the fork tube.

6. Install the right side axle holder (B, **Figure 1**) with its arrow mark facing up. Install the nuts and finger tighten.

7. Install the left side axle holder (**Figure 10**) with the arrow mark facing up. Install and tighten the upper axle holder nuts to the specification in **Table 3**. Then install and tighten the lower axle holder nuts to the specification in **Table 3**.

8. If the front axle is loose, tighten the front axle (C, **Figure 1**) as specified in **Table 3**.

9. Place the front wheel on the ground. Apply the front brake several times to reposition the pads against the disc. When the front brake is operating correctly, turn the front wheel so it points straight ahead. Apply the front brake again and pump the fork several times to seat the axle in the axle holders.

10. With the front wheel pointing straight ahead, tighten the right upper axle holder nuts (B, **Figure 1**), then the lower nuts, to the specifications **Table 3**.

11. Lightly lubricate the odometer cable O-ring with grease. Then install the cable by aligning the slot in the end of the cable with the raised tab inside the odometer gear box. Secure the cable with the screw (A, **Figure 1**).

CHAPTER TEN

Inspection

1. Inspect the seals (**Figure 11**) for wear, hardness, cracks or other damage. If necessary, replace the seals as described under *Front and Rear Hubs* in this chapter.

2. Turn each bearing inner race (**Figure 11**) by hand. The bearing must turn smoothly. Some axial play (end play) is normal, but radial play (side play) must be negligible. See **Figure 12**. If one bearing is damaged, replace both bearings as a set. Refer to *Front and Rear Hubs* in this chapter.

3. Clean the axle and collar in solvent to remove all grease and dirt. Make sure the axle contact surfaces are clean and free of dirt and old grease.

4. Check the axle runout with a set of V-blocks and dial indicator. Replace the axle if its runout exceeds the service limit in **Table 1**.

5. Check the brake disc bolts for tightness. To service the brake disc, refer to Chapter Thirteen.

6. Check wheel runout and spoke tension as described in this chapter.

7. Inspect the odometer gear box (**Figure 13**) for damage. Remove the gear and washers. Clean and dry all parts. Lubricate the washers and gear with grease and install them into the odometer gear box.

REAR WHEEL

Removal

1. Support the bike on a workstand with the rear wheel off the ground.

2. Loosen the rear axle nut (A, **Figure 14**) and slip the stopper plate (B, **Figure 14**) off of the swing arm pin.

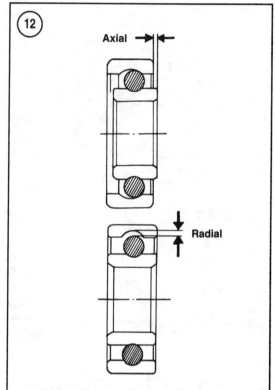

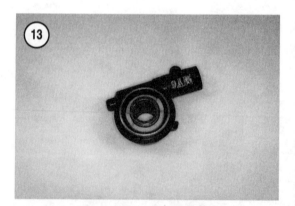

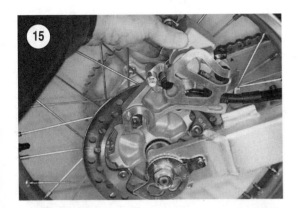

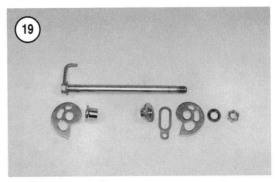

3. Move the rear wheel forward and slip the drive chain off of the driven sprocket.

4. Lift the brake caliper bracket away from the swing arm (**Figure 15**) and remove the rear wheel and axle assembly (**Figure 16**).

5. Secure the brake caliper bracket with a piece of stiff wire.

6. If necessary, remove the axle assembly as follows:

    a. Axle nut, washer, chain adjuster, stopper plate and collar (**Figure 17**).

    b. Axle, chain adjuster and collar (**Figure 18**).

7. Insert a plastic or wooden spacer block in the caliper between the brake pads.

NOTE
The spacer block installed in Step 7 will prevent the piston from being forced out of the caliper if the brake pedal is operated with the disc removed. If the piston is forced out too far, the caliper must be disassembled to reseat the piston.

Installation

1. If the rear axle was not previously removed, remove the axle nut, washer, chain adjuster and stopper plate from the right side of the wheel (**Figure 17**).

2. If removed, install the rear axle assembly (**Figure 19**) in the wheel as follows:

    a. Lubricate the axle and both seal lips with grease.

    b. Install the left (**Figure 20**) and right (**Figure 21**) axle collars.

NOTE
Install the axle adjusters with their marked side facing out. The axle adjusters are different—refer to the L (left) and R (right) identification marks.

10

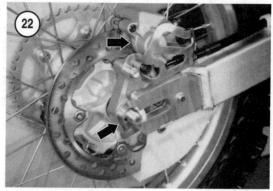

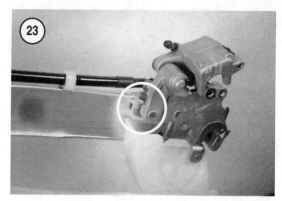

c. Install the left axle adjuster onto the axle and install the axle (**Figure 18**) into the left side of the wheel.

3. Position the rear wheel between the swing arm.

4. Install the brake caliper bracket (**Figure 22**) over the axle while positioning the brake pads over the brake disc. Then align the caliper bracket with the slide rail on the inside of the swing arm.

NOTE
Figure 23 shows the slide rail and caliper bracket engagement with the rear wheel removed for clarity.

5. Slip the drive chain over the driven sprocket.

6. Install the stopper plate (**Figure 24**) over the rear axle and hook it over the swing arm stopper pin.

7. Install the right axle adjuster, washer and axle nut (**Figure 14**).

8. Adjust the drive chain as described in Chapter Three. Tighten the rear axle nut to the specification in **Table 3**.

9. After the wheel is completely installed, rotate it several times while applying the rear brake to repo-

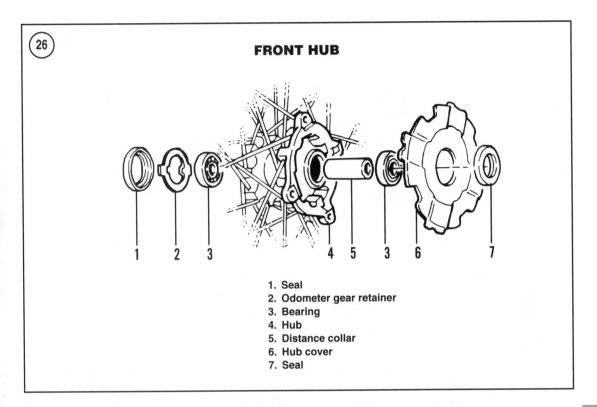

(26)

FRONT HUB

1. Seal
2. Odometer gear retainer
3. Bearing
4. Hub
5. Distance collar
6. Hub cover
7. Seal

sition the rear brake pads and to make sure the wheel rotates freely.

Inspection

1. Inspect the seals (**Figure 25**) for excessive wear, hardness, cracks or other damage. If necessary, replace seals as described under *Front and Rear Hubs* in this chapter.
2. Turn each bearing inner race (**Figure 25**) by hand. The bearing must turn smoothly. Some axial play (end play) is normal, but radial play (side play) must be negligible. See **Figure 12**. If one bearing is damaged, replace both bearings as a set. Refer to *Front and Rear Hubs* in this chapter.
3. Clean the axle and collars in solvent to remove all grease and dirt. Make sure all axle contact surfaces are clean and free of dirt and old grease.
4. Check the rear axle runout with a set of V-blocks and dial indicator. Replace the axle if its runout exceeds the service limit in **Table 1**.
5. Check the brake disc bolts for tightness. To service the brake disc, refer to Chapter Thirteen.
6. Check the driven sprocket nuts for tightness. Tighten the driven sprocket nuts as described under *Sprocket Replacement* in this chapter.

7. Check wheel runout and spoke tension as described in this chapter.

FRONT AND REAR HUBS

The front and rear hubs contain the seals, wheel bearings and distance collar. A brake disc is mounted onto each hub and the driven sprocket is mounted onto the rear hub. Refer to **Figure 26** (front) or **Figure 27** (rear) when servicing the front and rear hubs in this section.

Procedures used to service the front and rear hubs and wheel bearings are basically the same. Where differences occur, they will be described in the service procedure.

Pre-Inspection

Inspect each wheel bearing as follows:
1. Support the bike with the wheel to be checked off the ground. Make sure the axle is tightened securely.
   a. Grasp the wheel 180° apart and try to rock it back and forth. If there is any noticeable play at the axle, the wheel bearings are worn or damaged and require replacement. Have an assistant apply

10

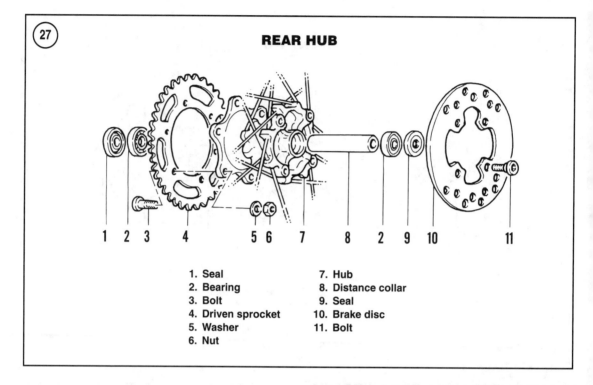

REAL HUB

1   2   3   4   5 6   7   8   2   9   10   11

1. Seal   7. Hub
2. Bearing   8. Distance collar
3. Bolt   9. Seal
4. Driven sprocket   10. Brake disc
5. Washer   11. Bolt
6. Nut

the brake and rock the wheel again. On severely worn bearings, play will be felt at the bearings even though the wheel is locked in position.

NOTE
When checking the rear wheel, re-move the drive chain before perform-ing substep b.

b. If there is no noticeable play, spin the wheel and listen for excessive wheel bearing noise. A grinding or catching noise indicates worn bearings.

c. To check any questionable bearing, continue with Step 2.

CAUTION
Do not remove the wheel bearings for inspection purposes as they may be damaged during their removal. Re-move the wheel bearings only if they are to be replaced.

2. Remove the front or rear wheel as described in this chapter.

CAUTION
When handling the wheel assembly in the following steps, do not lay the wheel down where it is supported by

the brake disc as this could damage the disc. Support the wheel on 2 wooden blocks.

3. Pry the seals out of the hub with a wide-blade screwdriver (**Figure 28**). Cushion the screwdriver with a rag to avoid damaging the hub or brake disc.

4. Turn each bearing inner race by hand. The bear-ing must turn smoothly. Some axial play (end play) is normal, but radial play (side play) must be negli-gible (**Figure 12**).

5. Check the bearing's outer seal (**Figure 29**) for buckling or other damage that would allow dirt to enter the bearing.

6. If one bearing is damaged, replace both bearings as a set.

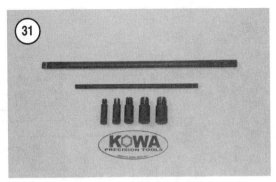

Disassembly

This section describes removal of the wheel bearings from the front (**Figure 26**) and rear (**Figure 27**) hubs. If the bearings are intact, one of the removal methods described in this section may be used. To remove a bearing where the inner race assembly has fallen out, refer to *Removing Damaged Bearings* in this section.

> *CAUTION*
> *When handling the wheel assembly in the following steps, do not support the wheel on the brake disc as doing so could damage the disc. Support the wheel on 2 wooden blocks.*

1. Pry the seals out of the hub with a wide-blade screwdriver (**Figure 28**). Cushion the screwdriver with a rag to avoid damaging the hub or brake disc.
2. Examine the wheel bearings for excessive damage, especially the inner race. If the inner race of one bearing is damaged, remove the other bearing first. If both bearings are damaged, try to remove the bearing with the least amount of damage first. On rusted and damaged bearings, applying pressure to the inner race usually causes the inner race to pop out, leaving the outer race in the hub.

3. On front wheels, remove the odometer gear retainer (**Figure 30**) from the right side of the wheel.

> *NOTE*
> *Step 4 describes two methods of removing the wheel bearings. Step 4A requires the use of the Kowa Seiki Wheel Bearing Remover set (**Figure 31**), available through a Honda dealership. Step 4B describes steps on how to remove the bearings with a drift and hammer.*

> *WARNING*
> *Wear safety glasses when removing the bearings in the following steps.*

4A. To remove the wheel bearings (**Figure 29**) with the Kowa Seiki Wheel Bearing Remover set:
   a. Select the correct size remover head tool and insert it into the right side hub bearing (**Figure 32**).
   b. From the opposite side of the hub, insert the remover shaft (B, **Figure 33**) into the slot in the backside of the remover head. Then position the hub with the remover head tool resting against a solid surface and strike the remover shaft to force it into the slit in the re-

10

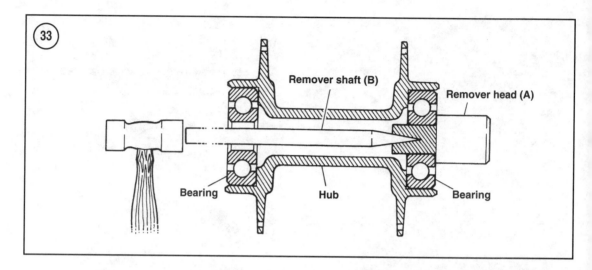

Remover shaft (B)

Remover head (A)

Bearing

Hub

Bearing

mover head. This will wedge the remover head tool against the inner bearing race. See **Figure 33**.

c. Position the hub and strike the end of the remover shaft with a hammer to drive the bearing (A, **Figure 34**) out of the hub. Remove the bearing and tool. Release the remover head from the bearing.

d. Remove the distance collar (B, **Figure 34**) from the hub.

e. Remove the left side bearing the same way (**Figure 35**).

4B. To remove the wheel bearings without special tools:

NOTE
Clean the hub thoroughly of all chemical residue before heating it with a torch in this procedure.

CAUTION
The hub and bearings will be hot after heating them with a torch. Wear welding gloves when handling the parts.

a. Heat one side of the hub with a propane torch. Work the torch in a circular motion around the hub, taking care not to hold the torch in one area. Turn the wheel over and remove the bearing as described in the next step.

b. Using a long drift, tilt the distance collar away from one side of the bearing (**Figure 36**).

NOTE
Do not damage the distance collar when removing the bearing. It may be necessary to grind a clearance groove

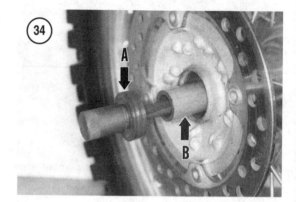

in the drift, to enable it to contact the bearing while clearing the distance collar.

c. Tap the bearing out of the hub with a hammer, working around the perimeter of the bearing's inner race.

d. Remove the distance collar from the hub.

e. Turn the hub over and heat the opposite side.

f. Drive out the opposite bearing using a large socket or bearing driver.

g. Inspect the distance collar for burrs created during removal. Remove burrs with a file.

5. Clean and dry the hub and distance collar.

Inspection

1. Check the hub mounting bore for cracks or other damage. If the bearings are loose, the hub mounting bore is damaged. Replace the hub.

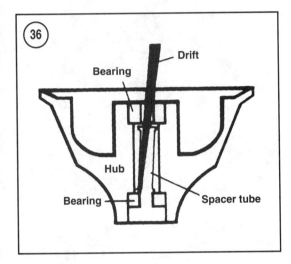

2. Inspect the distance collar for flared ends. Check the ends for cracks or other damage. Do not try to repair the distance collar by cutting or grinding its end surfaces as this will shorten the distance collar. Replace the distance collar if one or both ends are damaged.

CAUTION
The distance collar operates against the wheel bearing inner races to prevent them from moving inward when the axle is tightened. If a distance collar is too short, or if it is not installed, the inner bearing races will move inward and bind on the axle, causing bearing damage and seizure.

Assembly

Before installing the new bearings and seals, note the following:

  a. The front wheel seals are different.

b. The front wheel bearings are identical (same part number).

c. The rear wheel seals and bearings are different.

d. In each wheel, install both bearings with their closed side facing out. If a bearing is sealed on both sides, install the bearing with its manufacturer's marks facing out.

e. Install both seals with their closed side facing out.

f. When grease is called for in the following steps, use a Lithium based multipurpose grease (NLGI No. 2) or equivalent.

1. Remove any dirt or debris from the hub.

2. Pack the open side of each bearing (**Figure 37**) with grease.

NOTE
On the front wheel, install the right bearing first, then the left bearing. On the rear wheel, install the left bearing first, then the right bearing.

3. Place the first bearing squarely against the bore opening with its closed side facing out. Select a driver with an outside diameter slightly smaller than the bearing's outside diameter. Then drive the bearing into the bore until it bottoms out (**Figure 29**).

4. Install the distance collar and center it against the center race.

5. Place the second bearing squarely against the bore opening with its closed side facing out. Using the driver, drive the bearing partway into the bearing bore. Make sure the distance collar is centered in the hub. If not, install the axle through the hub to align the distance collar with the bearing. Then remove the axle and continue installing the bearing until it bottoms.

10

6. Insert the axle though the hub and turn it by hand. Check for any roughness or binding, indicating bearing damage.

NOTE
If the axle will not go in, the distance collar is not aligned correctly with one of the bearings.

7. Pack the lip of each seal with grease.

8. On the front wheel, install the odometer gear retainer (2, **Figure 26**) before installing the seal (**Figure 30**). Align the tangs on the odometer gear retainer with the slots in the hub.

9. Place a seal squarely against one of the bore openings with its closed side facing out. Then drive the seal in the bore until it is flush with the outside of the bearing bore (**Figure 25**).

10. Repeat Step 9 for the other seal.

Removing Damaged Bearings

When damaged wheel bearings remain in use, the inner races can break apart and fall out of the bearing, leaving the outer race pressed in the hub. Removal is difficult because only a small part of the race is accessible above the hub's shoulder. You only have a small and difficult target to drive against. To remove a bearing's outer race under these conditions, first heat the hub evenly with a propane torch. Drive out the outer race with a drift and hammer. It may be necessary to grind a clearance tip on the end of the drift, to avoid damaging the hub bore. Check this before heating the hub. When removing the race, apply force at different points around the race to prevent it from binding in the mounting bore once it starts to move. After removing the race, inspect the hub mounting bore carefully for cracks or other damage.

WHEEL SERVICE

Component Condition

Off-road riding subjects the wheels to a significant amount of punishment. It is important to inspect the wheel regularly for lateral (side-to-side) and radial (up-and-down) runout, even spoke tension, and visible rim damage. When a wheel has a noticeable wobble, it is out of true. This is usually

caused by loose spokes, but it can be caused by an impact-damaged rim.

Truing a wheel corrects the lateral and radial runout to bring the wheel back into specification.

The condition of the individual wheel components will affect the ability to successfully true the wheel. Note the following:

1. *Spoke condition*—Do not attempt to true a wheel with bent or damaged spokes. Doing so places an excessive amount of tension on the spoke and rim. The spoke may break and/or pull through the spoke

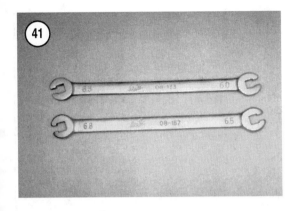

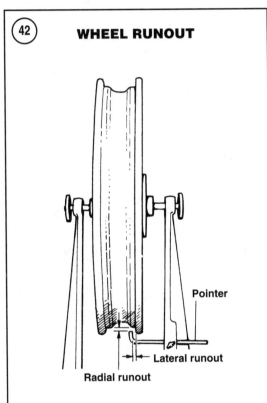

WHEEL RUNOUT

Pointer

Lateral runout

Radial runout

necessary to remove the tire from the rim and cut the spoke(s) out of the wheel.

3. *Rim condition*—Minor rim damage can be corrected by truing the wheel, however, trying to correct excessive runout caused by impact damage will cause hub and rim damage due to spoke overtightening. Inspect the rims for cracks, flat spots or dents (**Figure 38**). Check the spoke holes for cracks or enlargement. Replace rims with excessive damage.

Wheel Truing Preliminaries

Before checking the runout and truing the wheel, note the following:

1. Make sure the wheel bearings are in good condition.

2. A small amount of wheel runout is acceptable. Do not try to true the wheel to a perfect zero reading. Doing so will result in excessive spoke tension and possible rim and hub damage.

3. The runout can be checked on the bike by mounting a pointer against the fork or swing arm (**Figure 39**) and slowly rotating the wheel.

4. Perform major wheel truing with the tire removed and the wheel mounted in a truing stand. If a stand is not available, mount the wheel on the bike with spacers on each side of the wheel to prevent it from sliding on the axle.

5. Use a spoke nipple wrench of the correct size (**Figure 40**). Using the wrong type of tool or one that is the incorrect size will round off the spoke nipples, making adjustment difficult. Quality spoke wrenches (**Figure 41**) have openings that grip the nipple on four corners to prevent nipple damage.

6. Refer to the spoke nipple torque specifications in **Table 3** when using a torque wrench.

Wheel Truing Procedure

Lateral and radial runout specifications are listed in **Table 1**.

1. Position a pointer facing toward the rim as shown in **Figure 42**. Spin the wheel slowly and check the lateral and radial runout. If the rim is out of adjustment, continue with Step 2.

2. If there are many loose spokes, or if replacing the spokes, measure the rim to the base point off set clearance shown in **Figure 43** (front) or **Figure 44**

nipple hole in the rim. Inspect the spokes carefully and replace any that are damaged.

2. *Nipple condition*—When truing the wheels the nipples must turn freely on the spoke, however, it is quite common for the spoke threads to become corroded and make it difficult to turn the nipple. Spray a penetrating liquid onto the nipple and allow sufficient time for it to penetrate before trying to force the nipple loose. Work the spoke wrench in both directions and continue to apply penetrating liquid. If the spoke wrench rounds off the nipple, it will be

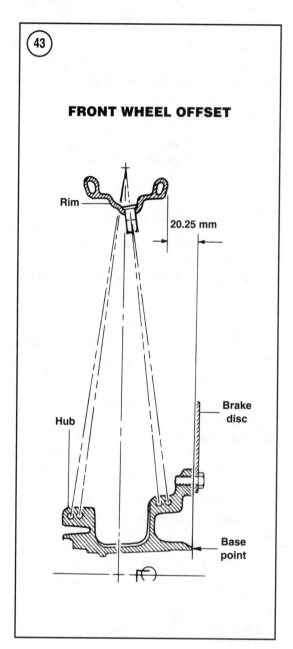

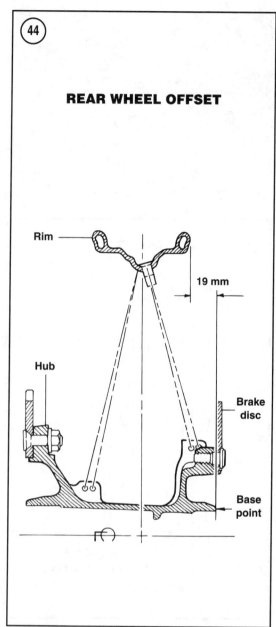

(rear). Reposition the rim and hub to obtain the correct off set clearance.

3. Lateral runout adjustment: If the side-to-side runout is out of specification, adjust the wheel, using **Figure 45** as an example. Always loosen and tighten the spokes (**Figure 40**) an equal number of turns.

NOTE
Determining the number of spokes to loosen and tighten in Steps 2 and 3

will depend on how far the runout is out of adjustment. Loosen two or three spokes, then tighten the opposite two or three spokes. If the runout is excessive and affects a greater area along the rim, loosen and tighten a greater number of spokes.

4. Radial runout adjustment: If the up and down runout is out of specification, the hub is not centered in the rim. Draw the high point of the rim toward the

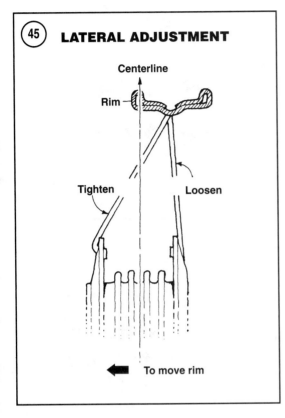

45 **LATERAL ADJUSTMENT**

Centerline

Rim

Tighten   Loosen

To move rim

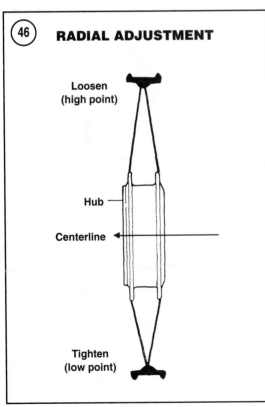

46 **RADIAL ADJUSTMENT**

Loosen
(high point)

Hub

Centerline

Tighten
(low point)

47

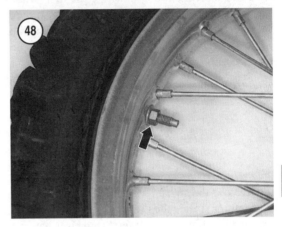

48

10

centerline of the wheel by loosening the spokes in the area of the high point, and tightening the spokes on the side opposite the high point (**Figure 46**). Tighten the spokes in equal amounts to prevent distortion.

5. After truing the wheel, seat each spoke in the hub by tapping it with a flat nose punch and hammer. Then recheck the spoke tension and wheel runout. Readjust if necessary.

6. Check the ends of the spokes where they are threaded in the nipples. Grind off any ends that protrude through the nipples to prevent them from puncturing the tube.

TIRE CHANGING

Removal

1. Remove the valve core (**Figure 47**) and deflate the tire.

2. Loosen the rim lock nuts (**Figure 48**).

3. Press the entire bead on both sides of the tire into the center of the rim.

4. Lubricate the beads with soapy water.

> *NOTE*
> *Use tire irons without sharp edges (**Figure 49**). If necessary, file the ends of the tire irons to remove any rough edges.*

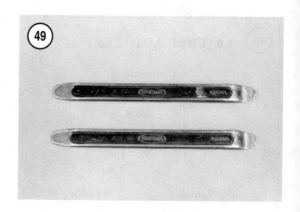

5. Insert the tire iron under the bead next to the valve (**Figure 50**). Force the bead on the opposite side of the tire into the center of the rim and pry the bead over the rim with the tire iron.

6. Insert a second tire iron next to the first to hold the bead over the rim. Then work around the tire with the first tire iron, prying the bead over the rim. Be careful not to pinch the inner tube with the tire irons.

7. Reach inside the tire and remove the valve from the hole in the rim, then remove the tube from the tire.

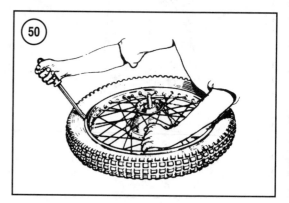

> *NOTE*
> *Steps 8 and 9 are required only if it is necessary to completely remove the tire from the rim.*

8. Remove the nut and washer and remove the rim lock(s) from inside the tire.

9. Stand the tire upright. Insert the tire iron between the second bead and the side of the rim where the first bead was pried over (**Figure 51**). Force the bead on the opposite side from the tire iron into the center of the rim. Pry the second bead off of the rim, working around as with the first.

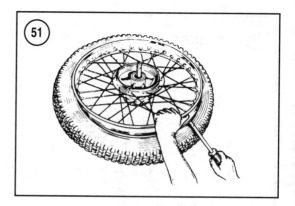

Inspection

1. Inspect the inside and outside of the tire for any damage.

2. Check the rim locks and replace if damaged (**Figure 52**).

3. Make sure the spoke ends do not protrude above the nipple heads and into the center of the rim. Grind or file off any protruding spoke ends.

> *NOTE*
> *If water and dirt are entering the rim, discard the rubber rim band. Wrap the rim center with 2 separate revolutions of duct tape. Punch holes through the tape at the rim lock and valve stem holes.*

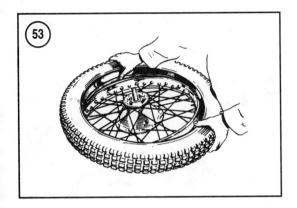

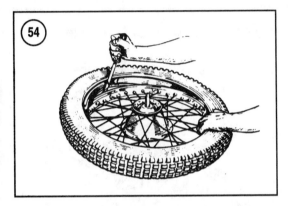

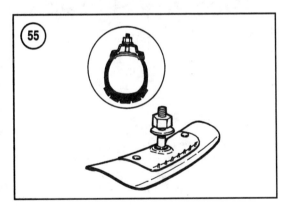

Installation

NOTE
Before installing the tire, place it in a hot place (in the sun or in a hot closed car). The heat will soften the rubber and ease installation.

1. If a rubber rim band is used, be sure the band is in place with the rough side toward the rim. Align the holes in the band with the holes in the rim.

2. Liberally sprinkle the inside tire casing with talcum powder to reduce chafing between the tire and tube and to minimize tube damage.

3. If the tire was removed, lubricate one bead with soapy water. Align the tire with the rim and push the tire onto the rim (**Figure 53**). Work around the tire in both directions (**Figure 54**).

4. Install the rim lock(s), lockwasher and nut. Do not tighten the nut at this time. Make sure the rim lock is positioned inside the tire.

5. Install the core into the inner tube valve. Put the tube in the tire, making sure not to twist it, then insert the valve stem through the hole in the rim. Inflate the tube just enough to round it out. Too much air will make installation difficult, and too little will increase the chances of pinching the tube with the tire irons.

6. Lubricate the upper tire bead and rim with soapy water.

NOTE
*Make sure to install the upper tire bead over the rim locks (**Figure 55**) in Step 7. If a rim lock is not installed correctly, it will be necessary to pull the side of the tire away from the rim to install it inside the tire. This increases the chances of pinching the tube.*

7. Press the upper bead into the rim opposite the valve. Pry the bead into the rim on both sides of the initial point by hand and work around the rim to the valve. If the tire wants to pull up on one side, either use a tire iron or a knee to hold the tire in place. The last few inches are usually the toughest to install and it is also where most pinched tubes occur. If possible, continue to push the tire into the rim by hand. Relubricate the bead if necessary. If the tire bead wants to pull out from under the rim use both knees to hold the tire in place. If necessary, use a tire iron for the last few inches.

8. Reach inside the tire and wiggle the valve stem to make sure the tube is not trapped under the bead. Set the valve squarely in its hole before screwing on the valve nut.

NOTE
*Make sure the valve stem is not turned sideways in the rim as shown in **Figure 56**.*

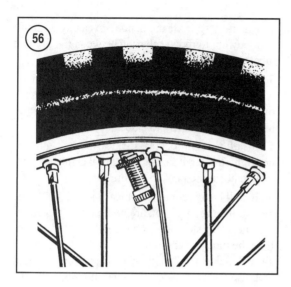

9. Make sure the bead on both sides of the tire fits evenly around the rim, then relubricate both sides of the tire. Inflate the tire to approximately 25-30 psi to insure the tire bead is seated properly on the rim. If the tire is hard to seat, release the air from the tube and then reinflate.

> *WARNING*
> *Do not overinflate the tube when try-*
> *ing to seat the tire onto the rim.*

10. Tighten the rim lock nut(s) (**Figure 48**) to the specification in **Table 3**.
11. Reduce the tire pressure to 15 psi (100 kPa). Screw on the valve stem nut but do not tighten it against the rim. Instead, tighten it against the air cap. Doing this will prevent the valve stem from pulling away from the tube if the tire slips on the rim.

DRIVE CHAIN

Refer to **Table 2** for drive chain specifications. Refer to *Drive Chain* in Chapter Three for routine drive chain inspection, adjustment and lubrication procedures.

Removal/Installation

1. Support the bike on a workstand with its rear wheel off the ground.
2. Turn the rear wheel and drive chain until the master link is accessible.

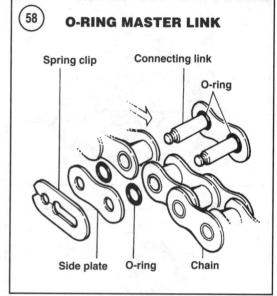

> *NOTE*
> *If the drive chain is equipped with a*
> *press fit master link, remove and in-*
> *stall it as described under **Press Fit***
> ***Master Link** in this section.*

3. Remove the master link spring clip with a pair of pliers (**Figure 57**). Then remove the side plate and connecting link and separate the chain. When disconnecting an O-ring chain, remove the four O-rings (**Figure 58**, typical).
4. Slowly pull the drive chain off the drive sprocket.
5. Install by reversing these removal steps while noting the following.
6. If an O-ring chain is used, install the four O-rings following the chain manufacturer's instructions (**Figure 58**, typical) or use the following guideline:

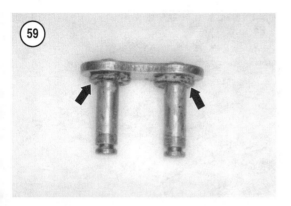

a. Install an O-ring on each connecting link pin (**Figure 59**).

b. Insert the connecting link (A, **Figure 60**) through the chain.

c. Install the remaining two O-rings onto the connecting link pins (B, **Figure 60**).

d. Install the slide plate (**Figure 61**). If the side plate is a press fit, refer to *Press Fit Master Link* in this chapter.

7. Install the spring clip (**Figure 58**) on the master link so the closed end of the clip is facing the direction of chain travel. See **Figure 62**.

8. Adjust the drive chain as described in Chapter Three.

10

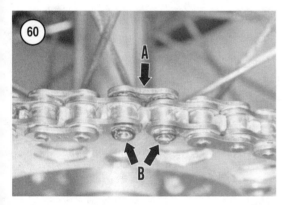

Press Fit Master Link

Many of the new drive chains use a press fit side plate (**Figure 61**), which helps to keep the chain connected if the spring clip pops off as the bike is being ridden. To remove and install this type of master link, special tools are required. To disconnect the chain, first remove the spring clip (**Figure 57**) from the master link, then use a chain breaker (**Figure 63**) to separate the side plate from the master link. To install the side plate, use a press-fit chain tool like the Motion Pro chain press tool (part No. 08-070) shown in **Figure 64**. Press the side plate onto the master link and pivot both ends of the chain at the master link. The chain ends must pivot smoothly with no sign of binding. If the chain is tight or binds at the master link, the side plate was pressed on too far. Usually, the side plate is properly installed when the grooves in the connecting link just show on the outside of the side plate. If the connecting link grooves are partially visible, the spring

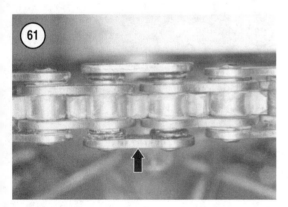

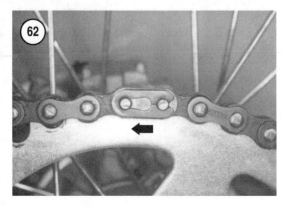

clip will not seat in the grooves properly and can pop off.

> *CAUTION*
> *Attempting to install a press-fit master link without the proper tools may cause you to damage the master link and drive chain.*

Cutting A Drive Chain To Length

Table 2 lists the correct number of chain links required for original equipment gearing. If the replacement drive chain is too long, cut it to length as follows.

1. Stretch the new chain on the workbench.

2. If a new chain is to be installed over stock gearing, refer to **Table 2** for the correct number of chain links. If the sprocket size was changed, install the new chain over both sprockets (with the rear wheel moved forward) to determine the correct number of links to remove (**Figure 65**). Make chalk marks on the two chain pins that will be cut. Count the chain links one more time or check the chain length to make sure it is correct.

> *WARNING*
> *Using a hand or bench grinder as described in Step 3 will cause flying particles. Do not operate a grinding tool without proper eye protection.*

3. Grind the head of two pins flush with the face of the side plate with a grinder or suitable grinding tool.

4. Press the side plate out of the chain with a chain breaker (**Figure 66**); support the chain carefully when doing this. If the pins are still tight, grind more material from the end of the pins and then try again.

5. Remove the side plate and push out the connecting link (**Figure 67**).

6. Install the new drive chain as described in this chapter.

Service and Inspection

For routine service and inspection of the drive chain, refer to *Drive Chain* in Chapter Three.

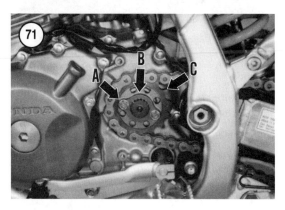

SPROCKET REPLACEMENT

This section describes service procedures on replacing the drive (front) and driven (rear) sprockets. See **Table 2** for sprocket sizes.

Inspection

Check drive chain and sprocket wear as described under *Drive Chain* in Chapter Three.

Drive Sprocket
Removal/Installation

Refer to **Figure 68**.

1. Remove the alternator wire (A, **Figure 69**) from the mounting bolt clamp.

2. Unbolt and remove the sprocket cover (B, **Figure 69**) and case saver (**Figure 70**).

3. Remove the two drive sprocket mounting bolts (A, **Figure 71**).

4. Turn the fixing plate (B, **Figure 71**) to align its splines with the countershaft splines, and remove the plate.

5. Pull the drive sprocket (C, **Figure 71**) off the countershaft, then disconnect it from the drive chain and remove the sprocket.

> *NOTE*
> *If the drive sprocket cannot be removed because the drive chain is too tight, loosen the rear axle nut and loosen the chain adjusters.*

6. Inspect the sprocket assembly as described under *Inspection* in this chapter.

7. Reverse these steps to install the drive sprocket, plus the following.

8. Install the drive sprocket (C, **Figure 71**) with its numbered side facing out.

9. Install the fixing plate (B, **Figure 71**) over the countershaft grooves, then turn it to align its holes with the sprocket holes.

10. Install the drive sprocket mounting bolts (A, **Figure 71**) and tighten securely.

11. Check the chain adjustment (Chapter Three).

10

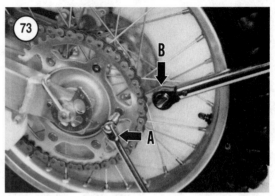

Driven Sprocket
Removal and Installation

> *NOTE*
> *The drive sprocket is attached to the rear hub with Allen bolts and nuts. Do not loosen these fasteners by turning the Allen bolt. Instead, hold the Allen bolt and loosen the nut to avoid damaging the Allen bolt head.*

1. Support the bike on a workstand with the rear wheel off the ground.
2. Hold one of the sprocket Allen bolts and loosen its mounting nut with a wrench. Repeat for each Allen bolt, washer and nut.
3. Remove the rear wheel as described in this chapter.
4. Remove the Allen bolts, washers, nuts and driven sprocket (**Figure 72**) from the rear hub.
5. Check the sprocket mounting tabs for cracks or other damage. Replace the hub if any damage is found.
6. Clean and dry the sprocket fasteners. Replace any nut or bolt with damaged threads or hex corners.
7. Install the new sprocket onto the rear hub with its marked or stamped side facing out.

8. Install the Allen bolts, washers and nuts and finger tighten.
9. Install the rear wheel as described in this chapter.
10. Hold the Allen bolts with a hex socket (A, **Figure 73**), then use a torque adapter (B) and torque wrench to tighten the driven sprocket nuts as specified in **Table 3**. Repeat to tighten all of the nuts.

> *NOTE*
> *B, **Figure 73** shows the Motion Pro torque adapter. For information on using a torque adapter and torque wrench, refer to **Torque Wrench Adapters** in Chapter One.*

11. Adjust the drive chain and tighten the rear axle nut as described in Chapter Three.

Drive and Driven Sprocket Inspection

1. Inspect the sprocket teeth. If they are visibly worn, replace the sprocket.
2. If either sprocket requires replacement, the drive chain is probably worn also. Refer to *Drive Chain* in Chapter Three. Always replace the drive chain and both sprockets at the same time.

Table 1 FRONT AND REAR WHEEL SPECIFICATIONS

Front tire	
Size	80/100-21 51m
Make/type	Dunlop K490G
Rear tire	
Size	110/100-18 64M
Make/type	Dunlop K695
Tire pressure	15 psi (100 kPa)
Wheel rim-to-hub offset	
Front	20.25 mm (0.797 in.)
Rear	19 mm (0.748 in.)
Wheel runout limit	2.0 mm (0.078 in.)
Axle runout limit	0.2 mm (0.008 in.)

Table 2 DRIVE CHAIN AND SPROCKET SPECIFICATIONS

Drive chain	
DID	520V8
RK	520M0Z6
Number of chain links	108
Stock sprocket sizes	
Drive sprocket (front)	15
Driven sprocket (rear)	45

Table 3 FRONT AND REAR WHEEL TIGHTENING TORQUES

	N•m	in.-lb.	ft.-lb.
Driven sprocket nuts	32	–	24
Front axle holder nuts	12	106	–
Front axle	88	–	65
Rear axle nut	88	–	65
Rim lock nuts	13	115	–
Spoke nipples	3.7	32.7	–

10

FRONT SUSPENSION AND STEERING

This chapter describes service procedures for the handlebar, steering stem and front fork. **Table 1** lists front suspension and steering specifications. **Tables 1-5** are at the end of the chapter.

HANDLEBAR

NOTE
This section describes service to the original equipment handlebars. When installing aftermarket handlebars and/or handlebar holders, refer to the manufacturer's instructions for additional service information.

Removal

1. Support the bike on a workstand.

2. Remove the fuel tank breather tube from inside the steering stem.

3. Remove the clamp securing the engine stop switch wiring harness to the handlebar.

4. Remove the engine stop switch (A, **Figure 1**).

NOTE
Inspect the engine stop switch while it is off the handlebar. Check for damage that could cause the switch to ground against the handlebar and cause a no spark condition.

5. Remove the clutch cable holder (B, **Figure 1**) mounting bolts and remove the holder and clutch cable from the handlebar.

6. Remove the decompression cable holder (C, **Figure 1**) mounting bolts and remove the holder and decompression cable from the handlebar.

NOTE
The following steps are shown with the right handlebar hand cover removed for clarity.

7. Remove the bolts securing the master cylinder to the handlebar and remove the master cylinder (A, **Figure 2**). Support the master cylinder so it does not hang by its hose.

8. Loosen the throttle housing screws (B, **Figure 2**).

9. Remove the handlebar holder bolts and the upper holder (**Figure 3**). Remove the handlebar while sliding the throttle housing off the handlebar.

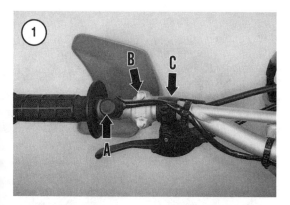

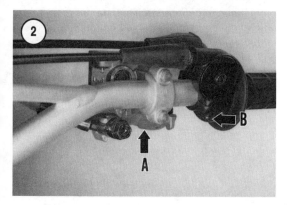

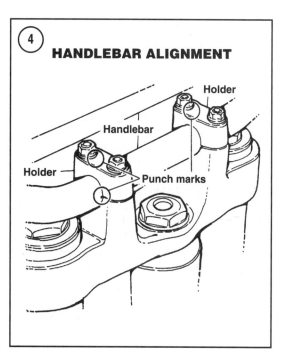

HANDLEBAR ALIGNMENT

WARNING
Never attempt to repair a damaged handlebar. These attempts can weaken the handlebar and may cause it to break while under stress (landing from a jump) or during a crash. Both instances can cause serious injury.

3. Inspect the handlebar mounting bolts for bending, thread strippage or other damage. Check the threaded holes in the lower holders for the same conditions. Clean the threads to remove all dirt and grease residue. Replace damaged bolts.

4. Clean the upper and lower handlebar holders and the knurled section on steel handlebars with a stiff brush and solvent or electrical contact cleaner. If an aluminum handlebar is used, clean the holder area on the bar with contact cleaner and a soft brush.

Inspection

1. Inspect the handlebar for cracks, bending or other damage and replace if necessary.

2. If equipped with an aluminum handlebar, inspect it for scores or cracks, especially at the handlebar, throttle and operating lever clamp mounting areas. If *any* damage is found, replace the handlebar. Cracks and scoring of the metal in these areas may cause the handlebar to break.

Installation

1. Slide the throttle housing over the handlebar. Position the handlebar in the lower holders and install the upper holders (**Figure 3**) and the mounting bolts. Install the holders with their punch mark (**Figure 4**) facing forward.

2. Turn the handlebar and align the punch mark on the handlebar with the lower clamp surface (**Figure 4**).

3. Install the four handlebar mounting bolts (**Figure 3**). Tighten the front bolts first, then tighten the rear bolts.

> *WARNING*
> *Do not ride the bike until the handlebar clamps are mounted and tightened correctly. Improper mounting may cause the bars to slip, resulting in loss of control of the bike.*

4. Align the clamp mating surface on the throttle housing with the punch mark on the handlebar (**Figure 5**). Tighten the front throttle housing screw first, then tighten the rear screw. Open and release the throttle grip, making sure it returns smoothly.

5. Install the master cylinder (A, **Figure 2**) as follows:

    a. Align the edge of the master cylinder clamp surface with the punch mark on the handlebar (**Figure 6**).

    b. Install the master cylinder holder with the UP mark on the holder facing up.

    c. Install and tighten the master cylinder mounting bolts. Tighten the upper bolt first, then tighten the lower bolt.

6. Align the edge of the decompression lever holder (C, **Figure 1**) clamp surface with the punch mark on the handlebar. Install the holder and tighten the two mounting bolts securely.

7. Align the edge of the clutch lever holder clamp surface with the punch mark (**Figure 7**) on the handlebar. Install the holder and tighten the two mounting bolts securely.

8. Install the engine stop switch by aligning the switch bracket with the punch mark on the handlebar (**Figure 8**). Tighten the bracket screw securely.

9. Sit on the bike and check the position of the handlebar and controls.

> *WARNING*
> *Make sure the front brake, clutch cable, decompression cable, throttle cables and engine stop switch are in good working order before riding the bike.*

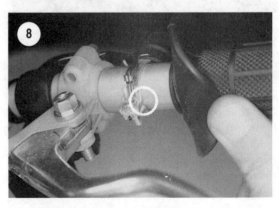

STEERING HEAD

The steering head (**Figure 9**) pivots on tapered roller bearings. The bearing inner races (mounted in the frame) and the lower bearing (mounted on the

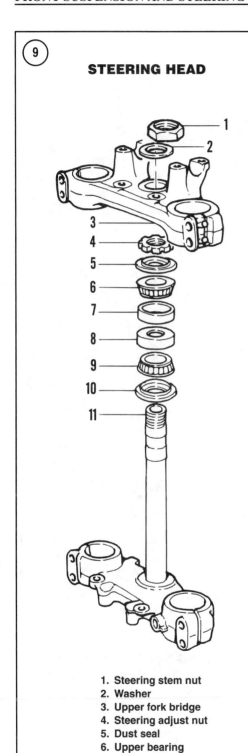

STEERING HEAD

1. Steering stem nut
2. Washer
3. Upper fork bridge
4. Steering adjust nut
5. Dust seal
6. Upper bearing
7. Upper bearing race
8. Lower bearing race
9. Lower bearing
10. Dust seal
11. Steering stem

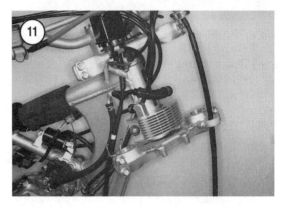

steering stem) should not be removed unless they require replacement.

Remove the steering stem and lubricate the bearings at the intervals specified in Chapter Three.

Disassembly

1. Note the cable and wiring harness routing before removing them in the following steps. See **Figure 10** and **Figure 11**, typical.

2. Remove the front visor (Chapter Fifteen).

3. Remove the odometer (Chapter Fifteen).

4. Remove the brake hose and odometer cable guides at the steering stem.

5. Remove the front wheel (Chapter Ten).

6. Remove the front fender (Chapter Fifteen).

7. Remove the handlebar as described in this chapter.

8. Remove the front fork as described in this chapter.

9. Remove the steering stem nut and washer (**Figure 12**).

10. Remove the upper fork bridge (**Figure 12**).

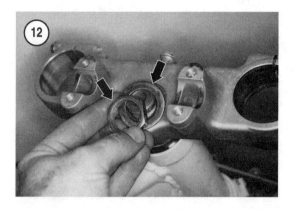

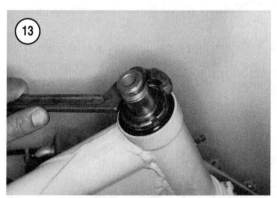

11. Loosen the steering adjust nut (**Figure 13**) with a spanner wrench.

12. Remove the steering adjust nut, dust seal (**Figure 14**) and steering stem (A, **Figure 15**).

13. Remove the upper bearing (B, **Figure 15**).

Inspection

Replace worn or damaged parts as described in this chapter.

1. Clean the bearings and races in solvent.

2. Check the steering head frame welds for cracks and fractures. Refer repair to a qualified frame shop or welding service.

3. Check the steering stem nut and steering adjust nut for damage.

4. Check the steering stem assembly for cracks and damage.

5. Check the bearing races in the frame for pitting, galling and corrosion. Compare the worn bearing race in **Figure 16** with the new race in **Figure 17**. If a race is worn or damaged, replace both races (and bearings) as described in this chapter.

6. Check the tapered roller bearings (**Figure 18**) for wear and/or corrosion damage.

7. When reusing bearings, clean them thoroughly with a degreaser. Pack the clean bearings with waterproof bearing grease.

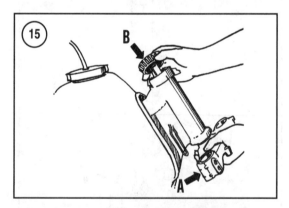

Outer Bearing Race Replacement

Do not remove the upper and lower (**Figure 17**) outer bearing races unless they require replacement. If replacing a bearing race, replace the tapered bearing at the same time.

1. Insert an aluminum drift into the frame tube (**Figure 19**) and carefully drive the race out from

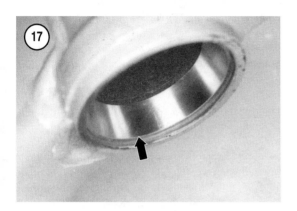

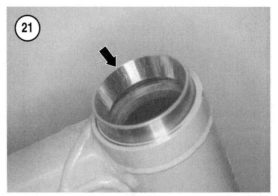

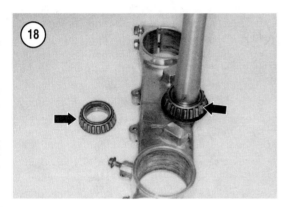

the inside (**Figure 20**). Strike at different spots around the race to prevent it from binding in the mounting bore. Repeat for the other race.

2. Clean the race bore and check for cracks or other damage.

3. Place the new race squarely into the mounting bore opening with its tapered side facing out (**Figure 21**).

4. To prevent damage to the race bore or races, install the races as follows:

   a. Assemble the puller (**Figure 22**) so the T-handle block can be used to hold the rod stationary while the race is pulled into position at the opposite end. If a block is not used, lock two nuts onto the rod and use a wrench to hold the rod stationary.

   CAUTION
   When using the threaded rod tool to install the bearing races in the following steps, do not allow the tool to contact the bearing race or it may damage it.

   b. To install the upper race, insert the puller (A, **Figure 23**) through the bottom of the frame tube. Seat the lower washer or plate against the frame as shown in B, **Figure 23**.

   c. At the top of the puller, slide the large washer down and seat it squarely on top of the bearing race (A, **Figure 24**). Install the required washers and coupling nut (B, **Figure 24**) that will work on the puller.

   d. Hand tighten the coupling nut (B, **Figure 24**). Make sure the washer is centered on the bearing race.

   e. Hold the threaded rod to prevent it from turning and tighten the coupling nut with a

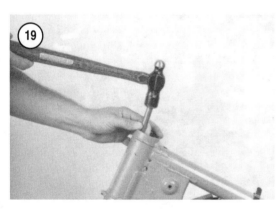

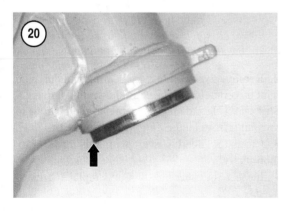

11

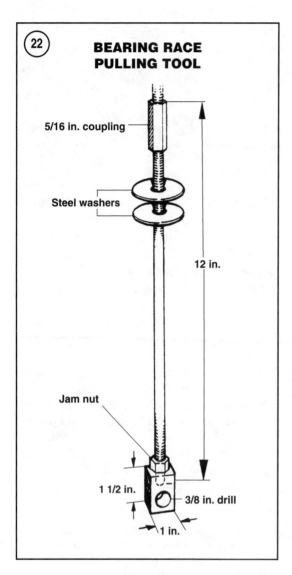

(22) **BEARING RACE PULLING TOOL**

5/16 in. coupling

Steel washers

12 in.

Jam nut

1 1/2 in.

3/8 in. drill

1 in.

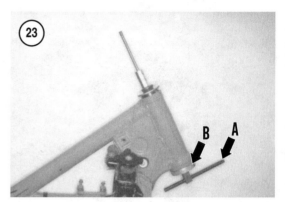

(23)

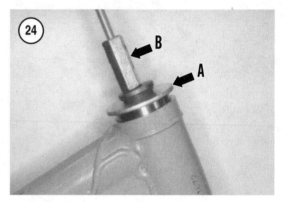

(24)

(25)

wrench. Continue until the race is drawn into the frame tube and bottoms out in its mounting bore. Remove the puller assembly and inspect the bearing race. It must bottom out in the frame tube (**Figure 25**).

f. Repeat to install the bottom race (**Figure 17**).

5. Lubricate the upper and lower bearing races with grease.

Steering Stem Bearing Replacement

Perform the following steps to replace the steering stem bearing (**Figure 26**).

1. Thread the steering stem nut onto the steering stem (**Figure 27**).

WARNING
Wear safety glasses while removing the steering stem bearing in Step 2.

2. Remove the steering stem bearing and dust seal with a hammer and chisel as shown in **Figure 27**. Strike at different spots underneath the bearing to prevent it from binding on the steering stem.

3. Clean the steering stem with solvent and dry thoroughly.

4. Inspect the steering stem and replace if damaged.

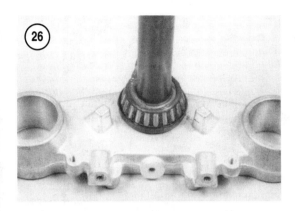

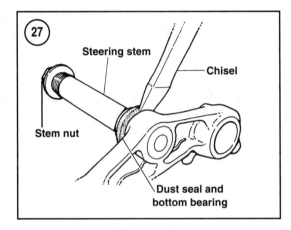

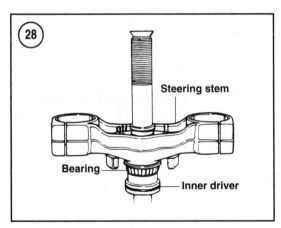

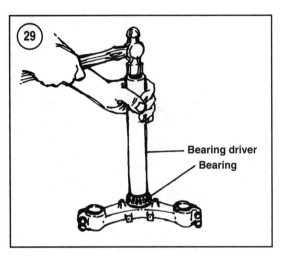

a. Install the steering stem and the new bearing in a press and support it with two bearing drivers as shown in **Figure 28**. Make sure the lower bearing driver seats against the inner bearing race and does not contact the bearing rollers.

b. Press the bearing onto the steering stem until it bottoms out (**Figure 26**).

8B. To install the new steering stem bearing with a bearing driver, perform the following:

a. Slide a bearing driver over the steering stem until it seats against the bearing's inner race (**Figure 29**).

b. Drive the bearing onto the steering stem until it bottoms out (**Figure 26**).

Assembly and Steering Adjustment

Refer to **Figure 9** when assembling the steering stem assembly.

1. Make sure the upper (**Figure 25**) and lower (**Figure 17**) bearing races are properly seated in the frame.

2. Lubricate the bearings and races with a waterproof bearing grease.

3. Install the upper bearing and dust seal (**Figure 30**) and seat it into its race.

4. Install the steering stem (A, **Figure 15**) through the bottom of the frame and hold it in place.

5. Install the steering adjust nut (**Figure 31**) and tighten finger-tight.

NOTE
Two methods are provided for adjusting the steering stem bearings. One

5. Lubricate the new dust seal lip (**Figure 27**) with grease and slide it over the steering stem.

6. Pack the new bearing with a waterproof bearing grease.

7. Slide the new bearing onto the steering stem until it stops.

8A. To install the new steering stem bearing with a press, perform the following:

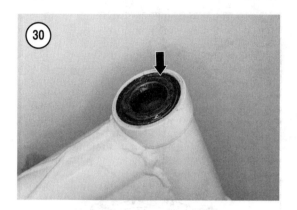

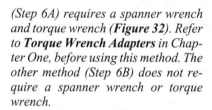

*(Step 6A) requires a spanner wrench and torque wrench (**Figure 32**). Refer to **Torque Wrench Adapters** in Chapter One, before using this method. The other method (Step 6B) does not require a spanner wrench or torque wrench.*

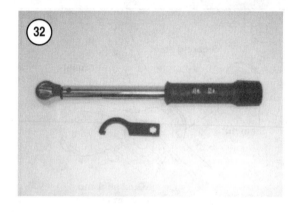

6A. To seat the bearings using a spanner wrench and torque wrench, perform the following:

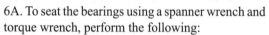

    a. Tighten the steering adjust nut (**Figure 33**) to the bearing seat torque specification listed in **Table 5**.

    b. Turn the steering stem from lock-to-lock several times to seat the bearings.

    c. Loosen the steering adjust nut (**Figure 33**).

    d. Tighten the steering adjust nut (**Figure 33**) to the final torque specification in **Table 5**.

    e. Check bearing play by turning the steering stem from lock-to-lock several times. The steering stem must pivot smoothly with no binding or roughness.

NOTE
Adjusting the steering play to a specific torque specification using a torque wrench and adapter can be difficult. If the steering stem is still too loose or tight after performing Step 6A, readjust it as described in Step 6B.

6B. If the tools described in Step 6A are not available, tighten the steering adjust nut as follows:

    a. Tighten the steering adjust nut (**Figure 31**) to seat the bearings. Turn the steering stem several times to seat the bearings. Loosen the nut completely. Use a spanner wrench or punch and hammer to tighten and loosen the nut.

    b. Tighten the steering adjust nut while checking bearing play. The adjust nut must be tight enough to remove play, both horizontal and vertical, yet loose enough so the steering assembly will turn to both lock positions under its own weight after an assist.

7. Install the upper fork bridge (A, **Figure 34**).

8. Install the washer and the steering stem nut (B, **Figure 34**). Finger-tighten the nut.

9. Slide both fork tubes into position and tighten the upper and lower fork tube pinch bolts.

10. Tighten the steering stem nut as specified in **Table 5**.

NOTE
Because tightening the steering stem nut affects the steering bearing preload, it may be necessary to repeat these steps several times until the steering adjustment is correct.

11. Check bearing play by turning the steering stem from side to side. The steering stem must pivot smoothly. If the steering stem is too tight, readjust the bearing play as follows:

a. Loosen the steering stem nut (B, **Figure 34**).

b. Loosen or tighten the steering adjust nut (C, **Figure 34**) as required to adjust the steering play.

c. Retighten the steering stem nut (B, **Figure 34**) to the specification in **Table 5**.

d. Recheck bearing play by turning the steering stem from side-to-side. If the play feels correct, turn the steering stem so the front fork is facing straight ahead. While an assistant steadies the bike, grasp the fork tubes, and try to move them front to back. If there is play and the bearing adjustment feels correct, the bearings and races are probably worn and require replacement. It helps to have someone steady the bike when checking steering head play.

12. Install the handlebar as described in this chapter.

13. Position the fork tubes and tighten the fork tube pinch bolts as described in this chapter.

14. Install the handlebar as described in this chapter.

15. Install the front fender (Chapter Fifteen).

16. Install the front wheel (Chapter Ten).

17. Install the brake hose and odometer cable guides at the steering stem.

18. Install the odometer (Chapter Fifteen).

19. Install the front visor (Chapter Fifteen).

20. After 30 minutes to 1 hour of riding time, check the steering adjustment. Adjust, if necessary, as described under *Steering Play Check and Adjustment* in this chapter.

**Steering Play
Check and Adjustment**

Steering adjustment takes up any slack in the steering stem and bearings and allows the steering stem to operate with free rotation. Any excessive play or roughness in the steering stem will make the steering imprecise and difficult and cause bearing damage. Improper bearing lubrication or an incorrect steering adjustment (too loose or tight) usually causes these conditions. Incorrectly routed clutch or throttle cables can also effect steering operation.

1. Support the bike with the front wheel off the ground.

2. Turn the handlebar from side to side. The steering stem should move freely and without any binding or roughness.

3. Turn the handlebar so the front wheel points straight ahead. Alternately push (slightly) one end of the handlebar and then the other. The front end must turn to each side from center under its own weight. Note the following:

a. If the steering stem moved roughly or stopped before hitting the frame stop, check the clutch and throttle cable routing. Reroute the cable(s) if necessary.

b. If the cable routing is correct and the steering is tight, the steering adjustment is too tight or the bearings require lubrication or replacement.

c. If the steering stem moved from side to side correctly, perform Step 4 to check for excessive looseness.

NOTE
When checking for excessive steering play in Step 4, have an assistant steady the bike.

11

4. Grasp the fork tubes firmly (near the axle) and attempt to move the wheel front to back. Note the following:

a. If movement can be felt at the steering stem, the steering adjustment is probably loose. Go to Step 5 to adjust the steering.

b. If there is no movement and the front end turns correctly as described in Steps 2-4, the steering adjustment is correct.

5. Remove the handlebar as described in this chapter.

6. Loosen the steering stem nut (B, **Figure 34**).

7. Adjust the steering adjust nut (C, **Figure 34**) as follows:

a. If the steering is too loose, tighten the steering adjust nut.

b. If the steering is too tight, loosen the steering adjust nut.

8. Tighten the steering stem nut (B, **Figure 34**) to the specification in **Table 5**.

9. Recheck the steering adjustment as described in this procedure. When the steering adjustment is correct, continue with Step 10.

NOTE
Because tightening the steering stem nut affects the steering bearing preload, it may be necessary to repeat Steps 6-9 a few times until the steering adjustment is correct. If the steering adjustment cannot be corrected, the steering bearings may require lubrication or are damaged. Remove the steering stem and inspect the bearings as described in this chapter.

10. Install the handlebar as described in this chapter. Recheck the steering adjustment.

FRONT FORK

Removal

1. Remove the front wheel as described in Chapter Ten.

2. Insert a plastic or wooden spacer block between the brake pads.

NOTE
The spacer installed in Step 2 will prevent the piston from being forced out of the caliper if the brake lever is ap-

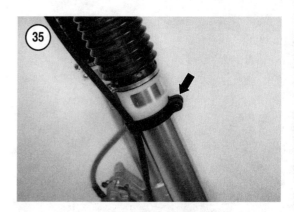

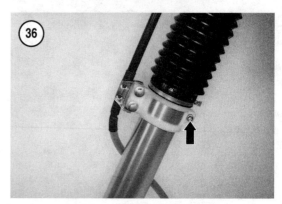

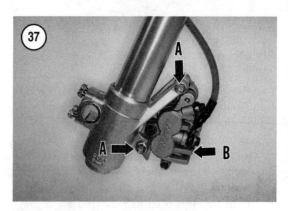

plied with the disc removed. If the piston is forced out, the caliper must be disassembled to reseat the piston.

3. Remove the front visor (Chapter Fifteen).

4. Remove the odometer clamp (**Figure 35**) from the right fork tube.

5. Remove the brake hose clamp (**Figure 36**) from the left fork tube.

6. Remove the brake caliper mounting bolts (A, **Figure 37**) and remove the brake caliper (B, **Figure**

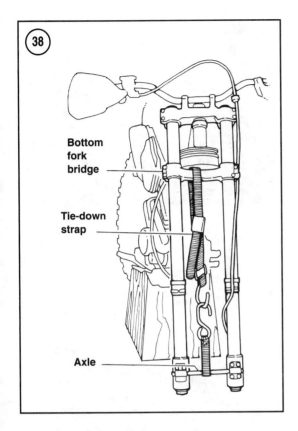

Bottom fork bridge

Tie-down strap

Axle

a tool is available to secure the cartridge when loosening and tightening the compression bolts.

7. To loosen the compression bolts on 1996-1997 models, do the following:

   a. Remove the front fender.

   b. Reinstall the front axle (without the wheel).

   c. Connect a tie-down strap between the bottom fork bridge and front axle. Tighten the tie-down strap (**Figure 38**) to compress the front fork tube approximately 5-10 cm (2-4 in.).

   d. Loosen, but do not remove, the compression bolt (**Figure 39**).

   e. Loosen the compression bolt on the other fork assembly.

   f. Remove the tie-down strap and front axle.

8. Loosen the upper and lower fork tube pinch bolts (**Figure 40**) and remove the fork tubes.

9. Clean the fork tubes, fork bridge and steering stem clamping surfaces.

10. Remove, clean and inspect the fork tube pinch bolts. Replace damaged bolts.

11

37). Support the brake caliper with a piece of stiff wire.

> *CAUTION*
> *Do not allow the brake caliper to hang from its brake hose.*

> *NOTE*
> *If the fork tubes require disassembly on 1996-97 models, loosen the compression bolts before removing the fork tube. On 1998 and later models,*

Installation

1. Clean the fork tube bores in the upper fork bridge and steering stem.

> *NOTE*
> *Install the fork tube equipped with the brake caliper mounting bracket (**Figure 37**) on the left side of the bike.*

2. Install one of the fork tubes into the steering stem. Align the lower fork tube groove with the top

surface of the upper fork bridge (A, **Figure 41**).
Tighten the lower pinch bolts (**Figure 40**) securely.
3. If the fork cap (B, **Figure 41**) was loosened earlier, tighten the fork cap to the specification in **Table 5**.
4. Repeat Steps 2 and 3 for the other fork tube.
5. Tighten the upper fork tube pinch bolts (**Figure 40**) securely.
6. If the fork boots were loosened or removed, position them so the air vent holes in each boot faces rearward. Make sure the lower end of each boot seats in its boot guide groove. Position the clamp screws so the screw heads face forward and then tighten securely.
7. Install the brake caliper as follows:
   a. Position the brake caliper (B, **Figure 37**) against the left fork tube bracket and secure it with two new mounting bolts. Tighten the brake caliper mounting bolts (A, **Figure 37**) to the specification in **Table 5**.
   b. Route the brake hose around the front of the fork tube and secure it with the clamp and mounting bolts (**Figure 36**).
8. Secure the odometer cable in place with the clamp (**Figure 35**). Insert the pin in the odometer clamp into the hole in the fork boot guide.
9. Install the front wheel as described in Chapter Ten. Turn the front wheel and squeeze the front brake lever a few times to reposition the pistons in the caliper. If the brake lever feels spongy, bleed the front brake (Chapter Thirteen).
10. If necessary, adjust the front fork compression and rebound adjusters as described in this chapter.

FRONT FORK SERVICE

Fork Tools

The following special tools are required to disassemble and reassemble the fork tubes and set the oil level:
1. Fork seal driver (A, **Figure 42**).

> *NOTE*
> *Before purchasing a fork seal driver, measure the outside diameter of the fork slider with a vernier caliper. Fork seal drivers are available in different sizes.*

2. Oil level gauge (B, **Figure 42**).

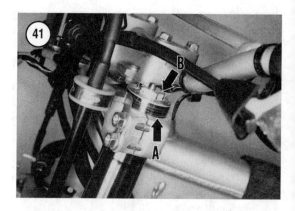

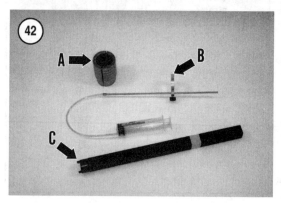

3. 1998-on: Honda damper rod holder attachment and holder handle (C, **Figure 42**).

> *NOTE*
> *See a Honda dealership for tools (**Figure 42**) and current part numbers.*

Disassembly

Refer to **Figure 43** when servicing the front fork.

> *NOTE*
> *When servicing fork tubes on 1996-97 models, loosen the compression bolts while the fork tubes are mounted on the bike. See **Front Fork Removal** in this chapter.*

1. Clean the fork assembly and the bottom of the compression bolt before disassembling the fork tube.
2. Remove the fork boot and boot guide.
3. Loosen the fork cap air screw (A, **Figure 44**) to release air from the fork tube.

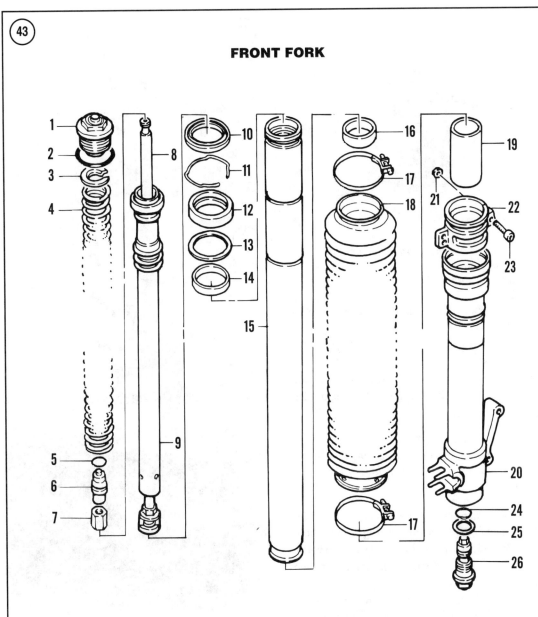

FRONT FORK

1. Fork cap
2. O-ring
3. Spring seat
4. Fork spring
5. O-ring
6. Rebound adjuster
7. Locknut
8. Piston rod
9. Cartridge
10. Dust seal
11. Stop ring
12. Oil seal
13. Back-up ring
14. Slider bushing
15. Fork tube
16. Fork tube bushing
17. Clamp
18. Boot
19. Oil lock piece
20. Slider
21. Nut
22. Boot guide
23. Bolt
24. O-ring
25. Washer
26. Compression bolt

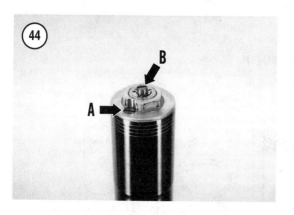

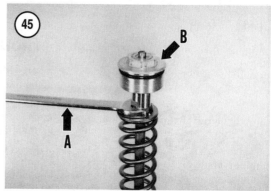

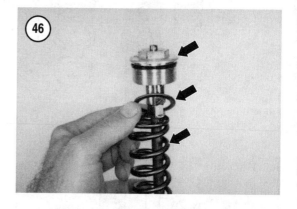

NOTE
In Steps 4 and 5, record the number of clicks so the adjusters can be set to the same positions.

4. Turn the rebound adjuster (B, **Figure 44**) counterclockwise to its softest setting.

5. Turn the compression adjuster (**Figure 39**) counterclockwise to its softest setting.

6. Hold the fork tube and unscrew the fork cap. Slowly lower the fork tube into the slider until it stops.

NOTE
If the fork cap is tight, install the fork in the steering stem, then loosen the fork cap.

7. Pull the fork spring down with one hand and install a wrench onto the locknut (A, **Figure 45**). Hold the wrench and loosen the fork cap (B, **Figure 45**).

8. Remove the fork cap, spring seat and fork spring (**Figure 46**).

9. Hold the fork tube over a drain pan and pump the fork tube to drain oil from the tube. Then pump the piston rod (**Figure 47**) to drain oil from the cartridge.

NOTE
*If only servicing the front fork to change the fork oil and set the oil level, stop at this point and go to the **Fork Oil Refilling** procedure in this chapter. To disassemble the front fork, continue with Step 10.*

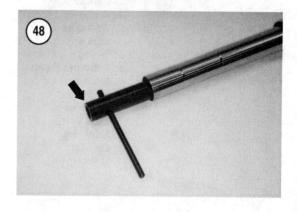

10. On 1998 and later models, loosen the compression bolt as follows:

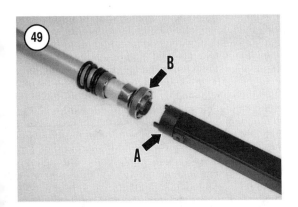

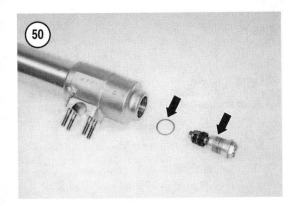

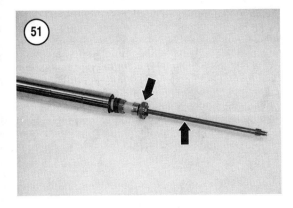

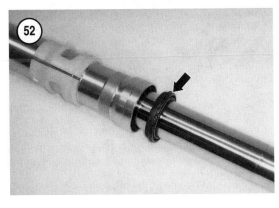

a. Bottom out the fork tubes, then clamp the axle holder on the bottom of the fork slider in a vise with soft jaws. Do not clamp against the side of the fork tube or fork slider.

b. Slowly push the piston rod into the cartridge until it stops.

c. Insert the Honda damper rod holder (or equivalent) into the fork tube and lock it into the top of the cartridge housing (**Figure 48**).

NOTE
Figure 49 *shows how the damper rod holder (A) locks into the top of the cartridge housing (B) with the cartridge removed from the fork tube for clarity.*

11

d. Hold the damper rod holder and loosen the compression bolt (**Figure 39**) with a socket.

11. Remove the compression bolt (**Figure 50**) and washer from the slider.

12. Remove the cartridge and piston rod assembly (**Figure 51**) from the fork tube.

13. Remove the fork slider from the vise.

14. Hold the fork over the drain pan and pump the fork tube to help empty any remaining oil from the fork assembly.

15. Carefully pry the dust seal (**Figure 52**) out of the fork tube.

16. Pry the stop ring (**Figure 53**) out of the groove in the fork tube.

17. Hold the fork tube and slowly move the fork slider up and down. If there is any noticeable binding or roughness, check the fork tube for dents or other damage.

18. There is an interference fit between the slider and guide bushings. To separate the fork tube from the fork slider, hold the fork tube and pull hard on

the slider using quick in and out strokes (**Figure 54**). This action withdraws the slider bushing, back-up ring and oil seal from the fork tube. See **Figure 55**.

19. Carefully pry open the end of the fork tube bushing (A, **Figure 56**) and slide it off the fork tube. To avoid damage to the bushing, do not pry the opening more than necessary.

20. Remove the following parts from the slider:
   a. Slider bushing (B, **Figure 56**).
   b. Backup ring (C, **Figure 56**).
   c. Oil seal (D, **Figure 56**).
   d. Stop ring (E, **Figure 56**).
   e. Dust seal (F, **Figure 56**).

21. Remove the oil lock piece (**Figure 57**) from the fork tube.

22. Clean and inspect the fork assembly as described under *Inspection* in this chapter.

Inspection

When measuring the fork components in this section, compare the actual measurements to the new and service limit specifications in **Table 1**. Replace parts that are out of specification or show damage as described in this section.

> *NOTE*
> *Handle the fork bushings (A and B, **Figure 56**) carefully when cleaning them in Step 1. Harsh cleaning can remove or damage their coating material.*

1. Initially clean all of the fork parts in solvent, first making sure the solvent will not damage the fork bushings or rubber parts. Then clean with soap and water and rinse with plain water. Remove all threadlock residue from the compression bolt and cartridge threads. Dry with compressed air.

2. Check the fork tube (15, **Figure 43**) for nicks, rust, chrome flaking or creasing, as these conditions will damage the dust and oil seals. Repair minor roughness with 600 grit sandpaper and solvent. Replace the slider if necessary.

3. Place the fork tube on a set of V-blocks and measure runout with a dial indicator. The actual runout is 1/2 of the indicator reading.

4. Check the slider's axle holder bore inner diameter for dents or burrs that could damage the compression valve O-ring when removing and installing

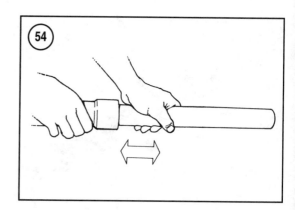

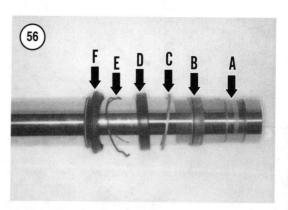

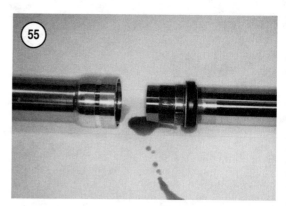

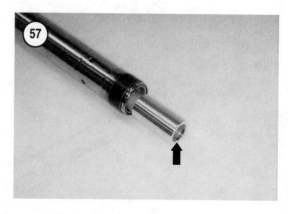

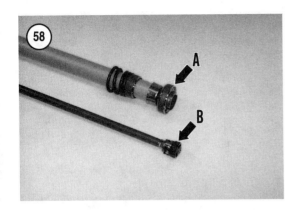

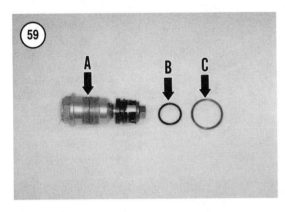

the valve. Remove burrs carefully with a fine grit sandpaper or a fine-cut file.

5. Check the slider (20, **Figure 43**) for:

    a. Outer tube damage.

    b. Damaged fork cap threads.

    c. Damaged oil seal bore.

    d. Damaged stop ring groove.

6. Make sure the cartridge (9, **Figure 43**) and piston rod (8, **Figure 43**) are straight and undamaged.

7. Check the piston ring on the cartridge (A, **Figure 58**) and piston rod (B, **Figure 58**) for excessive wear or damage.

8. Service the compression bolt (A, **Figure 59**) as follows:

    a. Remove the O-ring (B, **Figure 59**) and washer (C).

    b. Check the compression bolt (**Figure 60**) for damage.

CAUTION
*Do not disassemble the compression bolt (**Figure 60**). If further service or adjustment is required, refer service to a qualified suspension specialist.*

9. Check the slider and guide bushings (**Figure 61**) for scoring, scratches or severe wear. Check for discoloration and material coating damage. If any metal shows through the coating material, the bushing is excessively worn. Replace both bushings as a set.

10. Measure the fork spring free length with a tape measure (**Figure 62**). Replace the spring if it is too short (**Table 1**). Replace both the left and right side springs if they are unequal in length.

11. Service the rebound adjuster (6, **Figure 43**) as follows:

    a. Remove the rebound adjuster (6, **Figure 43**) from the fork cap and discard its O-ring.

    b. Check the rebound adjuster needle for damage.

    c. Lubricate a new O-ring with fork oil and thread the rebound adjuster into the fork cap. Set the rebound adjuster to its softest position.

12. Replace the fork cap O-ring if leaking or damaged.

11

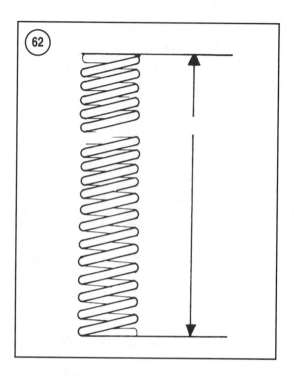

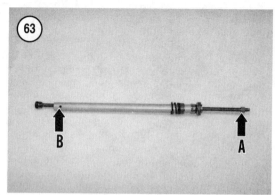

Front Fork Assembly

Unless otherwise specified, lubricate the fork components with the same fork oil used to refill the fork. See **Table 1** for the specified fork oil.

1. Before assembly, make sure all worn or defective parts have been repaired or replaced. Clean all parts before assembly.

2. Lubricate the inside of the cartridge and the piston rod piston ring with fork oil. Install the top of the piston rod (A, **Figure 63**) through the bottom of the cartridge (B, **Figure 63**). Slide the piston rod through the cartridge by hand and check for any binding or roughness.

3. Thread the locknut onto the end of the piston rod (A, **Figure 63**).

4. Lubricate the fork tube bushing and install it into the groove in the bottom of the fork tube (**Figure 64**).

5. Install the cartridge/piston rod assembly (**Figure 51**) into the fork tube and extend the cartridge (A, **Figure 65**) through the bottom of the fork tube.

6. Lubricate the oil lock piece (B, **Figure 65**) and install it onto the cartridge (**Figure 57**). Then push the oil lock piece into the bottom of the fork tube (**Figure 66**).

7. Slide the fork tube assembly (**Figure 67**) into the slider.

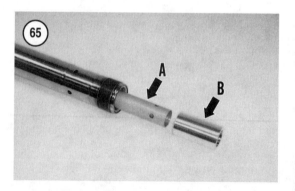

8A. On 1996-1997 models, temporarily install and tighten the compression bolt (B, **Figure 68**) as follows:

   a. Bottom out the fork tube inside the slider. Make sure the end of the cartridge is seating flush in the slider bore (**Figure 69**).

   b. Thread the compression bolt into the cartridge and finger tighten.

NOTE
On 1996-1997 models, final tightening of the compression bolt will occur after the front fork is assembled and temporarily installed on the bike.

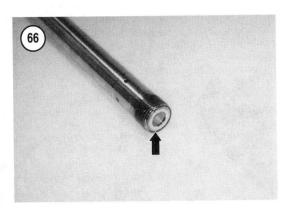

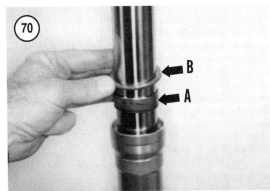

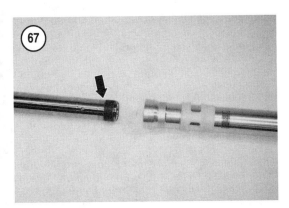

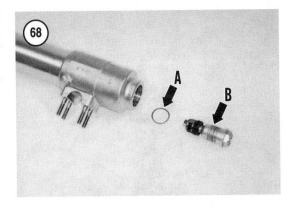

8B. On 1998 and later models, install and tighten the compression bolt as follows:

   a. Install a *new* washer (A, **Figure 68**) onto the compression bolt.

   b. Lubricate a *new* compression bolt O-ring with fork oil and install it into the compression bolt groove (**Figure 60**).

   c. Clamp the axle holder in a vise with soft jaws, then bottom out the fork tube against the slider.

   d. Insert the damper rod holder into the fork tube and lock it into the top of the cartridge body (**Figure 48**). Make sure the lower end of the cartridge still seats into the bottom of the slider bore (**Figure 69**).

   e. Remove any oil that may have dripped onto the threads in the bottom of the cartridge with an aerosol parts cleaner.

   f. Apply a medium strength threadlock onto the compression bolt threads.

> *CAUTION*
> *Do not allow the threadlocking com-*
> *pound to contact the O-ring, shim*
> *pack or the piston assembly.*

   g. Hold the damper rod holder to prevent the cartridge from moving, then install the compression bolt (B, **Figure 68**) through the fork slider and thread it into the bottom of the cartridge.

   h. Hold the cartridge body with the damper rod holder (**Figure 48**) and tighten the compression bolt (**Figure 39**) to the specification in **Table 5**.

   i. Remove the damper rod holder from the fork tube.

9. Lubricate the slider bushing (A, **Figure 70**) and slide it down the fork tube and into the top of the slider until it stops.

11

10. Install the back-up ring (B, **Figure 70**) over the fork tube and seat it on top of the slider bushing. Install the back-up ring with its chamfered side facing down.

11. Drive the slider bushing into the slider with an oil seal driver (**Figure 71**). Continue until the bushing bottoms out.

12. Lubricate the oil seal and dust seal lips with SF-3 grease or equivalent.

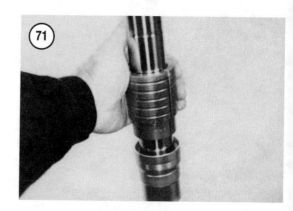

NOTE
SF-3 grease reduces friction on metal-to-rubber applications. It is an ideal grease to use on fork seals, as it resists wash-off and high temperatures.

13. To avoid tearing the oil and dust seals, cover the end of the fork tube with a thin plastic bag (**Figure 72**). Lubricate the bag with SF-3 grease or equivalent.

14. Slide the oil seal over the fork tube with its closed side facing down (**Figure 72**). Slide the oil seal down the fork tube and seat it squarely into the top of the slider.

15. Drive the oil seal into the slider with an oil seal driver (**Figure 71**). Continue to install the oil seal until it bottoms out or the stop ring groove in the slider is visible above the top of the seal.

16. Install the stop ring (**Figure 53**) into the slider groove. Make sure the stop ring seats in the groove completely.

NOTE
If the stop ring will not seat completely in its groove, the oil seal is not installed far enough into the slider. Remove the stop ring and repeat Step 15.

17. Install the plastic bag over the top of the fork tube again and relubricate it with grease, if necessary. Install the dust seal (closed side facing down) over the fork tube (**Figure 73**) and slide it down and into the top of the slider. Drive the dust seal (**Figure 52**) into the slider with the oil seal driver until it bottoms out evenly around the slider bore.

18. On 1996-1997 models, tighten the compression bolt as follows:

   a. Install the fork spring and spring seat into the fork tube.

   b. Thread the fork cap completely onto the piston rod, then thread the fork cap into the fork tube and tighten hand-tight.

   c. Repeat for the other fork tube.

   d. Install both fork tubes into the steering stem and tighten the upper and lower pinch bolts securely.

   e. Install the front axle and axle holders (without the wheel).

   f. Connect a tie-down strap between the bottom fork bridge and front axle. Tighten the tie-down

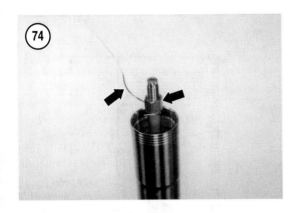

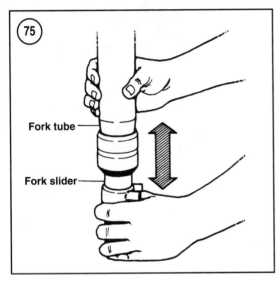

Fork tube

Fork slider

strap (**Figure 38**) to compress the front fork tube approximately 5-10 cm (2-4 in.).

g. Remove the compression bolt from one of the fork tubes.

h. Install a new washer (C, **Figure 59**) and O-ring (B) onto the compression bolt.

i. Lubricate the compression bolt O-ring with fork oil.

j. With an aerosol parts cleaner, remove any oil that may have ran down onto the threads in the bottom of the cartridge.

k. Apply a medium strength threadlock onto the compression bolt threads.

CAUTION
Do not allow the threadlocking compound to contact the O-ring, shim pack or the piston assembly.

l. Install the compression bolt (**Figure 39**) and tighten to the specification in **Table 5**.

m. Repeat for the other compression bolt.

n. Remove the fork tie-down and tubes from the steering stem.

o. Remove the fork cap, spring seat and fork spring from each fork tube.

19. Fill the fork with oil and set the oil level as described under *Fork Oil Refilling* in this section.

Fork Oil Refilling

See **Table 1** for recommended type of fork oil.

See *Fork Tools* in this chapter for a description of the tools used to set the oil level.

1. Install the locknut (**Figure 74**) onto the end of the piston rod until it bottoms against the rod. Then wrap a piece of stiff wire onto the piston rod, underneath the nut. This wire will be used to retrieve the piston rod when bleeding the fork and assembling the fork cap.

2. Bottom the fork tube into the slider. Then push the piston rod (**Figure 74**) all the way down.

3. Pour half the recommended amount of fork oil (**Table 2**) into the fork tube.

4. Hold the slider and slowly pump the fork tube (**Figure 75**) 8-10 times to removed air trapped in the lower part of the fork tube.

5. Bottom the fork tube into the slider and then push the piston rod all the way down.

6. Pour fork oil into the fork tube until it begins to flow from the end of the piston rod.

7. Pump the fork tube (**Figure 75**) and then the piston rod 8-10 times to bleed air trapped inside the cartridge.

8. Add the remaining recommended amount of fork oil. Pump the fork tube and then the piston rod 8-10 times.

NOTE
Use the recommended oil capacity as a guideline. The final step will be to adjust the oil level. The oil level reading is a more accurate means of adding fork oil.

9. Bottom the fork tube into the slider and push the piston rod all the way down.

10. Support the fork tube vertically and set aside for 5 minutes to allow any air bubbles to surface from the oil.

11

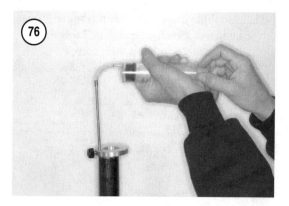

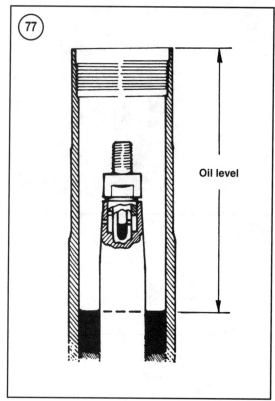

Oil level

11. To set the oil level, perform the following:

   a. Bottom the fork tube against the slider and place it in a vertical position. Push the piston rod all the way down.

   b. Using an oil level gauge (**Figure 76**), set the oil level to the specification listed in **Table 3**. See **Figure 77**.

> *NOTE*
> *If no oil is drawn out when setting the oil level, there is not enough oil in the fork tube. Add more oil and then reset the level.*

   c. Remove the oil level gauge.

12. Install the fork spring, with its narrow end facing down, over the piston rod and into the fork assembly.

13. Slowly pull the piston rod up. Remove the wire (**Figure 74**) from around the piston rod, then push the fork spring underneath the locknut (**Figure 78**) to prevent the piston rod from falling into the fork tube.

14A. On 1996-1997 models, install the spring seat (3, **Figure 43**) onto the fork spring and underneath the locknut.

14B. On 1998 and later models, install the spring seat (**Figure 79**) onto the fork spring, then push the fork spring and spring seat underneath the locknut to prevent the piston rod from falling into the fork tube.

> *CAUTION*
> *Install the fork cap carefully to avoid damaging the rebound adjuster needle inside the cap.*

15. Thread the fork cap (**Figure 80**) onto the piston rod until it is completely seated.

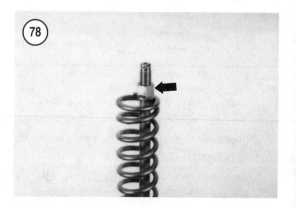

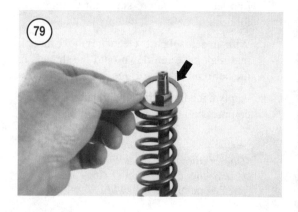

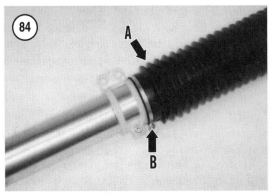

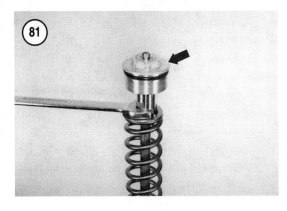

16. Hold the locknut and tighten the fork cap (**Figure 81**) to the piston rod locknut torque specification listed in **Table 5**.

17. Make sure the spring seat is positioned correctly against the fork cap and spring.

18. Pull the fork tube up and thread the fork cap (**Figure 82**) into the fork tube. Fighter-tighten the fork cap.

19A. Install the left boot guide as follows:

   a. Install the boot guide (A, **Figure 83**) into the groove in the fork slider, then align the tab on the boot guide with the slot in the slider (B, **Figure 83**).

   b. Secure the boot guide with the bolt, washer and nut (C, **Figure 83**). Install the bolt so that its head will face to the outside of the fork tube when the fork is mounted on the bike. Tighten the bolt securely

   c. Slide the boot over the fork tube and place its lower end into the boot guide groove (A, **Figure 84**). Position the lower hose clamp so the screw head (B, **Figure 84**) will face to the outside of the fork tube when the fork is mounted on the bike. Tighten the hose clamp screw securely.

19B. Install the right boot guide as follows:

   a. Install the boot guide (A, **Figure 85**) into the groove in the fork slider, then align the tab on the boot guide with the slot in the slider (B, **Figure 85**).

   b. Slide the boot over the fork tube and place its lower end into the boot guide groove (A, **Figure 86**). Position the lower hose clamp so that the screw head (B, **Figure 86**) will face to the outside of the fork tube when the fork is mounted on the bike. Tighten the hose clamp screw securely.

11

20. Install the fork tubes and tighten the fork caps and upper boot hose clamps as described under *Front Fork Installation* in this chapter.

21. Adjust the front fork compression and rebound adjusters as described in this chapter.

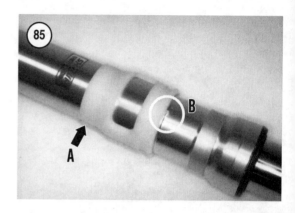

FRONT FORK ADJUSTMENT

The front fork can be adjusted to suit rider weight and riding conditions. Variables, such as fork oil level and compression and rebound adjustments, can be modified to overcome various handling complaints. When setting a suspension variable, make one adjustment at a time and then test ride the bike. Keep a record of the changes and how they affect the handling. Work in a systematic manner to avoid confusion and return to the original base settings if handling deteriorates. Make sure the steering stem, fork and front wheel bearings are in good condition before making any adjustments.

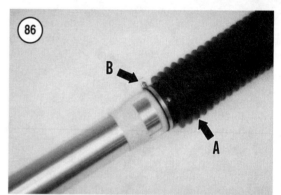

Air Pressure

These forks are designed to operate without air pressure. Before riding the bike, bleed the air out of the fork tubes as follows:

1. Support the bike with the front wheel off the ground.

2. Loosen the air screw (A, **Figure 87**) in the fork cap to release built-up air pressure. Then tighten the screw. Repeat for the other fork tube.

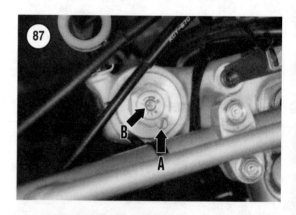

Rebound Damping Adjustment

The front fork rebound damping adjusters are mounted in the center of each fork cap (B, **Figure 87**). The rebound damping adjustment affects the front fork extension rate after compression. Turning the rebound adjuster clockwise increases (stiffens) the rebound damping; turning the rebound adjuster counterclockwise decreases (softens) the rebound damping. **Table 4** lists the standard rebound damping adjustment position.

To adjust the rebound damping adjuster to its standard position, perform the following:

1. Turn the rebound damping adjuster *clockwise* until it stops (B, **Figure 87**). This is the full hard position.

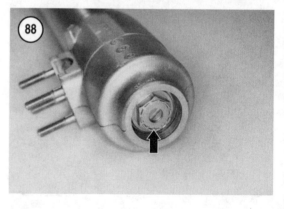

2. Turn the rebound damping adjuster *counter-clockwise* the standard number of turns listed in **Table 4**. This is the standard position.

3. Set both fork tubes to the same damping setting.

> *NOTE*
> *Make sure the rebound adjuster screw is located in one of the detent positions and not in between any two settings.*

Compression Damping Adjustment

The compression damping adjuster is mounted in the center of the compression bolt installed in the bottom of the fork tube (**Figure 88**). The compression damping adjustment affects the front fork compression rate. Turning the compression adjuster clockwise increases (stiffens) the compression damping; turning the compression adjuster counterclockwise decreases (softens) the compression damping. **Table 4** lists the standard compression damping positions.

To adjust the compression damping adjuster to its standard position, perform the following:

1. Turn the compression damping adjuster *clockwise* until it stops (**Figure 88**). This is the full hard position.

2. Turn the compression damping adjuster *counterclockwise* the standard number of turns listed in **Table 4**. This is the standard position.

3. Set both fork tubes to the same damping position.

> *NOTE*
> *Make sure the compression adjuster screw is located in one of the detent positions and not in between any two settings.*

Front Fork Oil Change and Oil Level Adjustment

The front fork must be removed from the bike and partially disassembled to change the fork oil and to check and adjust the oil level. When this type of service is required, refer to the front fork service procedures in this chapter.

11

Table 1 STEERING AND FRONT SUSPENSION SPECIFICATIONS

Steering angles	
Caster	25°
Trail	94 mm (3.7 in.)
Front wheel travel	280 (11.0 in.)
Fork fluid viscosity	Pro Honda Suspension Fluid SS-7*
Fork spring free length	
1996-1997	
Standard	510.4 mm (20.09 in.)
Service limit	505.3 mm (19.89 in.)
1998-on	
Standard	536.1 mm (21.11 in.)
Service limit	528 mm (20.8 in.)
Fork tube runout limit	0.20 mm (0.007 in.)
*Or use an equivalent 5 weight fork oil.	

Table 2 FRONT FORK OIL CAPACITY

	ml	U.S. oz.	Imp. oz.
1996-1997	570	19.3	20.0
1998-on	559	18.9	19.7

Table 3 FRONT FORK OIL LEVEL

	mm	in.
1996-1997	100	3.9
1998	116	4.6

Table 4 FRONT FORK COMPRESSION AND REBOUND ADJUSTMENT

	Approximate adjustment positions	Standard adjuster position
Compression damping adjustment		
1996-1997	20	14
1998	16	8
1999-on	14	8
Rebound damping adjustment		
1996-1997	12	5
1998-on	12	3

Table 5 FRONT SUSPENSION AND STEERING TORQUE SPECIFICATIONS

	N•m	in.-lb.	ft.-lb.
Compression bolt[1]	34	–	25
Fork cap	23	–	17
Front brake caliper mounting bolts[2]	30	–	22
Front brake disc mounting bolts[1]	20	–	15
Piston rod locknut	20	–	15
Rebound damping adjuster	27	–	20
Steering adjust nut			
Bearing seat torque	29	–	22
Final torque	4.5	40.0	–
Steering stem nut	98	–	72

1. Apply a threadlock onto fastener threads.
2. Install new ALOC fasteners during assembly.

CHAPTER TWELVE

REAR SUSPENSION

This chapter describes service procedures for the rear shock absorber, swing arm, and linkage assembly. **Table 1** lists rear suspension specifications. **Tables 1-4** are at the end of the chapter.

REAR SUSPENSION

The XR400R rear suspension is a progressive rising rate design. Compared to conventional suspension systems, this design allows for increased swing arm travel and provides ideal spring and damping rates over a larger operating range of the swing arm.

For example, when the swing arm is slightly compressed, the spring and damping rates are soft, for handling small bumps. As riding conditions become more severe, the swing arm travel increases. This causes the linkage system to pivot into a position to increase the travel of the spring and damper. This provides a progressively firmer shock absorbing action, greater control and better transfer of power to the ground.

The system consists of a single shock absorber and linkage (shock arm, link and pivot bearings) attached to the swing arm (**Figure 1**).

SHOCK ABSORBER

The single shock absorber is a spring-loaded hydraulically-damped unit with an integral oil/nitrogen reservoir.

Adjustment

To adjust the rear shock absorber (spring preload, rebound damping and compression damping), refer to *Rear Suspension Adjustment* in this chapter.

12

Shock Absorber Removal

1. Support the bike with the rear wheel off the ground.
2. Remove the subframe (Chapter Fifteen).
3. Remove the upper shock absorber nut and mounting bolt (**Figure 2**) and allow the rear wheel to drop to the ground.
4. Remove the shock arm-to-swing arm nut and bolt (**Figure 3**).
5. Remove the shock link-to-shock arm nut and bolt (**Figure 4**).
6. Remove the shock absorber with the shock arm attached (A, **Figure 5**).
7. If necessary, remove the nut, bolt and shock arm from the shock absorber.
8. Clean and service the seals, collar and bearing as described in this section.

Shock Absorber Installation

1. Clean and dry all shock absorber fasteners. Inspect for and replace damaged fasteners.
2. Apply a small film of grease onto the shock absorber and shock arm mounting bolt shoulders. Do not apply any grease onto the mounting bolt or nut threads. Wipe off any excess grease.
3. If removed, position the shock arm (A, **Figure 5**) between the lower shock mounts and install the mounting bolt (B, **Figure 5**) from the reservoir side. Install the nut and tighten to the specification in **Table 4**.
4. Install the shock absorber with its reservoir (**Figure 2**) on the left side.

> *NOTE*
> *Install all of the mounting bolts from the left side.*

5. Install the following pivot bolts and nuts. Tighten the mounting nuts to the specification in **Table 4**.

> *NOTE*
> *Wipe off all grease from the pivot bolt threads before installing and tightening the nuts.*

   a. Upper shock mounting nut (**Figure 2**).
   b. Shock arm-to-swing arm nut (**Figure 3**).
   c. Shock link-to-shock arm nut (**Figure 4**).
6. Install the subframe (Chapter Fifteen).

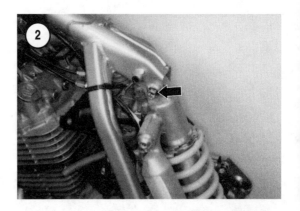

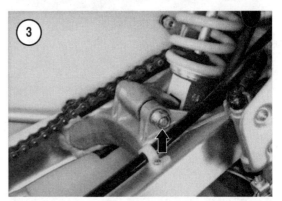

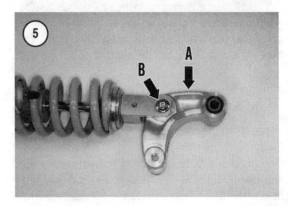

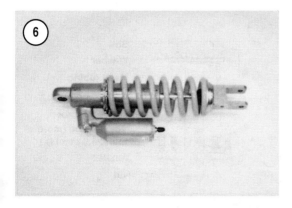

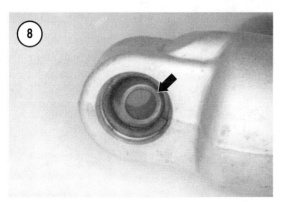

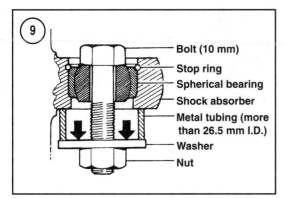

Bolt (10 mm)
Stop ring
Spherical bearing
Shock absorber
Metal tubing (more than 26.5 mm I.D.)
Washer
Nut

Shock Inspection

1. Inspect the shock absorber (**Figure 6**) for gas or oil leaks.
2. Check the damper rod for bending, rust or other damage.
3. Check the reservoir for dents or other damage.
4. Remove and inspect the spring as described in this section.
5. If the shock is leaking, or if it is time to replace the shock oil, refer service to a Honda dealership or suspension specialist.

Seals and Bearing Inspection and Replacement (1996-1997)

A spherical bearing is installed in the damper case at the top of the shock absorber.

1. Remove the dust seals from the damper case.
2. Pivot the spherical bearing (**Figure 8**) from side-to-side by hand. The bearing must pivot smoothly. If any roughness or damage is noted, replace the bearing, starting with Step 3. If the bearing is acceptable, go to Step 14.
3. To replace the spherical bearing, the following items are required:
   a. Metal tubing: inner diameter larger than 26.5 mm.
   b. Metal tubing: 25 mm outer diameter and 20 mm long.
   c. Large washer.
   d. 10 mm bolt and nut.
4. Assemble the metal tubing (inner diameter larger than 26.5 mm) and the 10 mm bolt and nut onto the shock absorber as shown in **Figure 9**. Place the metal tubing on the side opposite the bearing stop ring.
5. Hold the nut and tighten the bolt (**Figure 9**) to compress the bearing rubber and to gain access to the stop ring.
6. Remove the stop ring, then loosen the bolt and nut and remove the metal tubing. Discard the stop ring.
7. Install the metal tubing, washer, bolt and nut as shown in **Figure 10**. Then tighten the bolt to pull the bearing out of the damper case. Discard the bearing.
8. Clean the bearing bore in solvent, then check it for cracks or other damage.

12

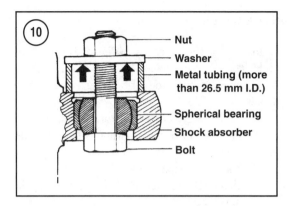

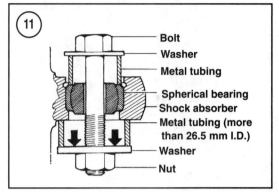

9. Lubricate the new spherical bearing with a waterproof grease.

10. Assemble the 2 metal tubes, bolt, flat washer and bearing onto the shock absorber as shown in **Figure 11**.

11. Tighten the bolt to press the bearing into the damper case (**Figure 11**). Install a new stop ring into the damper case ring groove.

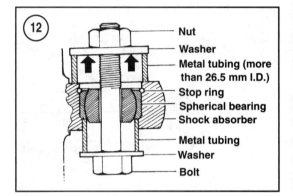

12. Remove the metal tubes and the fasteners, and then reassemble them onto the damper case as shown in **Figure 12**. Tighten the bolt to press the rubber portion of the spherical bearing into the stop ring.

13. Remove the metal tubes and fasteners from the damper case. Make sure the stop ring and bearing are properly installed.

14. On all models, lubricate the dust seal lips with grease, them install them into the damper case with their open side facing out (**Figure 7**).

Seals and Bearing Inspection and Replacement (1998-on)

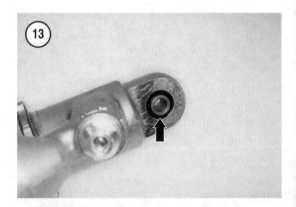

A needle bearing (**Figure 13**) is installed in the damper case at the top of the shock absorber.

1. Remove the collar (A, **Figure 14**) and seals (B) from the bearing bore.

2. Clean and dry the seals, collar and needle bearing.

3. Inspect the seals for cracks or other damage.

4. Inspect the collar for cracks, scoring or severe wear.

5. Inspect the needle bearing (**Figure 15**) for severe wear or damage. Check for loose or missing bearing needles or other visible damage. Lubricate the collar with grease and install it into the bearing and turn it by hand. The collar should turn smoothly. If

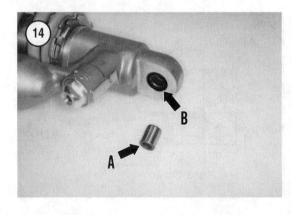

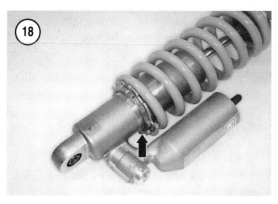

there is any roughness or damage, replace the needle bearing as described in Step 6. If the bearing is acceptable, go to Step 7.

6. Replace the needle bearing (**Figure 15**) as follows:

    a. Support the shock on a socket (**Figure 16**) large enough to accept the bearing and press the needle bearing out of its mounting bore. Discard the needle bearing.

    b. Clean and inspect the mounting bore in the shock absorber.

    c. Center the new bearing squarely in its mounting bore, then press it into the bore until its depth (measured from the bearing to the outer surface) is 3.5 mm (0.14 in.).

7. Lubricate the bearing and collar with waterproof grease.

8. Install the collar (A, **Figure 14**) into the bearing.

9. Install the seals (**Figure 17**) with their open side facing out.

Spring Removal/Installation

1. Remove the shock absorber as described in this chapter.

2. Measure the spring's preload length and record the length for installation.

3. Clean the shock threads with parts cleaner.

4. Mount the upper shock mount in a vise with soft jaws.

5. Loosen the locknut (**Figure 18**) with a spanner wrench and turn it all the way down. Then do the same for the adjuster to remove all preload from the spring.

6. Remove the stopper ring from the rubber seat. Then remove the spring seat (**Figure 19**) and spring from the shock.

12

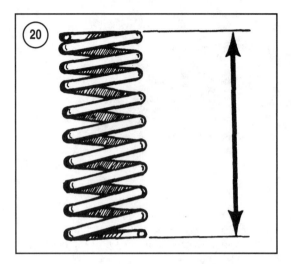

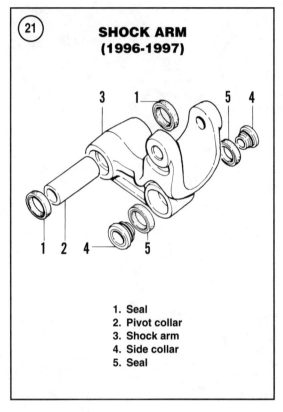

**SHOCK ARM
(1996-1997)**

1. Seal
2. Pivot collar
3. Shock arm
4. Side collar
5. Seal

7. Measure the spring free length (**Figure 20**). Replace the spring if it is too short (**Table 2**).

8. Install the spring and set the spring preload by reversing these steps, and perform the following:

    a. Install the spring with its narrow end facing down.

    b. Install the spring seat.

    c. Install the stopper ring into the rubber groove. Make sure it seats completely.

    d. Adjust the spring preload to the dimension recorded in Step 2, or set it to the standard installed length or within the adjustable length dimensions listed in **Table 2**. Hold the adjuster and tighten the locknut (**Figure 18**) securely.

> *CAUTION*
> *The spring preload must be maintained within the adjustable range specifications listed in **Table 2**. If the minimum specification is exceeded, the spring may coil bind when the shock comes near full compression. This will overload the spring and weaken it. Setting the preload beyond the maximum limit may allow the spring locknut and adjuster to loosen on the shock body and remove all preload from the spring.*

SHOCK LINKAGE

The shock linkage consists of the shock arm, shock link, pivot bolts, seals and bearings. The assembly must be periodically removed, cleaned and lubricated, due to the harsh operating environment.

Shock Arm Removal/Installation

Remove and install the shock arm as described under the *Shock Absorber Removal and Installation* in this chapter. See **Figure 5**.

Shock Arm Cleaning and Inspection

When inspecting the shock arm components, replace parts that show damage as described in this chapter.

> *NOTE*
> *Use a waterproof bearing grease when grease is called for in the following steps.*

1A. On 1996-1997 models, remove the side collars, pivot collar and seals from the shock arm (**Figure 21**).

1B. On 1998 and later models, remove the seals and pivot collars from the shock arm (**Figure 22**).

2. Remove the loose bearing needles (**Figure 23**) from their outer cage, making sure not to intermix them with the needles from the other bearings. Keep

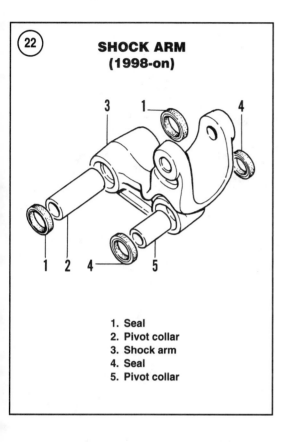

SHOCK ARM (1998-on)

1. Seal
2. Pivot collar
3. Shock arm
4. Seal
5. Pivot collar

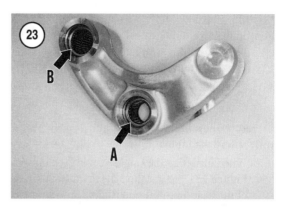

all of the loose bearing needles with their original bearing assembly. Do not remove a bearing cage unless the bearing will be replaced.

3. Clean and dry all parts. Remove rust and corrosion from pivot bolt surfaces.

4. Inspect the seals for cracks, severe wear or other damage.

5. Inspect the pivot collars for cracks, scoring, rust or other damage.

6. Inspect the loose needle bearings for cracks, flat spots, rust or color change. Bluing indicates the bearing has overheated. Inspect the separate bearing cages for cracks, rust or other damage. If a bearing is damaged, replace it as described in this chapter.

7. On 1996-1997 models, inspect the spherical bearing by pivoting its inner race by hand. If the inner race is stuck, tight, cracked or damaged from corrosion, replace it.

8. Inspect the pivot bolts for cracks, scoring or other damage.

9. Lubricate the bearing needles with grease and install them into their correct bearing cage.

10A. On 1996-1997 models, assemble the shock arm as follows:
    a. Lubricate the seal lips with grease and install them into the shock arm with their closed side facing out.
    b. Lubricate the pivot collar with grease and install it through the bearing as shown in **Figure 21**.
    c. Lubricate the side collars with grease and install them through the seals as shown in **Figure 21**.

10B. On 1998 and later models, assemble the shock arm as follows:
    a. Lubricate the seal lips with grease and install them into the shock arm with their closed side facing out.
    b. Lubricate the pivot collars with grease and install them as shown in **Figure 22**.

Shock Arm Needle Bearing Replacement

NOTE
*To replace the spherical bearing used in 1996-1997 models, refer to **Shock Arm Spherical Bearing Replacement** in this chapter.*

1. If removed, reinstall the individual needles into the bearing cage. These will support the bearing cage when pressing it out of the shock arm.

2. Measure the depth of the installed bearings (**Figure 24**). Measure from the outside of each bearing. In all cases, the bearing(s) should be centered in its mounting bore.

3. Support the shock arm in a press (**Figure 25**) and press out the bearing(s).

4. Clean and dry the shock arm. Inspect the mounting bores for cracks, galling and other damage.

12

5. Lubricate the new bearings with grease.

> *NOTE*
> *Install the bearings with the individ-*
> *ual bearing needles installed in their*
> *cage.*

6. Press the new needle bearings into the shock arm while noting the following:

    a. When installing the single needle bearing (A, **Figure 23**), the installed depth on both sides of the bearing is 5.0 mm (0.20 in.).

> *NOTE*
> *Install the double needle bearings*
> *with the manufacturer's marks on*
> *each bearing facing out.*

    b. When installing the double needle bearings (B, **Figure 23**), install the first bearing so its depth from the shock arm outer surface is 6.0 mm (0.24 in.). Then turn the shock arm over and install the second bearing so it seats against the first bearing.

Shock Arm Spherical Bearing Replacement (1996-1997)

This section describes replacement of the shock arm spherical bearing (**Figure 26**).

1. Support the shock arm in a press (**Figure 27**) and press out the spherical bearing using the Honda spherical bearing driver (part No. 07HMF-KS60100) or an equivalent bearing driver.

2. Clean and dry the mounting bore. Inspect the mounting bore for cracks, galling and other damage.

3. Lubricate the new spherical bearing with grease.

4. Press the new spherical bearing into the shock arm until the bearing depth from the shock arm outer surface is 7 mm (0.28 in.).

Shock Link Removal/Installation

The shock link (**Figure 28**) connects the frame to the shock arm. Both mounting points are secured with pivot bolts and nuts.

1. Support the bike with its rear wheel off the ground.

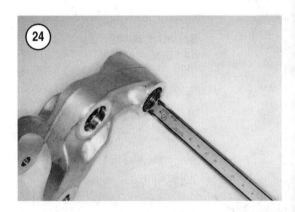

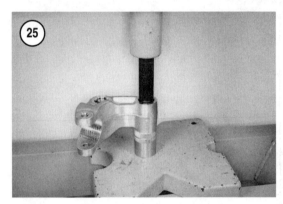

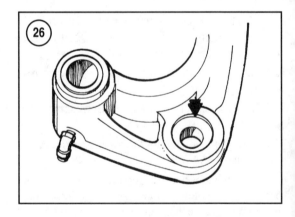

2. If the rear wheel is mounted on the bike, support the tire with wooden blocks to remove tension from the shock linkage pivot bolts.

3. Loosen and remove the shock link pivot bolt nuts (**Figure 28**). If used, remove the washer from the frame pivot bolt.

4. Remove the pivot bolts and shock link (**Figure 28**).

5. Clean and inspect the shock link and pivot bolts as described in this section.

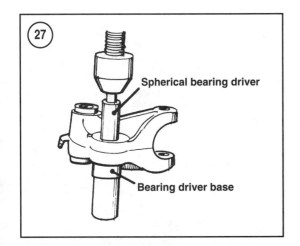

Spherical bearing driver

Bearing driver base

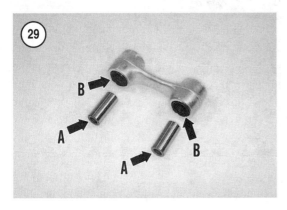

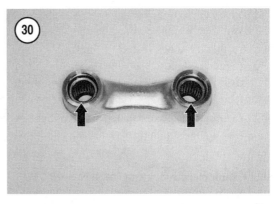

e. Install the shock link-to-frame pivot bolt nut and tighten to the specification in **Table 4**.

f. Install the shock link-to-shock arm pivot bolt nut and tighten to the specification in **Table 4**.

Shock Link Cleaning and Inspection

When inspecting the shock link components, replace parts that show damage as described in this chapter.

NOTE
Use a waterproof bearing grease when grease is called for in the following steps.

1. Remove the pivot collars (A, **Figure 29**) and seals (B) from the shock link.

2. Remove the loose bearing needles (**Figure 30**) from their outer cage, making sure not to intermix them with the needles from the other bearings. Keep all of the loose bearing needles with their original bearing assembly. Do not remove a bearing cage unless the bearing will be replaced.

3. Clean and dry all parts. Remove rust and corrosion from the pivot bolt surfaces.

4. Inspect the seals for cracks, severe wear or other damage.

5. Inspect the pivot collars for cracks, scoring, rust or other damage.

6. Inspect the loose needle bearings for cracks, flat spots, rust or color change. Bluing indicates the bearing has overheated. Inspect the separate bearing cages for cracks, rust or other damage. If a bearing is damaged, replace it as described in the following section.

7. Inspect the pivot bolts for cracks, scoring or other damage.

6. Install the shock link by reversing these removal steps, and perform the following:

a. Lubricate the pivot bolts with waterproof grease.

b. Install the shock link-to-frame mounting bolt from the right side. Install the washer, if used.

c. Install the shock link-to-shock arm pivot bolt from the left side.

d. Wipe off all grease from the pivot bolt threads before installing and tightening the nuts.

12

8. Lubricate the separate bearing needles with grease and install them into their correct bearing cage.

9. Assemble the shock link as follows:

   a. Lubricate the seal lips with grease and install them into the shock arm with their closed side facing out.

   b. Lubricate the pivot collars with grease and install them through their bearings.

Shock Link Needle Bearing Replacement

1. If removed, reinstall the individual needles into the bearing cage (**Figure 30**). These will support the bearing cage when pressing it out of the shock arm.

2. Measure the depth of the installed bearings (**Figure 31**). Both bearings should be centered in their mounting bore.

3. Support the shock link in a press (**Figure 32**) and press out the bearing.

4. Repeat for the other bearing.

5. Clean and dry the shock arm. Inspect the mounting bores for cracks, galling and other damage.

6. Lubricate the new bearing rollers with grease.

> *NOTE*
> *Install the bearings with the individual bearing needles installed in their cage.*

7. Press the new needle bearing into the shock link until its installed depth on both sides of the bearing is 5.0 mm (0.20 in.).

8. Repeat for the other bearing.

REAR SWING ARM

Swing Arm Bearing Inspection

  Periodically inspect the swing arm needle bearings for excessive play, roughness or damage.

1. Remove the rear wheel (Chapter Ten).

2. Remove the mud guard (A, **Figure 33**) from the air filter housing.

3. Remove the shock arm-to-swing arm nut and bolt (A, **Figure 34**).

4. Remove the shock link-to-shock arm nut and bolt (B, **Figure 34**).

5. Loosen the swing arm pivot shaft nut (C, **Figure 34**), then retighten as specified in **Table 4**.

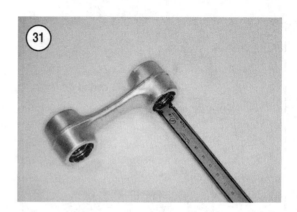

> *NOTE*
> *Have an assistant steady the bike while you perform Step 6.*

6. Grasp the rear end of the swing arm and try to move it from side to side in a horizontal arc. There must be no side play seen or felt.

7. Pivot the rear of the swing arm up and down through its full travel. The swing arm must pivot smoothly.

8. If play is evident and the pivot shaft nut is tightened correctly, or there is any roughness or binding,

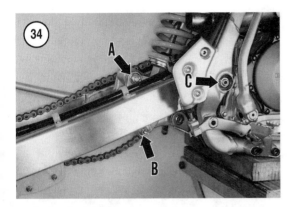

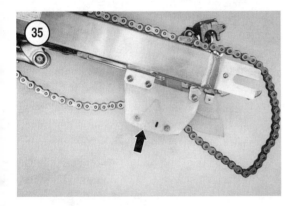

2. Remove the mud guard (A, **Figure 33**) from the air filter housing.

NOTE
Unless the caliper requires service, do not disconnect the rear brake caliper from its brake hose when performing Step 3.

3. Unscrew and remove the hose guides (B, **Figure 33**). Slide the rear brake caliper (C, **Figure 33**) off the swing arm. Secure the brake caliper with a piece of stiff wire.
4. Remove the shock arm-to-swing arm nut and bolt (A, **Figure 34**).
5. Remove the shock link-to-shock arm nut and bolt (B, **Figure 34**).
6. If the drive chain will not be disconnected, unbolt and remove the drive chain guide (**Figure 35**) from the swing arm.

NOTE
If the pivot shaft is hard to remove, it may be necessary to drive it out with a hammer and brass or aluminum rod.

7. Remove the swing arm pivot shaft nut (C, **Figure 34**), pivot shaft (A, **Figure 36**) and swing arm (B, **Figure 36**).
8. Clean, inspect and lubricate the swing arm bearings as described in this chapter.

Installation

NOTE
Use a waterproof wheel bearing grease when grease is called for in this procedure.

1. If removed, lubricate the pivot collars with grease and install them into the swing arm needle bearings.
2. Lubricate the dust seal cap lips (**Figure 37**) with grease and install them onto the swing arm (**Figure 38**).
3. Lubricate the pivot shaft with grease and set aside until installation.
4. Position the swing arm between the drive chain and then slide it into position in the frame.
5. Install the pivot shaft from the left side (A, **Figure 36**). Wipe off all grease from the pivot shaft threads before installing and tightening the nut in Step 6.
6. Install the pivot shaft nut (C, **Figure 34**) and tighten to the specification in **Table 4**.

remove the swing arm and inspect the needle bearings and pivot collars for severe wear or damage.
9. Reverse Steps 1-3 if the swing arm is not being removed. Tighten the following fasteners as described in **Table 4**:
   a. Shock arm-to-swing arm nut (A, **Figure 34**).
   b. Shock link-to-shock arm nut (B, **Figure 34**).

Removal

1. Remove the rear wheel (Chapter Ten).

12

7. Recheck the swing arm bearing operation as described under *Swing Arm Inspection*. If the swing arm movement does not feel correct in both directions, remove the swing arm and check the needle bearings and pivot collars for damage.

8. Lubricate the linkage pivot bolts with grease and set aside until installation.

9. Install the following pivot bolts and nuts. Tighten the mounting nuts to the specification in **Table 4**.

> *NOTE*
> *Install the following linkage pivot bolts from the left side.*

> *NOTE*
> *Wipe off all grease from the pivot bolt threads before installing and tightening the nuts.*

   a. Shock arm-to-swing arm pivot bolt and nut (A, **Figure 34**).

   b. Shock link-to-shock arm pivot bolt and nut (B, **Figure 34**).

10. Install the drive chain guide (**Figure 35**) and tighten the mounting bolts securely.

11. Slide the brake caliper (C, **Figure 33**) onto the swing arm rail.

12. Secure the brake hose onto the swing arm with the hose guides (B, **Figure 33**). Secure the hose guides with new screws.

13. Install the mud guard and secure it with its two screws.

14. Install the rear wheel (Chapter Ten).

15. Make sure the rear brake pedal and rear brake work properly.

Swing Arm Disassembly

Refer to **Figure 39** when servicing the swing arm bearings.

1. If necessary, remove the chain slider (A, **Figure 40**) and disc guard (B) from the swing arm.

2. Remove the dust seal caps and pivot collars (**Figure 41**) from each side of the swing arm.

3. Remove the seals (**Figure 42**) from each side of the swing arm and discard them.

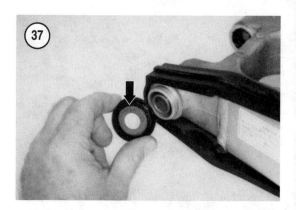

Swing Arm Inspection

Replace parts that show excessive wear or damage as described in this section.

1. Clean and dry the swing arm and its components.

2. Inspect the pivot collars (**Figure 41**) for scoring, severe wear, rust or other damage.

> *NOTE*
> *If a pivot collar is excessively worn or damaged, the mating needle bearings are probably worn also.*

3. Inspect the needle bearings (**Figure 43**) for cracks, flat spots, rust or other damage. If there is no visible damage, lubricate the pivot collar with grease and install it into the swing arm. Turn the pivot collar and check the bearings for any roughness, excessive play or other damage. To replace the bearings, refer to *Swing Arm Needle Bearing Replacement* in this chapter.

> *NOTE*
> *Replace all four swing arm needle bearings at the same time.*

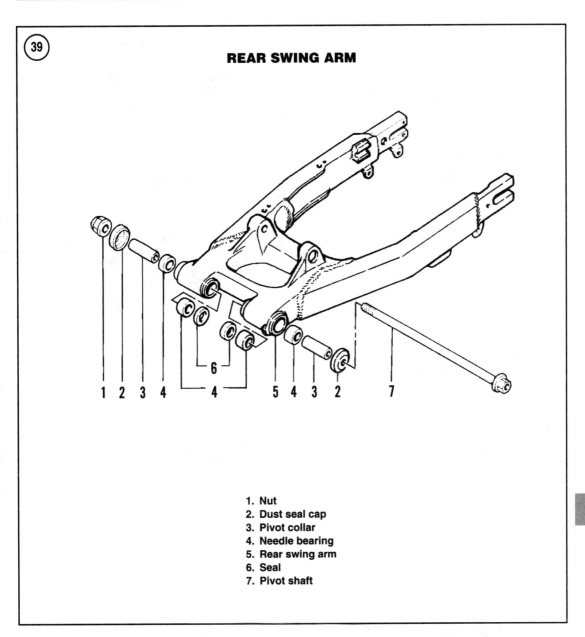

REAR SWING ARM

1. Nut
2. Dust seal cap
3. Pivot collar
4. Needle bearing
5. Rear swing arm
6. Seal
7. Pivot shaft

12

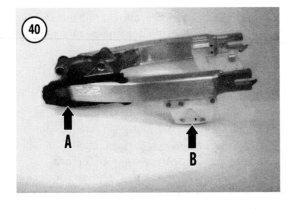

4. Check the swing arm for cracks, bending or other damage. Check the bearing mounting bore for cracks and other damage. Repair or replace the swing arm if damaged.

5. Inspect the chain slider (A, **Figure 40**) for excessive wear or missing fasteners.

> *NOTE*
> *The chain slider protects the swing arm from chain contact damage. Replace the chain slider before the chain wears completely through and damages the swing arm.*

6. Inspect the swing arm pivot shaft for cracks, rust, bending and other damage. Install the pivot collars onto the pivot shaft and slide them back and forth by hand. There must be no binding or roughness.

Swing Arm
Needle Bearing Replacement

Do not remove the swing arm needle bearings (**Figure 43**) unless you are replacing them. Two needle bearings are installed in each side of the swing arm (**Figure 39**). These are referred to as the inner and outer needle bearings. Replace all four needle bearings at the same time. The outer needle bearing on each side of the swing arm must be removed with a bearing remover. The inner needle bearings can then be removed with a press.

> *NOTE*
> *Special tools are required to safely remove the needle bearings from the swing arm. Because two needle bearings are used in each side of the swing arm, they should be removed separately. Do not attempt to drive both bearings out at the same time as they may bind and damage the mounting bore in the swing arm.*

1. Measure the depth of each installed bearing with a vernier caliper (**Figure 44**) and record the dimensions for reassembly.

2. To remove the outer needle bearing from each side of the swing arm, perform the following:
   a. Mount the Honda Needle Bearing Remover (part No. 07931-MA70000) onto one of the outer needle bearings (**Figure 45**).

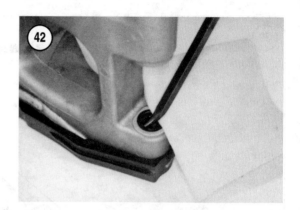

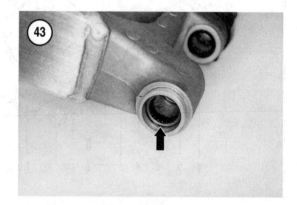

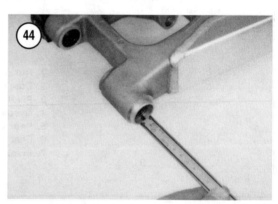

   b. Using two wrenches, turn the bolt head on the remover and withdraw the needle bearing from the swing arm.

   c. Turn the swing arm over and repeat to remove the other outer needle bearing.

> *NOTE*
> *A slide hammer equipped with the correct size bearing remover (**Figure 46**) can also be used to remove the outer needle bearings.*

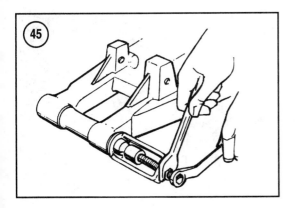

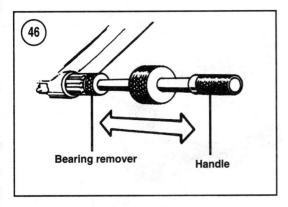

Bearing remover   Handle

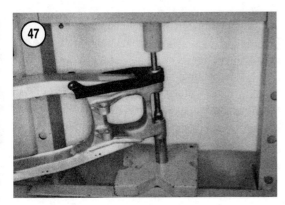

3. To remove the inner needle bearings, perform the following:

    a. Support the swing arm in a press and press out the inner needle bearing from one side.

    b. Turn the swing arm over and repeat to remove the other inner needle bearing.

4. Clean and dry the bearing mounting bores. Then check each mounting bore for cracks or other damage.

5. Lubricate the new needle bearing rollers with grease. Pack grease between the bearing rollers.

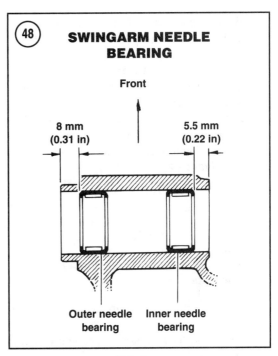

48

SWINGARM NEEDLE BEARING

Front

8 mm
(0.31 in)

5.5 mm
(0.22 in)

Outer needle   Inner needle
bearing   bearing

6A. To install the needle bearings with a press, perform the following:

    a. Install the bearings with their manufacturer's name and size code marks facing out.

    b. Support the swing arm in a press as shown in **Figure 47**, typical.

    c. Install the inner needle bearings until the depth measurement from the bearing to the inner swing arm surface is 5.5 mm (0.22 in.). See **Figure 48**.

    d. Install the outer needle bearings until the depth measurement from the bearing to the outer swing arm surface is 8 mm (0.31 in.). See **Figure 48**.

6B. To install the needle bearings with a threaded rod and bearing driver set:

    a. Assemble the fine-threaded rod tool shown in **Figure 49**. Place a socket or bearing driver (A, **Figure 49**) on the outer needle bearing's outside diameter (B).

NOTE
*When setting up the puller, make sure the socket or bearing driver (A, **Figure 49**) is of sufficient diameter to seat squarely against the needle bearing, but is small enough to slide through the swing arm bearing bore.*

12

b. Hold the inner nut and turn the outer nut to pull the bearing (B, **Figure 49**) into the swing arm.

c. Install the inner needle bearings until the depth measurement from the bearing to the inner swing arm surface is 5.5 mm (0.22 in.). See **Figure 48**.

d. Install the outer needle bearings until the depth measurement from the bearing to the outer swing arm surface is 8 mm (0.31 in.). See **Figure 48**.

Swing Arm Assembly

> *NOTE*
> *Use a waterproof bearing grease when grease is called for in the following steps.*

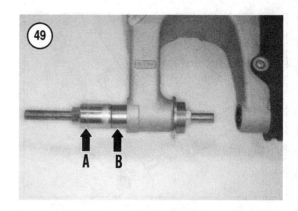

1. If removed, install the chain slider (A, **Figure 40**) and chain guard (B).

2. Lubricate the needle bearings with grease. Pack grease between the bearing rollers.

3. Lubricate the lips on both seals with grease. Install the seals into the swing arm with their closed side facing out (**Figure 50**). Install the seals so their outer surface is flush with the swing arm's outer surface.

4. Lubricate the pivot collars with grease and install them into the needle bearings (**Figure 51**).

5. Lubricate the lips on both dust seal caps (**Figure 37**) with grease. Install the dust seal caps over the swing arm (**Figure 38**).

6. Install the swing arm as described in this chapter.

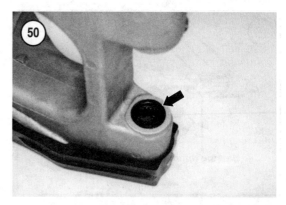

REAR SUSPENSION ADJUSTMENT

Shock Spring Preload Adjustment

The spring preload adjustment can be performed with the shock mounted on the bike.

1. Support the bike on a workstand with the rear wheel off the ground.

2. Remove the sub-frame as described in Chapter Fifteen.

3. Clean the threads at the top of the shock absorber (A, **Figure 52**).

> *NOTE*
> *Shock preload is adjusted by changing the position of the adjuster on the shock absorber.*

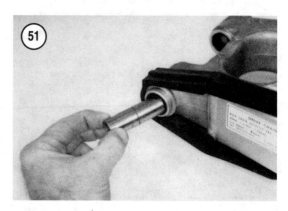

4. Measure the existing spring preload length (**Figure 53**) with a tape measure.

> *NOTE*
> *The bike's tool kit is equipped with a spanner wrench to turn the shock absorber locknut and adjuster.*

5. To adjust, loosen the locknut (**Figure 53**) and turn the adjuster (**Figure 53**) in the desired direction, making sure to maintain the spring preload length within the dimensions listed in **Table 2**.

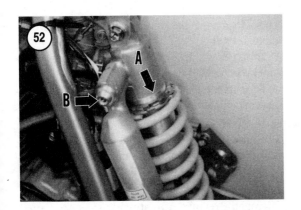

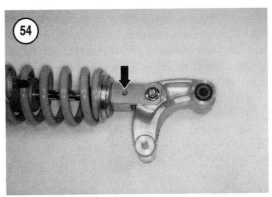

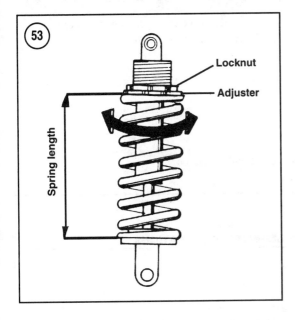

the spring locknut and adjust nut to loosen on the shock body and thus remove all preload from the spring.

6. After the desired spring preload is achieved, tighten the locknut (**Figure 53**) securely.

7. Install the subframe (Chapter Fifteen).

Rebound Damping Adjustment

The rebound damping adjustment affects the shock absorber extension rate after compression. This adjustment will not affect the action of the shock absorber on compression.

Rebound damping can be adjusted to the setting specified in **Table 3**. The adjuster screw is located at the bottom of the shock absorber (**Figure 54**). A clicker adjuster is used; each click of the adjuster screw represents one adjustment change.

For the standard setting, turn the adjuster screw clockwise until it stops (this is the full hard position). Then turn it counterclockwise the number of clicks (standard) listed in **Table 3**. When the standard setting is set, the two index marks on the adjuster will align.

To increase the rebound damping, turn the adjuster screw toward the "H" mark on the adjuster.

To decrease the rebound damping, turn the adjuster screw toward the "S" mark on the adjuster.

Make sure the adjuster wheel is located in one of the detent positions and not in between any two settings.

Compression Damping Adjustment

The compression adjustment affects the shock compression rate when the rear wheel hits a bump.

Tightening the adjuster increases spring preload and loosening it decreases preload.

> *NOTE*
> *One complete turn of the adjuster moves the spring 1.5 mm (0.06 in.) and changes the spring preload by 15.0 kg (33.1 lbs.).*

> *CAUTION*
> *The spring preload must be maintained within the minimum and maximum specifications listed in **Table 2**. If the minimum specification is exceeded, the spring may coil bind when the shock comes near full compression, overloading the spring and weakening it. Setting the preload beyond the maximum limit may allow*

12

This adjustment will not affect the action of the shock absorber on rebound.

Compression damping can be adjusted to the settings specified in **Table 3**. The adjuster screw is located at the top of the shock absorber reservoir (B, **Figure 52**). Each click of the adjuster screw represents one adjustment change.

For the standard setting on 1996-1997 models, turn the adjuster screw clockwise until it stops (this the full hard position). Then turn it counterclockwise the number of clicks (standard) listed in **Table 3** until the two index marks align. For the standard setting on 1998 and later models, turn the adjuster screw counterclockwise until it stops (this is the full soft position). Then turn it clockwise the number of clicks (standard) listed in **Table 3** until the two index marks align.

For the maximum setting, turn the adjuster screw clockwise until it stops.

To increase the rebound damping, turn the adjuster screw clockwise.

To decrease the rebound damping, turn the adjuster screw counterclockwise.

Make sure the adjuster wheel is located in one of the detent positions and not in between any two settings.

Nitrogen Pressure Adjustment

Refer all nitrogen pressure adjustment to a Honda dealership or suspension specialist.

Table 1 REAR SUSPENSION SPECIFICATIONS

Rear wheel travel	300 mm (11.8 in.)

Table 2 REAR SUSPENSION SERVICE SPECIFICATIONS

Shock absorber spring free length	
New	217.3 mm (8.56 in.)
Service limit	213.0 mm (8.39 in.)
Shock absorber spring preload length	
Standard	212.3 mm (8.36 in.)
Adjustable range	205.3-216.3 mm (8.08-8.51 in.)
Shock absorber	
Gas type	Nitrogen
Damper gas pressure	980 kPa (142 psi)
Recommended shock absorber oil	Pro Honda Suspension Fluid SS-8
Damper rod compressed force	
at 10 mm compression	15.4 kg (34 lbs.)

Table 3 REAR SHOCK ABSORBER COMPRESSION AND REBOUND ADJUSTMENT

	Approximate adjustment position	Standard adjuster position
Compression damping adjustment		
1996-1997	18	13
1998	18	14
1999-on	14	12
Rebound damping adjustment		
1996-1997	16	4
1998-on	16	10

Table 4 REAR SUSPENSION TORQUE SPECIFICATIONS

	N•m	in.-lb.	ft.-lb.
Chain adjuster stopper pin[1]	34	–	25
Chain slider screw[2]	4.2	37	–
Driven sprocket bolts	32	–	24
Rear brake disc mounting bolts[2]	42	–	31
Rear brake hose guide screw[2]	4.2	37	–
Shock absorber			
Compression damping adjuster	18	–	13
Damper rod end nut	30	–	22
Shock arm-to-shock absorber mounting nut	44	–	33
Spring locknut	88	–	65
Upper shock mounting nut	44	–	33
Shock arm-to-swing arm nut	69	–	51
Shock link-to-frame nut	49	–	36
Shock link-to-shock arm nut	44	–	33
Swing arm pivot shaft nut	88	–	65
Wheel setting plate fixing screw[2]	4.2	37	–

1. Apply threadlock to fastener threads.
2. Install new ALOC fasteners during assembly.

12

CHAPTER THIRTEEN

BRAKES

This chapter describes service procedures for the front and rear disc brakes.

Table 1 and **Table 2** list front and rear brake specifications. **Table 3** lists brake tightening torques. **Tables 1-3** are at the end of this chapter.

BRAKE FLUID SELECTION

Use new DOT 4 brake fluid from a sealed container.

DISC BRAKES

The front and rear disc brakes are hydraulically actuated and controlled by a hand lever or foot pedal on the master cylinder. As the brake pads wear, the brake fluid level drops in the reservoir and automatically adjusts for wear.

When working on the brake system, the work area and all tools must be absolutely clean.

Consider the following when servicing the disc brakes.

1. Do not allow disc brake fluid to contact any plastic parts or painted surfaces as damage will result.

2. Always keep the master cylinder reservoir and spare cans of brake fluid closed to prevent dust or moisture from entering and contaminating the brake fluid.

3. Use new DOT 4 disc brake fluid to wash and lubricate internal parts of the brake system. Never clean any internal brake components with solvent or any other petroleum-base cleaners. These will cause the rubber parts in the system to swell, permanently damaging them.

4. Whenever a brake hose banjo bolt is loosened, the brake system is considered opened and must be bled to remove air bubbles. Also, if the brake feels spongy, this usually means there are air bubbles in the system. Bleed the brakes as described under *Brake Bleeding* in this chapter

CAUTION
Do not reuse brake fluid. Contaminated brake fluid can cause brake failure. Dispose of brake fluid properly.

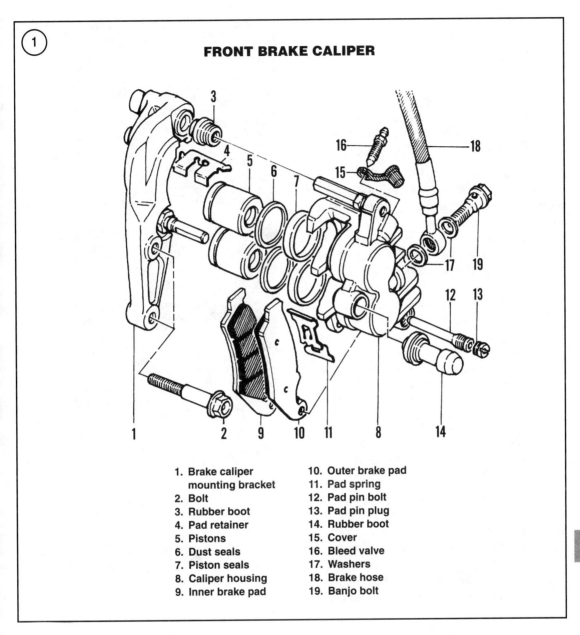

FRONT BRAKE CALIPER

1. Brake caliper
   mounting bracket
2. Bolt
3. Rubber boot
4. Pad retainer
5. Pistons
6. Dust seals
7. Piston seals
8. Caliper housing
9. Inner brake pad
10. Outer brake pad
11. Pad spring
12. Pad pin bolt
13. Pad pin plug
14. Rubber boot
15. Cover
16. Bleed valve
17. Washers
18. Brake hose
19. Banjo bolt

13

FRONT BRAKE PAD REPLACEMENT

Pad wear depends on riding habits and conditions. Replace the brake pads when excessively worn, damaged or when contaminated with oil and other chemicals.

Replace both brake pads at the same time. Never use one new and one used brake pad in the caliper.

Refer to **Figure 1**.

1. Read the information listed under *Disc Brake* in this chapter.

NOTE
Do not allow the master cylinder reservoir to overflow when performing Step 2. Brake fluid will damage most surfaces it contacts. If the brake master cylinder was recently filled, remove some of the brake fluid with a syringe.

2. Push the caliper body (from the outside) toward the brake disc. This will push the pistons into the caliper to make room for the new brake pads.

3. Loosen and remove the pad pin plug (A, **Figure 2**).

4. Loosen and remove the pad pin bolt (B, **Figure 2**).

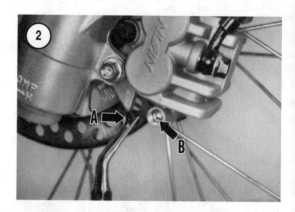

> *NOTE*
> *If the pads are to be reused, handle them carefully to prevent contamination and damage.*

5. Remove the brake pads (**Figure 3**).

6. Inspect the brake pads (**Figure 4**) for uneven wear, damage or contamination. Note the following:

   a. To remove surface contamination, lightly sand the lining surface with a piece of sandpaper placed on a flat surface. If the contamination has penetrated the lining material, replace both brake pads.

   b. Both brake pads should show approximately the same amount of wear. If the pads are worn unevenly, one of the caliper pistons or the caliper mounting bracket may not be working correctly. When one pad is worn more than the other the mounting bracket is not working correctly.

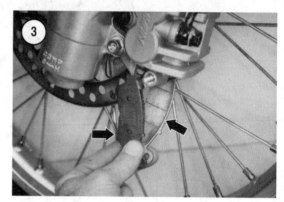

> *NOTE*
> *A leaking left side fork oil seal can allow fork oil to contaminate the front brake pads, caliper and brake disc.*

7. Check pad wear by observing the wear limit groove in the center of each pad (**Figure 4**). When the lining material is worn down to the bottom of the groove, replace both brake pads.

8. Check the caliper for signs of leakage around the pistons. If brake fluid is leaking from the caliper bores, overhaul the brake caliper as described in this chapter.

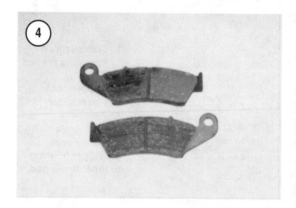

9. Clean the pad pin bolt and plug. Remove all rust and corrosion from the pad pin bolt and inspect for severe wear, grooves or other damage. Replace if damaged.

10. Inspect the brake disc for oil contamination (especially if the fork seal was leaking). Clean thoroughly with brake cleaner. Inspect the brake disc for wear as described in this chapter.

11. Make sure the pad spring (**Figure 5**) fits tightly against the brake caliper. If necessary, remove the spring and inspect it for corrosion and other damage. Replace the pad spring if damaged or if it will not stay in the caliper after being pushed into place.

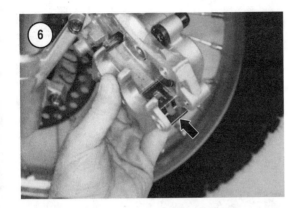

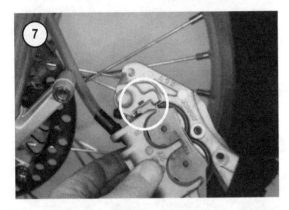

Figure 6 shows how the pad spring fits in the caliper with the caliper removed for clarity.

12. Install the inner and outer brake pads as shown in **Figure 3**. Push them in place so the upper end of each pad seats against the pad retainer (**Figure 7**) in the brake caliper mounting bracket.

13. Push both pads against the pad spring and install the pad pin bolt (B, **Figure 2**) into the caliper and through the hole in the bottom of each brake pad.

14. Tighten the pad pin bolt (B, **Figure 2**) to the specification in **Table 3**.

15. Install and tighten the pad pin plug (A, **Figure 2**) to the specification in **Table 3**.

16. Operate the brake lever a few times to reposition the caliper pistons against the brake pads. The brake lever should feel firm and be positioned away from the handlebar when applied.

17. Check the brake fluid level in the reservoir. If necessary, add new DOT 4 brake fluid.

> *WARNING*
> *Do not ride the motorcycle unless the front brake is operating correctly with full hydraulic advantage. If necessary, bleed the front brake as described in this chapter.*

FRONT BRAKE CALIPER

Refer to **Figure 1** when servicing the brake caliper in this section.

Brake Caliper Removal/Installation (Caliper Will Not Be Disassembled)

1A. To remove the caliper from the motorcycle, perform the following:

   a. Loosen the brake hose banjo bolt (A, **Figure 8**) at the caliper.

   b. Remove the bolts (B, **Figure 8**) holding the brake caliper mounting bracket to the fork slider. Lift the caliper off the brake disc.

   c. Remove the banjo bolt, two washers and brake caliper. Seal the hose to prevent leakage.

1B. To remove the brake caliper without disconnecting the brake hose, perform the following:

   a. Remove the bolts (B, **Figure 8**) holding the brake caliper mounting bracket to the fork slider. Lift the caliper off the brake disc.

   b. Insert a spacer block between the brake pads.

> *NOTE*
> *The spacer block will prevent the pistons from being forced out of the caliper if the front brake lever is applied with the brake caliper removed.*

   c. Support the caliper with a wire hook.

3. Install the caliper by reversing the preceding steps, and note the following:

13

4A. If the caliper was removed from the motorcycle, perform the following:

   a. Make sure the brake pads were not contaminated with brake fluid.

   b. Place a new washer on each side of the brake hose. Install the banjo bolt and finger tighten. Route the brake hose against the caliper as shown in **Figure 8**.

   c. Carefully install the caliper assembly over the brake disc. Be careful not to damage the leading edge of the pads during installation.

> *NOTE*
> *The brake caliper mounting bolts have a self-adhesive material applied to their threads (ALOC bolts). Discard these bolts and install new ones when installing the caliper.*

   e. Install two new brake caliper mounting bolts (B, **Figure 8**) and tighten as specified in **Table 3**.

   f. Tighten the brake hose banjo bolt (A, **Figure 8**) as specified in **Table 3**.

   g. Refill the master cylinder and bleed the front brake as described in this chapter.

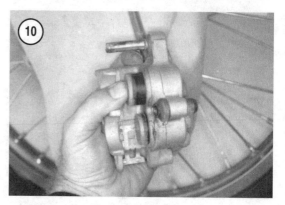

4B. If the caliper brake hose was not disconnected, perform the following:

   a. Remove the spacer block from between the brake pads.

   b. Install the caliper over the brake disc. Be careful not to damage the leading edge of the pads during installation.

> *NOTE*
> *The brake caliper mounting bolts have a self-adhesive material applied to their threads (ALOC bolts). Discard these bolts and install new ones when installing the caliper.*

   c. Install two new brake caliper mounting bolts (B, **Figure 8**) and tighten to the specification in **Table 3**.

5. Operate the brake lever a few times to seat the pads against the brake disc.

> *WARNING*
> *Do not ride the motorcycle until the front brake operates with full hydraulic advantage.*

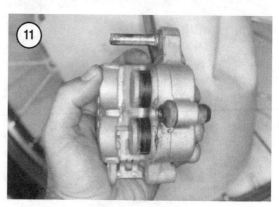

Caliper Removal/Piston Removal
(Caliper Will Be Disassembled)

Force is required to remove the pistons from the caliper. This procedure describes how to remove the pistons with the caliper connected to its brake hose.

1. Remove the brake pads as described in this chapter.

2. Remove the two brake caliper mounting bolts (B, **Figure 8**) and remove the brake caliper.

3. Remove the brake caliper mounting bracket (**Figure 9**) from the caliper.

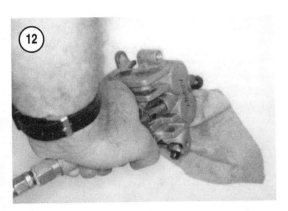

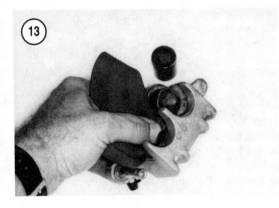

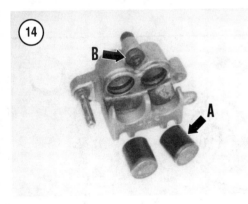

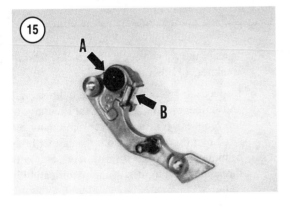

4. Wrap a large cloth around the brake caliper.

5. Operate the front brake lever to force the pistons partially out of the caliper bores. If one piston is stuck, block the other piston with a spacer block (**Figure 10**), and continue to operate the brake lever to force both pistons evenly out of their bore (**Figure 11**). To avoid brake fluid spillage, do not completely remove the pistons until the caliper is removed from the bike and placed on the workbench for disassembly.

NOTE
*If the pistons will not come out, remove them as described under **Disassembly** in this chapter.*

6. Remove the caliper banjo bolt (A, **Figure 8**) and both washers. Seal the brake hose to prevent leakage.

7. Take the caliper to the workbench for disassembly.

Disassembly

Refer to **Figure 1**.

1. Remove the brake caliper as described in this chapter.

2. Slide the caliper mounting bracket out of the caliper (**Figure 9**).

3. Make sure the bleed valve is tight.

WARNING
Compressed air will force the pistons out of the caliper under considerable force. Do not block or cushion the pistons by hand, as injury will result.

4. Cushion the caliper pistons with a shop rag, and be sure to keep hands away from the pistons. Apply compressed air through the brake hose port (**Figure 12**) and remove the pistons. If only one piston is blown out, remove it completely and then block its bore opening with a piece of thick rubber (old inner tube) or a rubber ball. Apply compressed air through the caliper once again (**Figure 13**) and remove the remaining piston. See A, **Figure 14**.

CAUTION
Do not rap the caliper with a hammer to remove the pistons. The aluminum caliper body is easily damaged.

5. Remove the rubber boots from the caliper body (B, **Figure 14**) and caliper mounting bracket (A, **Figure 15**).

13

6. Remove the dust and piston seals (C, **Figure 14**) from the cylinder bore grooves with a plastic or other soft-faced tool. Do not use a metal tool, which can damage the seal grooves or piston bore. Discard both seals.

7. Remove the bleed valve and its cover from the caliper.

8. Remove the pad retainer from the caliper mounting bracket (B, **Figure 15**).

Inspection

All models use a floating caliper design, which allows the caliper to slide or float on fixed shafts. Rubber boots around each shaft prevent dirt from damaging the shafts. If the shafts are worn or damaged the caliper cannot slide evenly. This condition will cause the pads to drag and result in uneven pad wear and brake system overheating. Inspect the rubber boots and shafts during caliper inspection as they play a vital role in brake performance.

When measuring the brake caliper components in this section, compare the actual measurements to the new and service limit specifications in **Table 1**. Replace parts that are out of specification or show excessive wear or damage.

> *CAUTION*
> *Do not get any oil or grease onto any of the brake caliper components. These chemicals will cause the rubber parts in the brake system to swell, permanently damaging them.*

1. Clean and dry the caliper housing and the other metal parts. Clean the seal grooves with a wooden or plastic faced tool. If the contamination is hard to remove, soak the caliper body in solvent and then reclean. If any of the rubber parts are to be reused, clean them with denatured alcohol or new DOT 4 brake fluid. Do not use a petroleum based solvent.

> *NOTE*
> *The caliper bore and seal grooves can be difficult to clean, especially if brake fluid was leaking past the seals. Clean the caliper carefully to avoid damaging the seal grooves and bore surface.*

2. Inspect the caliper mounting bracket, fixed shafts and rubber boots (**Figure 16**) as follows:

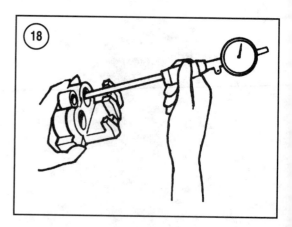

a. Inspect the rubber boots for cracks, tearing, weakness or other damage.

b. Inspect the fixed shafts on the caliper body and caliper mounting bracket for excessive or uneven wear. If necessary, replace a damaged shaft by unscrewing it from the caliper body or mounting bracket. Install a new shaft with threadlock and tighten to the specification in **Table 3**.

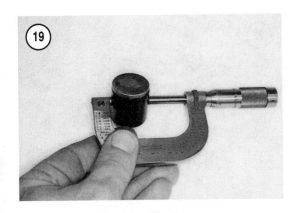

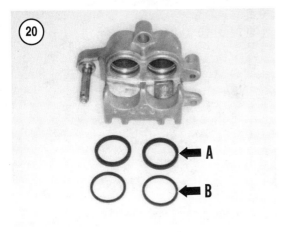

3. Check each cylinder bore (**Figure 17**) for corrosion, pitting, deep scratches or other wear.

4. Measure each cylinder bore with a bore gauge (**Figure 18**).

5. Check the pistons for wear marks, scoring, cracks or other damage.

6. Measure each piston outside diameter (**Figure 19**).

7. Check the bleed valve and cap for wear or damage.

8. Check the banjo bolt for wear or damage. Discard the washers.

9. Inspect the brake pads, pad spring, pad pin and pad pin bolt as described under *Front Brake Pad Replacement* in this chapter.

Assembly

> *NOTE*
> *Use new DOT 4 brake fluid when lubricating the parts in the following steps.*

1. Install the bleed valve and its cover into the caliper.

2. Soak the new piston and dust seals in a small container filled with brake fluid.

3. Lubricate the cylinder bores with brake fluid.

> *NOTE*
> *The piston seals (A, **Figure 20**) are thicker than the dust seals (B, **Figure 20**).*

4. Install a new piston seal into each rear bore groove (A, **Figure 21**).

5. Install a new dust seal into each front bore groove (B, **Figure 21**).

> *NOTE*
> *Make sure each seal fits squarely inside its groove.*

6. Lubricate the pistons with brake fluid.

> *NOTE*
> *The tight piston-to-seal fit can make piston installation difficult. Do not attempt to push the piston straight in; instead twist and push the piston past the seals. Once the piston is started past the seals, push it straight into the bore.*

7. Install each piston into its cylinder bore with its metal (**Figure 22**) side facing out. After installing the pistons past their seals, push them all the way in.

> *CAUTION*
> *In Step 8 use only silicone grease specified for brake use. Do not confuse silicone sealant (RTV) with silicone brake grease.*

13

8. Install the large rubber boot through the mounting hole in the caliper body (A, **Figure 23**). Make sure the boot opening faces toward the inside of the caliper. Partially fill the boot with silicone brake grease.

9. Install the small boot into the groove in the caliper mounting bracket (B, **Figure 23**). Partially fill the boot with silicone brake grease.

10. Hook the pad retainer (B, **Figure 15**) onto the caliper mounting bracket.

11. Hook the pad spring (**Figure 6**) onto the caliper housing.

12. Lubricate the fixed pins on the caliper body and caliper mounting bracket (C, **Figure 23**) with silicone brake grease.

13. Align and slide the caliper mounting bracket onto the caliper body (**Figure 24**). Hold the caliper body and slide the bracket in and out by hand. Make sure there is no roughness or binding.

14. Install the brake caliper assembly and brake pads as described in this chapter.

FRONT MASTER CYLINDER

Read the information under *Disc Brake* in this chapter before servicing the front master cylinder.

Refer to **Figure 25** when servicing the front master cylinder.

Removal/Installation

1. Support the motorcycle on a workstand.

2. Cover the area under the master cylinder to prevent brake fluid from damaging any component it might contact.

> *CAUTION*
> *Wipe up any spilled brake fluid immediately as it will damage the finish of most plastic and metal surfaces. Use soapy water and rinse thoroughly.*

3. Remove the master cylinder cap and diaphragm assembly. Use a syringe to remove brake fluid from the master cylinder reservoir. Discard the brake fluid. Reinstall the diaphragm and master cylinder cap.

4. To remove the hand guard/brake lever assembly, perform the following:

    a. Remove the pivot nut and collar from the pivot bolt (**Figure 26**).

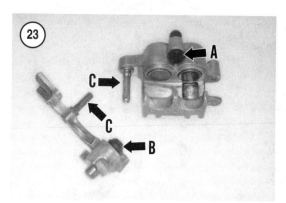

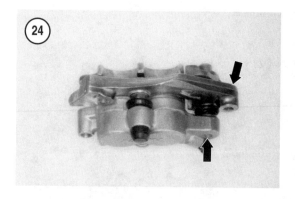

    b. Hold the brake lever and remove the pivot bolt and hand guard (**Figure 26**).

    c. Remove the brake lever and return spring (**Figure 27**).

5. Remove the banjo bolt (A, **Figure 28**) and washers securing the brake hose to the master cylinder. Insert the end of the brake hose into a small plastic bag to prevent leakage.

6. Remove the bolts and clamp (B, **Figure 28**) holding the master cylinder to the handlebar. Remove the master cylinder.

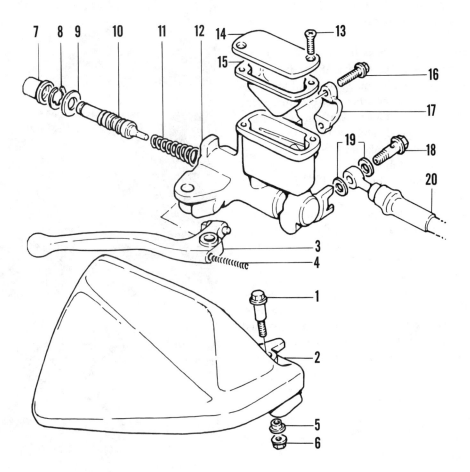

25

FRONT MASTER CYLINDER

13

1. Pivot bolt
2. Hand guard
3. Brake lever
4. Return spring
5. Collar
6. Nut
7. Dust cover
8. Circlip
9. Washer
10. Piston assembly
11. Spring
12. Master cylinder housing
13. Screws
14. Cover
15. Diaphragm
16. Bolts
17. Holder
18. Banjo bolt
19. Washers
20. Brake hose

7. Clean the handlebar, master cylinder and clamp mating surfaces.

8. Install the master cylinder holder with the UP mark on the holder facing up (B, **Figure 28**). Align the edge of the master cylinder clamp surface with the punch mark on the handlebar (**Figure 29**).

9. Install and tighten the master cylinder mounting bolts. Tighten the upper bolt first, then the lower mounting bolt.

10. Secure the brake hose to the master cylinder with the banjo bolt (A, **Figure 28**) and two *new* washers. Install a washer on each side of the brake hose. Center the brake hose between the arms on the master cylinder (A, **Figure 28**) and tighten the banjo bolt to the specification in **Table 3**.

11. If the hand guard/brake lever assembly was removed, install it as follows:

   a. Lubricate the pivot bolt with silicone brake grease.

   b. Install the return spring into the brake lever and then insert the return spring into the master cylinder hole and install the brake lever into position (**Figure 27**).

   c. Install the hand guard over the brake lever. Install the front brake lever pivot bolt (**Figure 26**) and tighten to the specification in **Table 3**.

   d. Install the collar and nut. Hold the pivot bolt and tighten the nut to the specification in **Table 3**.

12. Bleed the front brake as described under *Brake Bleeding* in this chapter.

> *WARNING*
> *Do not ride the motorcycle until the front brake works properly.*

Disassembly

Refer to **Figure 25**.

1. Remove the master cylinder as described in this chapter.

2. Remove the dust cover (**Figure 30**) from the master cylinder and piston.

> *NOTE*
> *Use a bolt and nut as shown in **Figure 31** to hold the master cylinder in a vise when removing and installing the piston circlip.*

> *CAUTION*
> *Do not pry the circlip out of its groove as doing so can damage the piston, circlip groove or bore.*

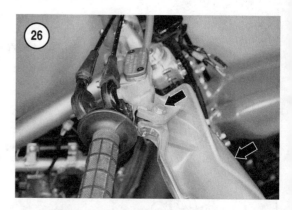

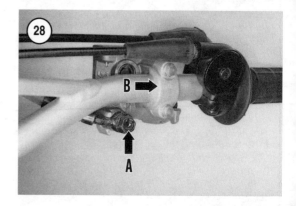

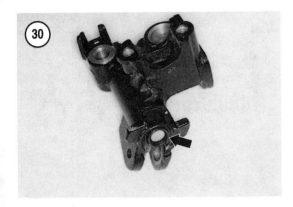

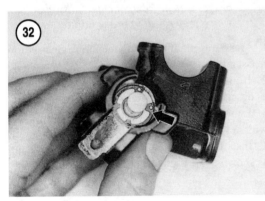

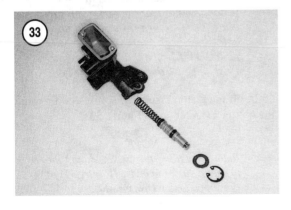

3. Compress the piston and remove the circlip (**Figure 32**) with circlip pliers.

4. Remove the piston and spring assembly (**Figure 33**) from the master cylinder bore.

5. Perform the *Inspection* procedure to clean and inspect the parts.

Inspection

When measuring the front master cylinder components in this section, compare the actual measurements to the new and service limit specifications in **Table 1**. Replace parts that are out of specification or show excessive wear or damage as described in this section.

> *WARNING*
> *Do not get any oil or grease on any of the master cylinder components. These chemicals will cause the rubber brake system components to swell, which may result in brake failure.*

1. Clean the master cylinder parts with new DOT 4 brake fluid or with denatured alcohol. Check for plugged supply and relief ports in the master cylinder. If using denatured alcohol, dry with compressed air.

2. **Figure 34** identifies the piston assembly:
   a. Spring.
   b. Primary cup.
   c. Secondary cup.
   d. Piston.
   e. Washer.
   f. Circlip.

> *CAUTION*
> *Do not remove the primary and secondary cups from the piston assembly to clean or inspect them. If the cups are damaged, replace the piston assembly.*

3. Visually check the piston assembly (**Figure 34**) for the following defects:
   a. Broken, distorted or collapsed piston return spring.
   b. Worn, cracked, damaged or swollen primary and secondary cups.
   c. Scratched, scored or damaged piston.
   d. Corroded or damaged washer or circlip.
   e. Excessively worn or damaged dust cover.

13

4. Measure the piston outside diameter with a micrometer at the point shown in **Figure 35**.

5. To assemble a new piston assembly, perform the following:

NOTE
*A new piston assembly consists of the piston, primary cup, secondary cup and spring. Because these parts come unassembled, install the new primary and secondary cups onto the piston. See **Figure 36**. Use the original piston and piston cups (A, **Figure 36**) as a reference when assembling the new piston assembly.*

a. Soak the new cups in new DOT 4 brake fluid for 15 minutes to soften them and ease installation. Clean the new piston in brake fluid and place it on a clean lint-free cloth.

CAUTION
Use extreme care when installing the piston cups. Do not pry the cups over the piston with any metal tool. Carefully stretch the cups by hand and guide them over the piston shoulder.

b. Install the secondary cup (B, **Figure 36**), then the primary cup (C, **Figure 36**) onto the piston.

6. Inspect the master cylinder bore for corrosion, pitting or excessive wear. Do not hone the master cylinder bore to remove scratches or other damage.

7. Measure the master cylinder bore (**Figure 37**) with a bore gauge.

8. Check for plugged supply and relief ports in the master cylinder. Clean with compressed air.

9. Inspect the reservoir cover and diaphragm for cracks and other damage.

10. Inspect the brake lever assembly for:
    a. Cracks or other damage.
    b. Excessively worn or elongated brake lever hole.
    c. Excessively worn brake lever pivot bolt.
    d. Weak, stretched or damaged brake lever spring.

Assembly

Refer to **Figure 25** for this procedure.

WARNING
Do not get any oil or grease on any of the master cylinder components. These chemicals will cause the rubber

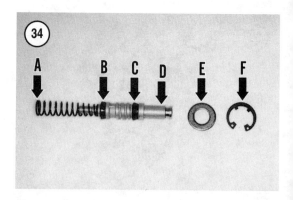

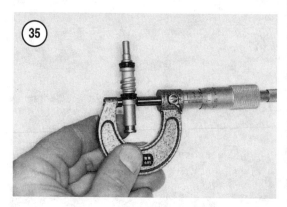

brake system components to swell, which may result in brake failure.

1. Make sure all of the components are clean before reassembly.

2. If installing a new piston assembly, assemble it as described under *Inspection* in this section.

3. Lubricate the piston assembly and cylinder bore with new DOT 4 brake fluid.

4. Install the spring, small end first, onto the piston as shown in A, **Figure 34**.

CAUTION
Use extreme care when installing the piston. Do not tear the piston cups or allow them to turn inside out. Lubricate the piston cups and bore with new DOT 4 brake fluid and carefully twist and push the piston into the bore.

5. Insert the piston assembly, spring end first, into the master cylinder bore (**Figure 33**).

NOTE
*Before installing the circlip, mount the master cylinder in a vise (**Figure 31**) as described under **Disassembly**.*

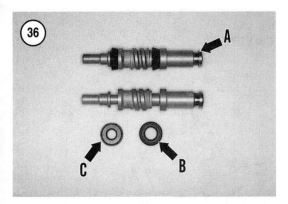

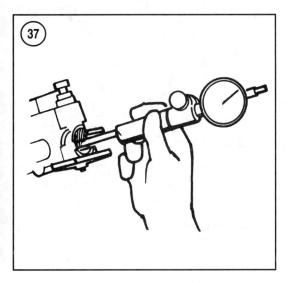

REAR BRAKE PAD REPLACEMENT

Pad wear varies with riding habits and conditions. Replace the brake pads when excessively worn, damaged or when contaminated with oil and other chemicals.

Replace both brake pads at the same time. Never use one new and one used brake pad in the caliper.

Refer to **Figure 38**.

1. Read the information listed under *Disc Brake* in this chapter.

CAUTION
Do not allow the master cylinder reservoir to overflow when performing Step 2. Brake fluid will damage most surfaces it contacts. If the brake master cylinder was recently filled, remove some of the brake fluid with a syringe.

2. Push the caliper body (from the outside) toward the brake disc. This will push the piston into the caliper to make room for the new brake pads.
3. Remove the pad pin plug (A, **Figure 39**).
4. Loosen and remove the brake pad mounting bolt (B, **Figure 39**).

NOTE
If the pads are to be reused, handle them carefully to prevent grease contamination.

5. Remove the two brake pads (**Figure 40**).
6. Inspect the brake pads (**Figure 41**) for uneven wear, damage or contamination:
  a. To remove surface contamination, lightly sand the lining surface with a piece of sandpaper placed on a flat surface. If the contamination has penetrated the lining material, replace both brake pads.
  b. Both brake pads should show approximately the same amount of wear. If the pads are worn unevenly, one of the caliper pistons or the mounting bracket may not be working correctly. When one pad is worn more than the other, the mounting bracket is not working correctly.
  c. Check the shims (**Figure 42**) on the back of each pad for corrosion. Each shim should be a tight fit on its pad.
7. Check pad wear by observing the wear limit groove in the center of each pad (**Figure 41**). When

6. Install the washer over the pushrod and set it on the piston.

7. Install the circlip over the pushrod with the flat side facing up.

8. Compress the piston assembly and install the circlip into the master cylinder groove. Make sure the circlip seats in the groove completely (**Figure 32**). Push and release the piston a few times to make sure it moves smoothly and the circlip does not pop out.

9. Slide the dust cover over the piston. Seat the large end of the dust cover against the circlip and install the small end into the pushrod groove (**Figure 30**).

10. Install the diaphragm, master cylinder cover and screws.

11. Install the master cylinder as described in this chapter.

13

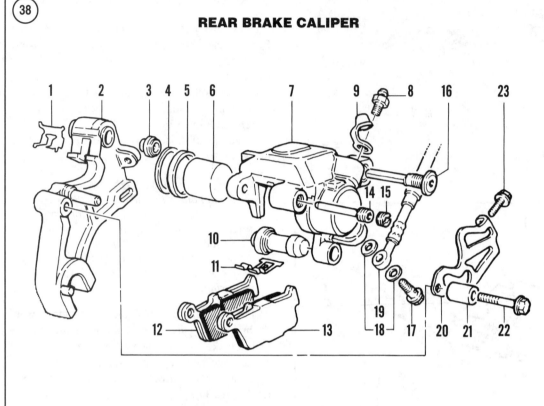

REAR BRAKE CALIPER

1. Pad retainer
2. Caliper mounting bracket
3. Rubber boot
4. Dust seal
5. Piston seal
6. Piston
7. Brake caliper housing
8. Bleed screw
9. Cover
10. Rubber boot
11. Pad spring
12. Inner brake pad
13. Outer brake pad
14. Pad pin bolt
15. Pad pin plug
16. Fixed shaft
17. Banjo bolt
18. Washers
19. Brake hose
20. Caliper guard
21. Collar
22. Bolt
23. Bolt

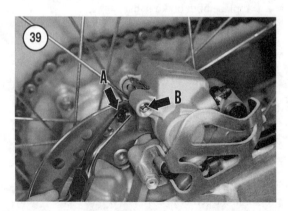

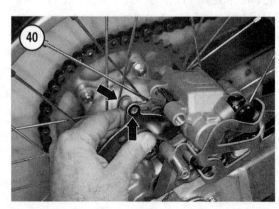

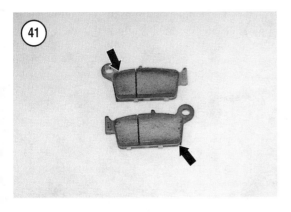

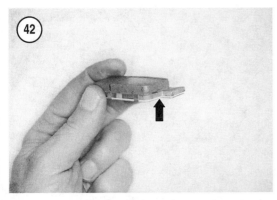

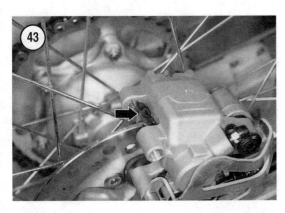

the lining material is worn down to the bottom of the groove, replace both brake pads.

8. Check the caliper for signs of fluid leakage around the pistons. If brake fluid is leaking from the caliper bores, overhaul the brake caliper as described in this chapter.

9. Clean the pad pin bolt and plug. Remove all rust and corrosion from the pad pin bolt. Inspect the pad pin bolt for severe wear, grooves or other damage. Replace if damaged.

10. Check the brake disc for oil contamination. Clean thoroughly with brake cleaner. Inspect the brake disc for wear as described in this chapter.

11. Make sure the pad spring (**Figure 43**) fits tightly against the brake caliper. If necessary, remove the spring and inspect it for corrosion and other damage. Replace the pad spring if damaged or if it will not stay in the caliper after being pushed into place. **Figure 44** shows how the pad spring fits in the caliper, with the caliper removed for clarity.

12. Install the inner and outer brake pads as shown in **Figure 40**. Push them in place so the upper end of each pad seats against the pad retainer (**Figure 45**) in the brake caliper mounting bracket.

13. Push both pads against the pad spring and install the pad pin bolt (B, **Figure 39**) into the caliper and through the hole in each brake pad.

14. Tighten the pad pin bolt (B, **Figure 39**) to the specification in **Table 3**.

15. Install and tighten the pad pin plug (A, **Figure 39**) to the specification in **Table 3**.

16. Operate the brake pedal a few times to reposition the caliper piston against the brake pads. The brake pedal should feel firm when applied.

17. Check the brake fluid level in the reservoir. If necessary, add new DOT 4 brake fluid to bring its level to the correct height.

WARNING
Do not ride the motorcycle unless the rear brake is operating correctly with full hydraulic advantage. If necessary, bleed the rear brake as described in this chapter.

REAR BRAKE CALIPER

Refer to **Figure 38** when servicing the rear brake caliper in this section.

13

Rear Brake Caliper Removal/Installation
(Caliper Will Not Be Disassembled)

NOTE
Do not drain the brake fluid or dis-
connect the brake hose if the caliper
will remain on the motorcycle.

1. Unbolt and remove the caliper guard (**Figure 46**).
2. Loosen the brake hose banjo bolt (**Figure 47**) at the caliper, then retighten it hand-tight so no brake fluid can leak out.
3. Remove the rear wheel (Chapter Ten).
4. Slide the brake caliper mounting bracket (**Figure 48**) off the swing arm stay.

5. If necessary, remove the banjo bolt, two washers and brake caliper. Seal the hose to prevent leakage.
6. If the caliper will not be removed during this procedure, insert a spacer block between the brake pads.

NOTE
The spacer block will prevent the pis-
ton from being forced out of the cali-
per if the rear brake pedal is applied
with the brake caliper removed.

7. Install the brake caliper by reversing these steps, and perform the following:
   a. If the brake hose was not disconnected, remove the spacer block from between the brake pads.
   b. Make sure the brake pads were not contaminated with brake fluid.
   c. Place a *new* washer on each side of the brake hose. Then install the banjo bolt and finger tighten.
   d. Hold the brake caliper mounting bracket with a large adjustable wrench (**Figure 49**) and tighten the brake hose banjo bolt to the specification in **Table 3**.
   e. Slide the brake caliper mounting bracket over the swing arm stay (**Figure 48**) and install the rear wheel (Chapter Ten).
   f. If the brake hose was disconnected, refill the master cylinder and bleed the rear brake as described in this chapter.
   g. Press and release the rear brake pedal to reposition the piston and seat the pads against the brake disc.

WARNING
Do not ride the motorcycle until the
rear brake operates with full hydrau-
lic advantage.

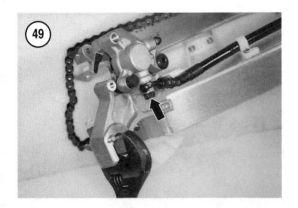

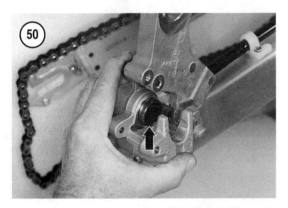

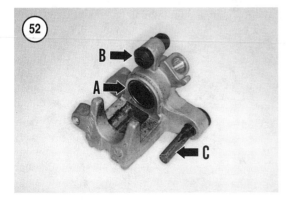

Caliper Removal/Piston Removal
(Caliper Will Be Disassembled)

Force is required to remove the piston from the caliper. This procedure describes how to remove the piston with the caliper connected to its brake hose.

1. Remove the brake pads as described in this chapter.
2. Remove the brake caliper as described in this chapter.
3. Wrap a large cloth around the brake caliper.
4. Grip the caliper with hands and fingers clear of the piston.

NOTE
To avoid brake fluid spillage, do not completely remove the piston until the caliper is removed from the bike and placed on the workbench.

5. Operate the rear brake pedal to force the piston (**Figure 50**) *partially* out of the caliper bore.

NOTE
*If the piston will not come out, remove it as described under **Disassembly** in this chapter.*

6. Hold the brake caliper mounting bracket with a large adjustable wrench, then loosen and remove the brake hose banjo bolt (**Figure 49**) and both washers. Seal the brake hose to prevent leakage.
7. Take the caliper to the workbench for disassembly.

Disassembly

Refer to **Figure 38**.

1. Remove the brake caliper as described in this chapter.
2. Slide the brake caliper mounting bracket (**Figure 51**) off of the brake caliper.
3. Remove the rubber boot from the caliper (B, **Figure 52**).
4. Remove the pad spring from the caliper body (**Figure 44**).
5. Make sure the bleed valve is tight.

WARNING
*Compressed air will force the piston (A, **Figure 52**) out of the caliper under considerable force. Do not block or cushion the piston by hand, as injury will result.*

13

6. Cushion the caliper piston with a shop rag, taking care to keep hands clear of the piston. Apply compressed air through the brake hose port (**Figure 53**) and remove the piston. See **Figure 54**.

7. Remove the dust and piston seals (**Figure 54**) from the caliper bore grooves.

8. Remove the rubber boot (A, **Figure 55**) and pad retainer (B) from the caliper mounting bracket.

9. Remove the bleed valve and its cover from the caliper.

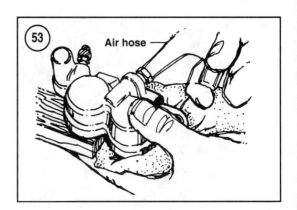
Air hose

Inspection

All models use a floating caliper design, which allows the caliper to slide or float on fixed shafts. Rubber boots around each shaft prevent dirt from damaging the shafts. If the shafts are worn or damaged the caliper cannot slide evenly. This condition will cause the pads to drag and result in uneven pad wear and brake system overheating. Inspect the rubber boots and shafts during caliper inspection as they play a vital role in brake performance.

When measuring the brake caliper components in this section, compare the actual measurements to the new and service limit specifications in **Table 2**. Replace parts that are out of specification or show excessive wear or damage.

> *WARNING*
> *Do not get any oil or grease on any of the brake caliper components. These chemicals will cause the rubber brake system components to swell, which can result in brake failure.*

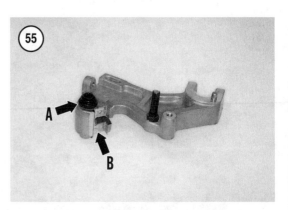
A
B

1. Clean and dry the caliper housing and the other metal parts. Clean the seal grooves with a wooden or plastic faced tool. If the contamination is hard to remove, soak the caliper body in solvent and then reclean. If any of the rubber parts will be reused, clean them with denatured alcohol or new DOT 4 brake fluid. Do not use a petroleum based solvent.

> *NOTE*
> *The caliper bore and seal grooves can be difficult to clean, especially if brake fluid was leaking past the seals. Clean the caliper carefully to avoid damaging the seal grooves and bore surface.*

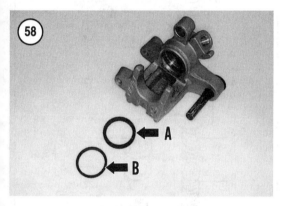

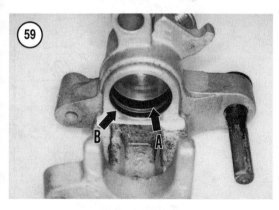

2. Inspect the caliper mounting bracket, fixed shafts and rubber boots as follows:

    a. Inspect the rubber boots for cracks, tearing, weakness or other damage.

    b. Inspect the fixed shaft on the caliper body and mounting bracket for excessive or uneven wear. If necessary, replace a damaged shaft by unscrewing it from the caliper body or mounting bracket. Install a new shaft with threadlock and tighten to the specification in **Table 3**.

3. Check the cylinder bore (**Figure 56**) for corrosion, pitting, deep scratches or other wear. Do not hone the cylinder bore.

4. Measure the cylinder bore with a bore gauge.

5. Check the piston for wear marks, scoring, cracks or other damage.

6. Measure the piston outside diameter (**Figure 57**) with a micrometer.

7. Check the bleed valve and cap for wear or damage.

8. Check the banjo bolt for wear or damage. Discard the washers.

9. Inspect the brake pads, pad spring, pad pin and pad pin bolt as described under *Rear Brake Pad Replacement* in this chapter.

Assembly

> *NOTE*
> *Use new DOT 4 brake fluid when lubricating the parts in the following steps.*

1. Install the bleed valve and its cover into the caliper.

2. Soak the new piston seal and dust seal in brake fluid.

3. Lubricate the cylinder bore with brake fluid.

> *NOTE*
> *The piston seal (A, **Figure 58**) is thicker than the dust seal (B, **Figure 58**).*

4. Install a new piston seal into the rear bore groove (A, **Figure 59**).

5. Install a new dust seal into the front bore groove (B, **Figure 59**).

> *NOTE*
> *Make sure each seal fits squarely inside its groove.*

6. Lubricate the piston with brake fluid.

> *NOTE*
> *The tight piston-to-seal fit can make piston installation difficult. Do not attempt to push the piston straight in, instead twist and push the piston past the seals. Once the piston is started past the seals, push it straight into the bore.*

13

7. Install the piston into its cylinder bore with its open (**Figure 60**) side facing out. After installing the piston past the seals, push it all the way in.

CAUTION
In Step 8 use only silicone grease specified for brake use. Do not confuse silicone sealant (RTV) with silicone brake grease.

8. Install the large rubber boot through the mounting hole in the caliper body (B, **Figure 52**). Make sure the boot opening faces toward the inside of the caliper. Partially fill the boot with silicone brake grease.

9. Install the small boot into the groove in the caliper mounting bracket (A, **Figure 55**). Partially fill the boot with silicone brake grease.

10. Hook the pad retainer (B, **Figure 55**) onto the caliper mounting bracket.

11. Hook the pad spring (**Figure 44**) onto the caliper housing.

12. Lubricate the fixed pins on the caliper body and caliper mounting bracket with silicone brake grease.

13. Align and then slide the caliper mounting bracket onto the caliper body (**Figure 51**). Hold the caliper body and slide the bracket in and out by hand. Make sure there is no roughness or binding.

14. Install the brake caliper assembly and brake pads as described in this chapter.

REAR MASTER CYLINDER

Read the information listed under *Disc Brake* in this chapter before servicing the rear master cylinder.

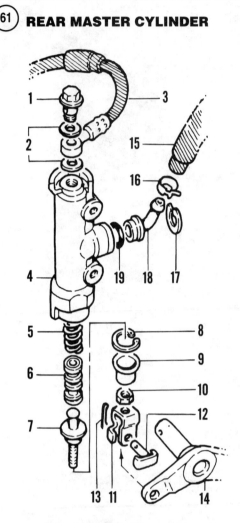

REAR MASTER CYLINDER

1. Banjo bolt
2. Washers
3. Brake hose
4. Master cylinder body
5. Return spring
6. Piston assembly
7. Pushrod/washer assembly
8. Circlip
9. Dust cover
10. Locknut
11. Pushrod joint
12. Clevis pin
13. Cotter pin
14. Rear brake pedal
15. Reservoir hose
16. Hose clamp
17. Circlip
18. Hose joint
19. O-ring

Refer to **Figure 61** when servicing the rear master cylinder in this section.

Removal/Installation

1. Support the motorcycle on a workstand.

> *CAUTION*
> *Wipe up any spilled brake fluid immediately as it will damage the finish of most plastic and metal surfaces. Use soapy water and rinse thoroughly.*

2. Drain the rear master cylinder reservoir as described in this chapter.

3. Unbolt and remove the master cylinder guard (**Figure 62**). Remove the washers installed between the guard and frame.

> *NOTE*
> *The two bolts used to secure the master cylinder guard are also the master cylinder mounting bolts.*

4. Remove the cotter pin and clevis pin that connect the master cylinder pushrod to the rear brake pedal (A, **Figure 63**). Discard the cotter pin.

5. Remove the banjo bolt (B, **Figure 63**) and both washers. Seal the brake hose to prevent leakage.

6. Pull the master cylinder away from the frame. Remove the brake reservoir hose circlip (**Figure 64**), hose and O-ring (**Figure 65**) from the master cylinder. Seal the reservoir hose to prevent leakage.

7. If brake fluid is leaking from the cylinder bore or if other service is necessary, overhaul the master cylinder as described in this chapter.

8. Lubricate a new O-ring with DOT 4 brake fluid and install it onto the reservoir hose joint. Push the reservoir hose joint into the master cylinder. Install the circlip (**Figure 64**) into the groove in the master cylinder.

9. Install the master cylinder, master cylinder guard, washers and new ALOC mounting bolts (**Figure 62**). Install the washers between the guard and frame. Tighten the rear master cylinder mounting bolts to the specification in **Table 3**.

10. Secure the brake hose to the master cylinder with the banjo bolt and two *new* washers. Install a washer on each side of the brake hose (B, **Figure 63**). Route the end of the hose so it sets against the

13

raised tab on top of the master cylinder and tighten the banjo bolt to the specification in **Table 3**.

CAUTION
Make sure the brake hose clears the rear shock absorber and all other moving suspension parts.

11. Connect the brake pedal to the master cylinder pushrod with the clevis pin (A, **Figure 63**) and a *new* cotter pin. Install the clevis pin from the outside. Bend over the ends of the cotter pin to lock it.
12. Refill the master cylinder with brake fluid and bleed the brake as described in this chapter.
13. Check the rear brake pedal adjustment (Chapter Three).

WARNING
Do not ride the motorcycle unless the rear brake is working properly.

Disassembly

Refer to **Figure 61**.
1. Remove the master cylinder as described in this chapter.
2. Loosen the locknut (A, **Figure 66**) and remove the clevis (B, **Figure 66**) and locknut from the pushrod.
3. Remove the dust cover (C, **Figure 66**) from the master cylinder.
4. Compress the piston, then remove the circlip (**Figure 67**) from the groove in the master cylinder using circlip pliers. Remove the pushrod assembly.
5. Remove the piston assembly (**Figure 68**) from the master cylinder bore.

Inspection

When measuring the rear master cylinder components in this section, compare the actual measurements to the new and service limit specifications in **Table 2**. Replace parts that are out of specification or show excessive wear or damage as described in this section.

WARNING
Do not get any oil or grease onto any of the master cylinder components. These chemicals will cause the rubber brake system components to swell, which can result in brake failure.

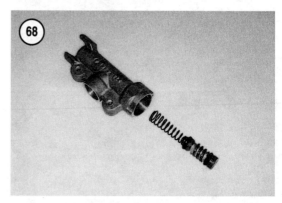

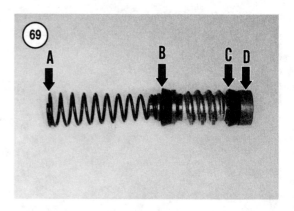

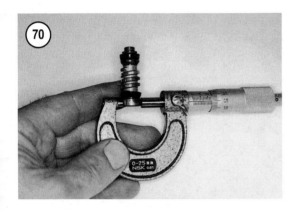

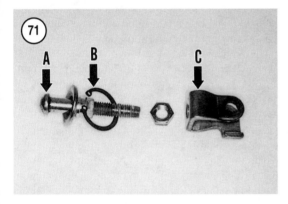

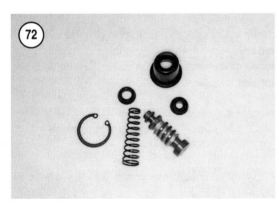

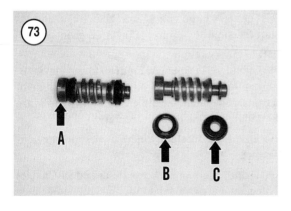

1. Clean the master cylinder parts with new DOT 4 brake fluid or with denatured alcohol. Check for plugged supply and relief ports in the master cylinder. If denatured alcohol was used, dry with compressed air.

2. **Figure 69** identifies the piston assembly:
   a. Spring.
   b. Primary cup.
   c. Secondary cup.
   d. Piston.

> *CAUTION*
> *Do not remove the primary and secondary cups from the piston assembly to clean or inspect them. If the cups are damaged, you must replace the piston assembly.*

3. Visually check the piston assembly (**Figure 69**) for the following defects:
   a. Broken, distorted or collapsed piston return spring.
   b. Worn, cracked, damaged or swollen primary and secondary cups.
   c. Scratched, scored or damaged piston.
   d. Excessively worn or damaged dust cover.

4. Measure the piston outside diameter with a micrometer at the point shown in **Figure 70**.

5. Check the pushrod assembly (**Figure 71**) for:
   a. Damaged pushrod (A, **Figure 71**).
   b. Weak or damaged circlip (B, **Figure 71**).
   c. Damaged pushrod joint (C, **Figure 71**).

6. To assemble a new piston assembly, perform the following:

> *NOTE*
> *A new piston assembly consists of the piston, primary cup, secondary cup and spring. Because these parts come unassembled, install the new primary and secondary cups onto the piston. See **Figure 72**. Refer to the original piston and pistons cups (A, **Figure 73**) when assembling the new piston assembly.*

   a. Soak the new cups in new DOT 4 brake fluid for 15 minutes, to soften them and ease installation. Clean the new piston in brake fluid and place it on a clean lint-free cloth.

> *CAUTION*
> *Use extreme care when installing the piston cups. Do not pry the cups over*

13

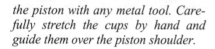

*the piston with any metal tool. Care-
fully stretch the cups by hand and
guide them over the piston shoulder.*

b. Install the secondary cup (B, **Figure 73**) and
then the primary cup (C, **Figure 73**) onto the
piston.

7. Inspect the master cylinder bore for corrosion,
pitting or excessive wear. Do not hone the master
cylinder bore to remove scratches or other damage.

8. Measure the master cylinder bore with a bore
gauge.

9. Check for plugged supply and relief ports in the
master cylinder. Clean with compressed air.

Assembly

1. Clean all of the components before reassembly.
2. If a new piston assembly is to be installed, assemble it as described under *Inspection* in this section.
3. Lubricate the piston assembly and cylinder bore
with brake fluid.
4. Install the spring, small end first, onto the piston
as shown in A, **Figure 69**.

CAUTION
*Use extreme care when installing the
piston. Do not tear or allow the piston
cups to turn inside out. Lubricate the
piston cups and bore with new DOT 4
brake fluid and carefully twist and
push the piston into the bore.*

5. Insert the piston assembly—spring end
first—into the master cylinder bore (**Figure 68**).
6. Compress the piston assembly and install the
pushrod, washer and circlip (**Figure 74**). Install the

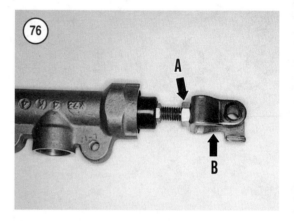

circlip with its flat side facing out (**Figure 67**). Push
and release the pushrod a few times to make sure the
piston moves smoothly and that the circlip does not
pop out.

NOTE
*The circlip must seat in the groove
completely (**Figure 67**).*

7. Apply silicone brake grease into the groove in
the pushrod.

8. Slide the dust cover over the pushrod. Seat the
dust cover's large end against the circlip and install the small end into the pushrod groove (**Figure 75**).

9. Thread the locknut (A, **Figure 76**) and clevis (B,
Figure 76) onto the pushrod. Adjust the position of
the pushrod joint to the dimension shown in **Figure
77** and tighten the locknut securely.

10. Install the master cylinder as described in this
chapter.

11. Adjust the rear brake as described in Chapter
Three.

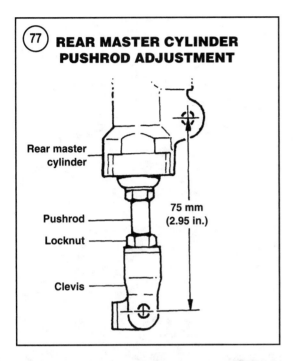

(77) **REAR MASTER CYLINDER PUSHROD ADJUSTMENT**

Rear master cylinder

Pushrod

75 mm (2.95 in.)

Locknut

Clevis

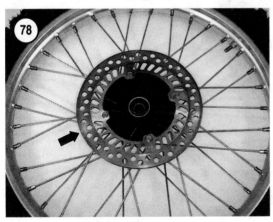

78

79

a. Install *new* sealing washers when installing the banjo bolts.

b. Tighten the banjo bolts to the specification in **Table 3**.

c. Fill the master cylinder(s) and bleed the brake(s) as described in this chapter.

d. Operate the brake lever or brake pedal while observing the brake hose connections. Check for a loose connection or other damage.

WARNING
Do not ride the motorcycle unless both brakes are operating properly.

BRAKE DISC

The brake discs are separate from the wheel hubs and can be removed after removing the wheel from the motorcycle. See **Figure 78** (front) and **Figure 79** (rear).

BRAKE HOSE REPLACEMENT

1. Drain the brake system for the hose to be replaced. Refer to *Draining Brake Fluid* in this chapter.

2. Before disconnecting the brake hoses, note how they are routed and mounted onto the master cylinder and brake caliper. Install the new hoses so they face in the same direction.

3. Remove the banjo bolts and washers for the brake hose to be replaced. To replace the rear brake hose, first remove the rear brake caliper as described in this chapter.

4. Install the new brake hose in the reverse order of removal and perform the following:

Inspection

The brake disc can be inspected while it is mounted on the motorcycle. Small marks on the disc are not important, but radial scratches deep enough to snag a fingernail can reduce braking effectiveness and increase brake pad wear. If these grooves are evident, and the brake pads are wearing rapidly, replace the brake disc.

See **Table 1** (front) and **Table 2** (rear) for standard and service limit specifications for the brake discs. The minimum thickness dimension is also stamped on the outside of each disc (**Figure 80**).

1. Support the motorcycle on a workstand.

13

2. Measure the thickness around the disc at several locations with a micrometer (**Figure 81**). Replace the disc if its thickness at any point is less than the service limit in **Table 1** or **Table 2**, or less than the dimension stamped on the disc (**Figure 80**).

3. Clean the disc of any rust or corrosion and wipe clean with brake cleaner. Never use an oil-based solvent which can leave an oil residue on the disc.

Removal/Installation

1. Remove the wheel as described in Chapter Ten.

2. Remove the bolts securing the brake disc to the wheel hub. Remove the brake disc. Discard the mounting bolts.

3. Inspect the brake disc flanges on the hub for cracks or other damage. Replace the hub if damage of this type is found.

4. Install the brake disc onto the hub with the side of the disc marked DRIVE facing out.

5. Apply threadlock to *new* brake disc mounting bolts and tighten the bolts as specified in **Table 3**.

6. Install the wheel as described in Chapter Ten.

DRAINING BRAKE FLUID

Before disconnecting a brake hose when servicing the brake system, drain as much brake fluid from the system as possible. This will help you service the brake system without having to deal with a large amount of leaking brake fluid.

An empty bottle, a length of clear hose that fits tightly onto the caliper bleed screw and an 8 mm wrench (**Figure 82**) are required to drain the brake fluid. A vacuum pump like the Mityvac (**Figure 83**) can also be used.

1A. Connect the hose to the caliper bleed screw (**Figure 84**). Then insert the other end of the hose into a clean bottle. Pour some new brake fluid into the bottle until it covers the end of the hose.

1B. When using a vacuum pump, assemble it and install it onto the caliper bleed screw (**Figure 85**).

2A. When draining the system manually, loosen the bleed screw with a wrench (**Figure 86**) and pump the brake lever or brake pedal to drain some of the brake fluid. When the lever or pedal reaches the end of its travel, hold in this position and tighten the bleed screw. Then release the brake lever or pedal. Repeat this sequence to remove as much brake fluid as possible.

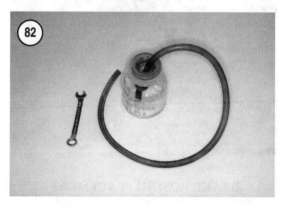

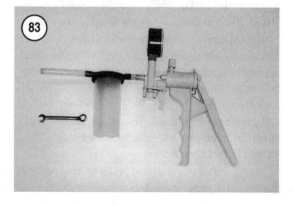

84

85

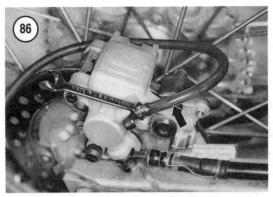

86

2B. When draining the system with a vacuum pump, operate the pump lever to create a vacuum in the line and then loosen the bleed screw with a wrench. Brake fluid will begin to flow into the vacuum pump bottle. When the fluid draining from the system begins to slow down and before the gauge on the pump reads 0 HG of vacuum, tighten the bleed screw. Repeat this sequence to remove as much brake fluid as possible.

3. Close the bleed screw and disconnect the hose or vacuum pump.

4. If necessary, use a syringe to remove brake fluid remaining in the bottom of the master cylinder reservoir.

5. Discard the brake fluid removed from the system.

BRAKE BLEEDING

Whenever air enters the brake system, bleed the system to remove the air. Air can enter the system when the brake fluid level drops too low, after flushing the system or when a banjo bolt or brake hose is loosened or removed. Air in the brake system will increase lever or pedal travel while causing it to feel

spongy and less responsive. Under excessive conditions, it can cause complete loss of the brake.

The brakes can be bled manually or with a vacuum pump. Both methods are described in this section.

When adding brake fluid during the bleeding process, use new DOT 4 brake fluid. Do not reuse brake fluid drained from the system or use a silicone based DOT 5 brake fluid. Because brake fluid is very harmful to most surfaces, wipe up any spills immediately with soapy water.

NOTE
When bleeding the brakes, check the fluid level in the master cylinder frequently. If the reservoir runs dry, air will enter the system.

Manual Bleeding

This procedure describes how to bleed the brake system with an empty bottle, length of clear hose that fits tightly onto the caliper bleed screw, and an 8 mm wrench (**Figure 82**).

1. Make sure both brake system banjo bolts are tight.

2. Remove the dust cap from the brake bleed valve and clean the valve and its opening of all dirt and debris. If a dust cap was not used, use a thin screwdriver or similar tool and compressed air to remove all dirt from inside the bleed valve opening.

CAUTION
Dirt that is left inside the bleed valve opening can enter the brake system. This could plug the brake hose and contaminate the brake fluid.

3. Connect the clear hose to the bleeder valve on the caliper (**Figure 86**). Place the other end of the

13

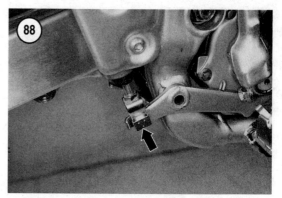

hose into a clean container. Fill the container with enough new brake fluid to keep the end submerged. Loop the hose higher than the bleeder valve to prevent air from being drawn into the caliper during bleeding (**Figure 84**).

> *CAUTION*
> *Cover all parts which could become damaged by brake fluid. Wash any spilled brake fluid from any surface immediately, as it will damage the finish. Use soapy water and rinse completely.*

4. Clean the top of the front master cylinder or the rear reservoir cap of all dirt and debris. Remove the cap and diaphragm. Fill the reservoir to about 10 mm (3/8 in.) from the top.

5. Apply the brake lever or brake pedal, then open the bleeder valve. This will force air and brake fluid from the brake system. Close the bleeder valve before the brake lever or pedal reaches its maximum limit or before brake fluid stops flowing from the bleeder screw. Do not release the brake lever or pedal while the bleeder valve is open. If the system was previously drained or new parts installed, brake fluid will not be seen draining from the system until after several repeated attempts are made. This is normal.

> *NOTE*
> *As the brake fluid enters the system, the level will drop in the master cylinder reservoir. Maintain the level at 10 mm (3/8 in.) from the top of the reservoir to prevent air from being drawn into the system.*

6. Repeat Step 5 until the brake fluid exiting the system is clear, with no air bubbles. If the system is difficult to bleed, tap the master cylinder and caliper banjo bolts with a soft faced mallet to release air bubbles trapped in the system.

> *NOTE*
> *If the brake lever or pedal feel firm, indicating that air has been bled from the system, but air bubbles are still visible in the hose connected to the bleed valve, air may be entering the hose from its connection around the bleed valve.*

7. The system is bled when the brake lever or pedal feels firm, and there are no air bubbles exiting the system. Tighten the bleeder screw and remove the bleed hose.

8. If necessary, add brake fluid to correct the level in the master cylinder reservoir. It must be above the level line.

> *WARNING*
> *Before riding the motorcycle, make sure both brakes are working properly.*

Vacuum Bleeding

This procedure describes how to bleed the brake system with a vacuum pump like the Mityvac pump (**Figure 83**).

1. Make sure both brake system banjo bolts are tight.

2. Remove the dust cap from the brake bleed valve and clean the valve and its opening of all dirt and other debris. If a dust cap was not used, use a thin

screwdriver or similar tool and compressed air to remove all dirt from inside the bleed valve opening.

CAUTION
Dirt left inside the bleed valve opening can enter the brake system. This could plug the brake hose and contaminate the brake fluid.

CAUTION
Cover all parts that could be damaged by brake fluid. Wash any spilled brake fluid from any surface immediately, as it will damage the finish. Use soapy water and rinse completely.

3. Clean the top of the front master cylinder or the rear reservoir cap of all dirt and debris. Remove the cap and diaphragm. Fill the reservoir to about 10 mm (3/8 in.) from the top. Insert the diaphragm to prevent the entry of dirt and moisture.

4. Assemble the vacuum tool according to the manufacture's instructions.

5. Attach the pump hose to the bleeder valve (**Figure 85**).

NOTE
When using a vacuum pump to bleed the system, the brake fluid level in the master cylinder will drop quite rapidly. This is especially true for the rear reservoir because it does not hold very much brake fluid. Stop often and check the brake fluid level. Maintain the level at 10 mm (3.8 in.) from the top of the reservoir to prevent air being drawn into the system. Suspend the vacuum pump with a piece of wire, so it is easier to check and add fluid.

6. Operate the pump handle several times to create a vacuum in the line between the pump and caliper, then open the bleeder valve with a wrench (**Figure 86**). Doing so forces air and brake fluid from the system. Close the bleeder valve before the brake fluid stops flowing from the bleeder or before the master cylinder reservoir runs empty. If the vacuum pump is equipped with a vacuum gauge, close the bleeder valve before the vacuum reading on the gauge reaches 0 HG of vacuum.

7. Repeat Step 6 until the brake fluid exiting the system is clear, with no air bubbles. If the system is difficult to bleed, tap the master cylinder and caliper banjo bolts with a soft-faced mallet to release air bubbles trapped in the system.

8. The system is bled when the brake lever or pedal feels firm, and there are no air bubbles exiting the system. Tighten the bleeder screw and disconnect the pump hose.

9. If necessary, add brake fluid to correct the level in the master cylinder reservoir. It must be above the level line.

WARNING
Before riding the motorcycle, make sure both brakes are working properly.

REAR BRAKE PEDAL

Removal/Installation

1. Disconnect the return spring (**Figure 87**) from the brake pedal.

2. Remove the cotter pin and clevis pin that connect the master cylinder to the rear brake pedal (**Figure 88**). Discard the cotter pin.

3. Remove the hitch pin and washer (**Figure 89**) from the brake pedal.

4. Remove the brake pedal and its washer (**Figure 90**).

5. Remove the seals from the brake pedal mounting bore in the frame.

6. Clean the brake pedal and seals of all old grease.

7. Replace the seals if worn or damaged.

8. Lubricate the lips of the new seals with grease and install them into the frame mounting bore.

9. Install the washer (**Figure 90**) onto the brake pedal.

10. Lubricate the brake pedal shaft with grease and install into through the frame mounting bore.

13

11. Secure the brake pedal with the washer and its hitch pin (**Figure 89**).

NOTE
If a cotter pin was used to secure the brake pedal, either install a new hitch pin or new cotter pin.

12. Secure the rear brake pedal to the master cylinder pushrod with the clevis pin and a new cotter pin. Install the clevis pin from the outside. Bend over the ends of the cotter pin arms to lock it.

13. Operate the rear brake pedal, making sure it pivots and returns correctly.

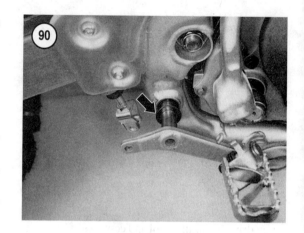

Table 1 FRONT BRAKE SERVICE SPECIFICATIONS

	New mm (in.)	Service limit mm (in.)
Brake disc thickness	3.0 (0.12)	2.5 0.10)
Brake disc runout	–	0.25 (0.010)
Master cylinder inside diameter	11.000-11.043 (0.4331-0.4348)	11.06 (0.435)
Master cylinder piston outside diameter	10.957-10.984 (0.4314-0.4324)	10.84 (0.427)
Brake caliper bore inside diameter	27.000-27.050 (1.0630-1.0650)	27.06 (1.065)
Brake caliper piston outside diameter	26.900-26.950 (1.0591-1.0610)	26.89 (1.059)

Table 2 REAR BRAKE SERVICE SPECIFICATIONS

	New mm (in.)	Service limit mm (in.)
Brake disc thickness	4.5 (0.18)	4.0 (0.16)
Brake disc runout	–	0.25
Master cylinder inside diameter	12.700-12.743 (0.5000-0.5017)	12.76 (0.502)
Master cylinder piston outside diameter	12.657-12.684 (0.4983-0.4994)	12.64 (0.498)
Brake caliper bore inside diameter	27.000-27.050 (1.0630-1.0650)	27.06 (1.065)
Brake caliper piston outside diameter	26.935-26.968 (1.0604-1.0617)	26.91 (1.059)

Table 3 BRAKE TIGHTENING TORQUES

	N·m	in.-lb.	ft.-lb.
Brake hose banjo bolt	34	–	25
Caliper bleed screw	5.5	49	–
Front brake caliper			
Fixed shaft[1]	23	–	17
Mounting bolt[2]	30	–	22
Front brake caliper mounting bracket			
Fixed shaft[1]	13	115	
Front brake disc mounting bolts[1]	20	14	–
Front brake lever			
Adjusting lever	6	53	–
Pivot bolt	6	53	–
Pivot bolt nut	6	53	–
Pad pin bolt	18	–	13
Pad pin plug	2.5	22	–
Rear brake disc mounting bolts[1]	42	31	–
Rear brake caliper			
Fixed shaft[1]	13	115	–
Pin bolt	27	–	20
Rear master cylinder			
Mounting bolts[2]	14	–	10
Pushrod locknut	18	–	13

1. Apply threadlock to fastener threads.
2. Install new ALOC fasteners during assembly.

13

CHAPTER FOURTEEN

OIL COOLER AND HOSES

This chapter describes service procedures for the oil cooler mounted on the steering head and the connecting oil hoses. **Table 1** (end of chapter) lists tightening torques.

OIL COOLER

Removal/Installation

Refer to **Figure 1** for this procedure.

1. Remove the front visor (Chapter Fifteen).
2. Drain the engine oil (Chapter Three).
3. Loosen the flare nut on each side of the oil cooler. See A, **Figure 2** and A, **Figure 3**.
4. Remove the bolts and washers (B, **Figure 2** and B, **Figure 3**) on each side of the oil cooler. Remove the oil cooler from the frame.
5. Locate the rubber cap (10, **Figure 1**) and reinstall it on the frame stay.
6. Reverse these steps to install the oil cooler, plus the following:

a. Install the oil cooler by aligning its stopper with the rubber cap on the frame stay (**Figure 1**).

b. Install the collars and dampers as shown in **Figure 1**.

c. Install the oil cooler mounting bolts and washers (B, **Figure 2** and B, **Figure 3**) and tighten securely.

d. Tighten the two flare nuts (A, **Figure 2** and A, **Figure 3**) to the specification in **Table 1**.

e. Refill the engine with oil (Chapter Three).

OIL COOLER OUTLET HOSE

The oil cooler outlet hose (**Figure 4**) is mounted above the oil cooler.

Removal/Installation

1. Remove the front visor (Chapter Fifteen).

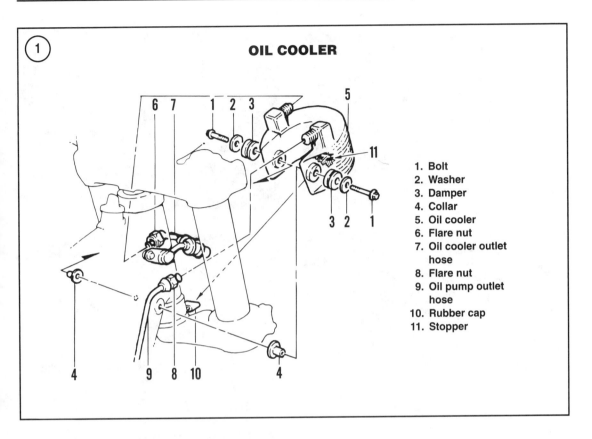

OIL COOLER

1. Bolt
2. Washer
3. Damper
4. Collar
5. Oil cooler
6. Flare nut
7. Oil cooler outlet hose
8. Flare nut
9. Oil pump outlet hose
10. Rubber cap
11. Stopper

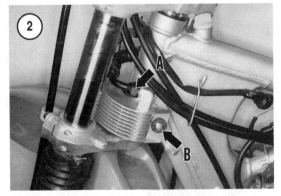

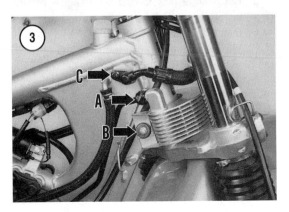

2. Drain the engine oil (Chapter Three).

3. Loosen the flare nut (A, **Figure 2**) on the left side of the oil cooler.

4. Remove the bolt securing the outlet hose (C, **Figure 3**) to the right side of the frame.

5. Remove the outlet hose. Remove the dowel pin and O-ring installed behind the oil hose (where it is bolted to the frame).

6. Reverse these steps to install the oil cooler outlet hose, and perform the following:

    a. Lubricate a new O-ring with engine oil and install it over the dowel pin.

    b. Tighten the flare nut to the specification in **Table 1**.

    c. Refill the engine with oil (Chapter Three).

OIL PUMP OUTLET HOSE

The oil pump outlet hose (A, **Figure 5**) connects the oil pump to the oil cooler.

Removal/Installation

1. Remove the fuel tank (Chapter Eight).

14

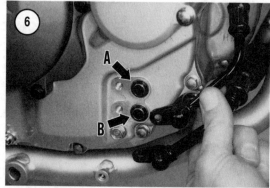

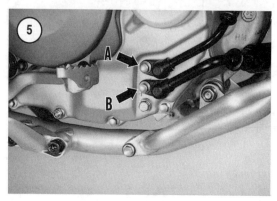

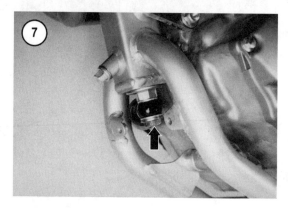

2. Drain the engine oil (Chapter Three).

3. Loosen the flare nut (A, **Figure 2**) at the oil cooler.

4. Remove the bolt securing the oil pump outlet hose (A, **Figure 5**) to the right crankcase cover and remove the hose.

5. Remove the dowel pin and O-ring (A, **Figure 6**).

6. Reverse these steps to install the oil cooler outlet hose, and perform the following:

   a. Lubricate a new O-ring with engine oil and install it over the dowel pin.

   b. Tighten the flare nut to the specification in **Table 1**.

   c. Refill the engine with oil (Chapter Three).

OIL PUMP INLET HOSE

The oil pump inlet hose (B, **Figure 5**) connects the oil pump to the frame's internal oil tank.

Removal/Installation

1. Drain the engine oil.

2. Remove the engine guard (Chapter Fifteen).

3. Remove the banjo bolt and washers (**Figure 7**) securing the oil pump inlet hose to the oil strainer.

4. Remove the bolt securing the oil pump inlet hose (B, **Figure 5**) to the right crankcase cover and remove the hose.

5. Remove the dowel pin and O-ring (B, **Figure 6**).

6. Reverse these steps to install the oil cooler inlet hose, and perform the following:

   a. Lubricate a new O-ring with engine oil and install it over the dowel pin.

   b. Install two new washers with the banjo bolt. Tighten the oil strainer banjo bolt (**Figure 7**) to the specification in **Table 1**.

   c. Refill the engine with oil (Chapter Three).

Table 1 OIL COOLER TIGHTENING TORQUES

	N•m	ft.-lb.
Frame downtube oil strainer screen	54	40
Oil cooler joint flare nut		
Left side (16 mm threads)	20	15
Right side (18 mm threads)	20	15
Banjo bolt at oil strainer	37	27

14

CHAPTER FIFTEEN

BODY

This chapter describes service procedures for the seat, side panels, subframe and other frame parts.

Table 1 is at the end of the chapter.

SEAT

Removal/Installation

1. Remove the two mounting bolts and collars (**Figure 1**) and remove the seat.

2. Install the seat by aligning the seat hook (A, **Figure 2**) with the mounting boss on the fuel tank (B, **Figure 2**). Also insert the arms on the bottom of the seat (C, **Figure 2**) underneath the front subframe rail (D, **Figure 2**).

3. Install the two mounting bolts and collars and tighten securely.

4. Lift up on the seat and make sure it is locked in place.

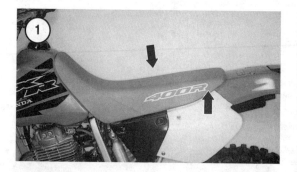

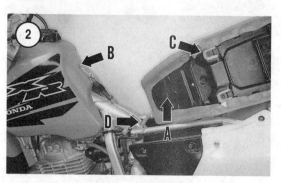

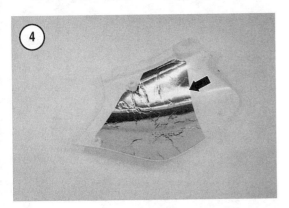

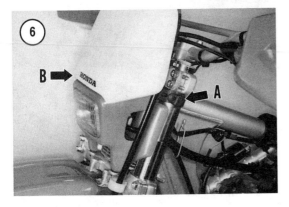

SIDE COVERS

Removal/Installation

1. Remove the seat as described in this chapter.
2. Remove the side cover mounting bolts (**Figure 3**) and remove the side cover.
3. On the right side cover, make sure the heat tape (**Figure 4**) is fixed to the inside of the cover.
4. Reverse these steps to install the side covers while also aligning the side cover tabs with the notches in the rear fender (**Figure 5**).

FRONT VISOR

Removal/Installation

1. Disconnect the rubber mounting bands (A, **Figure 6**) on both sides of the front visor.
2. Lift the front visor assembly (B, **Figure 6**) and place it on the front fender.
3. Disconnect the headlight and engine stop switch electrical connectors (**Figure 7**) and remove the front visor.
4. Locate the rubber grommets (**Figure 8**) and install them into the steering stem mounting bores.
5. Reverse these steps to install the front visor. Start the engine and check the headlight and engine stop switch operation.

FRONT FENDER

Removal/Installation

1. Remove the four bolts and washers (**Figure 9**).
2. Remove the front fender with the four collars.
3. Install by reversing these steps.

15

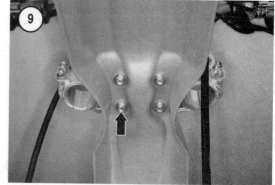

REAR FENDER

Removal/Installation

1. Remove the seat and both side covers as described in this chapter.

2. Disconnect the two wire harness clips mounted on the subframe.

3. Disconnect the taillight electrical connector (**Figure 10**).

4. Unbolt and remove the rear fender (**Figure 11**), while withdrawing the taillight wire harness through the frame.

5. Reverse these steps to install the rear fender, and perform the following:

    a. Route the wire harness (**Figure 12**) along its original path.

    b. Start the engine and check the taillight operation.

ENGINE GUARD

Removal/Installation

1. Support the bike on its sidestand.

2. Remove the bolts, washers and nut securing the engine guard (**Figure 13**) to the frame.

3. Reverse these steps to install the engine guard. **Figure 14** shows the engine guard assembly and its fasteners.

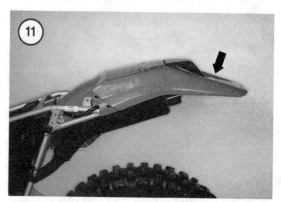

RIGHT SIDE FOOTPEG

Unbolt and remove the right side footpeg (**Figure 15**). During installation, tighten the footpeg mounting bolts to the specification in **Table 1**.

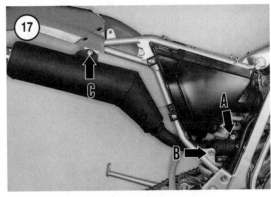

SIDESTAND

Removal/Installation

> *WARNING*
> *The return spring can slip and fly off*
> *when removing and installing it. Wear*
> *safety goggles to prevent eye injury.*

1. Disconnect the return spring (A, **Figure 16**) using a spring removal tool.
2. Remove the nut, bolt (B, **Figure 16**) and sidestand.
3. Reverse these steps to install the sidestand, plus the following:
   a. Lubricate the pivot bolt with grease and install it.
   b. Tighten the pivot bolt (B, **Figure 16**) as specified in **Table 1**. Then loosen the pivot bolt 1/8 to 1/4 turn.
   c. Hold the pivot bolt with a wrench and install the pivot nut. Tighten the pivot nut to the specification in **Table 1**.

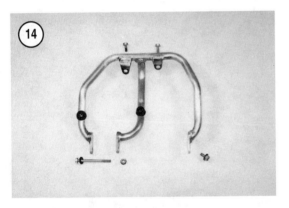

SUBFRAME

Removal/Installation

The subframe can be removed with or without the rear wheel installed on the motorcycle.
1. Remove the seat and the right side cover as described in this chapter.
2. Remove the muffler as follows:
   a. Loosen the clamp bolt (A, **Figure 17**).
   b. Remove the two muffler mounting bolts (B, **Figure 17**) and remove the muffler.
3. Disconnect the taillight electrical connector (**Figure 10**).

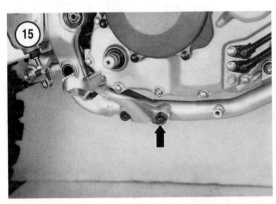

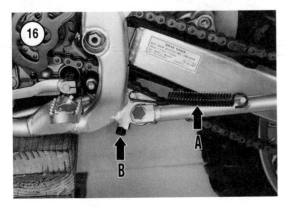

15

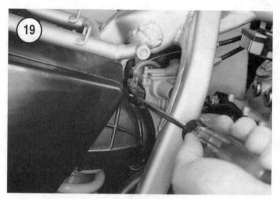

4. Disconnect the plastic band (A, **Figure 18**) and clip (B) from the subframe. and remove the taillight wire harness, carburetor air vent tube and crankcase breather tube.

5. Loosen the rear carburetor hose clamp (**Figure 19**).

> *NOTE*
> *It is possible to move the subframe away from the frame for component access without completely removing it. After removing the upper mounting bolt, loosen the lower mounting bolts and pivot the subframe away from the shock absorber.*

6. Remove the lower subframe mounting bolts (**Figure 20**).

7. Remove the upper subframe mounting bolt (C, **Figure 18**) and subframe (**Figure 21**).

8. Place a plastic bag over the air filter housing air boot.

9. Reverse these steps to install the subframe. Tighten the upper and lower subframe mounting bolts as specified in **Table 1**.

10. Recheck the muffler-to-exhaust pipe and air boot-to-carburetor connections.

11. Start the engine and check the taillight operation.

ODOMETER

Removal/Installation

1. Remove the front visor as described in this chapter.

2. Disconnect the odometer cable (A, **Figure 22**) from the meter.

3. Unbolt and remove the odometer assembly (B, **Figure 22**).

4. Install by reversing these steps.

Table 1 TIGHTENING TORQUES

	N•m	in.-lb.	ft.-lb.
Right footpeg mounting bolt	42	–	31
Sidestand			
Pivot bolt*	10	88	–
Pivot nut	39	–	29
Sub frame mounting bolts			
Upper	26	–	20
Lower	42	–	31
*Loosen the pivot bolt 1/8 to 1/4 turn after torquing it, then tighten the pivot nut to specified torque.			

15

INDEX

16

16

XR400R 1996-2000

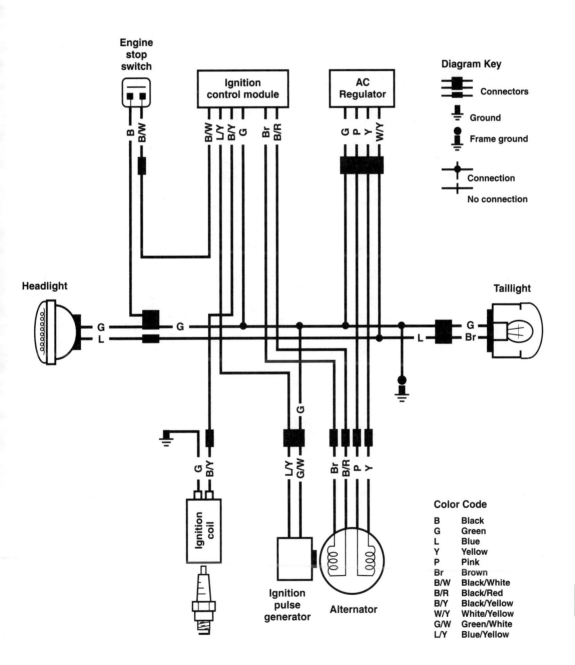

Diagram Key
- Connectors
- Ground
- Frame ground
- Connection
- No connection

Engine stop switch

Ignition control module

AC Regulator

Headlight

Taillight

Ignition coil

Ignition pulse generator

Alternator

Color Code
B	Black
G	Green
L	Blue
Y	Yellow
P	Pink
Br	Brown
B/W	Black/White
B/R	Black/Red
B/Y	Black/Yellow
W/Y	White/Yellow
G/W	Green/White
L/Y	Blue/Yellow

17

NOTES

NOTES

NOTES

NOTES

MAINTENANCE LOG

Service Performed	Mileage Reading				
Oil change (example)	2,836	5,782	8,601		